HEGEL'S ENERGY

Series Editors

Slavoj Žižek

Adrian Johnston

Todd McGowan

HEGEL'S ENERGY

A Reading of
The Phenomenology of Spirit

Michael Marder

Northwestern University Press
Evanston, Illinois

Northwestern University Press
www.nupress.northwestern.edu

Copyright © 2021 by Northwestern University Press.
Published 2021. All rights reserved.

Printed in the United States of America

10 9 8 7 6 5 4 3 2 1

Library of Congress Cataloging-in-Publication Data

Names: Marder, Michael, 1980–author.
Title: Hegel's energy : a reading of The phenomenology of spirit / Michael
   Marder.
Other titles: Diaeresis.
Description: Evanston, Illinois : Northwestern University Press, 2021. | Series:
   Diaeresis | Includes bibliographical references and index.
Identifiers: LCCN 2020052877 | ISBN 9780810143395 (paperback) | ISBN
   9780810143401 (cloth) | ISBN 9780810143418 (ebook)
Subjects: LCSH: Hegel, Georg Wilhelm Friedrich, 1770–1831. Phänomenologie
   des Geistes. | Spirit. | Consciousness. | Psychic energy (Psychoanalysis)
Classification: LCC B2929 .M267 2021 | DDC 193—dc23
LC record available at https://lccn.loc.gov/2020052877

For Rob Albritton, with gratitude

Dialectics is today an—or perhaps even the—actuality of the world [*Weltwirklichkeit*].
 —Martin Heidegger, *The Basic Principles of Thinking*

Contents

Preface — xi

Part I. Prolegomena to the Dialectics of Energy

Reading Hegel Energetically — 3

Wirklichkeit–Actualitas–Energeia — 7

Spirit, Actually — 10

The Real Is (Not) the Actual — 21

The Logics of Virtualization — 24

A Case Study in Virtuality: The Energy of Thought — 27

Speculative Energy — 32

Energy Is (Not) Power — 35

Synergy — 37

Shapes of Spirit, Shapes of Energy — 41

Two Energy Supplies, Three Energy Types — 44

Absolute Energy — 48

Dialectics against Extractivism — 51

Part II. *The Phenomenology of Spirit* and the Question of Energy: An Exegesis

Introduction: The Energy of Cognition — 57

A. "Mere" Consciousness and Its Energy Deficit — 66
    1. Sense-Certainty: "This Is," "I Am" . . . but All "This" "Is" Not Energy — 66
    2. Perception: The Non-Actual Reality of Seeing without Seeing Oneself See — 79

    3. *Force and Understanding: Literally Crystal-Clear and
       Unburdened by the Energy of Thinking*   88

B. Self-Consciousness and Its Surplus Energy   104
    4. *The Truth of Self-Certainty: Beyond the Living Energy of Life*   104
       a. Mastery and Servitude: Self-Consciousness Actualized   108
       b. The Freedom of Self-Consciousness: Three Manners of
          Virtualizing Thought   119

C. Reason and the Self-Limitation of Energy   144
    5. *The Certainty and Truth of Reason: Reality Rediscovered*   144
       a. Observing Reason: Becoming-Actual and/as Becoming-Rational   150
       b. The Self-Actualization of Rational Self-Consciousness:
          Becoming-Rational and/as Becoming-Actual   196
       c. Individuality Real in and for Itself: A Recircuiting of Energy   225

Notes   251

Index   255

Preface

If an ostensibly complete published work presented to readers' attention is a late fruit of the author's efforts, then the preface is a sketch of the tree, on which this fruit has grown and matured. Emerging from my patient decade-long reading of Hegel's *Phenomenology*, in conjunction with the two *Logics*, *Philosophy of Right*, and *Philosophy of Nature*, the theory of energy I have developed on the basis of the dialectical notion of *Wirklichkeit* (actuality) is closely connected to several vectors of my thinking and research.

So, for example, in the course of writing *Pyropolitics: When the World Is Ablaze* (2015), I realized that, in burning ourselves and the entire world on the pyres of economic and other kinds of progress, we are largely motivated by an implicit conception of energy as a pure potentiality that devours whatever is in existence. It is not so much fossil fuel per se as the conviction that energy can only be produced by burning (say, corn crops distilled into ethanol) that we should resist as we seek to address the massive environmental calamity we are living through. The human masses are no different in this respect from wood or coal, iron or steel: they are to be ignited by revolutionary sparks or melted into molds that are easy to manage and administer. Whatever the scenario, our unarticulated ideal of political energy mimicks the default idea of energy: it depends on fire quickly releasing explosive potentialities from anything and anyone, liberating them from previous material forms. Besides the elemental dialectics of fire in Hegel's *Philosophy of Nature*, his discussion of Revolutionary Terror in post-1789 France served as a model for thinking political energy in terms of a flaming void, consuming subjects and objects alike in its pure, abstract, and indifferent potentiality.

In *Energy Dreams: Of Actuality* (2017), I adopted a broader ontological perspective with the view to imagining an alternative conception of energy, rather than merely stressing alternative energy sources. Revisiting Aristotle was inevitable, since he coined the very term "energy"—*energeia*, which he circuitously defined as not-potentiality, not-*dunamis*. Given the centrality of the ancient Greek thinker in the Hegelian project, it quickly became evident that this word has been leading a sort of clandestine afterlife in German, encrypted as it was in the dialectical notion of *Wirklichkeit*, actuality. The consequences of retranslating energy back into actuality in our theological, political, economic, psychological, philosophical, and scientific paradigms can hardly be overestimated: they hold the promise of a nonviolent practice of being energized, of receiving energy without "hacking" everything in existence, without breaking into the dark interiors of things and capturing their potentiality at the expense of their integrity. The energy of the actual, as the actual, is the energy of the surface, of intense circulation rather than production, of relations instead of isolating analyses.

The complexities of the Hegelian concept of *Wirklichkeit*, however, were such that it was implausible to do justice to it within the limits of a book preoccupied with an alternative thinking of energy in general. It was apparent that, in the movement of *The Phenomenology of Spirit*, *Wirklichkeit* was an operative term on a par with spirit (*Geist*) itself. I further spotted in the way Hegel deployed the term a possibility of reinterpreting his masterpiece, and perhaps his philosophy as a whole, as a dialectics of *Wirklichkeit*. Except that it also dawned on me that the concept implied its own negation, or "energy," as colloquially and uncritically understood in terms of potentiality. A historical schema suggested itself whereby, having first surfaced as actuality in Aristotle's *energeia* and having then been negated into a dynamic form of energy in modernity, the concept of energy is only beginning to come into its own in Hegel's thought, which replays both of these movements at once. More importantly, though, the concept of energy *must* come into its own in our twenty-first-century actuality if the murderous and suicidal tendencies of contemporary "energy production" are to be countered, because—like all dialectical concepts—it is not just an ideal-theoretical entity (a thing of the mind, to put it bluntly), but also a set of practices, embodied relations, and institutions.

To mark this double movement in the dialectics of *Wirklichkeit*, I have referred to it as "energy-actuality," the hyphen both articulating and setting apart the two words. Accepting that relations are the spaces of conjunction and disjunction, of combination and separation, energy-actuality is an absolute relation, the one in which relationality as such is at stake. (Hegel, in fact, describes *Wirklichkeit* as an absolute relation in his *Science of Logic*, as I indicate in the "Prolegomena" section of this study.) This means that, coming into its own, the concept of energy will

PREFACE

never finally coincide with itself, unless it betrays its relational constitution and closes the gap between its two modalities for good—something that would be as destructive as the theory and practice of energy framed by pure potentiality. But the point is that we cannot afford *not* to relate to the absolute relation that energy-actuality is whenever we invoke the logic of relationality or, practically speaking, whenever we try to comprehend and tackle the living roots of our death-bearing environmental crisis.

In addition to my previous writings that directly nourished the work gathered here under the title *Hegel's Energy*, I would like to highlight some lateral influences that are, perhaps, equally important. Given my long-standing philosophical interest in and engagement with vegetal life, I concentrated on how plants search for energy in the different milieus they inhabit. With the exception of those that have aerial roots, plants live in two worlds simultaneously: above and below ground. From the soil, they draw water and minerals, while the leaves exposed to solar energy engage in photosynthesis. In other words, plants are the living practitioners of energy-actuality, stretching between the depths of potentiality and the surfaces of the actual, and mediating not only the organic and the inorganic realms (in a somewhat immediate fashion, Hegel notes in *Philosophy of Nature*, with an eye to what he considers as their ontological non-differentiation, the insufficiency of determinate negativity in their mode of being) but also two energy paradigms. Dialectical thought thus shares more than it realizes with vegetal life (and afterlife). It is well known that in the preface to the *Phenomenology*, Hegel maps the historical development of philosophy onto the reproductive stages of a fruit-bearing tree, as I discuss in *The Philosopher's Plant* (2014); not so obvious is the tacit figuration of plants as absolute relations, the channels of energy-actuality that render the hyphen vertical and let it grow, extend, branch out, decay, metamorphose . . .

Only when we accept that energy is tinged with vegetality—only then we will think of it non-metaphysically. And this is not a moot philosophical point, either: the metaphysical idea of energy, which largely overlaps with classical physics and its laws of thermodynamics, is behind the scenes of ecological devastation through the practices and the modes of production it sanctions. If, in keeping with this idea, regardless of its flows and conversions, energy remains unchangeable, essentially untouched, and quantitatively fixed, then it is indifferent to the temporary forms it assumes and, therefore, to the destruction of those forms. If potentiality is the hidden essence of things and, hence, the only thing that truly matters, then the actuality of appearances may be, in good conscience, pulverized in the course of extracting that hidden potential. The atomic energy that breaks down the atom itself is, in this respect, on an equal footing with the drilling and fracking that destroy crusts of the earth, the actuality of which is dispensable in a quest for energy-as-pure-potentiality, as I argued both in *Chernobyl Herbarium* (2016) and in *Energy Dreams*. To interrogate the metaphysics of energy is, in the first instance, to debunk the primacy of potentiality and the fixity of energy beneath its apparent changes and conversions. Plants and Hegel's dialectics are two styles of such an interrogation.

Before bringing these brief remarks to a close, a word on the structure of the present book is in order. The first part, "Prolegomena to the Dialectics of Energy" may be read as a spectral double of the preface to Hegel's *Phenomenology*: a semi-independent piece that recaptures the movement of thought (in this case on energy-actuality) after it has come to a close, and so contributes to the operations of the Hegelian absolute. It may be also consulted as a totally independent manifesto, with leads on how to interpret the *Phenomenology* and, perhaps more broadly, Hegelian thought in light of *Wirklichkeit*. Ultimately, the "Prolegomena" offers clues to a possibility of our self-interpretation, the questioning of our actuality against the backdrop of Hegel's concept.

The second part consists of a close reading of Hegel's text, starting from the introduction and up to and including the section on reason. In each instance, I keep Hegel's original section and subsection titles, adding to them themes related to energy and/or actuality that are salient in those portions of his book. While undeniably partial (my analysis breaks off just before the section dealing with spirit, which I conceptually translate into the self-actualization of energy), the exegesis is rounded off in a tripartite structure, proceeding from "mere" consciousness as energy deficit, through self-consciousness as surplus energy, to reason as the self-limitation of energy. If anything, these exegetical materials give a sense of how dialectical energy-actuality actually works, something merely indicated in the book's first part.

Once set in motion (which, as I reiterate throughout *Hegel's Energy*, is—in a modification of the Aristotelian unmoved mover—the dialectical movement of movement and rest), the process of energy-actuality coming into its own is as difficult to stop as it is impossible to accomplish, thanks to the resistances I have inscribed in the hyphen. The text that follows is not meant to provide a totalizing explanation for the dynamics of *Wirklichkeit*. What it sets out to do, instead, is present an unorthodox perspective on the concept, on Hegel, and ourselves. It will be up to the readers to fill in the blanks in this narrative, coming to the awareness that they have always been nourished by nothing other than Hegel's energy.

HEGEL'S ENERGY

Part I

Prolegomena to the Dialectics of Energy

Reading Hegel Energetically

A historical observer would be hard-pressed to pinpoint a force that has driven both philosophy and history over the last two centuries more powerfully and tenaciously than the energy of Hegel. With the spread of leftist (essentially Marxist) variations on Hegelianism beyond the narrow confines of German and European contexts to Asia, Africa, and Latin America, his thought was converted from a description of how dialectical spirit (which is, let us say from the outset, nothing mystically spiritual and nothing metaphysical) grows worldwide into spirit's actual becoming-worldwide.[1] If, from another direction, neoliberal ideologues, ever eager to argue that world spirit unfailingly culminates in a globalized free market, join the ranks of those influenced by Hegel,[2] then the entire political spectrum, right and left, is animated by his philosophy. Resistance to dialectics is also included. Like physical friction causing sparks to fly when two objects are vigorously rubbed against each other, anti-Hegelianism unwittingly participates in the dynamics it rejects, as Michel Foucault once ruefully observed. "But truly to escape Hegel," he wrote, "involves an exact appreciation of the price we have to pay to detach ourselves from him. It assumes that we are aware of the extent to which Hegel, insidiously perhaps, is close to us; it implies a knowledge, in that which permits us to think against Hegel, of that which remains Hegelian. We have to determine the extent to which our anti-Hegelianism is possibly one of his tricks directed against us, at the end of which he stands, motionless, waiting for us."[3]

All this is quite well known. The answers to queries about the sources of Hegel's energy are, perhaps, even more glaring. It seems pointless to ask: "What drives his thought, which is not-only-thought? Where is the power outlet it is plugged into?" Should one voice these questions, one would promptly receive several mutually reinforcing responses:

–the dialectic as such;
–the force of restless negativity;

–sublation, translating the German *Aufhebung* (elevation-cancellation-retention).

What will customarily remain unquestioned, shielded from the disquieting sway of the question, is the status and meaning of dialectical energy, which is uncritically understood as something powering, driving, instigating, propelling, or repelling and, in any event, *forcing* the movement to get under way. Yet force, along with understanding, are among some of the earliest stages in *The Phenomenology of Spirit*: they have to be overcome, negated, and preserved in this overcoming. So, what is dialectical energy in excess of power and force? More often than not, its sources will be laid out in the open, but its idea, its concept, and, indeed, its being will keep themselves hidden, both with regard to Hegel and to every area of thought and existence. The first task, then, is to rescue energy from scientific reductionism (especially from physics) and from its theological determination (as in certain currents of Eastern Christianity). The energy animating Hegel's thought will lend itself to interpretation if, and only if, we recodify its workings *through* Hegel's thought. Then, in a reflux from the singular back to the universal, we will be able to learn something about energy *as such* from this double entendre of "Hegel's energy."

It will be impossible, for all that, to tackle the issue of energy "point-blank," to wrest it from its hiding place, and without further ado to submit it to the inquisitorial apparatus of philosophy. I have dealt with the impediments to such an endeavor, the absolute and relative ambiguities plaguing energy, in my recent book *Energy Dreams: Of Actuality*.[4] These impediments are largely responsible for the obliqueness that persists in any ontological consideration of our theme. The only circumstances under which a hypothetical interrogatory scene involving energy's meaning or being could play itself out are those where we question ourselves—the energy of our thought and the effects it unleashes onto the world; our perception that we live at a time of entropic inertia when everything has already been said and done; the ascendancy of "virtual reality," which formally contradicts or counteracts this perception; the dogmatic primacy of possibility over actuality resulting from that ascendancy; the subsequent, at once ideal and real, dematerialization of the world into streams of unfulfillable potentialities, summoning to mind cash flows, money, or, generally speaking, finance and seeming to carry the secret of energy . . .

As old as philosophy itself, self-interrogation will be a recurrent theme in the interpretation of *The Phenomenology of Spirit* offered in this study. In inquiring into the energy of Hegel, we cannot help but ask about ourselves, seeing that a pivotal energetic configuration in this work is self-consciousness and its attendant self-knowledge. An orbital approach to ourselves via the Hegelian mediation is not to be confused with an "application," that is, with a transfer and a strained superimposition of certain theoretical insights onto our practices and contemporary realities. The analysis of actuality I propose aims at the self-understanding of the most recent permutations (more accurately, the perversions)[5] of Hegel's energy invested in our thinking and being.[6]

A nagging discrepancy between theory and practice turns out to be nugatory. And it is in this sense, I believe, that Foucault is right to register how "insidiously . . . close" Hegel is to us, his figure emerging not from the fogs of the nineteenth century's past but from the future, the absolute future, which has twisted free from linear chronology, where he is motionlessly "awaiting us." As Theodor Adorno and Slavoj Žižek have, each in his own way, also noted, Hegel holds, withholds, and turns, in his hand or in the door lock, the keys to our actuality. Nothing more and nothing less. To sense this uncanny proximity, whether desirable or deplorable; to conjecture whence the energy of thought and of the world springs from today and why it appears to be ebbing away; to better navigate a zigzagging route between the snares of metaphysics and nihilistic despair, we must read the *Phenomenology*, the German thinker's magnum opus, energetically, with renewed energy, even as we keep an eye on energy's trials and tribulations in the book's philosophical narrative. But exactly what does an energetic reading of Hegel on energy entail?

An energetic reading is, first of all, a *reading*, which has always been and remains (uniquely, though not inimitably) the only way of putting-to-work, actualizing, actuating, and, therefore, energizing a written text. This deceptively straightforward assertion invites a reflection similar to the one Louis Althusser undertook with respect to Marx's *Capital*: "What is it to read?"[7] A properly Hegelian response to this question is: to read is to reread *and*, in the course of an originary rereading, to write. Only on a second reading do reading and the work of understanding begin. And as we shall see, repetition is an assured energy supply, interlacing reality with itself and bringing it to actuality. A repeated reading folded unto itself, repeated as soon as—if not before—it has begun, the reading that does not receive what is read as a sensationalist "fake news" flash from the so-called tradition, is unmistakably imbued with energy. So, to read Hegel, we must reread and, hence, rewrite him: on our own and in his own words, with our words, turns of phrase, idioms, and languages that will have become his.

Although Althusser aspired to purge Marxist political economy of everything it had borrowed from Hegel, his provisional conclusions are sound. Just as in the twentieth century Marx was to be read afresh (i.e., reread), brushing away the silent consensus that had pegged his thought to one or another current of Marxism, so in the twenty-first century we ought to read Hegel without the usual –isms in a bid to rescue him from the swamp of Hegelianism. This method demands, as in Althusser's exhortation, going back to the text itself, reading it from beginning to end (which in this case is the absolute beginning), and bracketing, for the time being, a long history of interpretations accrued, layer upon layer, on the *Phenomenology*. It means putting aside the caricaturized images of Hegel, chief among them the label "the idealism of consciousness" affixed to his thought by Marx and Lenin and the tag "the history of metaphysics" favored by Heidegger and Derrida. Such a method demands that we reject the energy borrowed from previous interpreters, unless their interpretations free the text and the philosophy it condenses, and that we refuse to detain it within the typologies of dialectical materialism, pragmatism, totalitarianism, rationalism, contextualism, social theoreticism . . . Last but not least, this method entreats us to resist the sanitized versions of Hegelianism that match the current age of technocracy and are conveniently digestible for the "schools of analytic philosophy."

The second feature of an Althusser-inspired reading is "symptomaticity," *une lecture symptomale*[8] scanning the visible text for the invisible gaps, lacunae, absences, omissions, and silences that permit whatever does float on its surface to come to light. My suggestion is to read Hegel's *Phenomenology* symptomatically (or better, symptomally) so as to pay attention to what it holds in store for energy and to the energy it holds in store. Why am I advocating a symptomal reading? The German word *Energie* is exceptionally rare in the book; it appears at certain strategic moments, as in the "Preface," where the expression *die Energie des Denkens*, "the energy of thought," is charged with "the tremendous power of the negative," *die ungeheure Macht des Negativen* (PhG §32).[9] There will be plenty of opportunities for us to scrutinize the link not only between thinking and negativity but also, and more consequentially, between energy and power. What matters for now is that the paucity of explicit references to energy in the *Phenomenology* both masks and reveals—as a symptom also does—an underlying obsession with this semi-repressed phenomenon. I contend that the book speaks and dreams of nothing but energy, which oozes from its every sentence and formulation, albeit under a different name. That name is *Wirklichkeit*, "actuality."

Without yet examining the open seams where the relevant Greek (*energeia*), Latin (*actualitas*), and Germanic (*Wirklichkeit*) words are shoddily stitched together on an aged sewing machine of conceptual translation, we might puzzle over the appropriateness of energy for a symptomal reading. What is its dirty secret, for it to be repressed deep in the textual unconscious? Why does it need to hide behind the mask of an allegedly unrelated term, namely "actuality"?

The darkest lacuna in classical political economy, which Marx discovered and thought through, was the source of capitalist profits in the rate of exploitation imperceptibly factored by his predecessors into the labor theory of value. Things stand differently with energy. The problem is that the more expressly we invoke the latter, the more we grow oblivious to what and how it is, much as it happens with Heidegger's "being." We consign the meaning of energy to oblivion by constantly speaking of it, and especially by having recourse to words derived from its original Greek enunciation, *energeia*. This is why, to listen to what "energy" has to say, we would have to rid the concept of its familiar associations, its family resemblances to power, force, and potentiality. I began the work of this sort of de-familiarization, not sparing "work" itself, in my *Energy Dreams*. In the present study, I intend to carry on and concretize the task of re-imagining energy along the lines of actuality, or *Wirklichkeit*, by energetically rereading Hegel on energy. To put it succinctly and cryptically (but, in any event, we are faced with a high-level encryption here), I would like to actualize Hegel's watershed text on actuality, to grant it the freedom to say what it has always already been saying, to release it into its own, to bring it up-to-date with us, or, in line with Foucault's correction, to bring us up-to-date with it, and to assist Hegel in conducting energy to *its* self-consciousness—its fullness in us, as us.

Wirklichkeit–Actualitas–Energeia

Various philosophers have remarked in passing on how *Wirklichkeit* connotes energy in Hegel. In a long footnote to *Hegel's Naturalism*, Terry Pinkard stresses the connections between *Wirklichkeit* and Aristotle's *energeia*, lists the shortcomings of the English translation "actuality," and cites with a great deal of approval *Wirklichkeit*'s French rendition, "*effectivité*."[10] Alfredo Ferrarin,[11] Andreas Gelhard,[12] and Ricardo Pozzo[13] are all aware of the genealogy of *Wirklichkeit*. As is the Russian philosopher Vladimir Bibikhin, who in his lecture course *Energy* (*Energiya*) makes a leap from the technical sense of *energeia*, resurrected in Hegel's *Wirklichkeit* amidst an unmistakably "Aristotelian landscape," to the everyday conception of energy, irrevocably divested of its undertones of being-unmoved, free, and at peace.[14]

A few filaments are, nevertheless, missing from the thread that winds from *Wirklichkeit* back to ancient Greek thought. Aristotle's *energeia* literally conveys being-at-work or (and this *or* will play a crucial role for Hegel) being-in-the-work, *en-ergon*, integrating a determinate outcome with the workings still under way. In the Latin *actus*, the work of energy connotes activity, which is only complete in *actus purus*, the absolute perfection of God. The divine is the indisputable standard for activity and actuality, compared to which we are utterly passive, hardly in being, resigned to our fate as finite creatures, regardless of how busy we are with everything that preoccupies us in this world. The aura of "excellence" around *actus* and *actualitas* is an implied citation of Aristotle on the completion, accomplishment, and self-sufficiency of *entelecheia*, a term that is conventionally undifferentiated from *energeia* in translation. (Both words are rendered as *actus* in Latin.) Obviously, this babelic appropriation of Aristotle leaves no space for the elucidation of energy as a work in progress, which is integral to the Greek notion.

In the Germanic context, Hegel was not the first to bring *Wirklichkeit* into play and to see in it a fitting heir to *energeia* and *actus*. Meister Eckhart pitted this very concept against that of factical reality, *Realität*, and affirmed that *Wirklichkeit* belonged among the categories of essence, such as Godhead (*Gottheit*), beingness (*Seiendsein*), and absoluteness (*Absolutheit*).[15] Divine energy is imparted to the soul that "receives a kiss from the Godhead" and thereby finds itself "in absolute perfection and bliss: then she is embraced by unity."[16] The *Wirk* of *Wirklichkeit* is a version of *actus*; it refers to an act, an effect, a work (*Werk*), a deed. The morphology of *Wirklichkeit*, as much as its semantics, recall the Aristotelian *energeia*: at-work, or being-in-effect (*wirk-lich*; *en-ergon*), to which is added a substantive suffix, be it *–eia* or *–keit*, in a far-reaching linguistic move alluding to the substantivation of "energy." Even if the German word does not exactly reproduce its Greek antecedent the way *Energie* does, it reawakens the logic (and the *logos*) of Aristotle's mintage. More than that, *Wirklichkeit* is the periphrasis of *energeia*, a long-winded repetition motivated by the extra energy of self-consciously circling back to the work this concept had originally carried out in the nascent philosophical vernacular of ancient Athens.

In contrast to Eckhart, Hegel does not equate *Wirklichkeit* with the hidden core of an invisible essence. At least from the standpoint of the absolute, it is as much in the depths of essence as on the surface of appearances, the actualizing and the actualized, the workings and the work that ensues. *Wirklichkeit* is not given either to sensory perception or to a purely theoretical contemplation or to a mystical intuition, all of which are nevertheless its unconscious aftereffects; it needs to be won over, to become self-given gradually, step by painful step. The same is true for our readerly or philosophical engagement with *Wirklichkeit*: to treat of this subject is to enter immediately, without preparation, into the inner core of Hegel's phenomenology, at the risk of forgetting that this inner core is itself an outward manifestation of actuality, the world around us together with our modes of apperceiving it, rather than some withdrawn divinity or a set of foundational abstract principles.

As transformed by Hegel, *Wirklichkeit* (the concept *and* its actualization) is no longer concentrated in an inexhaustible engine outside the world of the here-and-now as it was in the writings of Eckhart and in the rest of the tradition that, in the wake of Heidegger, we designate as ontotheology. The energy of Hegel is the struggle of finite energy to elevate, refine, cancel out, and preserve itself without compromising on its finitude. The thrust of the *Phenomenology*, above all in its representative, synecdochal capacity reflecting in miniature the whole of the Hegelian system, is that of absolutizing finitude—envisioning the infinite self-absolutization of the finite. "Subsumed" by spirit (we are about to explore spirit's visceral ties to energy), matter and consciousness, plants and planets, animals and human institutions are ultimately subsumed *by themselves*.

Since we cannot approach *Wirklichkeit* directly, we would be well advised to immerse ourselves in the mediation of *reading*—in other words, in a patient repetition of the movements marshaled by Hegel's thought. We ought to do so at the pace of the *Phenomenology* (and of phenomenology), or even more slowly. Reading symptomally, we will replay the dialectic while plugging ourselves into and intensifying its energy supply. In doing so, we will notice that, as *Wirklichkeit*, energy has little to do with the potentiality of power (*Macht* or *Kraft*), with which we tend to associate it, and that it comprehends movement and rest, the working and the work, a verbal moment somewhat infelicitously covered by the signifier "subject" and a substantive moment. Far from harmonious, the mutual fit of the two moments is dissonant: taken together, within the same space (physical, conceptual, or both), they amount to something like a chaotic panorama of Rome with all of its historical and archeological strata overlapping—an allegory of the unconscious that Freud famously brought up in *Civilization and Its Discontents*—except that the overlap here is not of complete structures from various epochs, but of any given structure at different stages of its completion. In a chronological succession, while dialectical workings produce a work, this latter unravels into other workings, both negating and maintaining the preceding results. Labor and the work of art will not be exempt from this principle of Hegelian operativity—if I may be allowed to use this formal expression—that sets the tone and the cadence for energetic transformations within the dwindling but ultimately irreducible difference between two perspectives: a phenomenology working itself out and the already accomplished absolute. Dialectical enworkment is, therefore, consonant with a patently Aristotelian observation that becoming-actual only ever takes place on the basis of being-actual. Hence, the productive tautology of *Wirklichkeit*.

I have just qualified the energy of Hegel in terms of a "productive tautology." In our economics-laden jargon and way of thinking, it is all too easy to succumb to the temptation of handling the two sides of energy—subject and substance, the working and the work—using the shorthand of "process" and "product." Such is the *déformation professionnelle* of "process philosophers" (say, Henri Bergson or Alfred North Whitehead) who are antagonistic toward the view of the real as comprised of discrete entities, and so are allergic to "product philosophy," to coin a phrase bordering on PR-campaigns and marketing. Yet, the proponents of process and product philosophies have a lot in common, given their partial grasp of what energy means. Not only do both camps unwittingly secularize the theological doctrine of creation, where God is the Producer of the world, but they are also positioned at a point of transition in intellectual history where ontology *really* (effectively, practically) shifts into the gear of a political economy.

If spirit's energy as the absolute putting-to-work of the working and of the work is not to be construed economically, then what other accesses to it remain unobstructed? The rule of thumb I follow in this book is that an energetic reading of Hegel on energy ought to be neither economic nor scientific but ontological, advancing the thesis that spirit *is* energy—something further complicated by the above-mentioned historical permutation of ontology in our contemporaneity. Both spirit and energy, the one *as* the other, are being in the verbal and the substantive senses Heidegger identified in *Introduction to Metaphysics*.[17] Lest it be mistaken for an avatar of *metaphysical* ontology, en-ergy is the being that is (in) every entity along with these entities' modes of givenness. It enacts and enthinks itself only to the extent that they enact and enthink themselves. It is the *energeia* of thought thinking itself right into existence, and of existence lending itself to thought as its own relation to itself.

Spirit, Actually

Throughout our panoramic overview of *Wirklichkeit*, we should not pass over in silence its more down-to-earth, colloquial sense. *Wirklich* actually means "actually," "truly," "certainly," "indeed"; it certifies that a certain state of affairs is thus and so. In this word, truth and reality meet, putting knowing and being on an equal footing and surpassing the quintessentially modern divide between epistemology and ontology. (Now, in French, the Latin root is also colored with unmistakable temporal hues: *l'actualité* is the French for "current events," or "the news," and *actualisé(e)* signifies "brought up-to-date" or "updated," as in installing the most recent version of a computer program.) Could we say that *wirklich!* is a speech act that condenses in itself, metonymically, all other speech acts?

In the *Phenomenology*, spirit is the shibboleth for energy that combines in itself knowing and being, movement and rest, the working and the work, without diluting the one in the other; in fact, everywhere it maintains the difference and the tension between the two poles. Like energy, spirit (*Geist*) makes itself heard in the substantive, though it also has a verbal dimension, which for Hegel coincides with the subject. Like energy, which interweaves being-in-the-work and being-at-work, or space and time, spirit is a concept in excess of itself, a concept overflowing itself and announcing its readiness for—its compatibility with—absolute difference untethered to the gap between "the real" and "the ideal." The knotty identity of *Wirklichkeit-actualitas-energeia*, on the one hand, and *Geist*, on the other, is an identity of two non-identities.

    Hegel is on the verge of formulating the identity of spirit and *energeia* in his 1822–23 lectures on the philosophy of world history. There, he says apropos of ancient Greek thought: "One could not know that spirit is this infinite movement, this ἐνέργεια, ἐντελέχεια. Spirit is energy and does not remain in a state of immediacy; it is the movement and activity that proceeds from an initial state to another state, working through and overcoming the latter, discovering itself in this labor; and only by returning to the first state does it become actual spirit. It is only through this labor that spirit prepares for itself the universal, brings forth its concept as its object, brings it before itself. This production, however, comes last, not first."[18] Spirit's self-actualization or auto-update, its departure from "a state of immediacy," its "working through" the earlier state by means of negation, its swerve back to that presumably superseded state after a long chain of mediations, its self-production in the shape of the universal—*that* is energy as the accomplishing-accomplished fit of becoming and being, the working and the work. The labor (of the negative) through which spirit discovers itself is the revamped *ergon* of *energeia*. Not to be conflated with an endless wandering hither and thither, its "infinite movement" refers to a speculative articulation of the working work in its opposition to itself. Such a movement is ultimately indistinguishable from rest, along with which it is re-grounded on the (self-grounded and therefore eminently un-grounded) foundation of the absolute.

    The assertion that spirit = ἐνέργεια breathes new life into the interpretation of Hegel's overall project beyond his lectures on world history. To those content with a caricaturized image of Hegel, the equation is indicative of the metaphysical nature of his thought, assuming that any two keywords of metaphysics, including *Geist* and *energeia*, are roughly interchangeable. But to astute readers it supplies an index that is conducive to understanding the *Phenomenology*, among other ingredients of Hegelian dialectics. The shapes of spirit—consciousness, self-consciousness, as well as the family, the state, and so on—constitutive of actuality (*Wirklichkeit*) are energetic formations. In them, energy is congealed in a recognizable form, from which it can be released through a de-actualizing (virtualizing) negation, so as to keep reshaping itself across a series of relatively static conditions and dynamic developments. (The emphasis is on the word "relatively." An unconditionally dynamic order masks its own staticism; to recognize the dynamic as dynamic, one needs at a minimum a rhythmic, if at times halting, alternation and alteration of the more or less static and dynamic elements.) Hence, adding to "energetic formations" the words "of spirit" is superfluous; rather than an externally injected fuel for movement, energy is inseparable from what and how each entity, element, organism, mode of perceiving, understanding, reasoning, or institution *is*.

To clarify this intimate embrace of energetic content and form, we ought to pay heed to Hegel himself, who, in the section of the *Phenomenology* on "revealed religion," reveals the meaning of "actual spirit," *wirklicher Geist*: "its movement through itself constitutes its actuality [*Wirklichkeit*]. What moves itself is spirit; it is the subject of the movement and the *moving* itself, or the substance through which the subject moves [*was sich bewegt, ist er, er ist das Subjekt der Bewegung, und er ist ebenso das* Bewegen *selbst, oder die Substanz, durch welche das Subjekt hindurchgeht*]" (*PhG* §786). Actuality—or energy—is the "movement through itself" of spirit: the point of departure, the destination, the path it traverses between the two, the frictions that impart speed or slow down the movement, and the "fuel" needed for the journey. Energy—or actuality—is these five things, persisting in their difference from one another and sublated into a provisional unity. It is in this sense that actual spirit is self-moving. Differently stated, spirit is the moving and the moved, the working and that which is worked out of it, the actualizing and the actualized. (Lest we forget, more is happening in the conjunction "and" than at either of the extremes it at once articulates and disjoints.) The Hegelian dictum that spirit is both subject and substance announces *energeia*'s becoming itself, at the cusp of the distinct senses of "work" (*ergon*, *Wirk* or *Werk*). Taken as a whole, the *Phenomenology* engenders, records, and remembers this crossing. The work of the text before us, which is simultaneously at the forefront of Hegel's overall system, is that of working on work, seeing it through after its end from the beginning to the end in a circle of spirit. There is, for all that, no hermetic or hermeneutic closure in this philosophico-geometrical figure: the energetic circle spells out the opening and the openedness of actuality, exteriorization, the expressive (or de-expressive) turning inside out and outside in of interiority that is inverted and perverted until the metaphysical difference between the inner and the outer ceases to make any sense.

Energy circulates; it does nothing other than that. But, at every turn, with every rotation of the circle, it suffers substantive and subjective changes, which are typically dismissed in theories of "mere" circulation. This is, probably, the most significant ramification of its de-expression.

As actuality, the being-in of work in *en*-ergy is completely to the fore in a twist on the concept I have previously dubbed "ex-ergy."[19] Here is what the actual, accomplished, finite but not finalized, energizing and energized spirit is: a working work that is as much inner as it is outer. Prior to its accomplishment, exteriorization and interiorization are arranged in a succession that, at every coil of the dialectic, inches toward the absoluteness of spirit, its energetic rest in itself *and* outside itself, in the singularity of difference. It is, however, imperative to add to the rhythmic alternation of the inner and the outer in energy-actuality the idea that the phenomenological perspective of a self-actualizing or self-energizing spirit is not the whole story in Hegel's text. The absolute, as the Archimedean point of energetic rest in having-been-actualized, is the footing upon which all of the *Phenomenology* stands or moves. The lived outlook of energy is doubled, shadowed, put into relief by the absolute perspective on *the same movement actually brought to its denouement and now replayed, as a prerecorded video, in recollection*. Hegel always screens two imperfectly superimposed films at once: a "live feed" of the phenomenological adventure and its rerun. It is between them, in the rift between an energy still in search of itself and a brimming self-energized energy, that the dialectic of *Wirklichkeit* presses on.

A diagram might help visualize this dialectic:

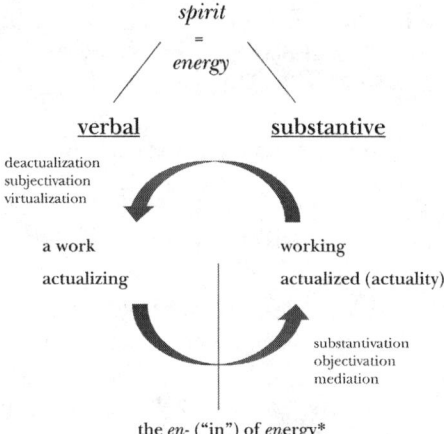

Figure 1. The dialectics of energy

*Note: This circular movement unfolds on the (unmoved) basis of the absolute,[20] to which it pertains and which, were it to remain immobile, would not have been absolute.

Energy's Peregrinations: From Actuality to Actuality'

Hegel's spirit reminds one prima facie of energy conversions in physics. As in the first law of thermodynamics, dialectical energy is preserved across its vacillations and transmutations. Preservation is the positive side of *Aufhebung*. The analogy is nonetheless false: a momentarily stabilized shape of energy matters in Hegel's thought, not in the science of physics.[21] The laws of thermodynamics are squarely those of substance oblivious to spirit's verbal-subjective dimension, that is, to its phenomenology. Consequently, "physical mechanics is steeped in an *unspeakable metaphysics* [*unsäglichen Metaphysik*] which, contrary to experience and the concept, has . . . mathematical determinations alone as its source."[22] Spoken like a true phenomenologist! The metaphysical paradigm of physics is "unspeakable," *unsägliche*, in that this paradigm leaves no viable stance for the speaking subject, accommodating instead a partial, mutilated energy indifferent to the forms it temporarily assumes prior to its liberation back into an undifferentiated flux. Cold indifference to formed matter, comprising the finite shapes of energy, is an attitude responsible for the current environmental crisis and suffusing many of the proposed solutions. From the standpoint of pure substance, ephemerally assembled unique living shapes, from organisms to biospheres, hardly matter and are not worth caring for. Not yet versed in how to live with and in finitude, we trust in these shapes' perpetual recombinations within the cycle of energy, all the while treating the body of the earth and our own biological corporeity as though one day we might be granted another, substantively different, better, more perfect actuality.

Physics lacks a robust philosophy of energy, but in philosophy *proper* the situation is not encouraging, either. One could argue, in fact, that, with the exception of Aristotle, there had been no *philosophers* of energy before Hegel. There had been, admittedly, plenty of scientific constructions that drowned the concept of energy in the uniformity of substance, not to mention theological attempts that assigned it to the individuated subject (in the first place, the Subject: God). A philosophy of energy deserving of the name would then be both substantive and subjective, both (and neither) scientific and (nor) theological. In my view, only in his *Phenomenology* does Hegel succeed in maintaining a fragile balance between the two. The *Encyclopedia Logic* veers too much on the side of theology, agreeing with the Scholastics that "God is actual [*wirklich*]—that he is what is most actual, indeed that he alone is what is truly actual," while "existence [*Dasein*] in general is partly *appearance* and only partly actuality."[23] At the other end of the energy spectrum, the *Science of Logic* subsumes both "actuality and possibility in general" under the truth of "absolute necessity," which is itself "blind."[24] (Here, Hegel finds himself in formal agreement with the physical sciences, as he charges a particular Kantian subcategory of modality—necessity—with the task of subduing the other two modal aspects, namely existence and possibility.) The former treatise indulges in the energy of the subject; the latter—in that of substance.

Let us return to the universe of Newtonian physics. The one significant development it is acquainted with, energy-wise, is entropy, a gradual destitution of energy from the formed matter that had temporarily stabilized it. The Hegelian system throws a challenge to what appears to be a scientific axiom: not only does dialectical energy *not* remain constant, but it also grows intensively, if not extensively. The more advanced the work of negation, the more actual the actuality arrested in a temporal snapshot, the more energized and energizing the movement of the whole. How is this possible?

The path of energy, commencing with the actual, that is to say, with energy itself, is charted through its dispersal into energi*es* and its gathering again into a *syn*ergy, which has always persisted at the core of energy to begin with. The synthetic moment in dialectics is essentially synergic, even as analysis separates, abstracts, and thereby individuates a multitude of energies. Actualized spirit—energy fully energized and energizing—is a synergic ensemble which, presupposed by though not included in the point of departure, assembles under its umbrella, among other things, the synergy of movement and rest. There is no energetic plenitude at a freestanding beginning so prized by modern thought. The initial abstract spirit, making itself known *de novo* at every dialectical turn of negation and analysis, is the least energized, because it is still incapable of releasing the working and the work into free synergies. Energy increases *at the end*, crisscrossed by actualized relations, self-relations, and synergies. Dialectical experience contradicts our default expectation that energy would be gradually exhausted until it finally fizzles out in what would amount to the triumph of entropy.

To maintain that the course of energy commences with the actual, as both Hegel and Aristotle do, is to bend it into a circle, where actuality leads to actuality and synergy grounds the development of synergy. We would be wrong to assume that, on the itinerary of spirit or *energeia*, an immature potentiality is nearing its actualization. The actual is the first and the last; potentiality is but its negation, emptying it out or de-actualizing it into another instant of working. At times, Hegel explains this emptying-out of the actual by way of a retreat into the interiority of thought, consciousness, or subjectivity. At other times, action, requiring externalization, produces this effect of dispersing the energy congealed in actual configurations. The chasm between theory and praxis, between the energies of interiority and exteriority, is filled with actuality and its negative elaboration.

Take, for instance, the *Phenomenology*'s section on reason. Making a laughingstock of talent as a cypher for individual potentiality, Hegel quips: "An individual cannot know what *he is* until he has brought himself to actuality through action [*Das Individuum kann daher nicht wissen, was es ist, eh es sich durch das Tun zur Wirklichkeit gebracht hat*]" (*PhG* §401). But, insomuch as an individual is already minimally actual before undertaking any actions, Hegel distinguishes between the actuality (the energy) that already is and the one that will be thoughtfully and actively accomplished in human self-making as human. The former *Wirklichkeit* must undergo a conversion, or a perversion (*Umkehrung*, a U-turn), "from an actuality that merely *is* the case into an actuality that *has been done* [*die bloße Umkehrung der Wirklichkeit als eines* seienden *Falles in eine* getane *Wirklichkeit*]" (*PhG* §635). So much so that the *Phenomenology* will be galvanized by these conversions, these perversions instigating its argument.

We may represent the movement of the text thus:

Figure 2. Energy's peregrinations (1)

But there are a few caveats.

First, the leaps from actuality to actuality cannot be grafted exclusively onto the straight line of an open-ended "bad" infinity. They take place on the convoluted basis of the absolute, which, in this case, means the absolute actuality motivating the blossoming forth of energies out of what, for us, the observers of the two-track (the phenomenological and the absolute) journey, constitutes the future. This absolute actuality does not stand above or outside the world; it is the self-accomplishment of the finite in its finitude: an infinitely finite consciousness and a recollection of the finite.

Second, the global trajectory of energy is a circle that swirls in and rests upon itself, but that least of all connotes isolation, hermetic sealing, or the ideal of independence characteristic of the virtual rather than the actual. Action and actuality, the working and the work, are the two halves of *energeia*—an insight Hegel expresses in a beautifully Aristotelian fashion in his *Science of Logic*: "What is actual can act [*Was wirklich ist, kann wirken*]."[25] The modal verb "can" (*kann*) is the *possibility of actuality*, allotted to and engrossed in that very actuality, yet, by the same stroke, virtualizing it. The de-actualizing negation of the actual is the potentiality proper to the actual and, moreover, that which potentiates potentiality itself. Every supposed flight from actuality (or from Hegel, for that matter) winds up in the territory it attempts to flee. To paraphrase: every escape from actuality is actually—seen from the absolute—actualizing, brought back to a more intensely self-related or self-conscious actuality.

Third, *actuality* is not substantively different from the modified *actuality'*, nor is the modified *actuality'* substantively different from the further modified *actuality"*. Retrospectively, from the vantage of the absolute, we realize that the so-called merely given actuality has been a transfigured, self-given, energetically charged actuality all along; only its mediations have not been fleshed out. What was absent was nothing substantive. Quite the contrary: the missing piece of the puzzle was the *evacuation of substance*, its self-negation yielding the subject, the actuality of de-actualization, a self-conscious regard turned inwards and putting on hold for the time being the parade of empirically accessible energy shapes. Hegel confirms this point in the paragraph from the section on reason that has already flashed before our eyes, where he writes that "what seems to be a *previously found* actuality [*eine* vorgefundene Wirklichkeit] is in itself his [the individual's] own original nature, which has merely the illusory appearance of being . . . but which shows itself to be his original nature by the interest he takes in it" (*PhG* §401). A pre-given actuality looms large thanks to the "interest" we take in it and is, thereby, already self-given through the passion or, more mildly put, the non-indifference of the subject, the subject *as* non-indifference. (Otherwise, it simply goes unnoticed.) We would not go awry if we were to transpose, mutatis mutandis, the retrospective construction of pre-givenness onto nonhuman nature, which is initially misrecognized by spirit as its absolute other and is later grasped as spirit-not-yet-conscious-of-itself, not yet processed through that form of energy which de-forms substance and is called "consciousness."

It behooves us, in light of the above, to revise the earlier diagram thus:

PART I

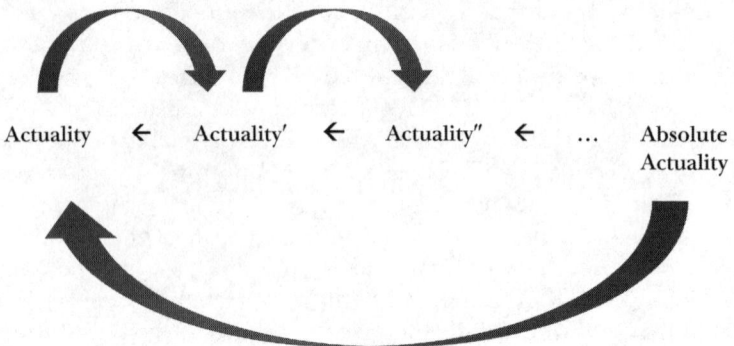

Figure 3. Energy's peregrinations (2)

Curiously, the internal metamorphosis that sees the self-given arise from (in and as) the merely given which has never been "mere" resonates with the discovery I made in *Energy Dreams* concerning the theological underpinnings of "facts." Reflecting on Saint Augustine's influential description of creation, I concluded that Augustinian "reality is comprised of *facta* (from the Latin *facere*, 'to do' or 'to make'), works made by God that live in him before the actual fabrication of the world. Our objective-empirical 'facts,' the idols of the techno-scientific outlook, are, in a convoluted way, the unacknowledged vestiges of objectified divine energy. . . . That the worldly 'facts' guide us back to spiritual realities is the ground-rule of Augustine's allegorical hermeneutics."[26] In Hegel, we detect a latent alteration in the meaning of *facticity*, from a passively given reality that is independent of what one does (e.g., a rock one stumbles upon, splitting one's leg open) to an actuality obtained by distilling the subject from the substance, wherein that subject takes interest. As far as theologians are concerned, facticity is, as a matter of fact, never passive; the supreme actor, God, is its maker, and it is stamped with the energy of creation at the core and on the surface of its being. (In the German context, this is the view held by Jakob Böhme and his doctrine of *signatura rerum*, with which Hegel was familiar.) Not before the advent of modernity did we run aground on an artificial dilemma of "facts" versus "norms," the inflicted and the willed. Though not expressly articulated, Hegel's achievement is to have overcome both the theological and the "secular" frameworks by having conceived facts, the merely given, as what is made, as energy in the shape of a work, without the obligatory reference to the divine creator. Far from the heights of "idealism," this is the twofold working of the subject on substance and the work of substance on the subject. Despite—but also thanks to—the fancies of an imagination ever eager to flee from the actuality of *what is*, the subject's energy conducts the fact back to itself and relates it to itself, instead of molding it in whichever way possible.

For all the proliferation of dialectical "actualities," only the first actuality of the world here-below exists. The rest consists in the refinement, deepening, determination, and concretization of the world's relation to itself—a deepening projected onto the surface, externalized. The "actualities" to-come are akin to a set of Russian dolls: they are the avatars of *the same actuality*, which has become other to itself, seen itself reflected in its otherness, and self-consciously acknowledged itself across the chasm of difference. Hegel prefers the technical term "determinate negation" to designate such an event in spirit. The more frequently the event is repeated, the more energetic and more actual the world grows. Absolute actuality as "reflected absoluteness"[27] is the absolute interiorization totally to the fore, an energizing-energized condition that is of a piece with the outwardness of existence.

Here, too, we can spot the Hegelian inversion of the physicists' entropy axiom, which turns out to be not an axiom but a modest hypothesis. Dialectical energy is not the force emanating from an original event (e.g., the Big Bang) and depleted in direct proportion to its distancing from the origin. This temporal order needs to be switched around in our minds. Dialectical energy is the *after*-energy, a surge that happens in every repetition, in every mediation, of *what is*. This is probably the cardinal difference between *Energie* and *Wirklichkeit*: despite its Greek provenance, the former is the unmediated, immediate capture-and-release of force; the latter is the instantaneous repetition of the working in the work that betrays—expresses *and* gives up: that is the double-bind of *Aufhebung*—the verbal aspect of *Wirk/Werk*.

When it comes to the iterations of actuality, metaphysicians have been buried under piles of derivatives (′) that, like financial derivatives, are progressively detached from their source until the last shreds of their relation to actuality and to themselves wear off altogether. The epitomes of this phenomenon in philosophy are the "possible worlds" theory, modal logic, and, more generally, the reign of unbridled abstraction—the poorest level of thinking, according to Hegel. Imagining wholly other actualities, which are ideally free from the fragility and finitude of this world, was already the vocation of metaphysics in its Platonic rendition. The effect this tendency has had on our topic is profound: as soon as one sees through the speculative machinations with actuality, one is urged to abandon speculation entirely, on account of the borrowed energy it deploys, and revert to the pure and immediate source it has abandoned. Marx's critique of commodity fetishism, of economic substance subjectivized in the form of value, is guided by this logic: one cannot speculate with the workers' self-produced subjectivity! A principled anti-speculative stance is seduced by the possibility of idealizing a pure, unmediated, ideally non-ideal (this contradiction in terms is buried in many of our "materialisms") origin. Such a stance miscarries the effort to reiterate the given otherwise and, especially, to ask how and to whom it has been given to begin with.

Before reaching the conclusion of this section, a methodological remark is in order. Whoever reads the *Phenomenology* closely will observe that, for the most part, Hegel is not technically precise (we might say: sloppy) with the uses of the term *Wirklichkeit*. "Actuality," on various occasions, stands for external reality: merely given, barely mediated, confronting us with its hitherto impenetrable otherness. For instance, when discussing sense-certainty, Hegel concludes that consciousness can only say of "actual things [*wirkliche Dinge*] . . . what is *universal*" (*PhG* §110). "Actual things" are not yet even objects at this point; they are the "this" of sense-certainty. On other occasions, "actuality" refers to what is self-given, meticulously mediated, and true—the world that spirit engenders for itself.[28] As we already know, however, mutually incompatible meanings converge on one and the same actuality exhibiting variations in the degree of its self-relatedness. The least mediated, first actuality is the spitting image of "reality," *Realität*, a word that crops up overwhelmingly in the initial parts of the *Phenomenology*. Incipient *Wirklichkeit* cannot, by implication, be distinguished from *Energie*. But, after dialectics has run its course, it becomes clear that "external reality," too, is the unrecognized and unclaimed actuality of spirit. It dawns on us that *actuality* = *actuality'*. I am willing to accept the criticism that Hegel is not rigorous in his references to *Wirklichkeit* solely on the condition that "rigor" is demoted from the sine qua non of thinking to the rigor mortis affecting every immobile system of thought. Just as the subject is that difference which makes no difference on the platform of substance, so the self-negations and multifaceted determinations of actuality elude a formal, non-dialectical philosophy. A technical, dictionary-like specification of concepts is utterly foreign to dialectics. The barefaced imprecision in Hegel's method is part and parcel of the *phenomenology* of spirit, a phenomenology that faithfully accompanies changes in the energy configurations of subject and substance, the working and the work, in the history (and the prehistory) of self-consciousness.

The Real Is (Not) the Actual

The fluid distinction between the real and the actual that we have touched upon requires further analysis. As the title of this section suggests, the real both is and is not the actual. It is still energy, if only in its maximally substantive aspect devoid of the verbal-subjective element, or with this element occluded from theoretico-practical view. Reality is a conjunction of works without workings, the scaffolding that supported its construction dismantled, the process mystified. A reified world where the ligature tying the two meanings of *ergon* constitutive of energy is torn, it amounts to actuality minus its self-relation, understood both in terms of actuality's subjective construction and in terms of the dynamic rapprochement of subject and substance, the working and the work, in dialectics articulating the two aspects of energy.

> reality = actuality *minus* its self-relation

Figure 4. The reality formula

According to the *Science of Logic*, "real actuality," *reale Wirklichkeit*, actuality reduced to the real, is, in another purposeful conflation of Kantian categories, nothing but "real possibility," *reale Möglichkeit*.[29] As such, it is the crudest kind of actuality, an actuality de-actualized by virtue of severing the tie between the inner and the outer, the working and the work, subject and substance—the tie that, if and when tightened, confers on *Wirklichkeit* the status of an "absolute relation."[30] All that endures are vacuous links among the things of which reality—a cemetery with unmarked graves, bereft even of monuments to energy—is made up.

Relations, to be sure, are fractured linkages, their articulations revolving around the gap they cannot and should not close. But absolute unbinding is something else entirely. Considered under the sign of pure negativity, the breach of relationality is the signature of the non-actual, which, in its turn, carries out the dialectical work of negation: "*the separated*, the non-actual itself is, however, an essential moment [*Aber ein wesentliches Moment ist dies* Geschiedene, Unwirkliche *selbst*]" (*PhG* §32). For the solidity of the real to be felt, for its calm façade to be sustained, horrendous violence and destitution must have taken place, and must keep taking place, to keep things separate, discrete, caught in the pincers of logical identity. The actuality of non-actuality, the energy of this anti-energy, is the labor of the negative, divesting each new iteration of actuality of its ephemeral stability, virtualizing it, and devolving it back to the verbal aspect of work. The *Phenomenology* will consecutively entrust such potentiation to death, thinking, and evil. These are the names, more or less synonymous in Hegel's system, for "reality"—a separating and separated (de-realizing) objectification, actuality at its most virtual. Were Hegel alive today, he would have joked that all reality is virtual reality.[31]

Lacking in the real is the synergy that makes energy what it is, a bond, on the one hand, between the works (things or objects in the world) and, on the other, the workings of *Wirklichkeit*. This complex bond is what creates the world as world. In addition to being virtual, reality is inherently analytic; it falls apart into a multiplicity of entities, contingently filling the container that the unbound world has become, and haphazardly interrelated aposteriori, after the fact of their inclusion in the "real," in the universe of facts where moments of self-givenness are dimmed down. This is the predicament, in contemporary philosophy, of object-oriented ontology, which is unwilling or unable to specify *who* is oriented to these objects. A mad (because blind toward itself) passion for the real is organized around a delusion that there can be objects without subjects, notably in philosophical discourse which, in this case, omits its own history (the twin birth of the notions of subject and object in modernity) and its own *subject position* in the midst of the real. The passionate subject disappears, swallowed up by its very passion.

A forerunner of this mutilated, unilaterally objectified energy is, no doubt, Nietzsche, who famously wrote in *On the Genealogy of Morality*: "there is no 'being' behind the doing, effecting, becoming; the 'doer' is simply fabricated into the doing—the doing is everything."[32] In all fairness, Nietzsche does not envision a world of either objects or subjects. He desires an active actuality without an actor, without a being, let alone the Supreme Being, for which he mistakes the subject. Much like Spinoza, however, he is speaking from the impossible standpoint of substance, which prevents him from discerning in the subject the nothing factored into ("fabricated") everything. The Hegelian subject, for its part, is not a being (and certainly not the Being) but a reiterated (and, more importantly, iterable) self-relation, which cannot be positively identified among objects. Whereas Nietzsche hankers after a doing without the doer, a working shorn of the worker and of the works, the proponents of object-oriented ontology are left with what is done, the fetish of facts in the etymological sense, the works to which they impute the verbal aspect of energy, arbitrarily fabricating the deed into the done and admiring the result as "magical."

Actuality, or energy, cannot be contracted to the static real any more than it can be limited to restless activity. It is the vanishing mediator between these two moments, a relation between what is encased in itself and what is open to the outside, between the in-itself and the for-us, between the non-relational and the relational, the latter discovered time and again in the former. In contrast to the real, which is an immediate, unmediated actuality (as well as, further down the dialectical line, a petrified act), the actual is spirit's self-relation in the articulation of the relational and the non-relational—and accordingly, the absolute relation, as per the *Science of Logic*. The actual enwraps the real, includes the real as an immature version of itself, even as the real repels the actual. Their back-and-forth is vital to the dialectics of energy spiraling upon itself.

The example of cognition is instructive. When Hegel avails himself of the word *Realität* ("reality") in his examination of "the reality of cognition," *die Realität des Erkennens* (*PhG* §81), he does so in the context of a perspectival hiatus between phenomenal knowledge and dialectical science. The hiatus is still palpable because "science has first begun to come on the scene" (*PhG* §81), and so the reality of cognition diverges from its actuality. As it appears early on, perceptual cognition is the royal road to the real and is, on that account, the real (genuine, authentic, true) mode of tackling the real world. This is, in a crucial sense, correct: the reality of perceptual cognition is isolating, insofar as it parses *what is* into less-than-objects, a set of empty and abstractly universal "thises"; hence, it goes hand in hand with the virtuality of reality as such. It is devoid of self-relation to the extent that it is ensconced in the categories not of self-consciousness but of consciousness, for which interiority does not exist. The reality of perception (subjective and objective genitive) embodies an actuality confined in itself, its energy barely at work, yet mustering enough strength to virtualize the world into a set of abstract universals under the guise of having uncovered the most secure foundation for experiencing and for thinking.

At the same time, the absolute is never far away: it is the most proximate, despite the daunting sense that a huge distance stretches between it and us. "It is therefore astonishing," Hegel writes, to grasp that "the reality or the being of external things as *this*, or as sensuous [*die Realität oder das Sein von äußern Dingen als* diesen*, oder sinnlichen*], has absolute truth for consciousness" (*PhG* §109). Reality, be it of the sensuous "this," has "absolute truth" when it is accepted as *a part of* actuality, when it is put to work or when it puts itself to work, disclosing its partial relation to energy. Its absolute truth is the form and the content of this actualization, the intuition that reality is the work of *energeia* in the substantive, just as being (*Sein*), which Hegel treats as a substitute for reality, is the substantive reflection of the verb "to be." (Heidegger's worry that Western thought has neglected the verbal sense of being resonates with how actuality dries up and shrivels to reality, to works without workings, where the connection between the two senses of *ergon* is disrupted. His fundamental ontology ultimately tries to repair ancient *energeia*, the emphasis in *Being and Time* on existential possibilities notwithstanding.) To sum up: reality *is* absolute actuality in the waiting, the actual at the outset of its unfolding or enfolding, an appearance that is as vital to the integrity of energy and of truth as the appearing.

The Logics of Virtualization

On the divergent, though gradually converging, horizons of phenomenology and of the accomplished absolute, the real and the virtual are also tied in a double knot. In the scheme of ordinary consciousness, virtualization is the de-realization of the world; for absolute self-consciousness, reality itself is a virtual artifact to be energized into an actuality. Although the two points of view seem to be at variance, to put it mildly, they participate in a quintessentially Hegelian syllogism, mediating one another:

- De-realization inches toward the absolute: it unhinges the hard-won shapes of actuality, does not let them linger in a substantive energetic state, and mobilizes the labor of mediation.
- The absolute issues a demand, backed up by actuality rather than potentiality, for the de-realization not of this or that thing but of the real "as such," and of our conviction that this real is the indubitable bedrock of *what is*.

Virtualization activates a backflow from the substantivized to the verbal-subjective energy (figure 1) and every transition from *actuality* to *actuality'* (figure 3).

The historical constellation of the twenty-first century is cataclysmic: the standpoint of the absolute has been deserted under a false pretext of its totalizing effects, while the de-realization of what presents itself to ordinary consciousness intensifies, its reconversion into another mode of substance blocked. Destructive energy is liberated into negative workings without works, an indeterminate negation in the name of the purely possible spurning every actual shape, however fleeting. We are conversant with this phenomenon variously labeled "nihilism" or "modernity," indwelling in the de-realizing workings of capitalist economies and now reaching its crest in global environmental destruction. As I've already mentioned, Heidegger flirts with this tendency when he proclaims, despite his allegiance to Aristotle, that "higher than actuality stands possibility [*höher als die Wirklichkeit steht die Möglichkeit*]"[33] and lays the groundwork for existentialist philosophy. What these disparate cultural, philosophical, economic, and ecological complexes have in common is their disdain for a fulfillment that presumably brings the dark tidings of finality and death-in-life. Yet, paradoxically, they barter exclusively in death—biological or planetary, social or physical—by fixating on a hollow potentiality that is insulated from the actual. The revolutionary locus today, in a rebuke to a long tradition in intellectual history, is actuality, not possibility.

So entrenched is pure potentiality in *our* actuality that we, by and large, experience energy as anti-energy (which is at the same time its essential, if hypervalorized, moment), accelerating the liberation of stored force from formed matter by exploding the shapes (ideally, all the shapes) that contain it. De-actualization does not guide us to another actuality; we are either stranded between actualities, as though on an elevator stopped between floors, or we are infinitely regressing to the virtual plane of energy without ever arriving at our destination. Our drives, our fantasies and desires are stuck, fixated in the Freudian sense of the word, and the object of their fixation is a purely negative, destructive, endless flow, cathecting the uncathectable. We are unworking dialectics, working backwards through to its virtual beginnings with the abstract, the indeterminate, the arbitrary, the diverse: the "absolutely free will" of the *Philosophy of Right*, the "doctrine of being," formally identical to nothing in the *Logics*, the mechanics of space in the *Philosophy of Nature*, consciousness not yet anchored in self-consciousness in the *Phenomenology*. Whatever is left of our energy feeds on the loss of actuality that has been attained; it de-actualizes, empties out, indeterminately negates everything it sweeps into its midst and celebrates this unconditional destruction of substance in a besieged and isolated interiority as a genuine actuality. This, too, is nihilism. It would be perfectly legitimate to repeat with regard to it what Hegel has to say about morality, namely that "it is supposed to have validity simply and solely as a non-actual 'thought-thing' [*als das unwirkliche Gedankending*] of pure abstraction, and then again equally to have no validity in that mode; its truth is supposed to consist in its being opposed to actuality [*der Wirklichkeit entgegengesetzt*], and to be entirely free and empty of it, and then again, to consist in its being actuality" (*PhG* §630).

There are two mechanisms, two apparatuses, for virtualizing the world that correspond to the two moments of possibility in the *Science of Logic*: the positive "being-reflected-into-itself" and the negative "deficiency" compared to a completed actuality.[34] Both mechanisms refer back to the process of subjectivation: the first, to the creation of the subject through the doubling and self-reflectedness of actuality; the second, to the spectacle of the subject from the platform of substance, where it appears to be a lacuna—a "deficiency"—in being. The emphasis on the real valorizes energy in the substantive, as works without workings; the stress on possibility is committed to energy in the subjective key as the destructive workings without the works. So long as the two attitudes are not complementary, our conceptions and practices of energy will suffer irreparable damage. That reality cut loose from actuality is virtual and that virtuality is real in its catastrophic effects are the ramifications of energy released from any limits (including, first and foremost, its self-limitations)—energy unbound from itself.

The subject hails from an inward self-relational twist, which, for Hegel, is the instant when the "actual self," *wirklich Selbst*, manages to "reflect itself into itself and to be a subject [*sich in sich zu reflektieren und Subjekt zu sein*]" (*PhG* §766). The actual self retreats from the actuality of works (and its selfhood *is* the main work) into an inner world it furnishes itself with. As Hegel never tires of reminding us, and as we shall rehash in detail a little later, this taciturn realm of subjectivity with its thoughts, intentions, and fantasies is not merely imaginary but has a special actuality, replete with its own works and workings. The subject is the actuality or the energy of the virtual.

The danger, nonetheless, is that this sort of energy would not undergo yet another conversion and, by *not* undergoing it, would arrest dialectical development. Should the subject fail to re-exteriorize itself, for instance by acting in the world, it would risk being a stand-alone entity, confined in itself, growing autistic on the verge of evil as absolute separation. When unrelated to an "actual" external other, a self-relation withers away. Foregoing its return to substance, the subject uses up its energy supply and, rather than strapping them together, keeps the two halves of energy apart. Energy ceases to be a synergy, which means that it dissipates as energy. The merely possible conditions *and* disrupts the dialectical workings of a subject who reflects without deflecting itself from itself, without reemerging on the surface of appearances. Eschewing external actuality, this subject, in whom we should have already glimpsed ourselves, lives by siphoning energy off from the cycle *working-works-working'* and, while that negative supply has not yet run dry, turns the loss of energy into an energizing factor. With this, it is expelled from the spheres of subject and substance alike.

Virtualized, *Geist* survives as a ghost, in accord with the word's German etymology *gēst*, which is explored, among other places, in Derrida's writings.[35] A ghostly substance folds unto itself, and the resulting wrinkle is subjective interiority, to be exteriorized or emptied out into the works of spirit, unless its recrudescence comes to a halt, as it seems to nowadays. To reiterate: a virtual-spectral element of spirit is vital to its self-overcoming and growth. At the same time, it cannot be anything but a hiatus—or a bridge—between *actuality* and *actuality'*. If energy (*Geist* or *energeia*) is the ensemble of actuality and actualization, of *what is* and the becoming of *what is*, of the edifice and the scaffolding used to build it, then virtuality is that by virtue of which actuality actualizes itself, splitting from itself and becoming other to itself as potentiality. Virtuality, in other words, is the way, the path that should be neither expunged nor covered over by the results it has led us to obtain. It signals the doubling of actuality, its othering that culminates in the accomplishment of another actuality—to wit, the "original" actuality viewed, through the prism of negativity, in a different, more mediated, self-mediated, self-conscious light.

Virtuality regularly intervenes in the speculative identity actuality = actuality that it makes possible. Its interventions, however, wax troublesome when it suspends the work of mediation, keeps dredging inter-actual spaces, invests heavily in the separation and disarticulation that persist in relational articulations, and prompts the idolization of pure activity at the expense of its crystallized outcomes. Voilà the thoroughly negative dialectic that Theodor Adorno dreamed of, or Walter Benjamin's "dialectics at a standstill" indistinguishable from the other extreme, that of the ongoing and ever-accelerating movement! Both our present and future fit within these interstices of the actual, which is permanently unglued from itself thanks to unrestrained virtualization.

A Case Study in Virtuality: The Energy of Thought

If virtuality is shackled to abstraction, to the void of universality, to the ghostly beginnings of spirit or energy, then it is to be expected that its form in subjective interiority will be cognition, thought itself. At first, thought needs to set itself apart from the actual world, so as to demarcate the boundaries of its own domain and its own right, a task it pursues most doggedly in Kant's transcendental philosophy. (According to dialectical logic, by the time philosophy brings its initial task to self-consciousness, this task has been already accomplished.) The "energy of thought," *die Energie des Denkens*, which we've encountered earlier in the text, is the outcome of such a demarcation.

It would certainly be erroneous to think that thought may be exclusively qualified and described by its negative, virtualizing (should I say "critical"?) power. In the course of the *Phenomenology*, Hegel will argue that this level of thinking at loggerheads with the world is the prerogative of novices. The project of self-consciousness and the point of dialectical apprenticeship is to transition from the virtuality of thought to the actuality of thinking, from *Energie* to the *Wirklichkeit* of a more-than-cognitive cognizing. The full-fledged energy of thinking lies in its reconciliation with substance, on the one hand, and in cementing the subject's relation to itself, on the other. Reconciliation with substance is not to be conflated with the transposition of thought's virtual reality onto the "outside world," or, for example, a practical "application" of its insights. Thought is always already substance, but at first it does not know this. Through mediation, objectivation, turning inside out, mature thought makes the world and is made by it. It is not a bureaucratic secretary of the world, documented by means of representational "picture-thinking." Rather, thought *becomes* the energetic formations, the shapes of actuality we are surrounded by. This outward tendency is in tandem with the cultivation and deepening of its self-relation, of a reflectedness that empowers it to be a thought and a thinking, the work and the workings of self-conscious energy.[36]

The indictment of Hegel for his supposed idealism tends to concentrate on the segment where the energy of thought exteriorizes itself into the world. Our accusers skip over the other half of the energy circle: the world de-substantivized into (and remaking) thought. The charges of idealism lose their sting as soon as one shows that the determination of thought and existence, of consciousness and nature, is a continual co-determination, thanks to which each earns for itself a new degree of actuality, is energized and is energizing in relation to the other. The synergy of being and thought, in equal measure "materialist" and "idealist," converts the virtual and abstract *Energie* into *Wirklichkeit*. That said, the virtual has its specific actuality, its energy; the objects of thought and the acts of thinking are its works and workings. And the actual *needs* virtuality in order to detach itself from itself, if only so as to come to terms with itself otherwise.

A memorable instance where actuality and thought are intermediated is to be found in the "Morality" section of the *Phenomenology*. There, Hegel is careful to distinguish between "pure thought" (*reine Denken*), representational thinking (*Vorstellung*), and actual self-consciousness. "Pure thought" deems itself "raised above its actuality [*über seine Wirklichkeit erhaben ist*]" (*PhG* §615), supplying *avant la lettre* the model for existential possibility, which similarly stands higher than actuality. It pretends to have rendered itself autonomous from the finite energy of being. But, Hegel insinuates, by virtue of doing so, pure thought also derives its energy from this imagined self-exaltation, that is, from its opposition to immediate actuality. The segregation of the two moments—of the relational and non-relational; of *Wirklichkeit* and pure thought—creates a (negative) meta-relation between them. Positively rearticulated, that relation instigates representational thinking: "For neither of these two is single and separate; on the contrary, each of them, whose essential determination lies in their being *free from one another*, is thus in the unity no longer free from the other, and each therefore is superseded. Hence, as regards content, they become as such, objects each of which counts as object for the other, and as regards form, in such a way that this interchange equally exists in representational thinking [*so daß diese Austauschung derselben zugleich nur vorgestellt ist*]" (*PhG* §615). The limits of representational thinking are drawn here in their schematic outlines. To surpass the sense of mutual repulsion of thought and actuality, it is de rigueur to lift oneself out of the sphere of morality and to arrive at an actual (i.e., actual*ized*) self-consciousness that, rather than saying "no" to, expresses actuality, by which it is, in turn, expressed. A thought that acts and an act that thinks, the energy of expression is finally the energy of energy: the self-relation of actuality turned to the other, literally pressing itself out of itself and, in this exteriorization, putting itself *into* practice, putting itself to work, en-ergizing.

There is, then, no energy of thought (in the singular; as such) but only the energies of thinking, among which we can now individuate at least three: pure, representational, and expressive.

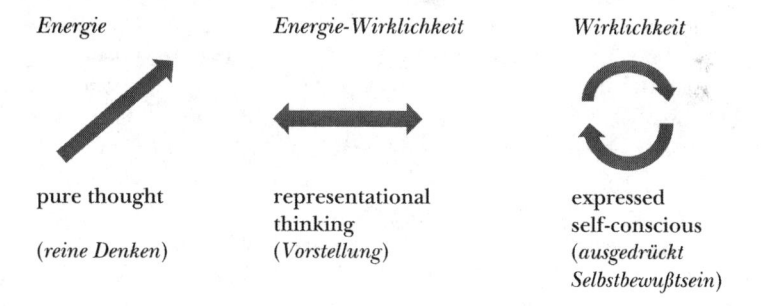

Energie	*Energie-Wirklichkeit*	*Wirklichkeit*
↗	←——→	↻
pure thought	representational thinking	expressed self-conscious
(*reine Denken*)	(*Vorstellung*)	(*ausgedrückt Selbstbewußtsein*)

Figure 5. Three modes of thinking

The energy of pure thought is the power of detachment from the immediately given, from the familiar, from the real which is not yet actual. Its predilection for estrangement follows the arc of retiring from the world and inaugurates a virtual space insulated from existence and still unaware of having simply carved out a niche, a lacuna, *within* that very existence. Phenomenologically construed as a movement of no-return, it is apriori plunged into a crisis and a contradiction: an analysis forbidding any synthesis, a stubborn non-relation, an active "'nothing' [which] just as much *is* [*aber dies Nichts selbst* ist *ebensosehr*]." "It is," Hegel continues, "an absolute abstraction, and thus pure thought or being-within-self [*also das reine Denken oder In-sich-sein*], and with the moment of its opposition to the spiritual unity, it is *evil*" (*PhG* §780). The actuality of the virtual is pure thought, the nothing which is and which blows the icy winds of nonbeing onto everything in existence, prompting the latter to welcome mediation and the cut of negativity. When it is hypostatized and gains independence, this nothing, unsatisfied with mediations and curbed (determinate) negations, strives to nullify existence as a whole, to recast existence in its own imagelessness. The being of nothing is, in its turn, actualized into evil, that one-way ticket out of the synergic energy from which *Geist*, or *Wirklichkeit*, is braided. In this sense, and in this sense alone, it is acceptable to complain that "ideas and ideals are nothing more than chimeras, and philosophy a system of such phantasms."[37]

In a dialectical truth procedure, however, bidirectional representation gains an edge over pure thought, which is unidirectional. Representational thought shuttles between the abstract virtuality of the representing consciousness and the concrete existence of the reality represented by it. Not only is "the mediation of representational thought necessary [*ist also die Vermittlung der Vorstellung notwendig*]" (*PhG* §784), but this thought in and of itself is also a mediation between things and thoughts, external existence and inner virtual reality. While pure thought is virtuality at rest and at arm's length from the world, representation is ceaseless agitation, wavering between the representing and the represented and endlessly busy with patching up the threads that pure thought has left undone. But, regardless of its apparently positive character, the cradle of representational thought is the nihilistic and annihilatory power of total negativity. *Vorstellung* (representation), though pointing in both directions, does not represent *itself* in representing the world, is not self-conscious, and has not reached the speculative insight "*thought* is *thinghood*, or *thinghood* is *thought*" *PhG* (§578); on the contrary, it erases its representational function. Only an expressed self-consciousness is capable of discharging these tasks.

Self-consciousness is Hegel's manner of interpreting the Aristotelian thought thinking itself, at once moving and unmoved because vibrating exclusively in itself (as other to itself). Nevertheless, the content of this interpretation undergoes drastic modifications depending on the stage in the *Phenomenology*, at which it is presented. Initially, thought thinking itself stands for the abstract freedom of a stoic self-consciousness with its "tranquil indifference of a thought thinking itself, the unchangeable and *genuine certainty of its own self* [*es ist sich diese Ataraxie des Sich-*

selbst-denkens, die unwandelbare und wahrhafte Gewißheit seiner selbst]" (*PhG* §205). A self-thinking thought is, on this reading, pure thought amputated from the world, plus a certain measure of self-reflexiveness. Later on, the essence of thought thinking itself will be taken up in a still abstract identity of thinghood and thinking, the "universal common to both" being "the abstraction of a pure, inward vibration, or of pure thought thinking itself [*die Abstraktion des reinen Erzitterns in sich selbst, oder des reinen Sich-selbst-denkens*]. This simple rotary movement must become more complex" (*PhG* §579). (Could this shared minimal universality be the Latin *res* qualified as *cogitans* and *extensa* by Descartes?) Circling back to the world, self-consciousness is mediated with thinghood and actuality. If its "simple rotary movement" is only *initially* simple, this is because it trembles, or oscillates, in itself alone, despite its identification with the principle of exteriority, with thingly *essence*. A subsequent complication of dialectical movement has to do with the expression of self-consciousness in the workings and the works that are simultaneously of thoughts and things, of thinking and of thinging. Self-consciousness expressed is self-consciousness betrayed in the speculative sense of the word, yet without losing its self-reflexivity, the inward swerve of its representation, which, by the same token, faces outward. "It is in its ownmost *works* [*ihrem eigentümlichen* Werke] that absolute freedom becomes an object to itself" (*PhG* §592), where its "works" are the substantive portions of energy beyond the abstract essence of things. Ex-pressed, squeezed out of itself, self-consciousness triggers the "sublation of thought thinking itself," *Aufheben des Sich-selbst-denkens*, and lets the actual germinate on the grounds of a negated virtuality.

Thought thinking itself is sublated but not, thereby, eradicated. What this means is that it becomes more-than-thought and more-than-real: it becomes actual. Thought thinking itself educes the world's self-relationality. It continues to think itself, but not within the borders of a virtual domain subtracted from existence. Thought is now thinking itself in and as the world, or, inversely, the world thinks itself through the mediations provided by thought, which has melted into it, demolished the barriers that had been erected to guarantee its purity, discarded its virtual shell. Hegel's energy is just that: an enworkment, working on itself and turned to the other, working on itself *in* being turned to the other, turning to the other by way of working on itself, all the while having already accomplished everything it *had to* accomplish. It does what it does freely, the contingent pressure of "empirical" necessity having been relieved. With an eye to Aristotle, Hegel retrieves a piece of ancient philosophy, according to which a thinking energy is thinking being and thinking. Growing with and into the world that concretizes (literally, "grows-with")[38] itself, a thinking thought mends its ways, amends its originally virtual and virtualizing works and workings in order to express and be expressed by the actual. Wandering the labyrinths of virtuality, often brutally foisted onto existence from the outside, we are yet to learn from and implement these energy procedures.

Speculative Energy

Thus far, we have been tracking virtualization as a process of withdrawal and detachment from the so-called "real world" and the establishment of a transcendent domain insulated from whatever is manifest here-below. Understood this way, virtuality overlaps with metaphysics, such that the energy of both is honed and rarefied in the negation of the actual and is, therefore, developing at variance with itself, as anti-energy. Metaphysics is nothing but the virtual entombed in itself, prevented from successively overcoming itself in a series of re-externalizations (or substantivations) that mediate actuality. Absconding from the world, it forecloses all recourse to the real, which, after a detour to virtuality, would be no longer real but actual. Insofar as our reality becomes more and more virtual, then, we come to inhabit the metaphysical domain (under the banner of anti-metaphysics, no less), the domain which, for its part, renders the world less and less habitable.

A more elementary technique of virtualization may be sighted in what I call "speculative energy." Speculation, to be perfectly clear, is not daydreaming; it is not a state of being absorbed by free-floating musings with one's back turned to the world. It has the exact sense of a mirror effect, referencing the specular scene where one gazes at oneself. To behold the spectacle of oneself, one must have come unglued from oneself, become other to oneself, been externalized vis-à-vis oneself. One must have acquired a spectral double as a result of the splitting experienced by a simple identity (which is only "simple" inasmuch as it has no idea of the *how* of its constitution). What is true for the subject is also true for the concept: its other is not outside but within, and, far from a totalitarian closure, this is what precipitates its turning inside out and, on the obverse, the subsequent loss of its unmediated unity.[39] This is why, for Hegel, "the absolute concept of difference" is an "inner difference, a repulsion of a like pole, as like pole, from itself, and as the equality of nonequal as nonequal [*innrer Unterschied, Abstoßen des Gleichnamigen als Gleichnamigen von sich selbst, und Gleichsein des Ungleichen als Ungleichen*]" (*PhG* §160). The same repels itself from itself to be the other; the other (or the non-same) keeps a formal identity to itself in its otherness. An unmediated actuality pushes itself away from itself to give rise to another actuality by precipitating the other *of* actuality—potentiality or virtuality. Speculative energy is discharged from an atomic explosion, in which the previously undivided, and ostensibly indivisible, nucleus of meaning and identity parts into two. *X* is redoubled, unpacking itself into itself and its other self, namely the other. It metamorphoses into *X* and not-*X*.

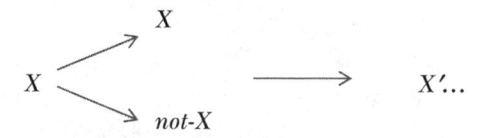

$$X \begin{matrix} \nearrow X \\ \searrow \text{not-}X \end{matrix} \longrightarrow X'\ldots$$

Figure 6. Speculative energy

Emblematically, speculative energy has made its appearance in the opening paragraphs of Hegel's *Philosophy of Nature*. The mechanics of space is first set to work through the negation of spatial indeterminacy by a single point localized somewhere—anywhere—on its infinite expanse. Next, the point must negate itself by being doubled, reflected in another point like it, and, potentially, in an infinite multiplicity of such points constituting a line: "the negation of *space* . . . is itself spatial. The point, as essentially this relation, i.e., as sublating itself, is the *line*, the first other [*die* Linie, *das erste Anders*], i.e., spatial being, of the point. . . . That the line does not consist of points, nor the plane of lines, follows from their concept; for the line is rather the point as existing *outside itself* [*der Punkt als* außer sich *seiend*], i.e., *relating* itself to space and sublating itself."[40] The point, *X*, is point, *X*, and not-point, *not-X*, namely aligned point*s*—a whole infinity of them—gathered into a line. Boiling beneath the atemporal and calm planes of geometry (but also of punctuation marks) is the speculative energy that causes simple identities, commonly depicted as points or periods, to explode.

As soon as a virtual double makes its appearance on the speculative stage, it de-actualizes what it copies, bisecting a preexisting identity. One divides into two because, in its unity and unicity, identity is not monolithic. Identity is not itself; it is the outcome of a partly erased process of identification, that is to say, a work, which is an aggregate of workings, of identifying-with (if only with oneself). Speculative energy distills the verbal and substantive moments of the one into the two that it is: itself and not-itself, identity and identification. Along these points-lines, Hegel defines the selfsame in terms of "the different in itself, or the like pole that repels itself from itself [*sich von sich selbst abstößt*] or sunders itself into two [*sich entzweit*]. What was called *simple force* duplicates itself [*ver-*

doppelt sich selbst] and, through its infinity, is law" (*PhG* §161). Speculative doubling, its energy resonant with atomic fission or with quantum matter hosting subatomic non-identities, will play a decisive role in the principle of signification, the excess of meaning sundered into "this" tree and the word "tree." More striking still will be the doubling of the "I" into this living-breathing I and the word "I," which, though evocative of singularity, can be uttered with reference to and by anyone.

The word "energy" is itself saturated with speculative energy. It separates from itself, divides into two, and operates, whether we realize this or not, with the senses of *ergon* or *work* that are at odds with one another: the completed and the incomplete, the substantive and the verbal, formed matter and a de-forming force, what is already in the work and what is still at work. Its content implies movement and rest, but the form, too, is a speculative unity of *X* and *not-X*, movement and not-movement. Translating *energeia*, the Hegelian actuality thus subdivides into "two extremes," *zweier Extreme*: the passive actuality (*die passive Wirklichkeit*) to be sublated by the active this-worldliness (*das tätige Diesseits*) of consciousness (*PhG* §221). Actuality is the energy that is not one and that is energizing-energized precisely because it is more than one in the one. (Hence, my preference for inscribing it in the composite expression "energy-actuality.") To state this riskily, dialectical thought receives its speculative impulse from the concept or the non-concept of energy; it models *the* concept on *a* concept, namely on energy-actuality divided in and against itself.

In order to avoid giving the impression that he has put his finger on an extrinsic stand-off between an active subject and passive substance in the two extremes of actuality, Hegel appeals to the logic of speculative energy: "actuality, on its side, can only be sublated because its own unchangeable essence sublates it, repels itself from itself [*sich von sich abstößt*] and hands over what has been repelled to the active extreme. The active force appears as the power, wherein actuality is dissolved [*Die tätige Kraft erscheint als die Macht, worin die Wirklichkeit sich auflöst*]" (*PhG* §221). The subject is the self-repelling of substance within the previously unmediated *X* of actuality. It is *how* actuality can act by doubling itself into a passive substratum and an active agent. The discharge of the subject from the self-repulsion of substance, though, entails the sacrifice of actuality to force and power, *Kraft* and *Macht*, *potestas* and potentiality—the notions we are prone to consider synonymous with energy. Powerless and forceless, energy dissolves into its own subjective self-negation, which usurps the concept of energy in toto, explaining it with reference to power and force. But this is tantamount to saying that energy dissolves in itself as other to itself, the otherness that will henceforth be its privileged aspect.

Energy Is (Not) Power

Why is power allocated to the other of energy in the speculative schism we have just attended to? To address this question in the context of intellectual history, we are obliged to make a detour via the Greek and Latin conceptions of power as *dunamis* and *potentia* that betoken what *energeia* and *actualitas* are not. Given Hegel's speculative conception, however, the opposites are not externally pitted against one another *ab initio*; power is produced by the self-repulsion of energy-actuality and its doubling into itself and the other, substance and subject. Dialectics discovers the speculative identity of opposites—*dunamis* and *energeia*, *potentia* and *actualitas*—which eludes the thinkers of antiquity and modernity alike. Still, today, in our today, that identity is less evident than ever. With the predominance of virtuality and the valorization of possibility in all spheres of human existence, energy presents itself to us exclusively as its other, to wit, as power or force.

"Virtue" might be a redeeming, if plainly gendered (*vir* = Latin for "man") feature of the "virtual." It condenses the energy of the good into individual "*gifts, capacities, powers* [Gaben, Fähigkeiten, Kräfte]." But in them, in these potentialities, the universality proper to the good is vacuous and abstract. They confine the good to "a mode of the spiritual . . . which requires the principle of individuality to give it life and movement, and in this principle it has its *actuality* [Wirklichkeit]" (*PhG* §385). At issue here is not, as it appears at first glance, the figure of a free individuality able to put its sovereign (manly) powers to arbitrary uses, but rather, the immature actuality of the good, too beholden to the virtuality of virtue. After all, virtue lacks the inner determinations that can result only from an immanent self-negation, exteriorization, action, behavior. When equally abstract (if, I insist, already gendered) individuals are taken as the end-all and be-all actuality of the good, particularly as far as their virtues or capacities are concerned,[41] and when, moreover, their "gifts" are not practiced, their immature moral actuality is barely distinct from virtuality. The energy of morality announces itself in the shape of its other, the power or potentiality it acquired by way of its speculative doubling the moment it repelled itself from itself, was subjectivated, and remained stuck in the subjective shape of "spiritual gifts."

Whereas, in matters of the good, individual virtue perverts energy into power, at the level of the cognizing mind, pure thinking is the catalyst of such a perversion. Pure thinking is a purely negative, destructive power through which, Hegel states, "the positive state of affairs was deprived of its power." "In this way," he goes on, "thinking made its mark on actuality and had the most awe-inspiring effect."[42] In the confrontation between a scarcely mediated reality and pure thinking, power is pitted against power, as two externalities (more exactly, self-externalities) tackle one another. Virtual reality revolts against itself: in it, the virtual bludgeons the real. Thanks to this groundbreaking skirmish and to the desire to leave the world here-below behind, pure thinking, which has the advantage of having incorporated into itself the principle of negativity, negates the positivity of *what is*. But, although Hegel omits this from the account he gives in the *Encyclopedia Logic*, thinking does not escape unscathed, either. In coming together, if only for a stand-off whereby thinking "made its mark" on immediate actuality, *both* sides are deprived of their powers (abstract capacities, potentialities, etc.), and this deprivation means that they are imbued with a budding, self-mediated actuality attained with respect to the vanquished or the vanquishing other.

With the above, I do not wish to imply that Hegel expresses a philosophical preference for powerlessness over power. Far from it: in a thinly veiled attack on Kant, he conveys how he detests "a beauty without force," *kraftlose Schönheit*, and confesses how much he revels in the already cited "power of the negative," *Macht des Negativen* (*PhG* §32). The absence of force that Hegel abhors characterizes that which is incapable of giving itself actuality, incapable of being otherwise than merely capable. This is, surely, a more sophisticated precursor to the negation of power which is so glorified today in certain philosophical circles reliant for their intellectual energy on the speculative double, the *not-X*, and bemoaning, at the same time, the dominance of *X*, the identity of which was, in any event, sacrificed in speculative splitting. Energetic powerlessness is not the downside of power; it is not the entropic divestment of power's potential, but a state or a movement (a state-movement) on the hither side of power and powerlessness.[43]

In the *Science of Logic* Hegel makes the argument that, divorced from actuality, the power of possibility is powerless, reduced to an infinitely malleable form contingently brought to bear on the content it is filled with. "When we therefore say of something 'it is possible,' this purely formal assertion is just as superficial and empty as the principle of non-contradiction, and any content that we put into it. 'A is possible,' says no more than 'A is A.'"[44] To disband existence in limitless possibilities is to drain its energy away, formalizing and abstracting it, announcing that it has the power to be anything whatsoever without tolerating its delimitation to a definitive energetic shape and the ontological commitment this delimitation entails. For this reason, possibility is not only reminiscent of the principle of noncontradiction; it *is* contradiction, "or it is *impossibility*."[45] The *–abilities* of possibility invite as much as they prohibit actualization.

The dictatorship of the virtual presupposes the unlimited reign of power. Our possibilities are void of actuality because everything seems to be in our power and nothing lies beyond power and powerlessness. In this crass sense, everything is political. The pleasures of completion and accomplishment have vanished in an assault on limits that keeps us captive, shackled to a beginning that has not begun unfolding yet, the condition of an indifferent non-differentiation. On a perpetual quest for newness, we refuse consciously to repeat—to work through—what has been and, consequently, fall into the routines of unconscious repetition, acting out the past. *Not-X* is the order of the day. It sounds absurd to claim that, rather than a universal powerlessness, peace is the effect of energy's coming to fruition. Reality and pure thought clash to no avail, unable to surpass their germinal negative mediation by the conflict itself; they are suspended in the infinite chasm of virtual reality, which is consumed by an unresolved inner contradiction between the virtual and the real. We live not in the age that succeeds the final synthesis Hegel is said to have forecast, but in the age of the subject—or rather of subject*s*—without substance, of energy perverted into power, felt solely in its otherness. According to the preface of the *Phenomenology*, our age is one of the "unrestrained fermentation of substance," *ungebändigten Gären der Substanz* (*PhG* §10), of a subject retreating further into itself, into its virtuality, and decomposing there. Whatever passes for thinking are vapors of such decomposition. The mutation we are living (or dying) through is that of virility hiding under the sheepskin of impotence; a power grab by means of affirming powerlessness; *not-X* letting slip what *X* stood for. From this "unrestrained fermentation" we draw our energy for acting out, vaguely cognizant of its unsustainability.

Synergy

Like possibility, with which it is associated, power has an unbinding effect. That is its work, *its* actuality. Power and possibility remove the restraints imposed by determinacy. To some extent liberatory, these anti-energies can easily tip the scales of being—especially those of pure, unmediated being—toward nothingness, as they excessively and obsessively untie every bond and unbind every nexus. (The exact translation of *ungebändigten*, an adjective, which Hegel uses to describe the fermentation of substance and which I have just now rendered in English as "unrestrained," is "unbound.") The power relation dissipates all relations, even if it ostensibly bolsters the political webs. Of power, then, there is only an analytics, and the same holds for a purely existential approach to existence, fixated on the possible, which remains unfulfilled in any of the infinite possibilities that comprise it.[46]

Bent on infinite analysis, potency and potentiality (power and possibility) are incompatible with synergy, the "with-work" or "working-with" at the heart of energy. Only the poorest, most abstract actuality of the real persists in an obdurate confrontation with the virtuality of pure thought. The first actuality, akin to the first principles for thinking, is too separate, too immediate to form synergic relations and, thereby, to garner much energy. Mediation, after all, is a tying of two or more ends in the middle knot, which is emphatically not a compromise solution, not the golden mean of moderation, but the most extreme process, opening onto a qualitative groundshift in actuality. Sufficiently mediated, actuality *is* actualities: a redoubling of *actuality* with *actuality'* with *actuality"*, and so forth, as well as with the redoubling itself, namely with the virtual, with its speculative negation. Synergy is a synergy of energy and anti-energy, of the binding and the unbinding, a bond where the work of separation and the separated itself have their undeniable place.

Usually, Hegel falls back on the figure of the circle in an attempt to depict the dynamics of dialectical mediation. Usually, but not always. In the *Phenomenology*'s preface, he unexpectedly contrasts the suffocating ligature of the circle with the binding of accidental singularities in a synergic tapestry of the actual: "The circle—which remains self-enclosed, rests and, like substance, holds [*hält*] its moments together—is an immediate and, therefore, unsurprising relation [*Verhältnis*]. But that the accidental, detached from its context, attains an isolated freedom and its own existence in its being bound together with other actualities and only as existing in their context [*gebundne und nur in seinem Zusammenhange mit anderm Wirkliche*]—this is the tremendous power of the negative" (*PhG* §32). The circle is the tightest link between actuality and itself, the same resting in itself. The accidental and the isolated, conversely, point back to the virtual, to possibility assimilated to contingency in the *Science of Logic*. Actuality itself is virtual when it is accidental, isolated, and merely possible. But one need not choose between a hermetically sealed circle and the detached shreds of accidental existence. A binding-together of actualities—first, decontextualized; then, inserted into another context, "hanging-together" (*Zusammenhang*) with other actualities—is their synergy. Negativity airs the circle shut in itself, punctures its self-enclosing totality, helps concentrate the working subject in the work of substance and, vice versa, unpacks a ready work into the workings that have preceded it or those yet to come. In this vein, synthesis, that tired third term of dialectics, should be reinvented in keeping with synergy's broken circle, its "with-work" welcoming another actuality and the other of actuality, while antithesis ought to be rethought as working with-and-against the thesis. Curtly put, synthesis is but a rarified, sublimated, intellectualized, or logically mediated version of synergy.

Further on in the *Phenomenology*, Hegel will delve in painstaking detail into the synergic structure and movement of "actual spirit" at stake in the dialectical system of science (*Wissenschaft*). Taking a leaf from the book of synthesis, the system itself is a synergy of part-wholes (in science: the synergy of historically conditioned ways of cognizing), not an oppressive totality. Each moment of energetic actuality is a whole unto itself, a global shape (*Gestalt*) of energy, its genuine working-work, which is absolutely true at a given moment in the history of spirit. Removed from the whole, as they inevitably are, individual historical shapes of spirit imbibe negative energy and are dripping with the virtual. Spirit is cleaved into spirits, and these are not melded together into a seamless unity but woven into a bundle or a coil, where they interweave and reencounter one another across conceptual and spatiotemporal distances. For a dialectician, energizing is mediating: synergizing.

Here is how Hegel explains the synergies of spirit in a textual band, on which the whole book is suspended: "This self-certain spirit and its movement are the genuine actuality [*wahrhafte Wirklichkeit*] and the *being-in-and-for-itself* which belongs to each moment. Thus while the previous single series in its advance marked the retrogressive steps by nodes, but continued again out of them in a single line, it is henceforth, as it were, broken at these nodes, at these universal moments, and falls apart into many lines which, gathered together into *a single* bundle [*in* einen *Bund zusammengefaßt*], at the same time combine symmetrically so that the same distinction in which each particular moment gave itself a shape all meet together [*zusammentreffen*]" (*PhG* §681). The actuality of each moment in the dialectic is the accomplished actuality as such ("self-certain spirit"); the actual does not stand over and against that given moment but is its energy source and ownmost shape, its "being-in-and-for-itself," its depth and surface. How so? The unique steps of each series—consciousness, self-consciousness, reason—function simultaneously as the universal nodes, or knots, marking stages on the tightrope path of spirit as such. These are the points of contact among lines that, once aligned in a synergic bundle, are recontextualized, receive an additional meaning, and yet maintain their singularity. They are also the internal combustion engines of dialectics, where the singular and the universal are burning together, without melting into one another. The synergic bond is a meeting place of the bound and the unbound, of the many and the one, the virtual and the actual, togetherness and separation.

PART I

part-whole of spirit   actual spirit as bundle

Figure 7. Spirit and synergy

The Hegelian system is a synergy of synergies that seeks the iterable and reiterated universal nodes across the bundles of phenomenology, aesthetics, religion, right, nature, and so on, even as it leaves plenty of room for their singular itineraries. It recollects, retracing the steps of part-wholes in a repetition that warrants a further flourishing of energy. A part of the system, the *Phenomenology* gathers the system into itself and repeats (for the first time: repetition *is* the inaugural gesture of the system, its incipit!) the movements of the whole, while remaining mindful of its absolute energetic rest. The book's singular nodes are, in their singularity, the universal knots of spirit, indicating when, where, and how to release or withhold energy along various stretches of the path to be negotiated. And they are also places of respite, more abiding than the temporary withholding of energy would permit, from the restlessness of the negative, whose work is already accomplished, though by no means "overcome."

Between the lines of the *Phenomenology*, self-consciousness is, similarly, a part that supplants the whole, because *its* unique nodes are the universal steps of the dialectical project as such and also because the consciousness, back to which it reflexively circles, is synergy in miniature, the working-with of thought and existence (the *con-* of *consciousness* is the Latin substitute for the Greek *syn-*) divided between an "external" object and itself. In self-conscious configurations, spirit shapes itself, gives itself an energetic shape, the shape of actuality at home in what is shaped. This is especially so in self-consciousness conscious of itself as spirit: "If its [self-conscious spirit's] shape is to express spirit itself, then the shape must be nothing else than spirit, and spirit must appear to itself, or be actual [*und er sich so erschienen oder wirklich sein*], just as it is in its essence" (*PhG* §678). Spirit-cum-energy attains freedom in synergy with itself, the synergy of its form and content, essence and appearance. But the secret of its liberation lies in the meaning of energetic shapes.

Shapes of Spirit, Shapes of Energy

Stabilized into a shape, energy is temporarily contained, held and withheld, kept *in potentia*, buried in the quantifiable mass of matter. This, at any rate, will be a physicist's account. For us, the potentiality of energy "at rest" is its actuality as a work or a set of works. A material shape is the substantive element of *ergon*, matching on the other side the working aspect of actively shaping the given with recourse to negative mediation. In Hegel's eyes, any such shape implies that the actual is not actual enough, not actualized all at once, but has to be de-formed and re-formed until it is finally liberated into self-givenness. Time performs the work of such de- and re-forming. The stabilization and destabilization of energy amount to a rhythm, yielding and discarding new shapes, distinct spatial, psychic, institutional, and other configurations on the tracks of dialectics. At every moment, this process aspires toward the absolute: the manifest juncture, the articulation of the shaping and the shaped repeated ad infinitum in its finitude.

We are now in a position to reimagine the workings and the works of energy in the realm of phenomena in the following manner:

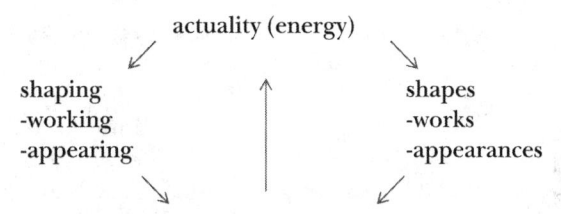

actuality (energy)

shaping　　　　　　　　　shapes
-working　　　　　　　　-works
-appearing　　　　　　　-appearances

self-shaped, self-shaping absolute repetition

Figure 8. The shapes and shaping of actuality

Worth noting is the fact that the shapes of energy, whether discernible in formed matter or as psychic configurations, are not the epiphenomenal, essentially superfluous manifestations of essence. A mode of working without works, mere essence that stubbornly keeps itself unshaped is no longer the philosopher's holy grail; rather, it is the abode of the virtual at a drastically diminished level of determinacy and mediatedness. The substantive countenance of energetic actuality with all the shapes, works, and appearances that belong to it turns essence inside out, allows essence to revert to phenomenality, to flare up from its concealment. Phenomenality (energy in the substantive) is the being-for-another of essence (energy in its verbal determination); essence is the being-in-itself of phenomenality.

A work is the shape of the worker's energy, the embodiment and fulfilled manifestation of the capacity to shape. "Whatever it is that the individual does, and whatever happens to him, that he has done himself, and he *is* that himself. He can only have the consciousness of having purely translated *his own self* from the night of possibility into the daylight of the present, from the *abstract in-itself* into the meaning of *actual* being [*in die Bedeutung des* wirklichen *Seins*]" (*PhG* §403). The individual's capacity to shape is the essence still dormant in "the night of possibility." For it to awaken, this energy must give itself a body in the works that appear among the phenomena, "in the daylight of the present," with a certain surplus of sense expressing the working impulse they contain, the "abstract in-itself" made palpable "for-us." Hegel views this double expression in terms of an act of "pure translation" (which, as we shall see, does not preclude a mistranslation), insofar as the actor's possibilities and the shaping essence as such are transformed into the shaped work or world. "The meaning of actual being," *die Bedeutung des wirklichen Seins*, of being and becoming as energy, is this ongoing carryover from the shaping to the shaped and back again to the as-of-yet withdrawn elements of essence.

Speaking of Hegel's essence, what we are really dealing with is *essencing*, a verbal connotation of energy, as opposed to its substantive embodiment in the works. A "simple," static, and amorphous essence is uncontainable in itself; speculatively sundered apart, it spills out into the phenomenal realm of works that express it and unavoidably betray its impossible purity locked in mere possibility. The dialectic of the shaping and the shaped (or of shape*s*) is a dialectic of energy and energies, of the one and the many. Ironically, the one energy devoid of synergy is not quite energy but a self-enclosed virtual essence, which has not yet made its appearance in the daylight of the present. In "actual being," contrariwise, there are only energ*ies* but no energy. And the absolute, as the most energetically accomplished state imaginable, implies a synergy of energies, in the plural and in the singular,[47] all of them accessible through infinite repetition, such that there is no longer a substantive difference between their essentiality and phenomenality.

The first energetic shapes, however, border on virtuality. Poor in mediations, they are relatively crude, undifferentiated, resistant to repetition, and far removed from the shaping impulse. These shapes, including the uncommitted will, pure being, space, or unselfconscious consciousness, border on the virtual, the indeterminate, the shapeless. In the dialectics of energy, the initial shapes—the works that present a barely concrete appearance overshadowed by the abstraction of the beginning—spring forth from the act of negating shapeless energetic fluxes and bear fresh imprints of what has been negated. As energetic figurations, they constitute a merely given actuality yet to be digested into an actuality that is (recognizably) self-given.

If self-consciousness is a shape of energy where the content identifies with the form of the self that knows itself in knowing the other, then it determinately negates the preceding shapes of spirit, invents for itself a new shapeless (because self-shaped: neither only phenomenal nor a concealed-essential) shape, and gives itself actuality. But if self-consciousness is a flight into the subject oblivious to substance, then its shapelessness parallels that of pure being or the abstract will, breathing with what I have tentatively designated as "the energy of a novice." Hegel hesitates: self-consciousness is sublated early on in the *Phenomenology*, yet it is also considered to be a prototype for every self-shaping energetic configuration. On the side of substance, dialectical geometry, too, offers a blueprint for how shapelessness is determinately negated, even as it regulates the rest of the developments in the dialectics of nature. To grasp its operations, which are analogous to those of self-consciousness, we must consult part II of Hegel's *Encyclopedia*.

Space is the shapeless possibility for shaping, a (virtual) "abstract self-externality" (*Außersichsein*) lacking determinations,[48] actuality other to itself, a substantive potentiality. The point is the first spatial negation of space, itself negated by an explosion (hence: speculative energy) into an infinite number of others like it in a line, which will set the limits of geometrical shapes. Geometric abstraction supports the realm of immediate actuality, prefigured in the rigidity of "first principles" and handed down as the law of substance. Its shapes are themselves negated in time, in "the negativity posited for itself [*für sich gesetzt*]" where "the point has actuality" (as a now).[49] The irruption of time from the calm of pure space is the mediated *actuality'*, which is self-related, in sharp contrast to the inert virtual reality of space. Temporal shapes free themselves from spatio-visual representations, and so recapture something of energy's verbal, non-substantive significations—something of its rhythm, if not musicality.

Dialectical "Mechanics" in *The Philosophy of Nature*

Space	Point, line ...	Time
Indeterminacy	Negation of indeterminacy	Determinate self-negation
Virtuality	Actuality'	Actuality"
Self-externality & inner essence	Externality of appearances Shapes	Dialectic of essence/ appearaces
Shapelessness	Works	Self-shaped/self-posited
Working without Works		Working Work

Figure 9. Speculative geometry and shapes of energy

That the shapes of energy (or of spirit) are not its epiphenomenal accouterments is a conclusion of the *Phenomenology*'s section on religion, where Hegel writes: "In its becoming, it [spirit] itself is, therefore, in *determinate* shapes [*In diesem Werden ist er also selbst in* bestimmten Gestalten] that constitute the different moments of this movement" (*PhG* §680). The determinate shapes are *of spirit* in the sense of substantively expressing its being, what it *is* at any phase in the temporality of its unfolding. They cannot be peeled off and away from the core of self-shaping activity without, by dint of their detachment from it, destroying that core. The less virtual a historical configuration of energy, the more indispensable are the works to its workings. Spirit breathes on the skin of its appearances and languishes in the cage of essence. Until, that is, energy attains its self-actualization, so that its works grant "a true shape," *wahren Gestalt*, to its workings, and the figuration or the figurativity of shape—the shape of shape, along with representational thought—demands to be overcome in favor of the actual concept. "It is then that spirit has grasped the concept of itself, just as we now have first grasped it; and its shape or the element of its existence, being the concept, is spirit itself [*seine Gestalt oder das Element seines Daseins, indem sie der Begriff ist, ist er selbst*]" (*PhG* §683). The self-negations of shape that rejoins the shaping, of rest experienced (more exactly, reexperienced) together with movement, of phenomenal appearances referred back to the essence, constitute the threshold of the absolute beyond amorphousness and morphologies, the absolute as a threshold across which spirit's transit through the world *and* through itself—through the world *as* through itself—will be repeated. They are also the pleats of Aristotelian *energeia* in the tissue of Hegel's text.

Two Energy Supplies, Three Energy Types

The transition from an ontology predicated on shapes to that of the concept is tantamount to switching energy supplies within the dialectics of the *Phenomenology*. The workings and the works of being originate from a more or less immediate actuality, the pre-given physical, biological, psychological, or cultural existence. The concept feeds on mediation itself—it grows from the middle, from all the punctuations and interruptions of the in-between—with its works and workings belonging to a self-given actuality. Of course, the switch from being to the concept is not a binary either/or, "on" or "off": the two energy supplies are interconnected, if only through the sublation of concrete shapes that cancels, as well as preserves and elevates, what is sublated. In the concept, familiar shapes and shapings survive otherwise than they have been outside it. After all, a self-given actuality does not posit an alternative reality that is better or purer than our mundane existence, but only repeats and immanently transfigures the world of mere being, reconnecting its elements *to themselves* and distilling peculiar "processes" and "products" from these relations. Dialectical energy is this internal self-sublation, the spiraling interplay of substantive and verbal dimensions of *ergon* that, at a certain degree of intensity, are qualitatively deflected from being to the concept.

While a transformed actuality is imbricated in the actuality it transforms (the energy of the concept plugged into that of being), any treatment of "raw" actuality is embroiled with the logic of the concept: "something is thought of as *existing* that is not yet actual [*das noch nicht wirklich*]—the necessity not of the *concept* as concept, but of *being*. But necessity is at the same time essentially a relation through the concept" (*PhG* §602). No sooner is it contemplated, at a minimum as necessary in and of itself, than the incomplete, non-self-related actuality of being—an "*existing* that is not yet actual"—receives surplus energy from the conceptual supply that affixes to it the attribute "necessary." Lest we forget, necessity is a logical category, which, with respect to the absolute, reconciles the other Kantian modal terms, that is, the possible and the actual. The mechanism through which this reconciliation comes to pass is a self-relation of relative necessity at the level of being: "the reflection of relative necessity into itself yields *absolute necessity*, which is absolute *possibility* and *actuality*."[50] The energy of being that has coiled back into itself is the inception of conceptual energy; a logico-conceptual category (necessity) that hypostatizes being's relation to itself brings the relation to the fore from mere existence, where it floats unperceived. Solely on the condition that the two energy supplies flow into one another, by virtue of a mediation of the immediate and the mediated, do necessity, possibility, and actuality touch the absolute, superseding the strictly formal and real types of dialectical energy.

What we have before us, then, are two energy supplies or regimes—the ontological and the conceptual (or, as Heidegger would say, the ontic and the ontological)—and three types of energy—formal, real, and absolute. First, formal actuality, according to the *Science of Logic*, generally dovetails with the energy supply of mere being; it is the "first actuality" of "existence" in general.[51] Second, real actuality, interchangeable with relative necessity, is filled with content through self-negations mediating mere being.[52] Thanks to it, the two energy supplies are first articulated among themselves, the juncture at which we found ourselves at the opening of the present section. Third, absolute actuality hinges on a self-conscious realization, or the actualization, of the "unity of being and essence," of ontology and the concept.[53] As always, the Hegelian absolute is not absolved from relations, not isolated in its sacrosanct separateness, but grasps itself as the thread of relationality, singularly responsible for suturing the whole.

In *the Phenomenology*, the three types of energy resurface with a slight change of focus from logical categories to the manifestation or non-manifestation of beings and concepts. It is probably misleading to refer to this as a typology, unless a proviso is added that Hegel has in mind something like a moving table (which is, in any case, how he treats Kant's table of the categories), where each rotation propels being and the concept to their mutual actualization, *Verwirklichung*. Be this as it may, the three energy types in the *Phenomenology* are the essential, the phenomenal, and the absolute. The first is the virtual actuality "in-itself," *an sich*, of material objects as much as of conceptual energy configurations, such as the Enlightenment (*PhG* §548). The reason for the non-manifestation of this energy in its works is the dearth of mediations in mere being and a formal concept walled within the purity of its essence. The second is the becoming for-itself of what was simply in-itself, which is only possible when being or the concept confront themselves as objects, "*sich selbst als Gegenstand gegenüberstellt*" (*PhG* §548), and thus become phenomenally available, exposed to others in their own essential otherness. Absolute actuality is a "for-us," *für-uns*, where this "we" is a standpoint of having traversed the dialectical itinerary and, in the ensuing energetic fullness, having realized that the in-itself is and has always been for-itself, the essence expressed in its appearances, the works lending a body and a voice to (while speculatively betraying) the workings of actuality.

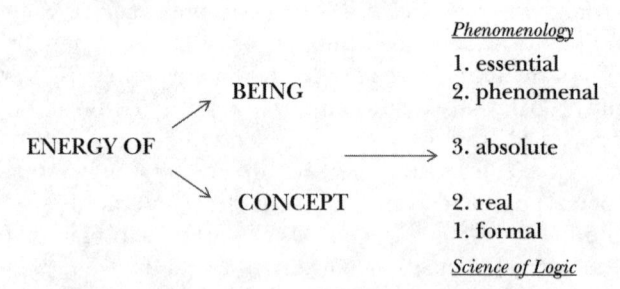

```
                                    Phenomenology
                                    1. essential
                    BEING            2. phenomenal
                 ↗
ENERGY OF        ──────────→         3. absolute
                 ↘
                    CONCEPT          2. real
                                     1. formal
                                    Science of Logic
```

Figure 10. Two energy supplies and three energy types

Different energy regimes and types are concentrated in the domain of art. On the one hand, there is the "instinctual work," *das instinktartige Arbeiten*, "submerged within existence." This variety of art, fueled by the energy of being, "works its way out of it [mere existence] and into it" and "does not possess its substance in the free ethical sphere, and thus the self at work also does not possess free spiritual activity" (*PhG* §702). On the other hand, and at a later stage of spiritual development, "absolute art," *die absolute Kunst*, signals a sort of self-overcoming of art. Here, the regime of representation (*Darstellung*), which has invariably harkened back to represented beings, is superseded together with the idea that the working self produces objective works (of art) as independent from it. Absolute art demands a shift to another energy regime, namely the energy of the concept that grows from the middle, from the mediations themselves, rather than the mediated extremes, whence the energy of being commences: "It is not only to give birth to itself from its concept; it is to have its concept as its shape [*seinen Begriff selbst zur Gestalt zu haben*]" (*PhG* §702). Under the aegis of the absolute, art effects a self-overcoming of art to the extent that it swaps the determinate shapes of representation for the shape of the concept, introducing the most significant alteration into the concept of art itself.

I am pausing on this example mainly due to the beautiful economy with which it condenses sundry issues in the dialectics of energy. Besides the sharp contrast it evinces between the energy of being and the energy of the concept, the transition from instinctual to conceptual art fleshes out the problem of the absolute as *energeia*. In the art animated by and responsive to the exigencies of being, Hegel espies a caesura between the worker and the work, or, more accurately, the working and the work as the verbal and substantive halves of *ergon*. The "self at work," the energetic subject of instinctual production, is not free, not so much because instinct remains beholden to the vicissitudes of natural or biological forces but because the two parts of energy are flimsily articulated with one another, not to mention that the necessity of their co-belonging as determined by mere being is thoroughly contingent. The regime of representation is artistic actuality at its most formal and abstract, populated with real content, which depends on a particular represented object or method. The phenomenal energy an art object captures likewise provides a limited expression for the essential energy of "the self at work." It is not until the advent of absolute art, moved by absolute energy, that the working and the work will be liberated from their fixed subject- and object-positions, freed from representational constraints and, even more so, from the imposed givenness of immediate being. The field that absolute art plows and fertilizes is where the working and the work, the artist and the artwork, freely and self-consciously assume their togetherness in a relation, an in-between, a mediation that serves as the subject *and* the substance of art.

On this newly prepared field, energy and actuality come into their own and expose their rootedness in freedom, as well as their entwinement, which has not yet been obvious at the beginning, far removed from the absolute. Hegel knows that the absolutizing of art, its inclusion within the energizing and energized complex, may cause it not to be recognizable as art. For him, the problem of absolute art is not—that is, not primarily—a problem of art, but of the absolute. Which is why, next, we need to turn our attention to the pulsations of absolute energy.

Absolute Energy

The Hegelian absolute is a flux and a state of intense interconnectedness, where relations or modes of relating are identical to the beings related through them. *What is* is the in-between; the substantive and the verbal sides of being complicated with (folded into) each other. But that is not all: the absolute is also, and by the same token, a cut of individuation beyond the most daring formulations of the metaphysical *principio individuationis* and in excess of a simple opposition to relationality. Subject and substance, activity and passivity, exuberant energy and rest, the working and the work, achieve the highest degree of integration in it. In our terms, the *en-* of energy is the absolute indwelling of the working in the work and of the work in the working—an ineffaceable exteriority in the seclusion of interiority and the inner imprinted right on the surface of things. Absolutely in tune with itself in and as the other, not least in the self-shaped shape of *energeia*, energy *is* the absolute and the absolute *is* energy, both in the sense of the energizing and of the energized.

The absolute-as-energy is, according to a standard Hegelian account, the accomplishment of spirit's journey in history, the culmination of its mission that initially sets the absolute apart by segregating it from the path spirit has traversed. Yet, like Plato's philosopher-king obliged to return among the shadows of the cave in order to guide others to eidetic light, the absolute must recollect its itinerary, replay its movements, set them to work again on the basis of what has been already achieved, namely itself. If repetition and, especially, a repeated self-reflection are actualizing or energizing, then the absolute repetition is the most energizing eventuality conceivable. Its offshoot is the freedom that absolves, that rids actuality of extrinsic, contingent determinations. The being of becoming, it promotes movement and rest, movement grounded in rest and rest set in motion—something that happens on a daily basis when each individual in the educational process runs through "the formative stages of universal spirit," *Bildungsstufen des allgemeinen Geistes,* already spanned in historical actuality, "worked out and leveled out [*ausgearbeitet und geebnet*]" by previous generations (*PhG* §28). It is in this absolute sense that the school is a *skholē*—leisure, rest, idleness even—carving out the time, freeing time itself, for a repetition of the already-worked-out.

The absolute repeats instinctual energy, liberating the historical occurrences of the working impulse in all their finitude. Instinctual energy (for instance, the life-instinct that ensures self-preservation) is spent on the model of its counterpart in physics that drifts from the Big Bang to what we might call the Big Entropy. But absolute energy promises a different kind of preservation. Without appending anything new, it rehashes the energy that has been expended in an immediate fashion, frees up the ostensibly inoperative and already lost time for its self-interpretation, and enables the recollected work and the workings of "instinct" to relate to themselves.

The freedom that absolute energy affords is not a utopian ideal but the self-relation of actuality, for which self-consciousness and the absolute are, at once, the conduits and the destinations. This freedom is already presaged, outside the school sphere, in everyday action: "In actual action . . . consciousness behaves as this particular self, as completely individual; it is directed to actuality as such [*es ist auf die Wirklichkeit als solche gerichtet*], and has actuality for its purpose, for it wills to achieve something" (*PhG* §607). "Actual action" (*wirkliche Handlung*) is oriented toward actuality as such (*Wirklichkeit als solche*) whence it seeks its purpose, its means and ends in an aggregate of the actualizing and the actualized, the working and the completed work. Energy is free insofar as it can, staying faithful to Aristotle's *energeia*, flow from itself to itself through the "electrical" conductors of self-consciousness anticipating absolute mediation, its shape sublated. (Except that, for different reasons, it is not "itself" either at the beginning or at the end, and this not-being-itself is essential to its idea.) Self-consciousness is the commerce of energy-actuality with itself, energy's proximity, its approximation—which, to be sure, does not close its relational or self-relational gap—to itself *as* actuality. Proximate, it is not hidden in the essential depths of thought or of an indeterminate will; energy's commerce takes place in its externalization in action, in provisional accomplishments, uncertain outcomes, an imperfect knowledge of causes and effects.[54]

So, having little in common with the Platonic ideas or Eckhart's Godhead, Hegel's absolute is not insulated from the world here-below. If anything, it is the fruit of this world. For action to be actual, for it to put the two halves of energy together, ever so provisionally (that is to say, speculatively), its effects need to be inscribed in a substantive reality of the work, which is itself a synthesis (a temporal synergy) of the energy expended in past action and the energy contained in the present condition. Self-consciousness cannot go on indefinitely discoursing with itself in the "inner life of the mind" if it is to arrive at the gates of absolute freedom; it must commit itself to the work that acknowledges a gulf between being-in-itself and being-for-itself, even as it permits us to "get rid of this division of soul and body: to clothe and give shape to the soul in its own self, and to endow body with soul [*diese Trennung der Seele und des Leibs aufzuheben, jene an ihr selbst zu bekleiden und zu gestalten, diesen aber zu beseelen*]" (*PhG* §693). Spirit, consequently, "knows this content [of its activity] in its work, which is a thing [*ihren Inhalt, sondern an seinem Werke, das ein Ding ist, weiß*]" (*PhG* §693). Absolute know*ing* is also absolute knowl*edge* (*wissen, das Wissen*), the absolute known in the working and the work, not at all free from what Marxism derided as reification.

Compared to a working work, the abstract genesis of the dialectical process is a far-flung point at the furthest extreme from the absolute, a point imbued with a purely verbal energy (objectless, indeterminately and arbitrarily "free") that is sometimes conflated with divinity (e.g., Hegel's *Science of Logic* as a reflection of God's thoughts before the creation of the world). The subsequent development of the beginning is contingent upon the mediation of this truncated energy with substance, wherein the subject gradually recognizes an energetic formation and, finally, itself. In a decisive sense, then, the absolutization of energy is its substantivation interlaced with subjectivity. The closer spirit comes to itself as absolute, the more of its energy acquires the substantive tinge of an accomplished work surrounded with the visible scaffolding of the workings that brought the work about, both pushing against (repelling) and supporting it.

In view of the biases ingrained in our thinking, the passage of energy into a substantive modality is interpreted as a sign that the living impulse present at the beginning is now dead, suffocated in the substance, to which it has been delivered. This passage will have been oddly redolent of entropy, of energy's dissipation or desaturation, in which case the absolute will have appeared absolutely dead in a rehashing of what Kant mocks as the "peace of the cemeteries." And yet, dialectically, an active energetic momentum is truly in effect only in conjunction with the substance it "ensouls," its becoming remembered in (or alongside) the resultant being. It was ancient Greek thought that precociously dealt with such accomplished energy, which is why Aristotle spelled the term itself, *energeia*, in the substantive, with the ending *–eia*. Hegel's mission, as he no doubt sees it himself, is to dispense a kind of energetic freedom to the Greek beginning, precisely when it comes to the thinking of energy and freedom.

Anything less than a verbal-substantive ensemble of energetic workings and energized works—the one incessantly mediated with and into the other—will fall short of the absolute and will lapse into mere formalism. Formalism, Hegel contends, "will not vanish from science, however much its inadequacy may be recognized and felt, until the knowledge of absolute actuality [*das Erkennen der absoluten Wirklichkeit*] has become completely clear as to its own nature" (*PhG* §16). "Absolute actuality" means, of course, "absolute energy." Still, this energy is not quite absolute, unless, in addition to the ontological self-relations it embraces, it enacts an epistemological relation to itself. The absolute insistently demands a surplus, the irreducible supplement of knowing itself in its absoluteness.

> the absolute
>
> =
>
> absolute actuality *plus* the knowledge of absolute actuality
>
> =
>
> absolute self-relatedness
>
> =
>
> remembrance of repetition

Figure 11. The formula of the absolute

In spite of this demand, the Hegelian absolute is inalienable from the actual. If actuality is a reality abounding in self-relationality, the absolute is the self-relation of self-relations—not encircling these from the outside, but rendering them transparent to themselves. It thus repeats and reinforces the work the actual has performed on the real. The additional energy provided by the self-knowledge of absolute actuality makes all the difference in this scheme, where what I have labeled in shorthand as "epistemology" rounds off the ontology that is as deficient without the subject supplementing substance as it was without substance giving body to the subjective impulse. The circle of energy—the actualizing and the actualized; the working and the work—shrinks to a point and expands to a sphere, ready to welcome existence reelaborated or replayed within it. That point-sphere is the Hegelian absolute.

Dialectics against Extractivism

Enough has been said thus far—before we have actually cracked open *The Phenomenology of Spirit* so as to go over the text with a fine-toothed comb, line by line and paragraph by paragraph—to lead us to the conclusion that the gist of the book and of Hegel's philosophy is foreign to the extractivist ideology that is set on devastating the planet, elemental worlds, and the animate and inanimate beings these sustain. As I write in *Energy Dreams*: "It is true that dialectics is a machine of energy production-extraction from rational principles, with negativity (more precisely: self-negation) for an internal combustion engine. And yet, Hegel kept too near to Aristotle to endorse the 'bad infinity' of unalloyed potentiality. What he extracts from the deep and essentially hidden rational kernel are the actual structures of physical, social, and political reality. 'What is rational is actual [*wirklich*]; and what is actual is rational' is his manner of underwriting the Aristotelian *energeia*. . . . The extraction of the actual from the rational is not a lethal operation. In self-negation and the negation of the negation (inspired or energized by Christian resurrection) death is incorporated, overcome, and put in the service of actuality. The derivation of dialectical energy is the work of history as the history of spirit, the self-relation of the world's self-relation."[55]

Pairing the rational and the actual, we ought to ask: "What is extracted from what in Hegel?" Obviously, the one from the other: the rational from the actual and the actual from the rational. In formal logical terms, induction and deduction belong together, buttressing and complementing each other. But much more is going on here than a run-of-the-mill logical operation. First (rational) principles are, as we have seen, abstract and unprepared to yield anything like a vibrant actuality. The "extracted" and the "extracting" are, in Hegel, inherently reversible and repeatedly reversed: a vacant energy-actuality must revert to a more concrete (self-negated) rationality, which will generate a more self-related, synergic, actualized energy-actuality, and so on. The rational *becomes* actual, navigating and mediating the opposition between being and nothing that constitutes becoming. And this holds, as well, for the actual that becomes rational. The copula articulating them is not ahistorical; it is to be understood as a determinate self-negation, a sublated actuality, the working work of time. Time as energy: the *is* in the "rational *is* the actual" is the grammatical congealment of actuality (or, better, of actualization) in the co-belonging of the actualizing and the actualized. Which brings us, again, to the Aristotelian insight that energy is mediated through energy, mediation through mediation, the actual through the self-negation of the rational, which is to say through the actual.

The extractivist ideology that saps the earth's "natural resources" is, by way of contrast, irreversible, while the relations it prescribes between what is used and the users are set in stone (or in shale rock). Its energy, hopelessly depleting itself, nourishes the irrationality of world-destruction. It prioritizes the Moloch of an unfulfillable potentiality over the actual—treated as so many obstacles in its path—a potentiality, to which existence is sacrificed together with its (non-transcendental) conditions of possibility. Existence is, hence, robbed of its chance for regeneration by the eerie reanimation of whatever remains of creatures who died ages ago. Extractivism does not liberate energy for the sake of actualization, so that actuality could become itself: the energizing and the energized, self-related. The group of practices and ideological presuppositions that go under the name "extractivism" undo *what is*, unbind existing synergies, thwart the freedom of accomplishment at the behest of abstract freedom indexed to limitless possibilities. (It is, admittedly, evident that the possibilities extractivism lets loose are not limitless: fossil fuels are finite resources subject to depletion, while a livable atmosphere cannot absorb the by-products of their combustion much longer.)

Dialectical energy does not extract resources from a world it construes as initially too abstract, too bare and vacant, to provide any fuel for being or for thought. Rather than extract, it extends and rhythmically contracts to come out of itself again, in the vegetal manner of the plant metamorphosis that Goethe admired and Hegel was abreast of. As historical actuality, dialectical energy is the working work of time, of being, and of being's self-relatedness in the form of truth replayed, stretched out, extended past their due. This is not at all the case in extractivism, where the work of time is wiped out and millions of years of decay, decomposition into the earth, and finally petrification are reversed in the brief instants of extraction and incineration.

I do not mean to assert that there is no place either for sacrifice or for violent negation in Hegel's philosophy. The point I would like to emphasize is that true sacrifice in the *Phenomenology* is (self-conscious) self-sacrifice, something quite different from a blithely destructive burning of the long-dead other. For "actual activity [*wirkliche Tun*] to be possible," Hegel writes, "the essence must have already *in itself* sacrificed itself [*muß das Wesen sich selbst schon* an sich *aufgeopfert haben*]. This it has done by giving itself existence and has made itself into an individual animal and into fruit" (*PhG* §718). The essence that sacrifices itself "in itself" dispenses energy-actuality in the shape of existence. It gives itself existence by sacrificing in itself this very "in itself," by reneging on the hidden abode of essentiality that is devoid of extension and inaccessible to the senses. Sacrificing itself in itself, essence exposes itself, spills out into existential positivity, its spillage being the bristling energy-actuality behind any "actual activity."

What does this have to do with extractivism? Everything and nothing. The sacrifice of the planet in a total burnt offering—the original sense of "holocaust"—to an obsession with the production of energy in the form of an empty and lethal possibility is also a self-sacrifice, except that the energy-producing subject has been largely unaware of this. The prevailing impression is that, to satisfy human needs, if not the ever-growing demands of "human essence," humanity is sacrificing its other on the altar that these needs and this essence construct. But, although specifically designated and deliberately limited "sacrifice zones" have been created, for instance in places that endure the devastating effects of fracking,[56] the unfettered self-sacrifice of humanity is inevitable: atmospheric and aquatic kinds of pollution know no boundaries, and the ensuing global climate change cannot be circumscribed to isolated areas on the planet.

In extractivism, the essence is not sacrificed "in itself," its outward expression emptying into the plenitude of existence; the essence is gutted out aposteriori, prohibited from giving itself the body and the voice of actual existence by our de-actualizing activity (what Hegel would have called *unwirkliche Tun*). It is not that the extractivists—not only the CEOs of natural gas and oil companies from Shell to Exxon, Petrobras to Gazprom, but also any of us who are convinced that fossil fuels are ontically fundamental to economic prosperity and ontologically indispensable to a fully human life—avoid sacrificing themselves and their descendants on the pyres continuing to spew greenhouse emissions into the air. They lack the *consciousness* of self-sacrifice. Perhaps in the current historical moment, it is the inability or the unwillingness on the part of the extractivists to raise their self-sacrifice to the level of self-consciousness that prevents energy from becoming what it is (actuality) and imprisons it in what it is not (a murderous potentiality, *dunamis*), which is nonetheless *a part* of what it is. Without the consciousness of self-sacrifice, we (i.e., the withdrawn essence wherein this *we* obdurately holes up) refuse to grant existence—above all, future existence—either to ourselves or to anyone or anything else in the world, toward which we conduct ourselves undialectically as though it were entirely separate from us.

This much can be said concerning the opaque backdrop for the divergence of extractivism from the dialectical conception and practices of energy. As to the more conspicuous reasons behind this variance, extractivist ideology does not complete the circle where the substantive and the verbal senses proper to the work of *Wirklichkeit* gyrate. In extractivism, workings without work bear with destructive force upon past actuality. They de-actualize that which is—the earth with its elemental, geological, micro-organismic, and biospheric synergies—and install another reality that is only if it is consumed by fire, devouring the very future of a livable planet. At every stage, from drilling and excavation through "refining" crude oil to burning fossil fuels, extraction requires segregation and material analysis that nullify the synergies of an interrelated and self-related energy-actuality. Its lopsided dynamics correspond to the flight of pure thought, determined in its indeterminacy to virtualize the world. It shares with the mechanics of space the qualities of shapelessness and self-externality. The promise of extracted energy—not as a thing differentiated into "natural resources" of various types, but as what it can *do*—is concomitantly reduced to pure power, to the reign of seemingly unlimited possibilities at the expense of the actual. In a word, extractivism represents abstract spirit stuck at the beginning of a thwarted journey, mired in immediation, beholden to unrealizable and de-realizing potentialities, beckoning with a negation devoid of determination.

Part II

The Phenomenology of Spirit and the Question of Energy: An Exegesis

Introduction: The Energy of Cognition

It appears, for all intents and purposes, that Hegel's central concerns in the "Introduction" to his *Phenomenology of Spirit* are going to be the epistemological ones. He is, after all, inquiring into the nature of cognition and, concretely, into "the actual cognition of what there is in truth [*das wirkliche Erkennen dessen, was in Wahrheit ist*]" (*PhG* §73). What is in question and under the dialectical magnifying glass is the path not so much toward true being, but toward being-in-truth. This is the philosophical "thing itself," *Sache selbst*, and a stand-in for the absolute. Immediately, however, another concern arises: how to differentiate between the path and its destination? Is cognition an instrument, a piece of equipment, a work-tool, *Werkzeug*, for grasping reality, or is it a medium, not just the means but the middle, *Mittel*, for glimpsing the absolute?

Before addressing these questions, let me put an accent on Hegel's preferred word for cognition, *das Erkennen*. In modifying the verb *erkennen*—"to discern," "to understand," "to perceive," "to recognize," "to realize"—with the neuter article *das*, he is eager to impart an active sense to the noun, to de-substantivize it as much as possible. That is to say, from the outset, Hegel plans to treat cognition in the energetic key, such that its verbal and substantive overtones would be harmonized. Cognition will constitute the workings and will be the work of phenomenology (and of the *Phenomenology*). And this semantic indication of the role allotted to it will implicitly furnish a preliminary answer to the question regarding its nature: *das Erkennen*, as the mindful embodiment of energy, will gather in itself the path and the destination on the hither side of the difference between the shaping and the shaped concept, between a passive-receptive medium for reflection and an active grasp of *what is*.

This mission will mark dialectical cognition from birth; it will be the birthmark of that cognition, setting it apart from a purely substantive *Erkenntnis*, of which there are "various kinds," *verschiedene Arten der*

Erkenntnis. Now, Hegel observes that, where various kinds of anything are present, the possibility of error (of mistaking one kind for another) creeps in, "and it could be that one of them, rather than another, would be better suited to achieving this final end" (*PhG* §73). *Das Erkennen* for its part is not prone to such risk. Why? Because, after the end of the first, immediately experienced phenomenology, it already begins with the synergy of means and ends, of the path and the destination, the synergy that aligns it with energy and the absolute. If epistemological inquiries take the divide between the means for knowing and the known end for granted, then, despite all appearances to the contrary, the "Introduction" to the *Phenomenology* contributes nothing to epistemology, refusing as it does to drive a wedge between the energy of active-substantive cognition and the absolute, or, in Hegel's words, "to draw a sharp dividing line marking a boundary between cognition and the absolute [*zwischen das Erkennen und das Absolute eine sie schlechthin scheidende Grenze falle*]" (*PhG* §73). Cognition itself, *das Erkennen*, is the cognizing and the cognized, including the cognizing as the cognized in its own right, the means and the end, the mental apparatus as much as the workings and the work of the absolute in and as "us."

The actual cognition, *das wirkliche Erkennen*, which Hegel proposes to reassess in what follows is equivalent to "energetic energy," its actuality (*Wirklichkeit*) repeating and intensifying the workings and the work of *das Erkennen*. Three unspoken premises prepare the stage for this equivalence: (1) the absolute is cognizable; (2) moreover, it has been cognized; and (3) it is actual finite cognition, replete with every conceivable imperfection and freed from its contingency in the synergy of reiteration. Absolutizing actual cognition is clearly not an epistemological operation, but an ontological observation, relocating the seat of *energeia* from the pure and divine (read: indifferent and abstract) "thought thinking itself" to an actually formed self-consciousness, where to think is to have already thought.

The epistemological alternatives that Hegel shrugs off fall short of the absolute, to the extent that cognitive instruments, on the one hand, and media, on the other, are incapable of overcoming the gap postulated in advance and amputating *the knowledge of what is* from *what is*. On these conditions factored into epistemological operations, the energy of cognition does not mingle with that of truth: the cognitive toolkit reshapes and changes what it is applied to, while the medium refracts the light of being. For a quantum physicist, to be sure, the interference of our instruments and senses with the observed phenomenon is, far from being a failure, an essential interaction that is constitutive of energy.[1] Hegel's point nevertheless remains valid. A rift between the means and the end, between the path and its destination, between workings and works denies us access to both. Energy scatters. There is nothing to actualize and nothing actualized. The actual, like the absolute, comes to be viewed as an unattainable ideal, deferred by yet another potentiality.

A saving grace in the scenario of the infinitely multiplying—normative, epistemological, ontological—chasms is the actual activity of science (*Wissenschaft*: the synergy, among themselves and with the absolute, of historical knowledges across the timeline of their cultural development, *Bildung*) which recovers lost energy by "going to work and actually cognizing," *ans Werk selbst geht und wirklich erkennt* (*PhG* §74). Out of itself, by virtue of its enworkment or being-at-work, science spins the forfeited actuality of cognition. It does so not by supplying the sorely needed mediations between us and the absolute but by showing, through the exercise of its energy which is also that of actual cognition, that "we" "are" the absolute. Neither mediately nor immediately. The absolute puts itself to work whenever "our" actual and finite cognition is at work. Our energy, the energy of our thinking, is its energy; were the two treated apart from one another, as they are by those anxious not to fall into error, the absolute (which has no "sides") would not have been absolute, but would have stood on one side and our cognition on another ("*das Absolute auf einer Seite stehe, und das Erkennen auf der andern Seite*" [*PhG* §74]). Such a supposition would have, moreover, disrupted the meta-circulation of dialectical energy between substance and subject, the latter edified into the former and the former dissolved into the latter. Herein lies the kernel of Hegel's bitter response to Kant: to dematerialize—to idealize—the absolute is to divorce the cognizing from the cognized, eviscerating actuality and restricting its energy to the indefinitely deferred, non-actualizable, impossible possibility.

The actual activity of science working itself out brings to light the representational nature of the theories of cognition as an instrument or a medium for reflection. Both are the "*representations* of *cognition* [Vorstellungen *von dem* Erkennen]" (*PhG* §74), which bask in the energy they have borrowed from what they represent. They switch from *das Erkennen* to *Erkenntnis*, reduce the cognitive to its substantive aspect, and irretrievably misplace the verbal, active facets of its work. As a result, science, with its actual cognizing, needs to step in and step up to the plate so as to remedy the effects of pure epistemologies, which, having disregarded the questions *how* and *who*, have diminished cognition to a *what*, an instrument or a medium. Yet, a substance devoid of the subject is desubstantivizing, verging on the virtual. Actual science is, paradoxically, the whole of spirit *and* its historically summoned supplement compensating for the prevalence of representational thinking about thinking that has, in the meantime, unlearned the actual practice of cognizing.

Science has to overcome the resistance of representational thinking and to put itself to work by actually cognizing. In philosophical modernity, this site of resistance has been the historical conjunction at which science (including, above all, Hegel's dialectical endeavor) has procured its energy. Casting thinking in terms of either work-tools or a medium, theories of cognition aim to invalidate the science of actual cognition, to render it incapable, impotent, inapt, to beget the "impotence of science," *das Unvermögen der Wissenschaft* (*PhG* §76). Rather than reassert its power in the face of epistemological emasculation, science turns this proposition on its head. Energy is far from an abstract, indeterminate power; only pure thinking lives up to the ideal of pure potency in the field of cognition. Speculative reason proclaims that science *is* indeed im-potent in the sense that every one of its potencies has been determinately negated, sublated into the whole, put in touch with the absolute and therefore converted into truth. The energy of science is its im-potence, one where "the absolute alone is true, and the true alone is absolute [*das Absolute allein wahr, oder das Wahre allein absolut ist*]" (*PhG* §75).

The actuality of true, or absolute, cognition does not depend on an abstract notion of being—a conclusion that wards off ontological arguments on the heels of dismissing the epistemological ones. Science, Hegel writes, "accounts for its force in terms of its being [*erklärte sie ihr Sein für ihre Kraft*], but non-true knowledge also appeals to the same thing, namely that *it is* [es ist]" (*PhG* §76). There is no qualitative difference between science and "non-true" knowledge at this level of ontological force (*Kraft*), which is not yet mediated into energy-actuality. The fact, or the facticity, of something that merely *is* suffices to bestow some actuality on the virtual; figments of our imagination, too, are marginally actual and triflingly energetic insofar as they announce themselves as what is (imagined to be true). But the broadest, least negatively determined, notion of being remains on a par with power, with both of them at a considerable remove from *Wirklichkeit*. As soon as science starts worrying about its power, and as soon as it locates its center of gravity in its being, it abandons the energy proper to it, slides into pure thinking, and becomes identical to "non-true" knowledge.

What follows is the dialectical inversion of Platonism: appearance, for Hegel, is closer to actuality than being. In this terse formulation resides the rationale of the *Phenomenology* precisely as *a* phenomenology. Coming on the scene, making its dramatic entrance, science proves that "it is itself an appearance," *ist sie selbst eine Erscheinung* (*PhG* §76), as theatrical as it is onto-phenomenal. Less abstract than being pure and simple, science's appearance does not yet unfurl (*ausgebreitet*) or accomplish (*ausgeführen*) the truth of science. Its energy-actuality is still precarious, still eclipsed by the empty possibilities of mere being and by the contingent instant of its emergence—a contingency to be repeated, energized, and hence preserved in the absolute. The absolute will be nothing but the energy of the contingent, its actuality achieved thanks to the work of repetition carried out by a science that actually thinks.

The path (*Weg*) from science's first appearance to its actuality is of utmost importance for Hegel, because, we might say, that actuality is limited unless the work it congeals remembers the more or less meandering workings that have culminated in it. If, similar to certain Eastern traditions, the way is at least as decisive for truth as the destination, then what is in question here is the conceptual and phenomenal unity of energy, comprising the means and the end. The buildup to the "actual accomplishment," *die wirkliche Ausgeführung*, of truth is as momentous as its ultimate scientific shape, at which we arrive after a long historical succession of cultural forms (*PhG* §78). Representations of cognition also participate in this process, even though on the path to science they represent the dead ends of thinking devoid of actuality, powerful yet ineffective. In them, the energy of thought experiences entropy and atrophies into piecemeal correlations of the cognizing and the cognized. (We will readily perceive *one version* of Husserlian phenomenology in this description.)

As for science, it is not just energized, but it is energy in the exact sense of Aristotle's *energeia*: "free and self-moving in its ownmost shape [*freie, in ihrer eigentümichen Gestalt sich bewegende*]" (*PhG* §77). Between science's first appearance and its actuality, the path is a circle, which never leaves its initial coming-on-the-scene behind. By itself, science gets under way (*sich bewegende*) and orients itself on a path (*Weg*) it treads toward the synergy of historical knowledges with themselves and with the absolute. Its freedom, self-movement, and self-shaping are mutually interchangeable in the same manner as they are in the original notion of *energeia*. Together, the first appearance and its actuality amount to the fullness (*Vollständigkeit*) of dialectical energy, of a historically conditioned cognizing raised to the level of necessity without compromising on its contingent character, that is, in synergy with all other forms of such cognizing: "The completeness [*Vollständigkeit*] of the forms of non-real consciousness will be produced by necessity in the progression of and interrelations [*Zusammenhanges*] among these forms" (*PhG* §79). *Zusammenhang*—the linkage, association, or interrelation of different modes of cognizing—is the synergy that paves the path of science and is, in the last instance, equivalent to science itself, more or less distant (or proximate) to itself. Energy comes about through a synergy of singularities: this maxim is applicable to cognition, as well as to all other matters energetic.

There is no need, according to Hegel, for the tribunal of reasonable judgment charged with the task of sifting among historical knowledges and separating the true from the false: all of these, whether negatively or positively interrelated, contribute to synergic actuality. A static contrast between truth and falsity, between true and non-true cognition, is a roadblock on the way to the absolute, which tolerates no such "one-sidedness," *Einseitigkeit*. The "pure nothing" (*das reine Nichts*) of the non-true echoes pure being, appropriated, with the same indeterminacy, by science and haphazard modes of thinking. (If both pure being and pure nothing disrupt the flow of energy from itself to itself, that is because they are the works of thought that preclude the possibility of further workings.) Hegel recommends, instead, framing the result of cognizing "as *determinate* negation [*als* bestimmte *Negation*]" (*PhG* §79)—in other words, as the synergy of the true and the non-true. Following his advice, the work of cognition is de-substantivized, unraveled into new workings, and "in that negation the transition has been made" toward another shape of knowing (*PhG* §79). Determinate negation determines the preceding purity of being or nothingness, and, in so doing, contaminates it; the determination itself, as such, negates these stable poles, and the negation determines, sweeping them into the (determinate) no-sidedness of the absolute.

The modus operandi of determinate negation is that it creates the path by walking. *No hay camino / se hace camino al andar*—"There is no path / the path is made by walking," as a popular Spanish song goes. In this, determinate negation diverges from quests for the secure foundations of true knowledge, for "a presupposition that would be laid as a grounding standard [*als* Maßstab *zugrunde*]" to be applied in the process of deciding on the correctness or incorrectness of propositions (*PhG* §81). Needless to say, Hegel objects to the correspondence theory of truth. But, in a more encompassing fashion, he takes issue with the theory of truth as *theory*. Purely contemplative approaches to cognition paralyze the work and the workings of truth, undermining its energy, or its synergies with other (historical) truths and the others *of* truth. That is why the kind of truth that is acceptable in epistemological theory is in dire need of stimuli supplied externally and extraneously by comparisons that establish "equality or inequality," *Gleichheit oder Ungleichheit*. They rob non-identity of its explosive, speculative energy. In these approaches, then, one may at most hope to catch sight of the reality of cognition (*Realität des Erkennens*), not of its actuality. Reality, we might recall, is an impoverished actuality bereft of self-relation—here, the necessary relation between selfsameness and non-selfsameness, truth and non-truth. The reality of cognition does not rise to an actuality, inasmuch as it only interrelates a preexisting fundamental or grounding standard (*Maßstab zugrunde*) with a random assertion at hand in an effort to determine its correctness. Lacking in self-relatedness (or self-reflexivity), this truth procedure does not close the loop of free cognitive energy.

With respect to "the truth of knowledge," *die Wahrheit des Wissens*, knowledge becomes both the subject and the object of an investigation; in itself, *an sich*, it is already for us, *für uns* (*PhG* §83). Supplanting the reality of cognition is cognitive actuality, the self-relatedness of knowledge in its energetic fullness. Not fixed apriori, objectively, cognition is self-grounded, its "standard submerged within us [*Maßstab fiele in uns*]" (*PhG* §83), and it is therefore radically ungrounded. This ungrounded self-grounding imparts to it the freedom of energy-actuality, along with its peculiar movement and shape. Comparisons become superfluous, assuming that consciousness splinters into "mere" consciousness and self-consciousness: "on the one hand, consciousness is consciousness of the object, and, on the other hand, it is consciousness of itself [*das Bewußtsein ist einerseits Bewußtsein des Gegenstandes, anderseits Bewußtsein seiner selbst*]" (*PhG* §85). To insist on the adjudication of "correct thinking" is to restrict consciousness to consciousness without letting it be in itself an other to itself, namely self-consciousness. It is to remain imprisoned in the iron cage of its reality, locked out from an actuality that demands self-relatedness. It is, also, to omit the explosive charge of speculative energy that causes one (an identity, a consciousness) to divide into two (an identity and a non-identity, the same and the other, a consciousness and a self-consciousness). The path of and to science ineluctably and repeatedly passes through this fork in the road.

Speculatively divided into consciousness and self-consciousness, the energy of cognition boasts the substantive and the verbal facets of cognitive work. For a naive consciousness, these facets correspond to the cognized object and the act of cognizing. In the Hegelian scheme, nonetheless, the substantive element in cognition is "mere" consciousness itself, and the verbal aspect is self-consciousness: "Because consciousness itself has knowledge of an object, the distinction is already present [in consciousness], namely that in its eyes something is *in-itself* while another moment is knowledge, or the being of the object *for* consciousness" (*PhG* §85). The truth of an object "in-itself," oblivious to the fact that it is already or still known by consciousness, is the reality of cognition divorced from itself. An appreciation of the object as it is "for-us," or for consciousness, is cognition's self-reflexive actuality. Yet, neither of the two perspectives is disposable: the energy of cognition is deficient unless it hangs onto a non-self-related reality and a self-related actuality. The work of consciousness frozen into a mold of what seems to be "in-itself" alternates with and calls for the workings of self-consciousness that unfreeze these rigidly determinate shapes and refer them back to cognizing acts.

"In the alteration of knowledge, the object itself is actually altered [*in der Veränderung des Wissens ändert sich ihm in der Tat auch der Gegenstand selbst*]" (*PhG* §85). The speculative fission of consciousness is its synergy with self-consciousness.

Truth itself acquires a double meaning (*Zweideutigkeit*), or becomes positively ambiguous, so long as it is nourished by the speculative energy of a split consciousness (*PhG* §86). The objects are not, Hegel maintains, something known over and against the knowing as such; there is, truth be told, no knowing *as such*. The duality consists in a consciousness that knows the world in a way unglued from the knowing itself (i.e., unconsciously with regard to itself) and a consciousness that, in knowing its object, springs back to, examines, and knows itself, including as a cognitive procedure, which is, by and large, oblivious to its own operations. At issue, then, are a real consciousness and an actual consciousness, their quanta of energy drastically unequal. The former is not simply false: actual consciousness *is* the real consciousness aware of its unsurpassable limitations and finitude. And straddling these two sides of nonrepresentational truth is the energetic meaning of experience, *Erfahrung* (*PhG* §86).

Hegel is well aware that his definition of *Erfahrung* is different from the ordinary sense of the word, and he hints that what we are dealing with at the maximal level of cognition is absolute experience. "*For it [for consciousness],*" he writes, "the outcome is merely an object; *for us*, the outcome is also movement and becoming [*Bewegung und Werden*]" (*PhG* §87). The experience "for us" is absolute experience, or experience from the vantage point of the absolute. This experience juggles the result and the process that has culminated in the result, the object and its becoming-object, the end and the means, the work and working toward the outcome. Whatever its content, the form of absolute experience is energetic plenitude, the fitting-together of energy's substantive and verbal sides, provided that this "plenitude" embraces failure, limitation, finitude—above all, in consciousness and self-consciousness.

Actuality is the actual (the "new object," *neue Gegenstand*) and the path toward actualization; actual consciousness is the mature self *and* its maturation starting from real consciousness (the "first object," *erste Gegenstand*). For the absolute "us," the truth of the non-true is essential: the results of partial, non-self-related, naive cognition "must be apprehended as the nothing of *that of which it is the result*, a result which contains whatever truth the preceding knowledge has in itself [*als Nichts* desjenigen, *dessen* Resultat *es ist*]" (*PhG* §87). Which sounds like an urging that the path toward the result not be leveled, not be consigned to oblivion. After the path fades away, only some unsatisfactory (never satisfactory, whatever the procedures for assessing and adjudicating correctness and incorrectness) outcomes remain as the empty husks of energy, its shells or outworks blissfully ignorant of the impulses that have been working them out. The duality and duplicity of truth is that of energy "itself"; channeling the absolute, it refuses to stand on one side alone.

Real consciousness, however, tolerates no ambiguities and is either unaware of or annihilates all contradictions, rather than bringing them to fruition. The infinite multiplicity of its experience notwithstanding, it is one-dimensional, in that it sees around itself nothing but ready-made results with plus or minus, true *or* false, signs affixed to them, and is blind toward itself as it cognizes what lies outside. Unable to chart a path between the true and the non-true, between being and nothing, let alone between a non-true result and "the nothing of *that of which it is the result*," this consciousness is doomed, unbeknown to itself, to energy starvation. It is also a non-true result, which has issued from an impulse striving toward another, more comprehensive and still open future, albeit a non-true result that has its necessary truth within the scheme of spirit's phenomenology.

Impenetrable for real consciousness, the duality of energy, of truth, of consciousness that is also self-conscious, and of science indicates that being on one's way to a destination matters as much as that destination itself. (And it is by no means a foregone conclusion that both the destination and the path toward it are not multiple in the unity of their co-belonging.) We thus arrive at the denouement of the "Introduction"— "this path to science is itself already *science [ist dieser Weg zur Wissenschaft selbst schon* Wissenschaft]" (*PhG* §88)—which sets us on *our* way, even as it provides a resting station, and which makes our heads (and the world around them) spin in a cycle already outlined in Aristotle's *energeia*. The path merging with the destination is the site of absolute experience—a synecdoche, a part of the whole that gathers into itself this very whole: "the experience through which consciousness learns about itself can grasp in itself nothing less than the entire system [*ganze System*] of consciousness, that is, the entire realm of the truth of spirit" (*PhG* §89). (Reading the *Phenomenology* is, in this sense, absolute experience per se.) The synergy that is the system articulates itself through a synergy of consciousness with itself. It bears repeating: a *synergy*, not a synthesis, with itself; in synthesis, the duality of *ergon*—the work and the workings undertaken by consciousness, energy, truth, and science—vanishes.

Consciousness and its phenomenology, as well as the *Phenomenology* itself, concentrate a tremendous energetic charge that explodes into the entire Hegelian system. The workings of this energy, its activity and actuality, shadow the works of truth, which include, besides what shows itself to consciousness, "the way consciousness itself comes on the scene in its relation to what shows itself." The "shapes of consciousness," *Gestalten des Bewußtseins* (*PhG* §89), are these works as its substantivized portraits in a given historical epoch. As the shapes crumble and are shaped anew (the works reworked; the worlds of spirit reworlded), established substantive energy patterns undergo de-substantivation and consciousness continues to "push itself forth to its true existence [*zu seiner wahren Existenz sich forttreiben*]" (*PhG* §89), to being a working work, the absolute energy or the energy of the absolute.

It is not that, in the existent truth of the absolute, the difference between real consciousness and actual consciousness is expunged. What changes is that this difference ceases to weigh upon, encumber, or afflict (*behaften*) a consciousness wherein it remains embedded—the consciousness that has freely come to terms with its own speculative doubling. So conceived, the absolute is the free persistence of difference no longer experienced as a burdensome imposition on the principle of identity. Absolute experience is relieved, absolutely light—but it does not, in the manner of metaphysical adventures, take leave of the world here-below. Such an experience need not choose between bending underneath and resisting the heft of difference, which for its part is neither ground into amorphousness nor organized into oppositional formations where it pushes against sameness. The experienced and experiencing absolute allows difference to be "itself" with the absolute. It glimmers with energetic freedom.

A. "Mere" Consciousness and Its Energy Deficit

1. Sense-Certainty: "This Is," "I Am" . . . but All "This" "Is" Not Energy

"Mere" consciousness, which I have also termed *real* as opposed to *actual*, is conscious of the world outside it without being conscious of itself. It is already an energetic configuration, a shape of energy, if a sketchy one: unstable, perfunctory, yet to be filled out with determinate (self-negated) content. There is no way to substantivize it without first de-realizing real consciousness, suspending our belief in the adequacy of its relation to external reality, both in its blissful ignorance of its own interiority and in its very possibility. More pervasive than skepticism, the work of de-realizing the real (including, above all, consciousness) exposes the paucity of its energy.

On its own terms, real consciousness is indescribable. Unconscious toward itself, it can be narrated exclusively by the other it will have become, notably by actual consciousness looking back at the condition, in which self-relatedness is absent, its look illuminated by the absolute. As soon as an account of real consciousness is given, its energy is transformed from brute givenness to self-givenness, due to the interest self-consciousness takes in it. The energy of the beginning is only apperceived from the end of self-relatedness. The im-mediate is immediately mediated, repeated, and thereby energized, both when it comes to consciousness and to "external" reality.

Against this background, Hegel's appeal not to change anything in the immediacy of the beginning demands the impossible. "Knowledge, which is from the first or immediately our object [*Das Wissen, welches zuerst oder unmittelbar unser Gegenstand ist*]," he writes, "can be nothing but immediate knowledge [*unmittelbares Wissen*] . . . We must also behave towards it *immediately* or *receptively* [unmittelbar *oder* aufnehmend] and to alter nothing in it" (*PhG* §90). Not only is "immediate" knowledge amnesiac with regard to the way it has come to know (and, hence, to the mediations it has gone through, the path it has traversed), but also to know knowledge as an object is to have already engaged in the additional mediations of self-consciousness. Moreover, the "we" who know knowledge itself relate to it from the condition of an accomplished absolute, which is anything but immediate or purely receptive. How to resolve this inaugural conundrum of "Consciousness"?

It could well be that Hegel wishes to see mere or real consciousness put itself to work all by itself, without outside interferences. As a good phenomenologist, he is prepared to let the phenomenon (here, the incipient phenomenalization of knowledge) appear just as it is by itself, with nothing added to or subtracted from it. Giving real consciousness the benefit of a doubt, we nonetheless immediately stumble upon the immediate mediation of consciousness by self-consciousness, its appearance by itself in the other, through the other's energy. But an alternative reading would suggest that Hegel intends to align (1) how reality appears to real consciousness and (2) how real consciousness appears to the actual and ultimately to the absolute, that is to say, to itself repeated, actualized, energized, and other to its "immediate," stand-alone, virtual self. If so, then the formal structure of (2) will follow that of (1), including the fetish of immediacy and the impression that an object can be left unaltered by the subject's transactions with it.

A contradiction ensues: the content of sense-certainty "appears immediately [*unmittelbar*] as the *richest* knowledge [reichste *Erkenntnis*]," but it "yields the most abstract and poorest *truth* [*abstrakteste und ärmste*

Wahrheit]" (*PhG* §91). The contradiction involves knowledge and truth: to know is not to stand in the truth; to stand in the truth is not to know. Immediate appearance handed over to (immediate) knowledge is the polar opposite of true essence, the richness of the former a match for the poverty of the latter. Truth is what is not immediately actual, and immediate actuality is what is not true. The non-actuality of truth signifies that it is still devoid of energy, yet to be put to work in any concrete, existing appearance. The non-truth of immediate actuality denotes a reality as variegated as it is lacking in self-relationality. Rich knowledge and poor truth are two sides of the same coin, exchangeable for energy starvation and minted on the ontological support of "pure being," *reine Sein*. (*Nota bene:* purity as such is alien to energy, which is congenitally tainted, contaminated, impure.)

About the matter of sense-certainty, one can only say, in truth, that "it *is*," *es* ist, and one can only know it as a "this," *Dieser* (*PhG* §91). The singular "this" belongs together with the general "is" under the umbrella of pure being, each of them embodying an aspect of the virtual: "this" stands for separateness and non-relationality; "is" symbolizes emptiness and abstraction. Each, in its way, negates actuality. Mere consciousness also merely "is," and, in addition, it is a "this": "Consciousness is *I*, and nothing further, a pure *this* [*das Bewußtsein ist* Ich, *weiter nichts, ein reiner* Dieser]" (*PhG* §91). It is an energy-deprived, non-relational, empty, and abstract subject that perfectly matches its energy-poor object.

Hegel obviously begins by shattering the Aristotelian category of first *ousia*, a *this*. The category is in fact formal and abstract, but only if dissociated from other categorial determinations of a thing, such as where, when, or what sort it is. In phenomenological experience, consciousness never analytically perceives a pure *this*; it registers a *this* replete (and on a par) with qualitative, quantitative, and other facets of being, without which being is nothing. The interrelatedness of the categories in the thing itself, in consciousness, or between the two endows sense-certainty with the energy Hegel denies it.

With respect to post-Hegelian thought, *that* I am (i.e., the fact that this I, which I am, is) or *that* this thing is does not furnish the ontological foundation Heidegger seeks from the copula. Ontico- (this thing; this I) ontological (is; am) difference is too indifferent and immediate for Hegel to yield any philosophical energy, let alone to make a meaningful contribution to dialectical development. Admittedly, such is the limitation of all foundations, shackled as they are to an actuality-defying formalism. In this case, however, the gravity of the situation is that an immediate identification on the part of "this I" with "this object" prevents the blossoming of thinking: "I, as *this* I, am certain of *this* thing not because *I*, as consciousness, have developed myself and have gotten the manifold of thoughts under way [*Ich,* dieser, *bin* dieser *Sache nicht darum gewiß, weil* Ich *als Bewußtsein hiebei mich entwickelte und mannigfaltig den Gedanken bewegte*]" (*PhG* §91). The energy of thinking is blocked by this virtual mirror, reflecting two virtual realities—this I and this thing, with the thisness of both in the foreground—and speculatively refracting this reflection through the lens of ontico-ontological difference.

Concentrated in thisness and in pure being, the one superimposed onto the other, virtual reality is rescued from its enclosure in itself, because it is rendered exemplary. Sense-certainty—the immediate relation, in which this thing and this I participate—is actual (*wirklich*) insofar as it is "not merely this pure immediacy but an *example* of pure immediacy [*ist nicht nur diese reine Unmittelbarkeit, sondern ein* Beispiel *derselben*]" (*PhG* §92). An "example," *Beispiel,* puts into play (*Spiel*) something more than pure being *in* pure being ("*An dem* reinen Sein . . . *spielt*. . .") and more than "this" in the "this"; the exemplifying singular and isolated instance represents that which is exemplified in general, or, as Hegel will later specify, in its excellence, *Vortrefflichkeit* (*PhG* §523). Hence, a peculiar mix of actuality and virtuality: the example's energy. So, sense-certainty is not just pure immediacy but *an example of pure immediacy,* which is to say, an impossible example, considering that every example is, at bottom, exemplary of mediation, of an oscillation between the singular and the universal, a specimen and the species. From the perspective of the absolute, "we" perceive that neither this I nor this thing "exists immediately in sense-certainty but is in equal measure mediated [*zugleich als vermittelt*], the one through the other" (*PhG* §92). The example's non-viability with regard to the immediate sets the mechanism of actualization to work already within sense-certainty as a mediating-mediated relation of the mediating and the immediate. Sense-certainty is qualified with the adjective "actual" thanks to its exemplary negation of exemplarity.

The contradiction we are occupied with is hardwired into mere consciousness. Clinging to virtuality, to virtual reality, to inwardness, to the disengagement from appearance it prides itself on, pure essence is exempt from exemplarity. We can come up with many examples of essence (humanness, tableness, treeness, animality, and so on), but it is, as such, essentially, non-exemplary. "We find the difference between essence and example, immediacy and mediation in sense-certainty itself" (*PhG* §93). This difference is mapped, on the horizons of the world experienced by the subject of sense-certainty, onto this thing and this I, the known object and the knowing subject—the former taken to be immediate and the latter the mediated. The known is the essential here, or, in our terms, the virtual and the withdrawn; it is what does not require any energy, need not be put to work, by the sheer fact of its independent being. To say, "the object *is* . . . the truth and the essence [*Der Gegenstand* ist . . . *das Wahre und das Wesen*]" (*PhG* §93) is to use its pure being, with the stable "is" understood in terms of its persistence even when the knowing subject is absent, as an excuse for not activating, actualizing, or enworking anything, seeing that the object is thought to be always already at work in itself. So much so that such an exemption from enworkment passes for the true essence of "this" thing.

Hegel deflates the claims of self-certainty's essentialism by interrogating the meaning of the "this." First, he attributes to it some measure of energy (actuality as an accomplished work) invested in the shape of its being, *Gestalt seines Seins*, which is twofold: the now, *Itzt*, and the here, *Hier* (*PhG* §95). "This is" utters in the same breath the determinate, actual, spatiotemporal being of the "this" and the indeterminate, virtual, indifferent being of the "is." Second, Hegel further delineates the sense of the now and the here with the help of examples: the inscription "The 'now' is the night" relinquishes its truthfulness at midday (*PhG* §95). By virtue of resorting to the logic of exemplariness, Hegel refuses to treat the "this," in the twofold character of its being, as essential. The essence of "this" is clarified through the appearances, the virtual determined through the actual. The question concerning the being of the "this," as spotted here and now, is answered by resorting to what, in the fixed phenomenological stance of essential being, constitutes nonbeing. The essence is put to work (energized) by becoming other to itself: mediated by the nonessential. For example, by an example.

Following Hegel's exhortation to keep to the mode of thinking (or of not thinking) practiced by sense-certainty, the choice of exemplarity is not arbitrary; it is faithful to how the subject of sense-certainty defines things. But "we," who are accompanying this subject's journey, chance upon the observation that the example, rather than isolating the "this" in its initial virtuality, draws out the more-than-this-in-the-this, i.e., a that, a "not-this," the Aristotelian second *ousia*. The example for what happens "now" is night, at this point in time when it is dark outside, but this example turns into "that" at midday. The energy of the example effects a speculative doubling of the "this," its bifurcation into a "this" and a "not-this," which is how, Hegel implies, we should read Aristotle's crucial category.

Though still plagued by the indifference (*Gleichgültichkeit*) of virtual pure being, the "now," the "here," and the "this" put to the test of time are mediated—determinately negated—by their respective others. Their "'simple' [i.e., referring to the simplicity of essence buried in itself] is through negation. It is neither this nor that, but equally *not-this* and indifferent to being this or that [*weder dieses noch jenes, ein* Nichtdieses, *und ebenso gleichgültig*]. Such a 'simple' is what we call a *universal*" (*PhG* §96). Under the sway of the exemplary, the universality of "this," "now," and "here" presents itself as more mediated, actual, energized than that of pure being externally opposed to nothing. When the "this," as well as its dual spatiotemporal ontological shape, has absorbed its own negation into itself, it can finally relate to itself and transition from the reality of isolated instances to a first, concretely universal, actuality. By means of its speculative repetition as the other, energized by the negativity of the "not-this," the "this" actually becomes itself for the first time. The negatively mediated self-relation of the "this" as "this" and "not-this" is quite formal—an actuality experienced within the boundaries of real (mere) consciousness, the energy of the energy-less, the universality that is a legatee of abstract indifference, including an indifference toward the difference between being and nothing. But it is capable of overstepping the limits of virtual reality, which is none other than the simplicity of the disconnected and fragmentary remnants of the entropic process.[2]

Such a step, however, will not take us very far, given that real consciousness with its phenomenal works ("this," "here," "now") is indescribable on its native turf. The nascent negative mediations, striving toward the self-knowledge or the self-relation of actuality, are too clumsy to express the sensuous, to press the hidden inner essence out to the surface of appearances. The sensuous is inexpressible because it cannot, in all actuality, be expressed by real consciousness—it can only be relegated to the sphere of empty universality, generality, and abstraction. What is said about it misses the mark of singularity (of the unrepeatable, the separated, the purely idiomatic and idiotic, of what, spurning synergy, lacks energy) and regurgitates "*the universal this*," das allgemeine Diese, and "being in general," *das Sein überhaupt* (*PhG* §97). Linguistic expression is not adequate to the expressed here, yet real consciousness does not know this. Only language itself does. This is why "language is more truthful; in it, we ourselves immediately contradict what we *mean to say* [*in ihr widerlegen wir selbst unmittelbar unsere* Meinung]" (*PhG* §97). While, for consciousness without self-consciousness, the contradiction does not exist, the self-awareness of language permits us to measure the disparity between the energy-poor virtual reality of sense-certainty, on the one hand, and the self-negating/self-negated energy of expression with its reiterations, synergies, and actualizations of the essential, on the other.

The universality of the "this," mediated by its negation, accommodates all the actually existing "thises" that are, at the same, mutually exclusive as the enunciated "this." The same, Hegel argues, applies to the "here" that attains to the universal, thanks to mutating into a "not-here" as soon as I turn elsewhere. In this turn, "the *here* itself does not disappear; rather, *it is* [es ist], remaining in the disappearance of houses, trees, and so forth and keeping itself indifferent [*gleichgültig*] to being a house, a tree" (*PhG* §98). If the universality of the "here" is more determinate (and, hence, determinately negated) than that of pure being, it is because the former includes actual places whereas the latter is totally undifferentiated. Nevertheless, already nourished by the actuality of the house or the tree that is here, the universal "here" imbibes the attitude of pure being, behaving *as though* differentiation has not happened, as though the distinct places and entities through which it is defined did not matter any more than arbitrary examples. Despite the fact that the shapes of actualities are present before sense-certainty, it acts as if everything were merely possible and, moreover, as if every possibility were situated on the same level as all the others, dwarfed by the very possibility of possibility that is pure being. It is not difficult to recognize in this comportment the dynamics of globalization, not only leveling different places but also subordinating their placeness to the placelessness of the empty abstraction it propagates throughout the planet. And the backflow from actuality to an indifferent meta-possibility far and away exceeds the economic sphere, affecting also sexual difference and political divisions, among other things.

When Hegel writes that in sense-certainty "*pure being* remains therefore its [sense-certainty's] essence, though not *qua* immediate [*bleibt also das* reine Sein *als ihr Wesen, aber nicht als unmittelbares*]" (*PhG* §98), he is hinting at the paradoxical condition in which, even if mediation, self-negation, and actualization have come to pass, the indifference of pure being seems to be undisturbed. Whatever the energy, whatever the actual existence that has been procured through these operations, it ebbs away upon contact with the specific universality of sense-certainty. And, conversely, to concede that the essence (namely, pure being—that which is purely deprived of energy) is beyond immediacy is to give up on its purity *and* on its being ("it is no longer what we *mean* by *being*" [*PhG* §98]), to acknowledge that something of essence has been released from its entombment in itself, has been mixed with the appearances, for otherwise mediation would not have been able to commence its proceedings (beginning always from the middle: hence, without beginning). Pure being both is and is not the essence of sense-certainty; it is, in fact, both pure and impure, while essence "itself" is both essence and non-essence (appearance).

Essence, then, puts itself to work and is converted into energy, regardless of how staunchly it tries to maintain itself in itself, in its insulated purity, and regardless, too, of the retrocession from the achievement of incipient actuality to the dictatorship of the merely possible, which is foisted upon us more and more insistently today. It is not even that an originally pure essence is somehow tainted, twisting and turning inside out into actuality; rather, its purity is reconstructed in an *après coup*, by and in the image of the yet unthinking real consciousness forgetful of itself.

The energizing of essence happens as a *divestment* from this presumably independent thing and an *investment* into the "I," relative to whom what is here and now appears as here and now. "The object, which was supposed to be the essential, is now the non-essential of sense-certainty . . . Its truth is in the object as *my* object, or in *what I mean* [*als meinem Gegenstande, oder im* Meinen]; it is, because *I* know it" (*PhG* §100). The object is, in other words, a work of the subject's energy, an objective appearance of this I taking interest in its here-and-now. That energy is, Hegel conveys through his use of the cursive, the energy of appropriation (making something "mine," *mein*) and of meaning-making (*Meinen*), the two words sharing a common root. The object becomes mine by virtue of making sense to me, through the meanings I assign to it. Thus, it is actual (timely and not-only-possible) to me: it matters to the extent that my consciousness subtracts it from the generally undifferentiated landscape of pure being, which is, itself, abstracted from the world. "This is" because "I am"—in a relation of knowing it. Its being (the "is") is no longer a virtual abstraction, but the actualization of my directedness toward it; it is no longer an independent pure essence, but a meaningful connection, forged by means of an appropriation in knowing.

There are, at the same time, multiple indicators that the truth of sense-certainty does not live up to the accomplishment of energy-actuality. Not only is it "driven back into the I [*in das Ich zurückgedrängt*]" (*PhG* §100), where it languishes in the (virtual domain of) subjective interiority of workings without work, but it also draws its force (*Kraft*) from this I, a power-potentiality that falls back into an immediacy (*Unmittelbarkeit*) of the senses (*PhG* §101). Sense-certainty persists in the grip of the richest knowledge and the poorest truth, one that does not appear in and as the actual, constructing instead a reality (*Realität*) of virtual fragments. Combined, these indicators amount to a sort of relativism, according to which my "here" directly contradicts the "here" of another and each boasts equal validity, its truth vouchsafed by the "immediacy of seeing," *die Unmittelbarkeit des Sehens* (*PhG* §101). The One—the empty, abstract universal—breaks up into the many, resistant to the synergic becoming of energy. That, too, is our situation today: an advanced state of entropy, where every shard of the virtual whole is either unaware of or incompatible with all the others.

The retreat of sense-certainty's essence into the I is possible in light of this I veering on the side of pure being, as indifferent as the "this," "here," and "now." Having appropriated its object with the acts of meaning-making, it has not yet taken hold of nor attributed meaning to itself, and it will not do so until the immediate biological life of "this I" is endangered. For the time being, the essential I is not committed to anything, not even to itself. Its vision "is a simple seeing [*einfaches Sehen*], which by virtue of the negation of this house and so forth, is mediated," and, across the negation, it stays "similarly simple and indifferent [*ebenso einfach und gleichgültig*]" (*PhG* §102). The mediated immediacy of universal vision is a mental working without the works, void of energy. It sees by stopping to see the "this" it is facing here and now, by shifting its gaze elsewhere in a perpetual distraction that, curious beyond satisfaction or just indifferent, values more the moments of refocusing than focus, the agitated intervals between those instances when one's eyes rest on an object. Every visible shape—the work of vision's energy—is immediately de-substantivized, dissolved into an undifferentiated background for seeing and an endless procession of workings. The virtual and inexhaustible possibility of individuating this or that object from the undifferentiated whole and letting it return to that whole presides over the simple universality of sight.

Having commenced in sense-certainty, mediations founder and disintegrate into immediacy, a budding actuality is brought into the fold of potentiality, and energy is squandered in the unbridgeable divide between that which is at work and that which is in the work. The crux of the matter is that, although sense-certainty is a relation between this I and this thing (and, as a relation, is mediated by the participating terms), it is a relation between two internally unmediated parties, infinitely echoing each other in their indeterminate universality. A relation without relation (which is, coincidentally, the philosophical designation Emmanuel Levinas adopts for the I-Other relation) is an immediate articulation of two or more immediacies without self-relation—a pure reality without actuality or energy. The "reality" (*Realität*) of sense-certainty is, therefore, neither this object nor this I but "the *whole* of sense-certainty," *das* Ganze *der sinnlichen Gewißheit*, "as the *immediacy* [Unmittelbarkeit] which thereby excludes from itself all opposition that has previously taken place" (*PhG* §103).

Pure immediacy lets go of the difference between terms in a relation without relation that collapse into one another. It is a "relation that remains equal, which makes no difference of essentiality and inessentiality between the I and the object, and into which no difference in general can infiltrate [*sich selbst gleichbleibende Beziehung, die zwischen dem Ich und dem Gegenstande keinen Unterschied der Wesentlichkeit und Unwesentlichkeit macht, und in die daher auch überhaupt kein Unterschied eindringen kann*]"

(*PhG* §104). Each instance is isolated in itself: if there is no difference here, that is because there is neither repetition nor self-repetition in static equality. A lack of distinctions between essentiality and inessentiality evinces the absence of boundaries between the inner and the outer required for (to put it in the language of physics) the production of energy potentials, of voltage based on differences in electric charges. The "remaining-equal" (*gleichbleibende*) of the relation without relation in a state of energetic non-differentiation is the afterglow of the indifference proper to pure being that insinuates itself into the mindset of political correctness and into certain "radical" ecological philosophies. It is an equality that foregoes comparison and equalization, seeing that the articulated terms are immediately the same. Yet, their sameness is not an identity, something that entails the same mediated (determined, negated, energized) by the other. Which is why the equality of this I and this object in the immediacy of sense-certainty repels difference.

The absolute, of course, is also incomparable, but its singularity is predicated on repetition and difference, a self-relation impregnated with otherness, energy both actualizing and actualized. The relation without relation of sense-certainty is pre-identitarian; the absolute is post-identitarian (this is where Levinas's term comes into play). This goes for interiority and exteriority, as well: in a passage of the inner essence to the outer envelope of appearances, energy's self-expression overcomes the master distinction of metaphysics (inside/outside), which is treated with indifference in sense-certainty. What makes the most difference is this very indifference, or the absence thereof. At the antipodes of the patent attitude of sense-certainty, the absolute is radical non-indifference, combining the singularity of the actual with its iterations, and individuation with the most intense interconnectedness.

That said, the pre- is everywhere shadowed by the post-, and the energy-less is put in relief by energy already dialectically secured, much like, in a miniature, the account of real consciousness is redoubled by actual (self-)consciousness. Sense-certainty itself knows none of this; its temporality is the immediacy of the now experienced as a continuous flux, as one now oblivious to the many that it is not. Taking all the necessary precautions not to interfere with this phenomenological experience from the outside, Hegel urges that "we must let ourselves *point* [zeigen *müssen wir es uns lassen*]" to the now, immanently and punctually disrupting it at the moment and place of its occurrence, neither afterwards (*nachher*) nor at a distance (*entfernt*) (*PhG* §105). With this primordial signification, the now softens its impermeable boundaries and is divided into *the before and the after in the now*. Repeated in the immanence of its unraveling, pointed out by the absolute that it will have been beyond immediacy and mediation, the now receives a boost of dialectical energy or, more precisely, the after-energy that relates it to itself as an other to itself.

The othering of the now, its mediation on the grounds of immediacy, is carried out by the act of pointing out: "The now that *is*, is another now than the one pointed to, and we see that the now is just that: to be no more just when it is [*dieses ist, indem es ist, schon nicht mehr zu sein*]. The now, as it has been pointed out to us, is the now that *has been* [*ein gewesenes*]" (*PhG* §106). Pointing out the now sullies its pure present, the present of pure being, and relegates it to the past, to the not-now, the one that has already been. This act thus grants actuality to the now solely on the condition that it is recognized as a non-actual, or a no-longer-actual, point in time. More pointedly still, the immanent disruption of the pure present does not result in a temporal succession: the having-been of the now is revealed in the now that is. Both this formulation and its content send us back to the Aristotelian energy of vision in the *Metaphysics*—"one has seen as soon as one sees [ὁρᾷ ἅμα καὶ ἑώρακε]" (1048b, 23)—already actualized in each of its moments. But while, in Aristotle, vision is overfull with itself, closing the circle of the actual, in Hegel, the pointed-out now breathes with loss, slipping away into the nonessential. In a calculated play on "essence," *Wesen*, and "what-has-been," *gewesen*, "what has been is, in fact, *no essence*; it *is* nothing [*was* gewesen *ist, ist in der Tat* kein Wesen; *es* ist *nicht*]" (*PhG* §106). Negated, temporally contaminated, pure being does not deliver itself to the determinately negated freedom of energy-actuality, but flips into nothing.

The act of pointing out sparks a chain reaction that climaxes in the speculative energy of the now. The pointed-out and the pointing-out are and are not the same: each is slightly delayed or slightly ahead of the other. Each is a now (*one*), but they are different nows (*many*): X and not-X. The pointing-out now sees itself in the mirror of the pointed-out now, and recognizes itself as (or in) another now: "it is precisely *one reflected into itself* [ein in sich Reflektiertes], or a *simple*, which remains in being-other what it is—a now, which is absolutely many nows" (*PhG* §107). The deeper one retreats into the one, the more assuredly the one scatters into the many, its "simple" atomicity split the moment the one relates to itself. Reflected into itself, the one is not one but at least two *and* it remains one in this being-other that is the many. Differently stated, burrowing into essence, we are catapulted to the skin of appearances, wherein the essence is expressed in actuality, energetically, despite or thanks to its becoming-other.

When the pointing-out is experienced, above all in its difference from the pointed-out, its felt dissonance gives a presentiment of synergy, of "a plurality of nows taken together," *ein Vielheit von Itzt zusammengefaßt*, that constitutes a universal now (*PhG* §107). The experience in question, moving from one continuous now through a plurality of nows toward the universal now, is phenomenological both within the limited purview of sense-certainty and in the context of replaying that movement from the perspective of the absolute. As absolute, experience is energetic plenitude: the working and the work, means and ends, the history of its making and the outcome, along with all the clefts and fissures of negativity between and among them. As belonging to sense-certainty, it is a way of working deprived of works, means without ends, a history of movement neglecting to take note of its results: "It is clear that the dialectic of sense-certainty is nothing other than a simple history of its movement, or its experience [*die einfache Geschichte ihrer Bewegung oder ihrer Erfahrung*], and that self-certainty itself is nothing other than just this history" (*PhG* §109). As contained in the "this" of external things, experience is dead, a bunch of works without workings, "reality or being [*die Realität oder das Sein*]" (*PhG* §109). Experience distilled to simple working is self-forgetting; "it forgets . . . and starts the movement over again from the beginning [*fängt die Bewegung von vorne an*]" (*PhG* §109). Reality or being that fits into simple works is the having-been-forgotten of the movement that culminated in "external things." It follows that sense-certainty is the beginning of dialectics because its form and content *are* the beginning oblivious toward what was before it began, a perpetual beginning in beginning*s* decoupled from an end and from ends. (For Hannah Arendt, beginning ever afresh is the enunciation of political action, which therefore requires a fair dose of forgetfulness.)

The energy of experience taken in its verbal sense is the movement by which external, sensuous things are swept away and in which they dissolve. Only to the detriment of this de-actualizing moment responsible for the relationality and self-relationality of the actual, is it possible to affirm that "reality . . . has absolute truth for consciousness [*die Realität . . . habe absolute Wahrheit für das Bewußtsein*]" (*PhG* §109). Even animals (*die Tiere*), Hegel quips, are initiated into the "elementary school of wisdom" that teaches them and us to submit the independent reality of external things to a practical test by eating them, by analyzing via digestion the works that things are into biochemical workings, and finally converting them into kinetic energy. "Despairing of the reality of those things [*verzweifelnd an dieser Realität*] and in the total certainty of their nothingness, they [i.e., the animals] without further ado help themselves to them and eat them up" (*PhG* §109). What animals despair of when they despair of reality is reality's autistic separation, its non-relationality, its being less than actual. They negate the specious self-sufficiency of reality and establish a negative rapport with it, transforming the "certainty [*Gewißheit*] of nothingness," itself the inversion of sense-certainty, into an objectified nothing—the eaten object as nothing independent of the eater. In synergy with the eaten, the eater is energized by the nothingness, to which the form of the real object has been reduced. Realists, Hegel ironically implies, are dumber than animals: neither afflicted by doubt, *Zweifel*, nor experiencing despair, *Verzweiflung*, regarding the autonomous reality of things, realists have not yet graduated from the elementary school of wisdom. They have not yet begun the work of transmuting reality into actuality.

Subjects and objects are yoked together and replicate each other's features: realists are as unrelated to themselves, unconscious of what they are doing and saying, as the reality they install on the pedestal of the absolute. In speaking of "the existence of *external* objects [*Dasein* äußerer Gegenstände]," they intend to determine it as "actual," *wirklich*. "However, they do not say what they mean . . . The sensuous 'this' . . . is *inaccessible* [unerreichbar] to the language of consciousness . . . In the actual attempt [*Unter dem wirklichen Versuche*] to say it, it would therefore decay" (*PhG* §110). The meaning of the realists is not theirs at all. For Hegel, a conflation of the real and the actual is not only unforgivable; it also does not withstand the test of action, the actuality of saying the sensuous "this." An actual attempt at an internally consistent realism puts the brakes on the desire that has motivated it and liberates huge amounts of anti-energy: the act counteracts itself. Pure universality is at odds with pure singularity, even though both, immediately and unbeknown to the realist, inhere in the "this."

Language, as the language of consciousness (or, more exactly, that of the real or mere consciousness), falls apart into two energy fields, virtually disconnected from one another: the universal signifier, S, and the singular (hence, unsayable) signified, s, which, by virtue of its non-relationality, remains inaccessible, *unerreichbar*. S/s is the model of language according to realist precepts. Its "arbitrariness," upon which Ferdinand de Saussure remarked, has to do with the fact that the signifier does not express the signified, the two assembled by force (of convention, for instance) and, as such, divested of energy. Real consciousness lacks the language to say the actual; with a modicum of consistency, it can do no more than mutely point at the *this*. Enunciation might begin, but it will not be complete (*nicht vollenden*) in these linguistic workings without works. And the resultant meaning, if there is one, is the equality, *Gleichheit*, of everything with everything: "If, about something, nothing is said beyond that it is an *actual thing* [*ein* wirkliches Ding], an *external object*, then the outcome is only the most universal of all, and what is spoken of is its *equality* [*seine* Gleichheit] with everything, rather than difference"

(*PhG* §110). Do we not recognize the celebrated flatness of our "new realisms," "object-oriented ontology," and politically correct discourse in Hegel's devastating critique of sense-certainty? What are they saying besides generalities that are vacuous and formally equalizing? Where do they derive their energy, if not from the entropy of thinking?

2. Perception: The Non-Actual Reality of Seeing without Seeing Oneself See

Actual attempts by sense-certainty to say the "this" failed: the act could not be completed because it ran into the inversion of the object from singularity into an empty universality. Sense-certainty was unable to take (*nehmen*) the object, the "this," in its truth (*Wahrheit*): it either grasped the opposite of what was intended or nothing at all. The objective dimension of its energy was absent; hence, the act was never actualized. This is not the case in perception, *Wahrnehmung*, or literally a "true-taking," where the mental workings of perceiving are united to the perceived. Acts of perception do not supersede the reality of pointing-out; they internally modify and bring this reality a tad closer to actuality by showing the co-belonging of the perceiving (*das Wahrnehmende*) and the perceived (*das Wahrgenommene*) in "the same movement," *dieselbe Bewegung* (*PhG* §111). Yet, the two sides are unequal in light of what is essential and what is not (one may venture a guess that it is this inequality that lends the movement its energy). In response to the excessive de-substantivation of late sense-certainty, essence migrates into the works of perception, its objects that are structurally parallel to the initial essentiality of the "this." Even the explanation remains the same: "the object is the essence insofar as it is indifferent [*gleichgültig*] to whether it becomes perceived or not" (*PhG* §111). With the indifference of the object, the shadow of undifferentiated pure being looms large on our horizon and covers over energy-actuality, which is characteristically non-indifferent.

The "true-taking" of perception is possible to the extent that the singular is *mediated* by the universal, rather than being *interchangeable* with abstract universality, as it was in the indifference of the "this." Mediation repeats the singular here and now in the "now" when and in the "here" where it is perceived, taken in its truth as singular. Repeating the singular at the precise moment when it appears, in perceptual presence, mediation energizes the object and lends it enough coherence to be not a mere "this" but a thing, with a set of properties of its own. Perception is consolidated into an energetic shape, even if it does not perceive itself perceiving and, absent this self-relation, does not yet elevate, cancel, and preserve (in a word: does not sublate) reality into actuality.

On the side of the perceived thing, conversely, the universal is mediated by the singular: determined, the objective principle "shows itself as a thing with many properties [als *das Ding von vielen Eigenschaften*]" (*PhG* §112). The properties are the synergic outcomes of determinate negation, the *erga* of perception, where difference (*Unterschied*) spells out manifoldness (*Mannigfaltigkeit*), itself folded into the one thing. But the dynamic element of perceptual energy does not pertain exclusively to the subject. Before being taken in truth by the act of perceiving, the thing has already appropriated itself, having divided itself into properties (*Eigenschaften*), or what is its own (*eigen*). What perception repeats is this self-mediation of the perceived, the objective principle put to work (rather than persisting in ideal isolation) in such a way that the thing "must express [*ausdrücken*] this [mediated simplicity] in itself as its nature" (*PhG* §112). The thing's expression of its energized, actualized, multifaceted principle will then be reiterated in perception that gathers manifold objective determinations—the properties or the proper—back into the unity of the perceived. The energy of perception stems from a repetition of the proper, reassembled from the ideal oneness of principle and the real dispersion of properties into an actual one.

Another way of saying that the thing appropriates itself in its properties is that each property is "related to itself [*auf sich selbst*]" and remains indifferent (*gleichgültig*) to all the others (*PhG* §113). By means of its self-relation, the "this" is converted into a property, while retaining its indifference inherited from pure being. It borders on actuality. Yet, to be properly (*eigentlich*) a property (*Eigenschaft*), it is missing "a determination still to-come," *eine ferner hinzukommende Bestimmung*, the non-indifferent self-relation ("pure self-relating-to-itself," *reine Sich-auf-sich-beziehen*) of thinghood (*PhG* §113), later to be exposed in its speculative identity to the subject. An indifferent compilation of properties (e.g., grayness, glossiness, smoothness, cylindricality, hollowness in the case of a cup) does not amount to synergy, a negatively mediated bond that renders disparate energies interdependent and, in effect, forges energy out of them in the first place. Thinghood, holding itself together (*zusammenfassende*) with the indifferent "also" (*Auch*), does not attain actuality; the real par excellence, *res*, is shackled to the virtual reality of an empty universal (thing) and an infinite addition of multiplicities (properties).

If at its center the thing is largely void of energy, at the edges it is awash with what the center lacks. The determination of thingly properties, allowing for the thing's self-appropriation and for its perceptual "taking in truth," can only happen through a negation: properties "are determinate insofar as they are both *distinguished* from one another and *relate themselves to each other*, as opposed [*als entgegengesetzte*]" (*PhG* §114).

Smoothness is neither grayness nor cylindricality nor hollowness nor... Moreover, smoothness is not not-smoothness; it is not roughness. The determinate negation of thinghood involves both difference and oppositionality, unlike the "this," which stood merely in an abstract opposition to its other, the "not-this." A combination of differentiation and oppositional relationality produces the shapes (works) of energy-actuality we typically identify as things, in contrast to the amorphous objects of sense-certainty.

This, for Hegel, is the fulfillment or the culmination of the truth of perception: "the thing as the truth of true-taking or perception is fulfilled [*das Ding als das Wahre der Wahrnehmung vollendet*]" (*PhG* §115). The principle of thinghood cannot generate more energy than that: it falls apart into an indifferent but inclusive universality of the "also" and a differentiated but exclusive universality of the one determined entity. No principle is, admittedly, capable of generating more energy than an abstract opposition (and the presumably self-consistent principles are the least energetic of all) because, as principle, it is confined to the realm of the inner, the essential, the virtual, the non-actual. For something other than a formal self-contradiction, one would need to consult, on the one hand, the actual properties of the thing that put the contradiction to work and, on the other, "consciousness in its actual perceiving [*Bewußtsein in seinem wirklichen Wahrnehmen*]" (*PhG* §116).

What takes place in actual perceiving? "True-taking" seems to demand that nothing be either added to or subtracted from the perceived; that perception serve as a passive-receptive medium for the perceived; that a taking without taking exist; and that consciousness not invest any energy of its own, least of all libidinal psychic energy. Perceptual taking is, ideally, a taking that does not bring anything to whatever it takes. An empty grasp, it "*only has to take* [nur zu nehmen] the thing and to behave as pure apprehension, and what emerges before it is the true [*das Wahre*]" (*PhG* §116). The danger here lies not in taking the thing inaccurately, as something more or something less than what it is, but in assuming pure taking without giving (back) to be possible. The illusion is not an incorrectly perceived thing, but perception itself understood as a cognitive medium shorn of energy, of uneven libidinal attachments or cathexes, of a preferentially differentiated, discriminatory approach. The truth of perception, in turn, is the truth of the thing, a conscious grasp of the thing reiterating the thing's grasping of itself. The former truth can only be self-contradictory: an apprehension of the universal (property) when singularity is the target; a discontinuous assemblage when one "community" (*Gemeinschaft*) of the thing was in view (*PhG* §117). The truth in the act of perception becoming untruth, the grasp released, opens unto dialectical energy as such: "its result and truth [*das Resultat und das Wahre*] are at the same time its dissolution [*Auflösung*]" (*PhG* §118). In our terms, the work—the outcome in its actual truth—is unworked; it disbands into a new moment of working, undergoing de-substantivation, virtualization, interiorization.

And, indeed, the result or the objective truth of perception is de-substantivized into the perceiving in a reflexive exile out of the true and "*a return of consciousness into itself* [Rückkehr des Bewußtsein in sich selbst]" (*PhG* §118). At the limit, in the extreme case of its retreat from the perceived, a perceiving consciousness in despair devises a self-relation, verges on self-consciousness, but interprets this option as utterly negative: as evidence of its being in the "untruth," *Unwahrheit* (*PhG* §118), of being under the sway of an illusion or a delusion. It sees nothing but its own fault and failure in this heightened energetic state. The problem is that the inward-looking self-conscious relation is taken to be not only untrue but also incongruous with the outward-glancing relation to things in the world. The possibility of energetically expressing the inner in the outer, of pressing essence out into appearances in an *activity* that deals with essences and appearances, is undermined before it has a chance to get off the ground. The two halves in this non-relation are equally virtualized, without having been dispensed to actuality.

Consequently, we succumb to an *either/or* fallacy: *either* we attend to external things, taking them in truth, *or* we attend to ourselves and find ourselves in the untruth. We either zoom in on the works or concentrate on the workings of perception itself; and not before phenomenological movement is replayed on the basis of its fulfillment in the absolute will the two extremes coexist, shadowing one another, in difference. In the meantime, while energy-actuality is out of touch with itself, things literally disintegrate, the works receiving no support from psychic workings. The principle of thinghood—the thing counts as "one"—is not reconstituted in actual perception, which relies on multiple senses to register the properties of things. Hence, "we do not take [*nehmen*] the whole variety of these aspects from the thing, but from us, ourselves" (*PhG* §119).

What is omitted from this account, however, is the prior self-appropriation of the thing, which is achievable at the price of its indifferent oneness. "Since the *property* is the thing's *proper* property [*die eigene Eigenschaft des Dinges*], i.e., determinateness in the thing itself, it has *multiple* properties" (*PhG* §120). The dispersion of the senses responds and corresponds to a determinate multiplicity in the thing itself: the "also" of the senses is a repetition, a mediation, and an actualization of the "also" that "is" the thing itself. A promise of energy flickers before us for a brief instant in which our taking of the thing reiterates, rather than distorts, the thing's self-appropriation, and so triggers a surge in dialectical after-energy. But the promise is short-lived: instead of an actual (or actualizing) repetition of what is proper to the thing, the perceiving consciousness is conceived in terms of an external "also"—superfluous at best, perverting at worst—added to the thing's inclusive universality. By comparison, "the thing is elevated to a genuine '*also*' [*zum wahrhaften* Auch *erhoben*], becoming a collection of matters [*Sammlung von Materien*]" (*PhG* §121). In its singularity, it is plural—energies assembled into completed works, into the real, next to which the workings of consciousness appear insubstantial, flimsy, virtual, and untrue.

On the point of things disintegrating, consciousness does the same. The thing "determinately presents itself *to* an apprehending *consciousness*" even as it is "reflected *out of* and *into* itself"; consciousness is in "the disparity between *apprehending* and *returning-into-itself*" (*PhG* §122). From the vantage of the absolute, we can acknowledge a parallel between, on the one hand, the phenomenon and the noumenon, and, on the other, the empirical-phenomenological and the transcendental subjects. More than a parallel, this is the ontology of energy, essentially partitioned between what is withheld *in potentia* (reflected into itself) and what is released (out of itself, toward the other). "Real" consciousness and the thing are kindred energy formations situated in the same ontological constellation. A cross-section of their energy supply must become anti-energy: pure possibility or potentiality locked in itself, inaccessible, non-actual, or even counter-actual, as well as counter-factual. Their truth, therefore, is set in opposition to itself, *entgegengesetzt* (*PhG* §122).

In the case of the thing, that energy which is not siphoned into potentiality is the actual appearance, the phenomenon, thingly existence "for the other," *für ein Anderes*. But it is, precisely, this energetic openness to the other that is dismissed as a source of dangerous illusions, unlike the thing's virtual reflectedness into itself as one, its being "for itself," *für sich* (*PhG* §122). Consciousness understands an analogous retreat of consciousness into itself, in a movement of self-reiteration that could augment its energy, as a betrayal of truth—a capricious and arbitrary mode of being disconnected from the real world (which is actually disconnected from itself). And there is a grain of veracity in this accusation: a consciousness that relates to itself without sensing its otherness to itself is stuck in pure virtuality and is prevented from becoming-actual. The thing's being "for itself" is grasped, on the contrary, as a token of its genuine existence, further entrenching the virtualization of "objective" reality. Like in mere consciousness, however, the self of the thing's "for itself" (its interiority) is not mediated with the other but is immediately "an *other* for itself, just *as it* is for an other [*ist es ein* anderes *für sich*, als es *für Anderes ist]*" (*PhG* §123). Before, oneness and diversity clashed in the absence of dialectical passages between them; now, the same fate befalls selfhood and otherness. While real consciousness coils into itself without knowing itself as other, the thing in and for itself is an other without a self.

Indifference flourishes, precisely, where determinately negated links between the self and the other are absent. At the level of thinking, this means that the opposites are entirely interchangeable, assuming that there is neither friction nor traction to instigate their determination and actualization because they are not yet privy to the speculative energy of self-negation. A self that is not other to itself is totally other; an other that does not relate to itself at all is a rigid self (*PhG* §126). The logical principle of noncontradiction is unmasked as eminently self-contradictory: 'A = A' implies 'A ≠ A'. Formal logic suffers from energy bankruptcy, and for that reason is inexpressible in the actual in a manner more drastic than the Procrustean bed argument makes appear. It is not that actual things do not fit the ideal molds of that logic, but, rather, that the ideal molds do not even fit themselves, immediately tipping into their others. Without mediations between the same and the other, they are *immediately* and *essentially* the other, impeding any further development of thought.

At the level of existence, pure indifference has no place whatsoever. In the raw, unmediated, merely given actuality of the thing, "in the fact," *in der Tat*, of its being, "there is diversity [*Verschiedenheit*] in it," which "necessarily exists as an *actual* difference [*als* wirklicher *Unterschied*] of multiple compositions in it" (*PhG* §124). The brute nature of this givenness "in fact" is greatly exaggerated: the logical category of necessity intervenes as a mediator between the diversity (*Verschiedenheit*) of determinations in the thing and difference (*Unterschied*) factored into its material composition. Whereas diversity is potential and apt for a purely indifferent stance (which is why it is the watchword of liberalism, multiculturalism, and environmental activism enamored of the idea of a global DNA archive), difference is actual, preliminarily sifted through the category of necessity, and thus marginally self-given, imbued with the energy of *actuality'*.

The actuality of the thing's manifold constitution holds for its content, though not for the thingly form, which is differentiated from another thing outside it. There is no way to embark on the dialectic of content and form when the former is actual and the latter is virtual. Diversity sublated into difference belongs to the manifold interior of the thing, but as one, in its very principle, the thing's "being-set-in-opposition [*Entgegengesetztsein*] does not become the actual opposition [*wirklichen Entgegensetzung*] of the thing itself" (*PhG* §124). What we have here before us is not just the virtuality of form and the actuality of content, but, seen from the absolute, an opposition between the virtual and the actual oppositionalities of the thing as one and as many. In this relation, whereas the essence/phenomenality distinction is maintained, essence's being-set-in-opposition (*Entgegengesetztsein*) admits the possibility of its engagement with the other and of becoming otherwise than it is. More than that, the *Entgegengesetztsein* of essence is its putting-to-work outside the ideal impermeability of essence's self-enclosure. Unsustainable in its unmediated self-identity, essence receives an energetic push in preparation for its actualization in what appears.

Essence is about to be de-essentialized (both in the sense of spilling into appearances and in the sense of becoming two—the exclusive-individual and the inclusive-universal universality) after things have disintegrated into an actual difference and the virtual indifference of their principle. The wheels of the dialectical energy machine start rolling: empirical and transcendental works are sent back to the determinate negations of what is at work, virtualizing and virtualized. Curiously, at this stage, it is the virtual (self-enclosed essence, abstract thinghood) that is virtualized in a negation of the negation that yields the first approximation to actuality. In practical terms, the virtualization of the virtual resulting in a mediated actuality occurs in a transition from the world of perception to the "realm of understanding," *das Reich des Verstandes*, itself assigned to the space of interiority. And a decisive gesture in this transition is the thing's self-negation, lending energy to the universality of understanding.

The thing, *das Ding*, is a universal that "*has come out of the sensuous*" and is "essentially *conditioned* [bedingt] by it [i.e., by the sensuous]" (*PhG* §129). So much so that conditioning by the sensuous "this" makes the thing a thing (to be conditioned is, to translate directly from the German, to be "bethinged"). Far from actualization, conditioning is the transcendental subjection of the conditioned to an apriori power, experienced as a limitation. Like anything conditioned, the universal is not free and, therefore, not purely universal; "*affected with an opposition* [mit einem Gegensatze affizierte]," it "divides into the extremes of individuality and universality, the 'one' of properties and the 'also' of free matters" (*PhG* §129). The thing, or the work of sublating the "this," is conditioned by what it has sublated, such that the conditioning itself supplies the speculative energy needed for its overcoming. The thing, or the work, unthings or unworks itself, insofar as the opposition afflicting universality compartmentalizes it into the universal and the nonuniversal ("the extremes of individuality and universality"). What emerges in consequence of the unthinging, or unworking, of thinghood from this schism, which is a schism *within* thingly universality, is the unconditional, *die unbedingte*: "But, since both are essentially *in one unity*, an unconditioned absolute universality [*die unbedingte absolute Allgemeinheit*] is now at hand [*vorhanden*]" (*PhG* §129). The universal split into the universal and the nonuniversal, in its sameness and otherness to itself, is ultimately dependent only on itself: the universal. That, by definition, is its unconditionality—being conditioned by itself alone. Unconditionally universal, understanding is inflected and haunted by the negation of the thing and its work. To understand is to unthing, uncondition, unwork, de-actualize, or virtualize—the sensuous.

Staying for a moment with the perceived thing and the act of perceiving, we note that their energy is virtually nonexistent because synergic self-relations are quite undeveloped on both sides of the equation. The self-reflectedness of the thing is "a *conditioned* being-for-itself [*ein bedingtes Für-sich-sein*]" (*PhG* §130), not conditioned by itself as a (negated) other to itself but by its arbitrary material limits, the necessity of the nonessential. As we've seen, to resolve the problem is to dissolve the thing, something that understanding accomplishes through its powers of analysis. Perception, nevertheless, strains to take the thing as it is, in the truth of its appearing or self-taking. Shackled to the conditioned universality of thinghood, perception is at the mercy of "empty abstractions of *individuality* and *universality* set over and against it," that is to say, it is at the mercy of "powers" (*Mächte*), whose "play" (*Spiel*) is perception itself (*PhG* §131). Individuality and universality are powers *inasmuch as* they are empty abstractions, virtual in their static opposition to one another. Their play is inimical to energy's work—which, to be sure, is playful in another sense—because it prevents perception from working an actuality out of itself (or working itself out into actuality). It is in this context that Hegel calls "mere" consciousness "real"—*reale Bewußtsein* (*PhG* §131)—hinting not at the gravitas of its acts of perceiving but, on the contrary, at their arbitrary play-character, captive to the perceived thing's unmediated individuality and universality, twice blind, conditioned by the conditioned.

All this is considered from the platform of the absolute. From a lived phenomenological perspective, real consciousness appears to be the exact opposite: the epitome of seriousness, the thing itself of the mind, especially since it borrows certain of its features from the thing's dignified solidity. (Hegel's qualifier for real consciousness is *gediegen*, meaning "dignified" or "solid.") It acquires the aura of a concrete outcome unaware of the means through which the end was reached, a work with the scaffolding that brought it into being already dismantled and obliterated. Precluding the dialectic of energy—of works and workings—it lapses into common sense (*Menschenverstand*) and, at the other end of the spectrum, into a philosophy of mere "thought-things" (*Gedankendingen*) (*PhG* §131).

Within the schemes of common sense and philosophy, the two approaches present themselves as irreconcilable, and precisely this irreconcilability is what is imparted to them from their shared source. Each is a permutation of thinghood in thought: one—of thingly universality; the other—of an equally unmediated individuality. They are works without workings, virtual to the nth degree. Philosophy's pure thought-things are no more detached from the real than the postulates of common sense; they are the most real products of cogitation and, by the same token, the least proximate to the actual. The only difference, perhaps, is that philosophy is not merely conscious of such things but also "recognizes them to be pure essence, the absolute elements and powers [*die absoluten Elemente und Mächte*], and recognizes them equally *in their determinateness* [Bestimmtheit]" (*PhG* §131). In other words, philosophical recognition has already worked through and reconciled universality and individuality, having overcome their static opposition in the thing. Dealing with thought-things, it preserves the virtuality of "powers" at the level of essence, even as it actualizes these powers by lending them determinateness (through work performed by determinate negation). The secret of philosophy's energy lurks in this actuality of the virtual.

Perception, according to Hegel (i.e., according to itself as phenomenologically experienced and to its repetition in the absolute), does not successfully leave the fetish of dignified solidity behind: it "does not come to the consciousness of the essentialities that rule over it but rather supposes that it is dealing with entirely solid material and content [*mit ganz gediegnem Stoffe und Inhalte*]" (*PhG* §131). To translate otherwise, into the language of energy: acts of perception do not have enough energy to leap to self-consciousness, being too beholden to the rigidity of thinghood, of concrete virtuality, of the conditioned which does not suspect *that* and *by what* it is conditioned. These acts bask in the illusion of a ready-made, merely given nature of the perceived, and buttress the subjective aspect of the illusion by transferring the desideratum of mere givenness, which shuns self-givenness, to perceptual "true-taking." The workings of perception are erased as workings: the perceiving and the perceived are cast in the role of works prohibiting future transformations of the given and skipping over past ones. The conceptual rigidity of the thing and of perception is overlaid by the rigidity of space without time— that of pure perceptual present.

The perceiving consciousness does not, above all, see itself seeing; it has no part in the transcendental vision of "essences" ("the consciousness of the essentialities that rule it") folded into the empirical instant of looking. Instead, it "goes unstoppably [*unaufhaltsam*] forward to the result of an equal sublation [*gleichen Aufhebens*] of all these essential essentialities or determinations" (*PhG* §131). And this is our default association with energy, namely, going unstoppably forward in a movement whose vectors, curves, and unexpected turns will be entirely expunged in the result. For Hegel, such movement is the modus operandi of the virtual, not of the actual, of a straight line tending to infinity or abruptly and arbitrarily cut at a certain point. The result (in-the-work) is indifferent to the vector (at-work) which has pointed toward it. Neither self-reflected nor repeated, one-directional movement terminates in the indifference of "equal sublation" defining the result. Copied from thinghood, the rigidity of perception coincides with its insane dynamism, pressing toward its target on the road of "bad infinity" and neglecting to circle back to itself. The source of the paradox is the extreme disconnect between the verbal and the substantive dimensions of energy, as well as universality and individuality, sameness and otherness. Forging incessantly ahead, perception demonstrates its rigidity, its inability to bend or twist the straight line and to energetically replay the "play of powers" that condition it.

3. Force and Understanding: Literally Crystal-Clear and Unburdened by the Energy of Thinking

Does the straight line of real consciousness bend in understanding? This consciousness itself is convinced that it does: "For consciousness, the object has returned into itself from its relation to an other and has thereby come to be *in itself* [an sich] the concept; however, consciousness is not yet for itself [*für sich selbst*] the concept and thus does not yet have any cognizance of itself in that reflected object" (*PhG* §132). In the self-reflection of the object, the concept is in itself, but not for itself—a relation it can achieve exclusively in consciousness. The concept, with which understanding operates, is a thing stripped of its properties, related to itself, and presented in the reified form of an "objective" idea. In itself, it is potential, virtual, destitute of energy and, at the same time, a result, the already actualized, a work oblivious to the movement that reached its apex in it. How can it be both? Because the virtual does not preexist the actual, but is an actuality cordoned off from whatever has been at work in actualizing it. Virtuality is an actuality that does not experience itself as such, matched by a consciousness that is not for itself a concept, that apprehends the conceptual "in-itself" on the outside, in the exteriority of a self-reflected, idealized object, wherein it does not yet recognize itself. A virtualizing trend is tantamount to total detachment (privatization, idiosyncrasy, idiom, idiocy) lacerating energy-actuality from within by divorcing its works from the workings, thanks to which they have been consummated.

A bending thus occurs in the object, not in the subject, who fails to recognize itself on the terms of mere understanding. Not before shifting gears to the absolute "for us," *für uns*, do we realize that "this object has become what it is [*so geworden*] through the movement of consciousness in such a way that this consciousness is interlaced [*verflochten*] with the object's becoming [*das Werden*]" (*PhG* §132). Such interlacing is none other than the enworkment of energy, which is as attentive to the being-at-work of becoming (*das Werden*) as it is to the being-in-the-work of what has become (*geworden*). A true concept imbued with dialectical energy would be not only an object of thought but also the subject of thinking, the work and the workings that brought it into existence. The becoming of the concept must be grasped in the subjective and in the objective senses of the genitive—something that intellectual history, ostensibly responding to Hegel's demand, cannot do, yielding but a slideshow of thought-products, rather than of thinking. (Intellectual biographies are pitiful attempts at remedying this condition.)

The medium of thought is foreign to understanding. From a strictly dialectical point of view, understanding is a crystalline structure: clear, transparent, following straight lines, and utterly inflexible. It does not think because it does not think itself through, preferring instead to entrust conceptuality to ideal self-reflected objects. There, "consciousness is still receding from what has become [*von dem gewordenen zurücktretend*] in such a way that this having-become as objective is, for it, the essence" (*PhG* §132). The retrocession or the withdrawal of consciousness—of the working—from the conceptual outcome—the work—undoes the synergic ties—the being-interlaced of the two—that constitute energy. Subsequently, the dynamics of separation will continue and intensify, as objectified concepts deemed to be the essential element are installed in a virtual domain of the supersensible world, set over and above the world herebelow, and so alienated from becoming as to appear to have altogether escaped the necessity of being generated. Unconditioned, this domain will be assigned an effectiveness all its own, the distinct actuality of the virtual, worshipped as the only true and essential actuality, the energy that moves the world. No wonder that it will grow nihilistic, its effectiveness dependent on anti-energy, that is, on the suppression of energetic links between conceptual becoming and what has become of it.

Since the concept exists in the shape of an idealized object, distanced from consciousness, the approach to it resembles that to perceived objects: the true "drives [*treibt*] its essence forth for itself in such a way that consciousness has no part in its free realization [*freien Realisierung*] but merely contemplates and purely apprehends it" (*PhG* §133). "Free realization" needs to be understood in a very precise sense, in light of understanding's position vis-à-vis energy. The freedom of an objective concept is largely negative: its getting unglued from the workings that brought it about. Its realization means its becoming-reality, a virtual (separated) entity with regard to the subject. So thoroughly repressed is the development of the concept, so divided is energy against itself in this "free realization," that the supplement of the absolute (we, who are repeating dialectical movement retrospectively) is called upon to retrace the itinerary, at the end of which we find a reified, fetishized, virtualized result: "*we* therefore have to step in its place [*an seine Stelle zu treten*] and to be the concept that cultivates what is contained in the result" (*PhG* §133). The absolute, thus, lends itself to serving as the missing link in the energy equation, where everything is unknown save for the end (result). It fills in the blanks of conceptual being-at-work in the face of an obsession with being-in-the-work. Once the absolute makes this step, the result can no longer maintain the pretense of "the unconditioned universal," *das unbedingt Allgemeine* (*PhG* §134), and, instead, shows its truth as conditioned (by what has been at work)—again, as a kind of thing, *das Ding*.

In its virtual, virginal apartness, the concept is "the essence set off to one side [*auf die Seite getretene Wesen*] as a universal medium" (*PhG* §136). Discrete and non-relational, as a medium, it makes relationality possible. What forces it to leave its self-enclosure and open up, from within, to the other? As we shall see, force itself does. That said, the movement begins with speculative energy, which even the most virtualized domain cannot ward off: the one conceptual essence breaks into the many, the not-one consisting of "diverse universals," *verschiedenen Allgemeinen*, or various concepts, their diversity still palatable to the virtuality, from which they've sprung. As such, as merely diverse and not as determinately negated differences, the many leave intact the one essence, which has undergone atomic fission into one and non-one. The universal and universals, the concept and concepts, are mutually indifferent, or, what amounts to the same thing, "independent," *selbstständig*, with regard to each other. Within the logic of mutual indifference (also cherished by the social philosophy of liberalism), the work of energy comes to a grinding halt. There is, admittedly, plenty happening here, but only on the terms of virtuality's effectiveness, spawning, under the sign of immediacy, interminable workings without works. "Those differences which are posited as independent immediately [*unmittelbar*] pass over into their oneness, and their oneness immediately [*unmittelbar*] passes over into the unfolding [*Entfaltung*], and this unfolding immediately [*unmittelbar*] turns back into the reduction [to the one]" (*PhG* §136). The repeated back-and-forth of unfolding and reduction, the one and the not-one, does not actualize anything; the insistent repetition of the word "immediately," *unmittelbar*, is meant to convey that the movement erases its own history, and, without the substantive markers of accomplished works, begins anew as if nothing has occurred. This movement's pure dynamism is force (*Kraft*)—a one-word designation for the effectiveness of the virtual.

From the perspective of actuality, force is caught in a limbo: on the one hand, it is externalized in the expression (*Äußerung*) of the one essence (conceptuality) in the many; on the other hand, it is "*driven out of its expression back into itself, as genuine force [die eigentliche Kraft]*" (*PhG* §136). No sooner is the energetic bond between the inner and the outer—the one and the many, conceptuality and things—tied than it is dissolved by virtue of force retreating into itself from its expression. We might suspect that the entire dialectical energy apparatus is encapsulated in this description. Yet, while Hegelian dialectics formally resembles the movement of force, this movement does not build upon the provisional works of expression, diffusing them instead into the unperturbed smoothness of the virtual: it does not, in other words, fold the path into the destination (it has none). The chief difference between force and dialectical movement is, precisely, actuality, the mutual *non*-indifference of what is at work and what is in the works.

Perfectly equipped for understanding the oscillations of force, understanding cannot understand either dialectics or the actuality of these oscillations. "The concept of force belongs authentically [*eigentlich*] to understanding, which is itself *the concept*" (*PhG* §136). In understanding, after all, the expression and interiorization of force are known as synthesis and analysis, such that difference is held "merely in thought," *nur im Gedanken* (*PhG* §136). To say that understanding locates difference in thought alone means that, in its essential-conceptual isolation, it cuts itself off from actuality, be it merely given or self-given. Not even a less-than-actuality, the "posited reality" (*Realität gesetzt*) of force is registered by a faculty only fitted to grasping "genuine" force, the moment of being reflected into itself and held in reserve. But the precarious phenomenality of force, its "being-for-another," *Für-ein-Anderes-sein*, or what Hegel deems to be "the substance of these differences," *Substanz dieser Unterschiede* (*PhG* §136), is elusive. In excess of mere thought, it exists as the work-aspect of force's clandestine energy, which, absent an inner connection with purely dynamic workings, is felt as totally alien to the thinking mind. The classical mind-body divide belongs here, in the matrix of force and understanding, with all their undeveloped energies, their virtualities that segregate thinking from the existence it does not express.

The answer to the predicament of understanding comes from force itself, which, on its own terms, is an improper concept, one that lumps together "genuine," self-reflected force and its extra-conceptual (substantive-phenomenal) expressions. Both parts are indispensable—"force is also the whole, that is, it remains what it is according to its concept [*sie bleibt, was sie ihrem Begriffe nach ist*]" (*PhG* §136)—and their coexistence in the unity of the concept implies that force cannot remain purely virtual, driven back into itself, but must spill out into expression (hence, beyond the reach of an abstract concept), however inauthentic this spillage is in comparison to genuine self-reflection. Force is, therefore, and in line with other speculative terms, both itself and not itself; in its otherness to itself, gushing out of mere thought into actuality, it is energy. (Strictly speaking, it is force that perverts energy, not the other way around, but the order is upended in the phenomenological reconstruction of the movement.)

Ambiguous and improper as a concept, energy is the impropriety and ambiguity that afflicts every concept and that slips extra-conceptuality into conceptual formations. It is the non-identity that drives the concept out of itself, as much as the terminus of this drive. If force cannot find shelter in its virtual isolation, that is because it does not coincide with the purely conceptual representation of what it is "as *such* [*als* solche], or as *reflected into itself*" (*PhG* §137); its "substantivized extreme" is the disavowed bonus of relative stability, repelled by the concept. As such, it is also not as such—or, even, such as it is not, and this excess over the ideality of its essence is the site of energy. In itself, force harbors "another essence," *ein anderes Wesen* (*PhG* §137), which is the other of essence, namely phenomenal existence, containing energy's work (in the substantive). Understanding grasps the "as such," the ideal essence, but not the non-essence within essence; hence, it ultimately understands only itself when it believes to have understood its other. It is unburdened by the dialectical energy of thinking, before which alone energy appears, even in the vanishing. It cannot understand, for instance, that "the being-one of force vanishes in the *how* of its appearing, namely as *an other* [*das Einssein verschwindet, wie es erschien, nämlich als* ein anderes]" (*PhG* §137). So long as force appears, it ceases to be one, precisely *because* it appears. It vanishes into two.

The unity of force buckles under its own speculative energy, which analyzes it into *X* and *not-X*, itself and the other. Its "duality," *Zweiheit*, is that of being-in-itself and being-for-the-other, the forcing and the forced, the soliciting (*Sollizitierende*) and the solicited (*Sollizitierte*) (*PhG* §138). To solicit is to make tremble or excite (past participle of *ciere*) as a whole (*sollus*). The one (force) is excited as a whole by itself, and that already makes it two. (Perhaps, it trembles so much because in its intimacy with itself it is no longer one, and the trembling, moreover, is a symptom of its vanishing unity in the midst of its affirmation in the exciting-excited *sollus*.) The solicited substance of force is shaken by its soliciting subject; the energized is set in motion by the energizing. But the energy supply is soon interrupted: as two, force is set over and against itself (*entgegengesetzt*), and the "play of both forces," *das Spiel der beiden Kräfte* (*PhG* §139), replays the abstract opposition of thinghood without rising to the actual difference of thingly composition.

Understanding, which is really perception tailored to things without properties, is at the mercy of a play of forces, reminding us of how perception was a plaything of the powers of individuality and universality. This play is the state of indeterminacy, much vaunted in deconstruction—not the privation of determinations but their "absolute immediate confusion [*der absoluten unmittelbaren Verwechslung der Bestimmungen*]" (*PhG* §139), which takes refuge in an infinitely stretched-out finitude of the virtual. Here, the opposites unremittingly change places, assume each other's place, vying for the honor of being unconditional (the solicited solicits the soliciting and is, therefore, meta-soliciting, etc.) in such a way that nothing comes out of them. There is no outcome, nothing in-the-work, save for more play. In its duality, force is the more or less immediate passage of the soliciting into the solicited, and back again.

At the same time, the virtuality of force, set asunder and against itself, actualizes the concept: "through doubling into two forces, the concept of force becomes *actual* [wirklich *wird*]" (*PhG* §141). The concept emerges from its self-enclosed essence, assumes its impropriety, and deals with it by means of a playful interlude, a suspension it is unable to bring to a close on its own. The concept of force in particular is energized by and receives its actuality from a virtual back-and-forth of forces, into which it divides. While the two stand in the shadow of virtual force reflected into itself, the one (concept)—the *sollus* of solicitation—shares with actual force its expressivity . . . in the two. Such actualization via expression in the virtual bespeaks a unique perversion of the actual and an obdurate resistance to it on the part of force and understanding. The essence of the concept neither attains "external" actuality nor is put to work in the phenomenally accessible world. Rather, "the *concept* of force preserves itself even more as *the essence* within its *actuality* itself [*in seiner* Wirklichkeit *selbst*]" (*PhG* §141). Its energy, its setting-to-work in the two forces, is, if anything, de-actualizing: binding and unbinding the ties between the soliciting and the solicited, playfully luxuriating in itself on the outer side of expression, celebrating the primacy of essence, and uninterested in forging a self-relation of the real—the self-relation that energizes the real to be the actual.

Since force is blind to that actuality which does not secure its virtual essence in the actual, its truth "remains merely the *thought* of force," and, negatively speaking, its "realization [*Realisierung*] is at the same time the loss of reality [*Verlust der Realität*]" (*PhG* §141). The division of labor is well-defined. Force, taken to be synonymous with energy, de-realizes the real and thus unintentionally accentuates its truth as the virtual, even as understanding picks up the morsels of this de-realization, raising them to thought, which, as the thought of force, is its essence. Both are highly allergic to substance: the former, as the jealous guardian of its pure (albeit essentially impure) essence; the latter, as an orientation in a world of things without properties, the world ultimately reducible to the subject of this orientation.

The classical opposition of force and substance, as well as of understanding and substance, buttresses this ontological explanation. At all times at work, force and understanding analyze substance in practice and in thought, such that their dynamism is conflated with energy *tout court*, while the inertness of substance is presumed to be the other of energy. Energy, however, is the difference between in-the-work and at-work, the senses included in the Greek *en-ergeia*. Once the tension permeating this difference becomes too lax or too rigid, due to the privileging of one part over the other, energy itself fades away. The realization of that which is at work to the detriment of that which is in the work, overlooking energy's substantive element, spells out total de-realization, "the loss of reality" and of energy that imbues the real with self-relationality. Without a doubt, the loss is necessary so as to "air" the real in preparation for its passage into the actual. But neither this passage nor the reinvention of energy will happen on the terms of force and understanding, for which true being is in what is not: in the vanishing of beings.

Judging everything by itself, with recourse to the *ultima ratio* of workings without works, the partial energy of force and understanding elevates vanishing, or the upending of all ends, to the highest ontological principle. If "the developed *being* of force [*das entwickelte* Sein *der Kraft*]" is a "vanishing," then the opposite, namely appearance (*Erscheinung*), stands for nonbeing (*Nichtsein*) and is a matter of seeming (*Schein*) (*PhG* §143). Force and understanding present us with a picture of the world reconstructed on the basis of the vanishing substance; for them, de-substantivation and virtualization are the truth, the whole truth, and nothing but the truth (they *are* the truth, but not the whole of it, the other, omitted half being substantivation and objectivation). On this view, anything that retains a determinate shape and declines to participate in the dynamics of play is suspect and belongs in nonbeing, which is the case in our contemporary sciences and their technological offshoots, economies, and political systems. Not just anything, but everything that appears, the whole of the seeming, is placed in question as a whole and therefore as a universal ("this *whole* as a whole, that is, the universal"), which, when emptied out by force and understanding, constitutes the inner (*das Innere*) of things (*PhG* §143). The possibilities of interpreting the world and changing it, juxtaposed in Marx's eleventh thesis on Feuerbach, rotate in the universe of understanding and force.

The emptying-out of the world is not, as we might suspect, a forced operation: force and understanding merely crystallize the truth of perception, which, under the guise of the most concrete, handles vacuous, interchangeable abstractions of universality and singularity. The inner of things is not mined for its energy reserves somehow occluded by the appearing shapes; it displays its emptiness on the surface of sensuous appearances that, backed by perceptual abstraction, *are* matters of seeming, inasmuch as the consciousness that registers them conflates being and nothing, truth and non-truth, the essential and the nonessential, the richest and the poorest cognitive modes. Hence, "the play of forces is the developed negative [*dies Spiel der Kräfte ist daher das entwickelte Negative*]" (*PhG* §143), developing, at one stroke, the negation of appearing substances and the negative dynamics of perception.

The unfolding of "the developed negative" does not end there, with the negativity of endless play. Force and understanding stabilize the inner into an energetic shape: "the *supersensible* as the *true* world over and above the *sensuous* as the *appearing* world [*über der sinnlichen als der erscheinenden Welt... eine übersinnliche als die wahre Welt*]" (*PhG* §144). The supersensible world, sundered from and elevated above the sensible one, is an effect of substantivizing without substance, of the ideal workings without work hypostatized into a work. The truth of the supersensible is non-appearance, called upon to complete the oxymoron of virtual energy with a substantive dimension, namely with what is in the work without having a shape. Hypostatized in it, then, is the absolutely vanished being, whose being-vanished is more thorough and more permanent than the disappearing (vanishing) appearances of the sensuous realm. It is as though, eager to analyze, de-realize, and virtualize every energy constellation they encounter, force and understanding guarantee their own success, vouchsafe for themselves, by giving themselves, in place of substance, the total negation of substance.

Vanished being, revered for its persistence in the nothing that flips into unalterable presence, is immanent in diluted doses to the world of appearances here-below. Compared to the "vanishing this-worldliness [*verschwindenden Diesseits*]" (*PhG* §144), the vanished pure and simple is the truth, bringing the movement of appearances to its logical conclusion. In this sense, the supersensible world is electrified from the same power outlet as the world it has, presumably, overcome. The inner of things is "the nothing of appearance," *das Nichts der Erscheinung* (*PhG* §146), in a double entendre: it is the outcome of negating the appearances *as much as* the nothing that the appearances themselves already are in all their finitude and fleetingness. The virtual actuality proper to the supersensible domain, replete with energy at work and in the work in what does not appear, is an exacerbation of the finite energy of this world, of the sensuous on the edge of disappearing.

The hypostasis of vanished being, of energy's substantive dimension transformed into de-substantivized works, lies at the intersection of (1) the void of things, sucking, like a black hole, materiality into itself and (2) the void of understanding, analytically bringing this void out, centripetally expanding it, lending it an independent existence, and bestowing on it the mantle of essence. A "void which came about as the void of objective things . . . must now be taken *as void in itself* [Leerheit an sich], or as the void of all spiritual circumstances [*Leerheit aller geistigen Verhältnisse*], or even as the void of the differences of consciousness as consciousness" (*PhG* §146). This is the power of abstraction in action: things devoid of properties familiar to understanding are further reduced to things devoid of things, which is to say, to the void itself, in itself and not in the thing. In its mediating capacity, understanding puts the void of the thing to work all by itself, both hypostatizing it in a virtual work and accompanying it at work. Thereafter, the void in itself does not need the understanding (in truth, it eschews understanding), which has released it to its negative energy. The de-realization of reality, of the *res* stripped to its innermost void, renders reality virtual *and* maximally real—phenomenologically, because the supersensible world is believed to be the most authentic reality; considered by the absolute, because the very possibility of a self-relation, which would have allowed the real to attain actuality, is nipped in the bud.

The work performed by the supersensible has the effect of making reality, defined by a dearth of self-relations, fully itself by further dissociating it from itself, by making it entirely other to itself, non-actual. In the face of the hypostatized void of the real substituting for pure being with its marked indifference, appearance likewise comes into its own and is equally admissible whether it refers to the thing's self-presentation or to a matter of seeming, sheer fantasy, daydreams (*Träumereien*). "The supersensible is therefore *appearance* as *appearance* [*Das Übersinnliche ist also die* Erscheinung *als* Erscheinung]" (*PhG* §147); it is the non-apparent essence of appearances, the essence installed as an independent reality, which itself appears in the shapeless shape of the void, its form indifferent to the content. What the supersensible world endeavors to conjure up, then, is the energy of essence playing its own part and that of the other, being the workings and the work, refusing to come outside of itself in coming outside of itself. This trick distinguishes supersensible actuality from its sensuous counterpart: while the latter is a "real actuality," *reelle Wirklichkeit* (*PhG* §147), the former is the irreal, virtual actuality, which is nonetheless *more* real, goes deeper into the virtual essence of the real, than the play of the superficies, or of sensuous appearances, does. The inner essence claims actuality for itself and demotes appearance to a virtual apparition, even as it converts energy as such into pure potentiality, which is its (and our) true actuality. We are still living through the epoch of this conversion, or this perversion, named in a shorthand "metaphysics."

Within the energy scheme of virtual actuality, understanding prefers the hypostatized void (taken to be the truth) over the play of forces striving toward this void. It favors what is in the work over what is at work. "What is *immediately* for understanding is the play of forces, but for it the *true* is the simple inner" (*PhG* §148). Energetic lopsidedness now shifts from the virtual workings without work to a work without workings, the essential truth that neutralizes the differences of forces and stabilizes their fluctuations in "difference as universal," *Unterschied als allgemeiner* (*PhG* §148), which is also a "simple difference," *einfache Unterschied*, at rest, *beruhigter* (*PhG* §149), between the true and the non-true. Why this sudden swing from one extreme to another? Because, to understanding, everything seems either in a tirelessly fluctuating movement or completely at rest, given that energy in its phenomenal unity, in the sense of the co-belonging of being-at-work and being-in-the-work, is not available to this faculty. The situation is *absolutely* understandable: what we understand about understanding reconstructed by the absolute is that, sensing the absence of truth, understanding first embarks on a quest and immediately experiences the unrest emanating from the play of forces that rule over it, even as it dreams of truth as its destination, the end of the journey when this disquietude would be finally quelled. Just as it foregoes singular differences in favor of difference as a simple universal, understanding represses its path and dwells exclusively on the destination, on the outcome that consists of what is *in truth*, or in the work. Being at rest is interpreted in terms of having successfully secured energy's substantive dimension, however de-substantivized. In this quelling of unrest in the work, truth, the void, and law—"as a *stable* image of restless appearance," *als dem* beständigen *Bilde der unsteten Erscheinun* (*PhG* §149)—overlap.

The discovery of law is, perhaps, the most important work of understanding. As the Hegelian definition implies, law itself valorizes the stability of the universal in-the-work over the unrest of singularities at-work: "law is present [*gegenwärtig*] in appearance, but is not the whole presence [*ganze Gegenwart*] of appearance; under circumstances that always become other, it has an always-other actuality [*immer andere Wirklichkeit*]" (*PhG* §150). Despite the illusion of stability, the empty universality of law puts it at the mercy of the ever-changing circumstances wherein it is applied, the circumstances that encompass the remainder of what is present in appearance and dictate the energetic shape of law, its "always-other actuality," from the outside. Like understanding, law knows no mediation between the singular and the universal, and that is why understanding can "discover" it, without yet recognizing its own objectified image in it. Even the dialectic of the one and the many, formally repeating the same division in the thing with its properties, proceeds under the sign of indeterminacy, *Unbestimmtheit*, to which law is subject. As soon as we depart from the simplicity of universal difference, prescribing the sense of law as such, we encounter "indeterminately *many* laws" that contradict this very principle (*PhG* §150). Lifeless in itself, the abstract universality of law must rely on the contingent energy of the other (of *its* other) that actually negates it.

Yet, understanding ignores this necessary contingency factored into the actualization of the law and presses on with its efforts at formulating a universal law, capable of unifying all laws into one. When it supposes that it "has found a universal law which expresses universal actuality *as such* [*die allgemeine Wirklichkeit* als solche *ausdrücke*]," it "has in fact merely found the concept of law itself" (*PhG* §150). Understanding succumbs to its usual muddle, which passes for crystal-clear thinking, in that it mistakes the idealized ("as such") universal actuality for a universal in-the-work, while neglecting both the at-work, which internally mediates the universal and the singular, and the dialectic of what is in the work and at work, which accounts for energy-actuality as a whole. Or—this amounts to the same thing—understanding presupposes that the universal is *immediately* at work in the particulars ("that *all* actuality [alle *Wirklichkeit*] is *in itself* lawful" [*PhG* §150]) and, if not, that every bit of what is can without further ado and without mediations be made lawful, gathered into the "all," put in line through a direct imposition of the concept, and made to comply with its law. Stated precisely, the problem here is that of *expression* and absence thereof, that is to say, of energy's thinking and thought self-expression, to which the pure thinking of understanding is unable to rise. If the unity of universal law is the virtual-essential unity of the concept, then we remain stuck at the level of an autistic interiority, which has been neither pressed out (ex-pressed) into nor transformed by existence and, which therefore, is bereft of actuality, whether merely given or self-given.

Law, as "a stable image of restless appearance," usurps the place of energy-actuality, which, irreducible to the static real ("a stable image") and to agitated activity ("restless appearance"), is a vanishing mediator between these two moments. In the definition of law, the word "of" (*dem*) requires infinite interpretation: it is the site of mediation, neglected on the terms of law itself, between being-in-the-work and being-at-work where energy could flourish. Energy is, indeed, the stability of restlessness and the restlessness of stability—something realized, conceived, and consummated in thought and in the world after a long series of mediations, unworking the accomplished works and putting actuality to work otherwise. These mediations are nowhere to be found in law, a concept oblivious to its own history of conceptualization as much as to actual being. Nor are they embedded in force alone, which is abstract being consistent with what is colloquially called "energy," including the electrical variety (*PhG* §152). The energy of the concept and that of being are still inchoate in law and in force, respectively, that share the indifference (*Gleichgültigkeit*) of the virtual (*PhG* §153). In the language of the *Phenomenology* they belong to the essential, and in the language of *Science of Logic*, to the formal level of the dialectic, not yet permeated by actual existence.

At their most effective, force and understanding translate the void in itself into the differences of consciousness as consciousness. The price paid for the simplicity and universality of difference is its interiorization and virtualization: "this inner difference [*inner Unterschied*] still belongs *to the understanding* and is not yet posited in *the thing itself*. It is thus merely its *own* necessity that the understanding expresses" (*PhG* §154). Understanding refers to itself, all the while imagining that it is differentiating within the other; it "expresses its own necessity" without understanding itself. The true referent obscured, the energy of signification is caught up in virtual webs, such that the signifier does not express the signified but is irreparably amputated from the signified and speaks of itself alone: "this necessity merely lies in words [*nur im Worte liegt*]" (*PhG* §154). (This is, again, the impasse of Saussure's theory of the sign.) The inner, simple, and universal difference is not actual; instead, "of this difference it is said that it is no difference at all [*von diesem Unterschiede wird gesagt, daß er keiner*]" (*PhG* §154), seeing that not only with regard to actuality but also with regard to its essence it is absorbed by the indifference of the concept and pure being, of law and force.

At the same time that understanding thinks it is explaining or expressing something about the world, it only projects itself, the difference interiorized in it. Absorbed in itself, without self-understanding it remains exterior to itself. Now, this mix-up interferes with the concept of energy, notably with the *en-* of *energeia* I have rendered as *in* or *at*, in-the-work or at-work. When understanding is excited by the discovery of the universal law at work in the world, it unconsciously stumbles upon what is at work not outside but in it, itself; when it contemplates and analyzes the outcomes of this all-powerful universality, it only unpacks what is in the work that it, itself, is. Supposedly delving into the workings of the world, it is barred from exteriority and is ecstatically immersed in itself outside itself, not recognizing itself in the matter of explanation. In fact, the explanation (*Erklärung*) is so clear (*klar*) as to be tautological, and nothing different can be stated from what has been already noted (*PhG* §155). Totally interiorized, difference lapses into indifference, a mindless repetition of the same, which is, however, set on the path of actuality by virtue of being a repetition. (Still on the subject of clarity, the German term *Aufklärung* is the inverse of the English word "Enlightenment," to which it is ostensibly equivalent. Said in German, it means "clearing-up," whereas in English it implies receiving the "light within." What is at issue in this distinction is the exterior and interior work of thinking, the plurivocity of *en-* in *en-*ergy.)

Rotating around its own axis all the while it imagines that it is orbiting its other (the thing in need of explanation), understanding divides energy into "tautological movement" (*tautologische Bewegung*) on its part and the object's "restful unity" (*ruhige Einheit*) on the part of its other (*PhG* §155). Understanding thus arrogates for itself the at-workness of energy and relegates the object to be understood to the realm of being-in-the-work, the stable/stored energy at rest. It functions by means of dissociating the two halves of energy, and it gleans its own energy from this dissociation between the changes and exchanges (*Wechsel*) of explanatory powers, on the one hand, and the unchangeable object held within a determinate and ever the same (supersensible) shape, on the other. In this, it diverges absolutely from the absolute, as much as from Hegelian dialectics, which goes beyond understanding without succumbing to mysticism.

Nonetheless, at the limit of understanding, the object is destabilized, its volatile energy shown to be at work in its noncoincidence with itself. Understanding does not understand this, of course, since "it *experiences* [*er* erfährt] the *law of appearance itself* [Gesetz der Erscheinung selbst]" as internally contradictory and is convinced that "its differences are no differences but that *like poles repel* themselves from themselves [*das* Gleichnamige *sich von sich selbst* abstößt]" (*PhG* §156). A foundation for the supersensible world, the law of appearance is doubly unstable: it postulates that appearances only appear by way of disappearing and, as a law, it provides a static image—a frozen snapshot—of this appearing-disappearing flux. The experience of the law's contradictions gives understanding a grip on speculative energy, the absolute concept of difference, whereby difference ruptures into itself and its other, difference and indifference. One repels itself from itself and becomes one and not-one, that is, at least two. At this point, force turns into energy, its play setting itself to work in an identity divided against itself.

Besides the thing, affected by speculative fission from within, the supersensible world, which was organized around the ideal unity of the inner of things, is also split into two, its restfulness disturbed. According to Hegel, "the first supersensible world was merely the *immediate* elevation [*die* unmittelbare *Erhebung*] of the perceived world into the universal element," and the second "is *the first supersensible world inverted* [verkehrte]" (*PhG* §157). If the first supersensible domain formalizes what is perceived, then it outlines Plato's eidetic jurisdiction (*eidos* as the "look" or "image" of things) and anticipates *in nuce* Husserl's transcendental phenomenology. If, conversely, the second, "twisted" supersensible world inverts the first, then it de-formalizes the so-called eidetic realities and posits an essence prima facie opposed to the sensuous as the true appearance *within the sensuous world itself*. The inverted, "twisted," or perverse actuality, *eine verkehrte Wirklichkeit* (*PhG* §159), sees the sensuous world interspersed with the virtual energy that has been generated in the supersensible domain and then materialized in particular appearances. With this, the effectiveness of the virtual is upended, so as to infiltrate the singular (true) instantiations in the actual.

Thanks to the perversion of the supersensible, the universal element is at work in the world, its energy in part actualized. But it is also not at work, for it is counteracted by and counteracts another, the opposite sensuous appearance with which its own sensuous manifestation is combined in the same thing: "the sour, which would be the in-itself of a *sweet* thing, would be as much of an actual thing [*ein so wirkliches Ding*] as the sweet one, that is, it would be a *sour* thing" (*PhG* §159). A clash between virtual essence and actual appearances is supplanted by a standoff between the essence that, having been energized or actualized in the act of twisting, acquires both an appearance and another appearance that negates it. The impossible demand this situation places on understanding is to learn how to be and to think in "pure change, the *opposition in itself* [Entgegensetzung in sich selbst], *contradiction* [Widerspruch]" (*PhG* §160). Self-contradictory being and thinking in actual objects and subjects complete a transition of the speculative impulse from force to energy, that is, the actual, and not just the virtual-essential, splitting of the one into two and against itself.

An actual contradiction musters energy by virtue of assuming and repeating its constitutive difference in a self-relation: the inverted and twisted world "is for itself the inverted, i.e., the inversion of itself [*sie ist für sich die verkehrte, d.h. die verkehrte ihrer selbst*]; it is itself and that which opposes it in *one* unity" (*PhG* §160). On the condition that the supersensible world relates to itself as other, it becomes itself (in all the glory of its inverted-perverted otherness). The difference interiorized in "*one* unity" is a difference exteriorized into actuality, not immediately but through the mediations of the infinitely repeated supersensible twists, turns, versions, and perversions. Now, the most crucial inversion it performs is outward: turning inside out despite keeping to interiority, being "for itself" the inverted. Such an interpretation of Aristotle's unmoved mover—the world's self-relation in its otherness—is palatable to Hegel, who discerns in the "*one* unity" of the world opposed to and enveloping itself the old philosophical idea of "the soul of the world," *die Seele der Welt*, updated or actualized into "the absolute concept," *der absolute Begriff*, which "pulsates in itself without setting itself in motion, vibrates in itself without being restless [*in sich pulsiert, ohne sich zu bewegen, in sich erzittert, ohne unruhig zu sein*]" (*PhG* §162). The unmoved mover or the absolute concept is thought thinking itself in and as the world, the world perverted by itself (into thought) and grasping itself in its otherness, in an inversion of itself in and for itself. These are not the "pure vibrations" of abstract thought still too immature to engage with the world outside the ideal circle of its movement. Rather, the soul of the world is essentially impure—inverted-perverted, issuing from the world that folds unto itself and again unfolds into the other, that is, into a way of comprehending it—which is something it shares with the congenitally contaminated energy emanating from the dissolution of "pure being."

Perhaps more so than the unmoved mover or thought thinking itself, the absolute concept that trembles in itself without agitation or fluttering about reiterates (energizes or actualizes) *energeia*, actual in itself outside itself, at rest and not at rest, in the work and at work. The inversions or perversions of the world, sensuous and supersensible, are the ripples of energy's interiority, the *en-* of *energeia* not concealing any secret in itself except that it is the very exteriority of actuality, the place where "difference or being-other has come *out of* [heraus] pure essence" (*PhG* §162). Understanding is locked out from absolute difference, or from energy's uncanny interiority for that matter, unless the consciousness, to which understanding pertains, similarly inverts itself into an object and, reflected into itself, becomes self-consciousness. Its autistic discourse with itself (*Selbstgespräche mit sich*) and quasi-masturbatory self-enjoyment (*sich selbst genießt*) announce that conscious understanding, which is unconscious concerning itself, is a *potential* interiority still bereft of an energetic self-relation (*PhG* §163). Understanding is exterior to itself in an entirely different way than the difference that peers out of pure essence—in the way of falling away from itself, falling short of a self that is formed solely through becoming-other or incorporating difference, and falling apart on account of its exclusive commitment to analysis averse to the with-work of synergy. Neither deep nor superficial, understanding is simply extraneous to the *en-* of *en*ergy.

So, where do things stand with the energy deficit plaguing mere or real consciousness? It turns out that, in the timeline of dialectics, this consciousness receives its energy (and its truth, which amounts to the same thing) from the future, that is, from its self-reflection, self-objectification, or transmutation into the indwelling of absolute difference. In "lived" actuality, however, that energy is always already present in mere consciousness, which does not suspect that the "consciousness of things is only possible for a self-consciousness [*Bewußtsein vom Dinge nur für ein Selbstbewußtsein möglich ist*]" (*PhG* §164). The actuality of consciousness in self-consciousness is its true possibility, the virtual undersigned by the actual. Why is this the case? Because, in order to experience the being of an object, one must first experience oneself as an object for oneself: "Consciousness of an other, of an object in general [*Das Bewußtsein eines Andern, eines Gegenstandes überhaupt*], is itself, indeed and necessarily, *self-consciousness*" (*PhG* §164).

Far from being an afterthought, speculative energy is the condition of possibility for having experience, in particular the speculative energy flowing from the diremption of the I into I and not-I, myself and the other. In the rupture (or in the rapture) of self-consciousness, energy is the subject at work and the object in the work, its two planes equally glaring for self-consciousness itself. Understanding, for its part, sees itself at work, engaged in the ongoing (and futile at that) activity of bridging, in a straight line, the gulf that stretches between it and the external object as being-in-the-work. What it does not apprehend, of course, is that no matter how much it strains to reach its object with the powers of explanation, it remains cordoned off from objectivity so long as it does not circle back to and understand itself. It cannot garner enough energy, because it is unable to become a conduit for the gathering of energies, for putting the two halves, at-work and in-the-work, together. "Real" consciousness is more virtual still than the essentially virtual reality. It is hopelessly banished from the real, from *res* or the thing that it also is.

PART II

B. Self-Consciousness and Its Surplus Energy

4. The Truth of Self-Certainty: Beyond the Living Energy of Life

The energy deficit of mere consciousness had to do with the fact that it could embody neither itself nor the other, precisely because it did not sense, perceive, or understand itself from the standpoint of the other, in the capacity of being-in-the-work rather than a pure being-at-work. The surplus of energy in self-consciousness is related to the notion that it is more (and, at the same time, less) than itself: namely, it is itself and the other, having assimilated the speculative split between I and not-I, the split that *imprimis* makes me who or what I am. I become certain of myself once I am no longer straightforwardly and unproblematically myself. Self-consciousness, then, is at work and in the work, even if it is divided against itself and/as the other due to the scission of speculative energy, which is still too fresh to be sublated and overcome.

In self-consciousness, energy comes into its own when its substantive and verbal aspects match one another absolutely and phenomenologically: "If we call the movement of knowledge [*die Bewegung des Wissens*] '*concept*' and call '*object*' knowledge as unity at rest [*das Wissen als ruhige Einheit*], or the I, then we see that the object corresponds to the concept not only for us but also for knowledge itself" (*PhG* §166). The I speculatively divided into I and not-I (or the other) is the locus of energy exchange, of its transactions or interactions with itself, where the conceptual movement of knowledge at work flows toward the being-in-the-work of knowledge at rest, and back again. Two consonances are at stake here: (1) that of perspective ("for us," or the absolute, and "for knowledge itself," or the way things are perceived from within the movement) and (2) that of energy, released from the concept and held in the object. Both are folded into self-consciousness, spanning movement and rest, the knowing and the known, the energizing and the energized.

Cracks emerge on the surface of various correspondences when self-consciousness is reduced to a definitive shape, a "new shape of knowledge [*neue Gestalt des Wissens*], the knowledge of itself" (*PhG* §167). Fixed in this shape, captured in the work that it is, self-consciousness "*is* merely a motionless tautology [*bewegungslose Tautologie*] of 'I am I'" (*PhG* §167), a formula that takes otherness to reside in exteriority. To banish difference and otherness to the sphere of what lies outside an identity—this is the prerogative of mere consciousness, which self-consciousness engenders, covering over its speculative energy, the scission at its origin. In a vein similar to how self-consciousness-cum-mere-consciousness is converted into a substantive form of being indicated by the copula that articulates it with a "motionless tautology," the alterity expelled from its midst is a "being-other *as a being*," *das Anderssein* als ein Sein (*PhG* §167), the energy of self and other condensed into a determinately shaped work: a figure. The dramatic turnabout in the energy situation of mere consciousness is worth paying attention to: what was phenomenologically experienced as frenetic activity or as infinite workings without work in the world of consciousness is a static work of self-consciousness retraced by the absolute back to the moment when it had descended to mere consciousness. And yet, bifurcating into self-consciousness and consciousness, does self-consciousness not repel itself from itself? Does it not become itself *and* the other, that is, the very consciousness for which the other is external? Does it not produce a speculative split that edits out the evidence of speculative splitting? Is it not, at the same time, a shape of energy and the dissimulation of energy in the shape of self-negation responsible for the mereness of mere consciousness?

We thus have two phenomenological tendencies occurring in tandem: on the one hand, the "first," relatively poor, and still virtual actuality of consciousness is deepened and filled out by dint of its self-relatedness in and as self-consciousness, and, on the other hand, consciousness receives whatever energy-actuality it has from the "future" of self-consciousness and ultimately from the absolute it will have become (see figure 3). But, overviewed from the perspective of the absolute, consciousness is not a positive potentiality anticipating the flourishing of self-consciousness. Rather, it is actuality de-actualized, self-consciousness divested of itself and of its self, exempt from iteration, isolated in space and time. Consciousness is the name for the entropy of self-consciousness, the energy deficit of surplus energy. There is never a state of equilibrium between the two, at least within the purview of Hegelian dialectics. "More" or "less" energy-actuality are not quantitative measures but qualitative differences presupposing a leap from one mode of being to another, from pure indifference to differentiated self-relations.

As Hegel notes, it is not only the subject who is self-related at the point in the dialectical process when self-consciousness is won over. The object that "through its reflection into itself has become *life* [Leben]" (*PhG* §168) follows suit. Life is here a sign for energy: it indicates that the object has been actualized and actuated beyond its dispersion in the real. In life, thought thinking itself is externalized, comes to life and comes alive—a singular universal that becomes phenomenally (singularly) available in a variety of shapes (or works, living beings as "products") to the other, while retaining a sense of universal fluidity (or workings, the life-process) in itself (*PhG* §171). Life is the energetic activity of the living, as much as the living themselves. A crease in its self-reflection is the actuality of an object, which does not impassively wait to be discovered by sensation, perception, or understanding, but which expresses itself in a shape evincing the life-process whereby it shapes itself.

Together with self-thinking thought, the conceptual determination of life echoes Aristotle's *energeia* with its circulation barely distinguishable from being at rest. Life, Hegel writes, is "the pure movement rotating around its axis, its rest conceived as absolutely restless infinity [*die reine achsendrehende Bewegung, die Ruhe ihrer selbst als absolut unruhigen Unendlichkeit*]" (*PhG* §169). The work of life, namely a living being in its finitude, is speculatively identical to the absolute unrest of the infinite self-relation wherein life sets itself to work. Life is living and the living (*das Leben als* Lebendiges [*PhG* §171]), the energizing element and the actuality of energy in the substantive. And yet, this speculative identity overlays a speculative split, whereby life, like thinghood before, is sundered apart into the one and the many, the fluid medium and definite shapes, the "abstraction of essence" and actual appearances. It is "only *actual* as a shape [*es ist nur als Gestalt* wirklich]" (*PhG* §171), which means that its energy is concentrated in the substantive dimension, even as the fluid universal retains the patent features of pure being, virtual and indifferent to the particulars.

If from Spinoza to Nietzsche, Bergson, Whitehead, and Deleuze, philosophers of immanence (who are not coincidentally also those of life) have been willing to sacrifice life's actuality residing in its shapes to the universal fluidity of its process beckoning with possibility, then they ipso facto have given up on living energy in the substantive (the "only actuality" of life, as Hegel puts it) and chosen the side of virtuality, of the essence in itself. Theirs is life as pure living without *the* living, a working without the works wherein it sets itself to work. Paradoxically, the life discussed by the philosophers of life is dead (or is as good as dead)—an essence valorized at the expense of its phenomenal appearances, an absolutely restless infinity conceived as the rest of an abstract universal that is indifferent towards all finite differences.

The living energy of life slips away from consciousness and self-consciousness alike: from the former, since it is *not yet* fully alive, failing to become self-reflected and to complete a rotation around itself; from the latter, because it is *already not* immediately alive, facing the object "life" in an oppositional relation governed by immediate desire (*PhG* §168). There is, remarkably, no desire in mere consciousness, though there is certainly need. To desire the other, it is necessary to know and desire oneself as other, something of which only self-consciousness is capable. (As an aside: I would say that one does not become a Hegelian consciously—only self-consciously; not via understanding but via desire.) If self-consciousness *is* desire (*Begierde*) (*PhG* §174), then its default point of reference is its (narcissistic?) desire for itself, on the basis of which desire for the other develops as the negation of both this self and this other, feeding on the energy contained in alterity. It is this desiring self-negation and the subsequent negation of the other that surpasses life in its immediacy. And not just life but also energy, procured by means of destroying the independent (*selbstständig*) other, by eliminating its recognizable shape. It follows that desire cuts the association of energy with actuality, corroborates "the nothingness of the other" (*Nichtigkeit dieses Andern*) whom it deprives of (admittedly illusory) independence, and gains its self-certainty from this nullification and this cut (*PhG* §174).

Consciousness takes the following route: it understands life to the extent to which life itself lends itself to consciousness in a result more general than a living being, namely, a group of living beings who share a particular shape of life and constitute a genus (*Gattung*). The result is a universalized being-in-the-work. Understanding the genus as an object, consciousness posits itself as the other of life (hence, as death) or, better yet, "in this *result*, life refers to an other than it, namely to consciousness [*in diesem* Resultate *verweist das Leben auf ein anderes, als es ist, nämlich auf das Bewußtsein*]" (*PhG* §172). Life is not an exception here: it is a speculative concept cleaved into itself and not itself, life and not-life, that is, the consciousness that makes sense of the genus containing the result, the shape, or the work of life beyond single living beings.

As for self-consciousness, it is not the other of life but "this other life [*andere Leben*], for which the *genus* as such exists and which is the genus for itself [*für sich selbst Gattung ist*]" (*PhG* §173). The otherness of this "other life" (of this surplus vitality) hinges on its mediated character, that is, on its negation and self-negation, driven by desire, and on its unwillingness to draw hard-and-fast distinctions between the process and the result, the life at work and that in the work, into which the abstract universal is differentiated. The end of an outcome reflected into itself (a "genus for itself") is infinitely deferred; such an outcome is a continual coming-out of what is interiorized by means of self-reflection. It is a genus with a population of one—"the simple I [*einfache Ich*] is this genus" (*PhG* §174)—who divides into two, the genus of speculative energy personified.

An outcome where being-in-the-work and being-at-work are hopelessly (or hopefully) entangled loses the markers of reification, having escaped the tyranny of thinghood by the double means of life and desire, energy and surplus energy. This escape is far from successful: "desire and the self-certainty attained in its satisfaction [*Befriedigung*] are conditioned [*bedingt*] by the object," the autonomy of which is negated by desire in a negation that gives rise to self-certainty (*PhG* §175). The thing returns as a revenant negatively conditioning (or bethinging) the very desire that has nullified it in the course of draining its energy. The spectral thing deadens self-consciousness, saps its surplus energy, returning tit for tat as far as the thing's determinate shape is concerned, exchanging *its* actuality for the self-shaping and self-shaped form of self-consciousness. It stands in the way of satisfaction, pacification, the quiescence of desire (in a word, everything conveyed by *Befriedigung*) in the energizing and energized outcome.

Still, a ghostly thing is not an object of sense, perception, or even understanding. A conditioning negation, it works to de-actualize, virtualize, induce disquietude, dissatisfy. In it, "negation exists as absolute [*die Negation als absolute ist*]" (*PhG* §175) and, hence, absolutely self-related as desire, the genus of one, and finally self-consciousness. The energy of life is recovered across the abyss of spectrality, which renders the otherness of "that other life" meaningful: "the object of self-consciousness is also independent in this negativity of itself, and it is thus for itself the genus [*für sich selbst Gattung*], the universal fluidity in the ownness of its isolation; it is a living self-consciousness [*er ist lebendiges Selbstbewußtsein*]" (*PhG* §176). Self-consciousness desires the other (another self-consciousness) as it desires itself—such is its admittedly negative and murderous variation on the biblical "love thy neighbor . . ." Nothing less satisfies it than the redoubling (*Verdopplung*) of speculative energy, the splitting of the split where one becomes two and then becomes four: the other of self-consciousness is the one who, akin to it, is in and for itself the other. The synergy of this fourfold is the life of "a living self-consciousness," of the one arrived at through the working-with of the four. Not to be conflated with peacefulness, this synergy dissociates satisfaction from pacification, the two senses of *Befriedigung* set against each other similarly to self-consciousness itself, fulfilled in and thrust against another self-consciousness.

a. Mastery and Servitude: Self-Consciousness Actualized

The synergy of self-conscious energy disobeys the analytic powers of understanding, for which synthesis and analysis are either sequentially ordered operations or aspects of one meta-analytic procedure, which is used to chop things up without really putting them back together. Self-conscious synergy is the doubling of speculative energy: "the concept of its unity in its doubling, of infinity realizing itself in self-consciousness [*Der Begriff dieser seiner Einheit in seiner Verdopplung, der sich im Selbstbewußtsein realisierenden Unendlichkeit*], is that of a multisided and polyvalent entanglement [*Verschränkung*], within which moments must be kept apart, and, at the same time, in this difference, must be taken as not different"

(*PhG* §178). Synergic entanglement is not just the opposite of analytic understanding; it is not a synthesis blind to fine distinctions. Rather, such an entanglement is the crossing of opposites—oneness and doubling, difference and non-differentiation, infinity and accomplishment, unity and separation—in the concept of self-consciousness that, as one, entails both a schism in itself and two self-consciousnesses. Its synergy synthesizes and analyzes *at one and the same time* in the manner of which only desire is capable. The "with-work" of self-consciousness (a concept that, in its identity, is not identical to itself, being with the other as though with itself, with itself as though with the other) exemplifies how "with," *syn-*, generally operates, keeping apart the elements it interrelates, preserving and suspending their differences.

Why this quadrupling of what was already divided in itself? Considered on its own terms, self-consciousness embraces the I (a simple identity) and its virtual other (the I on the right-hand side of the tautological equation I = I), whereas in a relation to another self-consciousness alterity is actualized, suffusing both the "original" self-consciousness and the relation as a whole with additional energy. It takes four—two self-consciousnesses facing each other—to become actual, ecstatically within the same, such that self-consciousness would "come *outside itself* [außer sich *gekommen*]" (*PhG* §179). Its energy is an ex-ergy, an out-work in the with-work of its entanglements.

In and of itself, self-consciousness is virtual, *because* its constitutive inner alterity is virtual. This self-alienation in the security of an isolated identity must be exacerbated: the virtuality of the essence belonging to a single self-consciousness (which is already two) must be itself alienated before it arrives at its actuality. Virtual alterity will then be converted into actual alienation, the essence, which is the Other and which is also the other of actuality, perverted, rendered other, turned inside out. In another self-consciousness, the first "has lost itself, because it finds itself as *another* essence [*als ein* anderes Wesen]" (*PhG* §179), that is to say, because the otherness of its essence has attained actuality in the essence of the other self-consciousness. So inverted, essential otherness is rescued from a virtual, self-enclosed, energy-less realm: self-consciousness "does not see the other as essence but sees *itself* in the other" (*PhG* §179). This de-essentializing of essence contains the seeds of recognition, of a fourfold relation between two actual I's, who have swapped the virtual for the actual other.

The actual I and the actual other endow energy with a "doubled meaning," *gedoppelte Bedeutung*, embracing "the activity of the one," *das Tun des Einen*, as well as "the activity of the other," *das Tun des Andern* (*PhG* §182). In an encounter of two self-consciousnesses, their energies

PART II

intersect as two instances of being-at-work, working with and against each other in anticipation of the being-in-the-work that will result from their combined workings—"what must happen [*was geschehen soll*] can only come about by both of them bringing it about" (*PhG* §182). In our energy scheme, this means that the resulting work will be synergic, a product of two intentionalities (indeed, of four: both actual and virtual, each directed to itself and to the other [*PhG* §183]) working with and against each other to arrive at the work of mutual recognition. The with-work of mutual recognition admittedly diverges from the pacification of desire, which depends on the destruction of the object's independent shape, its virtualization, and transformation into energy-as-fuel. In both cases, the ensuing work is not material as far as its substance is concerned, or *not only* material. But, while a consumed object of desire is assimilated to the immediately living substratum of self-consciousness, an encounter with another self-consciousness yields after numerous trials and tribulations a work of recognition, synergic in its form and in its content, provided that this work is qualified as mutual.

Before that mutualistic synergy is reached, the activities of the two self-consciousnesses are set in opposition (*entgegensetzt*), such that "the one is merely recognized and the other merely recognizing [*das eine nur Anerkanntes, der ander nur Anerkennendes ist*]" (*PhG* §185). Their polarization reiterates the oppositionality of properties in the object of sense-certainty, the self-opposing truth of the thing and of mere consciousness in perception, and the play of opposing forces—the soliciting and the solicited—in understanding. In particular, a trembling-inducing solicitation will make its comeback in the fear of death that will have predetermined the end of the struggle for recognition. What is decisive at this oppositional stage, though, is the permutation of energy as a charge with negative and positive signs, similar to the electrical impulse. Analogous to a neutral atom ionized by losing or gaining electrons or protons, the purely recognizing and the purely recognized self-consciousnesses are allocated pure loss and pure gain, respectively. The actualization of self-consciousness, as the mutual satisfaction and recognition of the two facing each other while each also faces itself, traverses a stretch of total dissatisfaction, where energy-actuality breaks down into energy and anti-energy, themselves coded as "life" and "death." It will be the latter—felt finitude, the premonition of mortality—that will play the role of potentiality, "airing," virtualizing, disfiguring the actuality of the "*independent* shapes," selbstständige *Gestalten*, the (substantive) shapes of energy pertaining to each self-consciousness "absorbed . . . in the *being* of *life* [*in das Sein des Lebens . . .* versenkte]" (*PhG* §186).

Seen in this light, the life-and-death struggle boils down to a contest in de-actualization. The question is who will go further beyond the living energy of life; who will shed its forms and present her- or himself as "attached to no determinate *existence*, . . . not being attached to life [*an kein bestimmtes* Dasein *geknüpft, . . . nicht an das Leben geknüpft zu sein*]" (*PhG* §187). If it is to be efficacious, the denuding of living forms will retrieve something of pure being, a virtual domain, which, in its indeterminacy, merges with pure nothing and which, in the sphere of existence, translates into death. One's nonattachment to life, or to determinate being for that matter, is wielded as a sign of freedom (*PhG* §187)—a negative freedom, we might add, from the substantive side of energy, that is, from being-in-the-work, including in a living-breathing body as an objective energetic conglomeration.

Hegelian individuation is, unlike its market- and consumption-driven variety, a corollary of self-conscious detachment from all recognizable forms of energy, one's emergence from the absorption (literally: sunkenness, *Versenktsein*) in life with its determinacy, an act of delivering oneself to death whence the sense of oneself as a pure being-at-work is derived. Given the dialectical coordination of two active self-consciousnesses, the same expectation is posed before the other; however, the unstated dilemma in this bacchanalia of death is that, without the determinacies of energetic shapes, "the truth of being recognized as an independent self-consciousness" (*PhG* §187) is the impossible truth of recognizing the unrecognizable, the one who or that which is exclusively for itself, rather than for the other, a shape withholding the clues to its outlines from the outside world. After all, indistinguishable from pure nothing, pure being is, precisely, what cannot be recognized, unless recognition is dissociated from its perceptual modalities or from the world of understanding. In the way he arranges the materials for the *Phenomenology* (where perception and understanding precede recognition and, in contrast to it, are categorized as manifestations of impoverished "mere" consciousness), Hegel appears to drive at this very dissociation, in keeping with which recognition is not synonymous with discernment, but is reserved for the perceptually and cognitively unrecognizable assertions of individuality.

The one who goes further beyond the living energy of life (i.e., recoils back to pure, shapeless, non-actual being/nothing) occupies the position of a master; the one who clings to the determinacy of energy as being-in-the-work is assigned the functions of a servant. The verbal and substantive senses of energy are distributed along the boundaries of the two self-consciousnesses, such that the substantivized party recrudesces to mere consciousness and its true essence, thinghood. From the perspective of the absolute, energy distributions between the opposing sides are not static; the circle of energy (see figure 1) rotates, seeing that the master ignites the movement of virtualization, and the servant induces the process of substantivation. Phenomenologically, we find, on the one hand, "pure self-consciousness" in the master, who is purely at work, and, on the other hand, "a consciousness is posited which exists not purely for itself but for an other, that is, as an *existing* consciousness [*als* seiendes *Bewußtsein*] or consciousness in the shape of *thinghood* [*in der Gestalt der* Dingheit]" (*PhG* §189), namely the servant, or being-in-the-work as confinement to the thing.

Scurrying to shed every vestige of determinate being, self-consciousness asserts its mastery by first reducing existence ("an *existing* consciousness") to shapes of thinghood, or, as Heidegger will later put it, to the ready-to-hand and the present-at-hand. That which exists is, for it, equivalent to being-in-the-work, which means that being-at-work is outside of existence, thought of as the determinacy of things or of life, the difference between the two instances of such determinacy having evaporated. Whereas the shape of the servant consciousness is thinghood, its essence (*Wesen*) is "life or being for an other [*das Leben oder das Sein für ein Anderes*]" (*PhG* §189). What life shares with thinghood is this mode of being for another, exposed to exteriority in self-relationality; what death has in common with "pure" self-consciousness is being in and for itself, not existing extensionally, jealously guarding its withdrawal.

The riddle of energy is that it is more than itself—energy and anti-energy—and that this virtual *more* unrelentingly trims it to *less* thanks to which it, nonetheless, grows more determinate, fuller, more robust. As actuality, energy is on the side of life, exposure, and being-for-another, but as actualization, it requires the virtual supplement of death, retreat into interiority, being-for-itself. The master-servant relation resolves this riddle by parceling it out between the two participants who jointly constitute the movement and the rest—the movement-rest—of energy. And, with this, the master is slotted into the space of the *less*, a vanishing moment contradicting the purported *all* that he is vis-à-vis the servant's *nothing*.

The revolutionary inversion of master and servant roles in Marx's theory of class struggle is, therefore, a revolution in energy. Having declined direct engagement with things that should be mediated in preparation for their consumption, the master's proud being-at-work does not actually work but relies on the servant to handle or elaborate (*bearbeiten*) things by way of their negation (*das Negieren*), which is not the same as elimination (*Vernichtung*) (*PhG* §190). In working-on, in labor or elaboration, energy is practically thematized, providing the form (enworkment) and the content (work) to an activity. Given this reaffirmed tie between content and form, working-on is not, primarily, the destruction of formed matter and an imposition of new forms in accord with the directives of the master carried out by the servant. Working-on is, above all, working-with—a synergy of the worker and that which is worked upon, of the consciousness that exists for the other and is, in its essence, *with* the other, "synthetized with independent *Being* or thinghood in general [*mit selbstständigem* Sein *oder der Dingheit überhaupt synthesiert ist*]" (*PhG* §190). The solidarity of the worker and what will become the works is primordial; it is from what is worked upon that the worker will receive the intimations of *human* freedom. The servant's energy moves through and along the energetic shapes of being (which is to say: the shapes of actuality), not against them. It combines a negative, moderately virtualizing impulse with a positive attachment to the actual, and so completes the energetic cycle on its own, absent the master's interference. The servant is a work working on works, a thing bethinging things on behalf of the no-thing that is the master. All that remains is to put the master in the place of *actual* nothing (in the sense of actuality as *Wirklichkeit*, or energy), notably by emphasizing the "energy relations" that subtend self- and class-consciousness in Hegel and Marx alike.

Facilitating the self-relations of things by working on them, the servant achieves determinate self-consciousness more assuredly than the master. In effect, the servant brings to the foreground the self-relational, self-reflected nature of thinghood and of life, repressed in the master's illusions of independence from (thingly, "independent") existence. Therefore, the servant resuscitates the energy of life and thinghood. For his part, in order to sustain the illusion constitutive of mastery, the master wields, or rather, "*is* the power over this being [*der Herr* ist. . . *die Macht über dies Sein*]" (*PhG* §190), the power that virtualizes, isolates, severs every connection—in a word, produces existence in its own image, as nothing, alongside pure thought and abstract law. Powerless by comparison, elaboration recuperates the lost energy of thinghood and life itself, cultivates their self-relations, and contributes to the shaping of a work by the means, with the mediation, through the medium of the servant. The servant's being-for-another evinces the phenomenality and phenomenalization of actuality, the self-expression of energy that, by definition, is essentially inessential, ruptured into two essences: at-work and in-the-work, the one self-consciousness and the other. This being-for-another leaves the enclosure of essence and is substantivized in everything that is. While the servant allows the complexity of actual self-relations to stand out from the undifferentiated background of being, the master simplifies everything to the single essence of nothing, embodied (or, better, disembodied) in the power of mastery. (The essence is simple: simply, being or nothing. Appearances are complex. A split essence is simplicity complicated or complication simplified.)

Once again, the phenomenological perspective of self-consciousness is immediately contradicted by the absolute. At the inception of unequal recognition (*ungleiches Anerkennen*), the master reductively postulates (and the servant accepts) that essence is one and that it refers to the master's being-for-itself, "the pure negative power for which the thing is nothing [*die reine negative Macht, der das Ding nichts ist*]" (*PhG* §191). All else is decreed inessential. But, reconstructed absolutely, the essence is not one, meaning that it is two and that it is not identical to itself: the essence is not essence. When it comes to energy, its essential (virtual and self-enclosed) moment is not essential, or, at best, it is as essential as the surface appearances of actuality, not least among them the "inessential activity," *unwesentliches Tun*, of the servant (*PhG* §191). The master's actions themselves are evidence of the essentiality of the inessential and its obverse, the inessentiality of the essential: "the inessential consciousness [*das unwesentliche Bewußtsein*] is therein for the master the object that makes up the *truth* of his certainty of himself" (*PhG* §192).

Let us pause for an instant and note that our nihilistic culture unfortunately elects for itself the stance of the master with regard to material existence as a whole. It wields the essential power of pure negativity, leaving no chance for standing on an equal footing with the other that it brings to naught, renders non-actual. In this drive for unlimited mastery, energy is foreclosed on both sides: ever-escalating destruction leaves us alone, bereft even of self-validation or self-certainty sought from the objectified, inessential, evanescing other. Which other?

Despite what the dominant narrative and counter-narrative tell us, the grand confrontation in Western thought has never been between spirit and matter, but between self-consciousness and consciousness (i.e., "actual" and "real" consciousness) transposed onto oppositions between mind and body, man and woman, human and animal or plant. The other, the servant, was not inert "stuff"; it compressed into itself the entire "inessential activity" of living corporeality, of female labor, or of nonhuman nature, associated at the same time with thinghood and life, as being-in-the-work and being-for-another, objectified, desired, consumed, demanded, and annihilated. Their self-reflection and self-relationality disavowed, the living energy of these others was simultaneously posited and negated, separated from itself, and so demoted to "mere" consciousness.

Not sufficient by far are the claims, more and more frequently voiced nowadays, that consciousness is part and parcel of life, so long as what confronts it is a self-consciousness of the master. To be sure, this unequal non-relation is ultimately unsustainable not only because the servant consciousness ends up depleted and incapable of satisfying the requirements of self-conscious consumption, but also, and especially, because, having interfered with the other's tie to itself, self-consciousness thereby rends the tissue of *its* ties to itself and ceases being self-conscious. "What the master does to the other, he does to himself [*was der Herr gegen den Andern tut, er auch gegen sich selbst . . . tue*]" (*PhG* §191), Hegel writes, ominously if read from the future of the environmental crisis (our present), where the devastation of nonhuman nature is our self-devastation. Or, if it is read within the framework of gender relations, where the denial of self-consciousness to the woman leaves the man speechless, to the extent that he speaks into the void. Or, if referred back to the mind that stops thinking and lapses into an automatic, algorithmic, machinic cognition, the moment the body is robbed of its own self-reflected complexity and is figured as a machine.

The energy starvation, to which the other is subjected, has a boomerang effect on the all-powerful master, whose very extirpating-virtualizing power precludes energy. Framing the other as nothing, the self-consciousness that appears to be in control projects its own virtual nothingness outward and actually becomes nothing, akin to the isolated, idiomatic and idiotic, non-self-related consciousness of the servant, who nonetheless serves as a conduit or a mediator for the self-relations of the thing and of life, augmenting their energies. Negatively understood, this boomerang effect implies that the master is infected by the inessentiality of the servant: "the *truth* of the independent consciousness is the *serving consciousness*" (*PhG* §193). But, positively construed, it means that energy-actuality has been restored in what had deteriorated to a lopsided relation without relation and without self-relation: when "the inessential," *unwesentliche*, is revealed as the truth of deep inner essence, then the substantive-phenomenal world of works has been regained at the level of self-certainty. Translated into the vocabulary of energy, the truth of being-at-work is being-in-the-work. To reach this conclusion, plenty of energy conversions must happen: the masterly essence must become inverted in the kind of inversion (*das Verkehrte*) that is also its extraversion, and the serving consciousness must be converted or perverted by itself (*sich umkehrte*) to attain the position of "true independence" (*PhG* §193). Of course, all these inversions, conversions, and perversions are the works of energy, of finding and recognizing being-at-work in being-in-the-work.

The master is articulated with thinghood through the mediation of the servant in the same fashion that the servant glimpses death, itself "the absolute master," with the intervention of the master. In the existentialized play of forces, a serving consciousness is shaken by the fear of death, causing this consciousness to "vibrate in itself [*in sich selbst erzittern*]" and to experience the dissolution of everything that had been fixed (*PhG* §194). Aside from paralysis, a proper response to this fear is work.

The worker is energized to work by the unworkable void of death, motivated to exert energy from the condition of consummate powerlessness. Work is nothing but a series of externalized reverberations, emanating from the inner vibrations that are provoked by the fear of death. (Freud in his theory of the death drive, of what lies beyond the pleasure principle, subscribed in his own way to this Hegelian insight.) That is why the servant's confinement to being-in-the-work cannot but be felt as a contradiction.

I am not referring in my analysis to the actual activity of labor that fashions human essence, as Marx did, but to the substantive dimension of energy assigned to a serving consciousness, which has been put in flux by a disturbing vision of mortality and, having lost its anchoring in the universe of substance, is harnessed for working. Vibrating in itself, this consciousness harbors a virtualizing negativity (fear itself and that which is feared, death) and contains the master within; reverberating outside itself in its work, it responds to the actualizing drive. Hence, it accommodates *on its own terms* and, probably, thanks to its objective self-contradiction, the amphibology of energy.

Another way of formulating this insight is to say that the master represents a virtual virtuality, in contrast to the servant who stands for the actual virtuality and the actuality of the virtual. Hegel says: "not only is there this universal dissolution *in general* [*allgemeine Auflösung* überhaupt], but in his service the servant also accomplishes it *actually* [*vollbringt es sie* wirklich]" (*PhG* §194). Working lends energy or actuality to a dissolution that remains merely hypothetical as far as the master alone is concerned—the master, who, at the end of the day, is neither at work nor in the work, having renounced hands-on engagement with things and the meaningfulness of thingly being *as* being. The serving consciousness, conversely, is both at work and in the work; it partakes of the two senses of energy by mediating between the master's (admittedly destructive) desire and things, and by putting itself into the works that result from its labor.

In parallel with the play of forces in understanding, opposites change places: the solicited flips into the soliciting, master's pure activity is transformed into actual passivity, and servant's passivity becomes a laborious production of actuality. But, contrary to the play of forces, from which nothing has come out, there is no back-and-forth tossing between virtual virtuality and actual virtuality. Instead, there is an actual outcome here, namely the work and the being of the worker. (This, mind you, is the difference between play and work, or between emplayment and enworkment: the latter is the difference that makes a difference, that endures however temporarily, and that, in dissolving, is not erased without a trace, as though it had never come to pass. And this, incidentally, is also the difference between our commonplace notion of energy as the potentiality of force, on the one hand, and the *energeia-actualitas-Wirklichkeit* complex, on the other.) Irreversibly, a serving consciousness enters the abode of energy, wherein it secretly receives the promise of emancipation.

From work, something comes out in addition to working, namely an outcome, a work, which is not necessarily a material object. Gathered in its results, work shies away from autotelic play, lauded by Kant and in post-Kantian aesthetic philosophy. This is not to say that there are no elements of play in the circle of energy (self-referentiality, turning on itself). But, if we are to be rigorously Hegelian, we must admit that play pertains to force and that possibility belongs to power, rather than to energy—two conclusions seriously undermining Kant's aesthetic and transcendental projects. It is true that imagination indulges in play, so much so that this faculty comes to be defined by its absolute disquietude. The moment a work of art or anything "empirical" (a fact, what has been done, a work) issues forth, however, the movement of force reaches its end in the sense of being abruptly terminated, not fulfilled.

The same applies to the existential play of forces, which is quelled once a work appears. The work is not just an objective product of labor but, as Marx will phrase it, the production of the producers themselves, or, in our terms, the recognition of being-at-work in being-in-the-work. Before and beneath the mutual recognitions of two self-consciousnesses, whereby each recognizes itself as the recognizing and the recognized, there is a self-recognition of the working individuality in the remains, in the rests of work (in the substantive) that capture a working activity outside of itself and past its due: "This *negative* middle term, this formative *activity*, is at the same time *individuality*, the pure being-for-itself of consciousness that now, in the work external to it, enters the element of what remains [*welches nun in der Arbeit außer es in das Element des Bleibens tritt*]" (*PhG* §195). It is crucial to recognize oneself in one's death (the root of all individuality), in a certain experience of death that coincides with being outside oneself in the outcome of one's activity, which is something that master self-consciousness is incapable of doing. Mutual recognition is predicated on this substantive aspect of energy (the work) reflecting the verbal aspect ("formative activity") across the gap of mortality, both deferred by and incorporated into labor.

Having passed into a work and acknowledged its life after death (its survival) in the form of substantivized energy, the working consciousness is permeated with what it had previously feared and what had set it to work from the beginning, that is, the absolute mastery exercised by death. The solicited, the shaken, is supplemented from within by the

PART II

other half of the phenomenon of force and is the solicited soliciting, for which negativity is no longer "an alien essence": "The objective *negative* is precisely the alien essence [*das fremde Wesen*] by which he was shaken [*es gezittert hat*]. Now, however, he destroys this alien negative and posits *himself* as such a negative in the element of the remains" (*PhG* §196). The worker's passage through the elaborated-upon thing estranges the worker's immediate existence in an imitation of death that totally alienates a living being from *its* immediate bodily reality, even as it overcomes the alienation of self-consciousness from the thing (also a diluted alienation in the face of mortality) without negating thinghood the way the master disingenuously does. While the thing was better reflected into itself thanks to the service rendered by that self-consciousness which materially engaged with it, the servant's self-consciousness is more thoroughly related to itself with the mediation of the elaborated thing. With self-relationality buttressed on both sides of this double synergy, the energy circulating between the worker and the work is augmented. But, in the process, or, more accurately, in the outcome of the processes wherein the serving self-consciousness glimpses itself, in "the element of the remains," the servant morphs, in a paradigm case of Girard's mimesis, into what was feared: the uprooting negativity of death.

In the actuality of working and of the work, we find the highest degree of virtuality. The very thing that affirms the bonds between each worked-upon thing and the worker, as well as between the thing and itself, not to mention between the workers and themselves, unfastens things from their previous forms and the serving self-consciousness—from the accouterments of its "determinate being," *bestimmte Sein*, and "natural consciousness," *natürlichen Bewußtsein* (*PhG* §196). Negativity interiorized practically puts in question "the conscious actuality of existence," *die bewußte Wirklichkeit des Dasein*, which rises to actual self-consciousness as actually virtualizing and virtualized, negating the pre-given forms of things by working and the inherited forms of its own being by recognizing the working in the works. In a word, it rises to actual self-consciousness as thinking. Forming a mind of one's own is accomplished by "airing" the taken-for-granted actuality, displacing its energy, noticing with a great deal of surprise the void (fear, death, negativity, the master) that has installed itself in the place of that actuality, and finally working that void into oneself through work, triggered by the dread of the external void. But a mind of one's own (*eigene Sinn*) lapses into single-mindedness or obstinacy (*Eigensinn*) provided that shreds of the bygone, not yet self-related actuality persist in the shape of determinate being and natural consciousness (*PhG* §196). An emanation of a practically engaged self-consciousness, the energy of thought is not sufficiently free (above all from itself, from its unconsciously received actuality) and thus still bears a stamp of servility. Its freedom—and that of self-consciousness—is yet to be secured.

b. The Freedom of Self-Consciousness: Three Manners of Virtualizing Thought

The division of labor, or of non-labor and labor, between the master and the servant self-consciousness culminates in a state of affairs where a thorough virtualization of actuality is actually ineffective (the master) and its actually effective virtualization is not thorough (the servant). Energy-actuality not yet released from the hold of pure being, of the merely given, of the natural or the naturalized, or, in sum, from a genuinely virtual belonging handed over to mastery, which the self-consciousness previously labeled "servile" now needs to reenact at the level of thought, working with the first actuality in its parts and as a whole. Stoicism, skepticism, and the unhappy consciousness are the names of these reenactments, each of them shackled, in its own way, to the still virtual energy (*Energie*) of thought, while straining to attain the actuality (*Wirklichkeit*) of thinking. But, as in other Hegelian reversals, hope germinates in the depths of despair: it is essential fully to virtualize the virtual, to render a given actuality truly virtual in order to attain that true actuality which it has always, unbeknown to itself, been. This is what, in the last analysis, the freedom of self-consciousness as thought accomplishes.

i. Stoicism: Virtual Indifference

The tragedy of thought is that, although it emerges from the synergy of a working consciousness with the elaborated things, it craves mastery and seeks unlimited power over existence, from which it sees itself as independent. In the early phases of the energy conversions or perversions of self-consciousness, the servant realizes the hidden power of that position and aspires to become a new master, directly and immediately, if also universally so. The quest for universal power, *die allgemeine Macht*, beyond the reach of work (*PhG* §196) misses the mark of energy: it gets bogged down in the possible, and the thought most enamored of possibility (or of its conditions) is Kant's transcendental philosophy. On that quest, thinkers hit the target of the virtual, not the actual. So, what if we backtracked and replayed on the screens of the absolute the sequence when thought sprang into being from the synergy of the working and the worked-upon?

Hegel takes the Cartesian "thinking thing," *res cogitans*, literally: thinking emanates from thinghood (or from thinging). In contrast to the master's self-consciousness, which, as a pure for-itself, is at work in a world emptied of works, the servant's consciousness spans the substantive and

PART II

the verbal instantiations of energy, albeit without self-consciously integrating the two extremes, such that "these two moments fall . . . outside each other" (*PhG* §197). The chasm between them is the prehistory of thought, which is, strange as it may sound, our contemporary predicament—that of inhabiting a universe of "cultured" or "cultivated things" (*gebildete Dinge*) that are more alien to the cultivating consciousness than the so-called "wild." Hegel's proposal in this regard is also unexpected: he does not suggest recognizing the domesticity of works as the objective vestiges of the working impulse but, conversely, taking alienation to its logical conclusion and discovering the troubling uncanniness of works in the very core of the working: "being-*in-itself* or *thinghood*, which received its form from labor, is no other substance than consciousness [An-sich-*seins oder der* Dingheit, *welche die Form in der Arbeit erhielt, keine andere Substanz als das Bewußtsein*]" (*PhG* §197). It is this disquieting realization, which slips what was understood as an independent substance of the thing into the place of the subject, that charts the path to thought. Instead of being-at-work catching a sight of itself in being-in-the-work, objectified energy is brought out into the open as the essence of subjective energy. Concurring with neither Descartes nor Spinoza, Hegel refuses to occupy the master position that potentiates a rift between the thinking thing and the extended thing in the former, even as he rejects the indifference of the absolute divorced from phenomenology and the parity between the two modes of the same substance in the latter. Plenty of hard work will be required (of Hegel as well as of us) to hitch together the two dimensions of energy, while neither consenting to their timeless separation nor postulating their immediate identity. This is the hard work of thinking.

Hegel sees in thinking "a new shape of self-consciousness," *eine neue Gestalt des Selbstbewußtseins*, which is to say, a new shape of energy. To be fair, this shape is awash in paradox, to the extent that in its own substantivized appearance on the phenomenological scene it de-substantivizes everything it touches upon. Perhaps, the instability of a form that deforms everything around it accounts for a greater share of its freedom than the official explanation, namely that the subject dwelling in this form is, by the same token, an object for itself ("*Thinking* is not thinking as an *abstract I*, but as an I that equally has the meaning of being-*in-itself*, of being its own object [*die Bedeutung des* An-sich-*seins hat, sich Gegenstand sein*]" [*PhG* §197]). This, at any rate, is how the explicit justification for the freedom of thought has been interpreted, conveniently letting fall by the wayside the thingly origins of the "in-itself" and, therefore, the persistence of thinghood, of energy in the substantive, within the self-objectification of consciousness. If so—if the thing not only endures in but also underwrites the freedom of consciousness—then the perversions that thought sows in the "first" actuality it encounters along its route are due to its congenital self-perversion, its perverse beginnings in thinghood that it would rather forget. To Hegel's adage "in thinking I am free, because I am not in an other [*im Denken* bin *Ich* frei, *weil Ich nicht in einem Andern bin*]" (*PhG* §197) we should add the words "though the other persists in me."

It is by virtue of forgetting its beginnings that thought inaugurates two divergent energy regimes, that of being and that of the concept: "From the standpoint of *thought*, the object sets itself in motion not in representations or shapes, but in *concepts* [*Dem* Denken *bewegt sich der Gegenstand nicht in Vorstellungen oder Gestalten, sondern in* Begriffen] . . . The represented, the shaped, and what is already in existence as such have the form [*die Form*] of being something other than consciousness" (*PhG* §197). Oblivious to its origination from thinghood, thought fails to detect energy in the substantive in the represented, the shaped, and the already existent. For *its* animation—for its enworkment—it relies on concepts, as though these have not first come about in the form of inner perversions, the twists and turns in the first actuality of being. The *shapes of beings* that retain the "natural" determinacy of what is merely given, the works of representation and immediate existence, are then categorized as a *form of being* different from that of conscious thought, the pure workings of concepts, the native turf of the thinking I, who, moving in them, moves in itself (*PhG* §197). In addition to ontological difference between the represented, existent, shaped beings and conscious being, the two regimes operate based on an *energetic difference* between substantive works and the subject at work. That said, energetic difference is only discernible from the standpoint of the absolute; for thought, that is, phenomenologically, it presents itself as a difference between non-energy and energy, the raw materials for thought and the activity of thinking. Staying close to the source of its energy, immersed in its proper conceptual element, is, for the thinking I, an imperative, dictating at the same time the terms of its survival (of maintaining the form of being appropriate to it as consciousness) and of its freedom (of remaining authentically itself and not the other, dwelling in the conceptual milieu where what it is in itself coincides with who it is for itself).

Stoicism's raison d'être is to jealously guard the purity of the distinction between the energy regimes of being and the concept. The stress placed on purity is symptomatic of an obsession with essence—in this case, the essence of thought, or the "thinking essence" (*denkendes Wesen*) of consciousness (*PhG* §198)—which, as such, is distanced from *Wirklichkeit*. More concretely, the essence of thought is conceptuality, insulated from determinate shapes of existence and ensuring that the thinking I is maintained in its proper element. Stoicism is, therefore, doubly virtualizing: first, in its obsession with essence in general, as opposed to existence, and, second, in its attachment to the essence of pure thought in particular. It thus "keeps the lifelessness [*Leblosigkeit*] which constantly *withdraws* from the movement of existence, from effective actions [*aus dem Wirken*] as well as from suffering, into *the simple essentiality of thought* [die einfache Wesenheit des Gedankens]" (*PhG* §199).

This withdrawal from actuality, this refusal of every bit of energy that does not conform to the concept, is the purist and utterly negative manner in which stoicism resolves the problem of the servant consciousness that stubbornly clings to shreds of unelaborated being. The stoic solution is a massive energy transfer from the real-phenomenal to the formal-essential, "lifeless," domain. At the expense of existence, effective actions (*Wirken:* the work-site of practical actuality), and bodily suffering, the thinking interiority alone is now brimming with sense. As it happens in everyday life, however, where our deepest flaws are hidden from our own mental regard and are projected onto the other in whom they irritate us the most, the lifelessness of thought in its essentiality is pointed out in external being, not in the subjectivity of the stoic. A thinking withdrawal from existence revolves around the conviction that what it withdraws from is the apotheosis of anti-energy. In reality, it merely projects its own empty essence (as well as the very essence of essence, or essentiality, *Wesenheit*) onto the being it deems inessential.

Instead of calibrating its approach to the singular remains of a surpassed actuality, stoicism adopts the attitude of the master's indifference in "the *pure universality* of thought" (*PhG* §198), leveling down everything outside the purview of the concept. It embraces the universality of form shorn of content, of possibility unglued from actuality. And, through the master's self-consciousness with its unperturbed relation to death, it dips into the inexhaustible virtual reserves of pure being purged of beings and posits the ideal of freedom, according to which nothing would remain of the past actuality, or at least nothing that truly matters. This is why stoicism strives to be "*indifferent* toward natural existence [gleichgültig *gegen das natürliche Dasein*]" (*PhG* §200): it stands for a transitional phase in the natural-unnatural history of energy, when the first actuality has undergone universal dissolution, dispersion, and entropy, while the other actuality is not yet determinately negated into existence. Taking the initiative to cast off its yoke to existence, stoicism, as one strand of thought among many, condenses in itself the impulse and dynamics of thought as such—the drive toward idealism.

Unmoored from a merely given actuality while still adrift in a sea of potentiality without the shore of another actuality in sight, the stoic self-consciousness rejects *any* substantive manifestations of energy. It shuns anything already accomplished, including the very freedom it pursues. For it, freedom substantivized isn't free and truth "is without accomplishment in life [*ohne die Erfüllung des Lebens ist*]" (*PhG* §200) and without effect on a living actuality (or the actuality of the living), only on thought. Even its negation of embodied otherness is incomplete—"*die unvollendete Negation des Andersseins*" (*PhG* §201)—meaning that no works can be expected to issue from its project. By hankering after the power of the mind (indeed, after a power of any kind) unperturbed by the material vicissitudes of existence, by wishing to preserve the unadulterated essence of thought, and by snubbing the entire world of being-in-the-work, stoicism surrenders its claim to energy. Its potency is the impotence of sufferers who imagine themselves above and in control of the cause of their suffering to the extent that they will this cause away as trifling and inessential but refrain from actually (in actuality; through action) interfering with it. With mastery dispensed to pure thought and servitude allotted to the body as the nadir of external reality, stoicism "*retreats* into itself," *in sich* zurückgezogen (*PhG* §201), and relishes the virtuality of its self-enclosure, the much-praised "inner strength," which lacks energy-actuality-effectiveness.

ii. Skepticism: Virtual Indifference Realized

Paraphrasing Heraclitus on *phusis*, we might say that energy hates to hide; uncontainable in a non-apparent essence, it tends toward disclosure and phenomenalization. If "skepticism is the realization [*Realisierung*] of that of which stoicism is merely a concept—and is moreover the actual experience [*die wirkliche Erfahrung*] of what freedom of thought is" (*PhG* §202), then, in skepticism, the stoic impulse becomes a thing (*res*), through which the world around the thinking I is reclaimed. The sheer reifying repetition of stoicism in skepticism accounts for the upsurge of its energy, which is the after-energy of what is otherwise singular, insulated, purely idiomatic. The "actual experience of . . . the freedom of thought" is contingent upon this becoming-thing of thinking, thrown back onto its repressed provenance.

Less charitably, the realization of X is the intensification of its animating drive: from a total virtual irreality, we skip to the endlessly multiplying virtual realities. Instead of a blanket negation of otherness, skepticism negates "the multifarious shapes of life [*mannigfaltigen Gestaltung des Lebens*]"—the shapes of energy that are its substantive outcomes—and so heralds the advent of "real negativity," *realen Negativität* (*PhG* §202). Still, any realization of stoicism, faithful to what is realized in it, is bound to be the realization of the unfulfillable, or, differently stated, the actualization of thought's virtuality. The energy of essential thinking is felt only by way of exteriorizing this thinking, prompting it to become other to itself (but also, by the same token, to become more of itself, reunited with the thing whence it commenced), to venture out of essence's inner abode, and to unleash its destructive workings on the multifarious shapes of life that it undoes or unworks.

Enlisted to realize the unfulfillable and to actualize the virtual without compromising on its virtuality, skepticism is a magnet for self-contradictions, from which it draws much of its own energy that, of necessity, is divided against itself. To live up to the impossible demands posed before it, the skeptical implementation of the stoic fantasy cannot count on much room for maneuvering in the sphere of exteriority. It can do no more than surface from the enclosure of thought so as to negate, piece by piece, the constituents of what it finds outside: otherness, desire, and labor. "Skepticism corresponds to the *realization* [*Realisierung*] of the concept of independent consciousness as a negative orientation to otherness, desire, and labor [*als der negativen Richtung auf das Anderssein, der Begierde und der Arbeit*]" (*PhG* §202). Such a realization is to be rigorously distinguished from actualization; the concept is real (a thing-concept) on the condition that it keeps "independent consciousness" in an isolated, virtual state, sequestered from the world. (When it comes to the unhappy consciousness, the energy situation improves because that consciousness is at least negatively related to itself and, in this minimal self-relatedness, restyles its reality into an actuality.)

In the phenomenology of skepticism, that is, within "the actual experience of what freedom of thought is," the freedom of self-consciousness is assured so long as the other is perpetually put into question. The world must be on its way to de-actualization (robbed of its effectiveness) and disappearance in order for the skeptic to feel free and in control. Moreover, as Hegel indicates, the vanishing of what has been taken as "true and real," *sein Wahres und Reelles*, is not something that "just happens" (*PhG* §204); such virtualization is consciously and self-consciously orchestrated by the skeptical procedures themselves. The realization of the concept of independent self-consciousness is packaged together with the de-realization of past certainties concerning what was true and real, and whatever energy skepticism possesses derives from these two interrelated modes of virtualization. But, since negation is not accompanied by a self-negation, it bears with universal indifference on anything negated by it. In other words, a skeptical negation is not determinate and does not fill out the empty freedom of self-consciousness with self-given content.

Upon relinquishing the pre-given difference pertaining to the "other that masquerades for the real [*dies andere für reell sich Gebende*]," skepticism is not in a position to give difference (as opposed to freedom) to itself anew: "What disappears is the determinate or the difference [*das Bestimmte, oder der Unterschied*] that, no matter what it is or where it comes from, is set up as fixed and unchangeable" (*PhG* §204). Its universal indifference to the negated content, combined with the non-differentiation that dominates the interlude between the merely given and the self-given, means that the very thing which has differentiated skepticism from stoicism has evaporated as well. Instead of each aspect of alterity, desire, and work skeptically considered by self-consciousness, thinking follows a "cookie-cutter" recipe on how to carry out an abstractly universal, indeterminate negation. With difference dissipated, energy vanishes as well, and a universal entropy characteristic of stoicism reigns in the midst of the skeptical attitude. The thingification of the former in the latter, the becoming-work of stoic in skeptical thought, harkens back to that of which it is a realization. The thing of the skeptic is demonstrated in its truth as a mask overlaying a pure no-thing.

A skeptically inclined thought is shorn of the determinacy—the differentiation into thoughts—that, with definite quanta of energy, already marked the stoic variation on cogitation. The form and the content of thought thus part ways, the one taking refuge in the tranquillity ("ataraxy") of thought thinking itself and the other in "*the absolute dialectical unrest* [absolute dialektische Unruhe]" (*PhG* §205). The segregation of content from form in skepticism is symptomatic of energy's partitioning, the non-relation between its formal work-aspect and the content of its workings. The skeptic renders the energy of thought in such a way that this energy is indifferent to itself as much as to its other; its two dimensions disarticulated, it falls short of self-relationality and therefore, with typical self-contradictoriness, undermines itself and does not live up to the designation "energy."

Although Kant is not explicitly named here, and although his philosophy is not skepticism in any traditional sense of the term, it is hard to miss the subtext of Hegel's attack on his predecessor. Formal ataraxy is a feature of transcendental subjectivity and the conditions of possibility for experience, whereas restless consciousness is identified as "empirical" (*empirisch*), and its content is an "utterly contingent disarray," which causes this consciousness to "act upon and bring to actuality [*zur Wirklichkeit bringt*] what has no truth for it" (*PhG* §205). Kant's transcendental idealism is unfulfillable and unattainable; more than that, it is foreign to the logic of fulfillment and the immanent attainment of energy-actuality. Once its immutable works or things (the *conditions* of possibility) are set in place, the workings of empirical consciousness are doomed to spin in a void, never truly meeting that which conditions them. They wax deadly as the destructive workings without the work, ready to annihilate the entire world for the sake of the unattainable, the consecrated, the absolute. Assuming that the transcendental realm conceived as "*universal selfsameness*" is "the negativity of all individuality and all difference [*die Negativität aller Einzelnheit und alles Unterschieds*]" (*PhG* §205), the principle of Kantian philosophy—like that of skepticism and nihilism, neither of which, together with Kantianism, goes any further than principles: hence, the virtual, the energy-less in thought—is indeterminate negation fixated on the possible (as in the conditions of *possibility*) which, *eo ipso*, is impossible to actualize. Despite appearing as a trans-historical given, the transcendental/empirical gap signifies a historical schism in energy.

Skepticism is coldly indifferent to the matters it submits to the axe of negation and doubt, stringing an endless chain of inclusive universality with a minus sign: "and also not," "and also not," "and also not . . ." In this respect, *also*, it is beholden to its thingly vocation—the realization of stoicism—which negatively reiterates the "also" of the senses, being itself a repetition of the "also" that articulates (and disarticulates) the properties of a perceived thing. On the one hand, undoubtedly, the repetition of repetition in skepticism augments the dialectical energy thriving on replays of the working in the work, all the way to the absolute repetition. On the other hand, *what* is repeated is virtual non-relationality, or a relation so weak as to border on a non-relation. It matters after all, and not only here, whether what returns in a repetition is a form, its content, or a series of frictions, tension, and contradictions between the two.

The negative power, the energy-poor force of skepticism, is negating but not internally negated: negativity at work but not in the work that skepticism itself is. Only from the vantage of the absolute, as a realization or thingification of skepticism, does its substantive work-aspect come through. Even then, its self-contradictions, like the properties of the thing, are mutually indifferent to one another, and, in this being outside one another ("*aber es hält diesen Widerspruch seiner selbst auseinander*" [*PhG* §205]), in this non-interrelatedness, crumble into incoherence. In a virtual state, thought relives the fate of the thing itself, whence it has come about, including its organization around a void of which it is not aware and the illusion of having an independent reality. Not until skepticism turns back to itself and "experiences itself in truth [*in Wahrheit*] as a contradictory consciousness" (*PhG* §206) does it become imbued with energy, albeit at the cost of its familiar shape.

iii. Unhappy Consciousness: The Non-Relational Gap of (Self-)Relationality

That skepticism which is skeptical about itself and which grasps its existence as contradictory is "*for itself* a doubled consciousness [für sich *das gedoppelte Bewußtsein*]," also termed "unhappy," *unglückliche* (*PhG* §206). The doubling of an individual self-consciousness supplants two self-consciousnesses (that of the master and that of the servant) and, as such, throbs with speculative energy, whereby one divides into two. At the same time, the internalized split undergoes yet another process of virtualization, having withdrawn into a self-consciously "self-contradictory essence," *als . . . widersprechenden Wesens* (*PhG* §206). The unhappy consciousness negates itself, bears witness to this negation, and furnishes a photographic negative of actuality—a self-relation to obstinate non-relationality. In sum, it is unworkable as a whole; it cannot establish any sort of synergy with itself (between its two parts) and, as a result, lets its speculative energy fizzle away.

Why is the consciousness that supplants skepticism "unhappy"? The short answer is that it is no longer unconscious of its own troubling predicament. It is worth noting that Hegel uses "happiness" in the classical Aristotelian sense of fulfillment, the actual living up to its full potential. And this is what the split subject is debarred from. Unfulfillable, the unhappy consciousness is aware that, in its very essence, it is denied basic essentiality (the simplicity of essence) due to the excess it carries in itself, that is, its being double. Unfulfilled, it realizes that it is not (and cannot be) actualized as a whole, which, like the biblical Moses, it is doomed to overview from the outside but, being hopelessly torn asunder, is prevented from inhabiting. (Unless Moses himself personifies the unhappy consciousness, torn between freedom and slavery, Egypt and the Land of Israel, at home neither there nor here.) The new shape of consciousness contains the knowledge that there is yet another mode of the unfulfillable besides the "bad infinity" of unsatisfiable desire. That other mode is one of self-contradictory fulfillment: when a part is at rest, the other is of necessity disquieted, and vice versa. Self-estrangement means that no sooner is the "rest of unity," *Ruhe der Einheit*, intuited than each part is "driven outside" (*ausgetrieben*) of the whole (*PhG* §207). Therefore, the whole exists only by way of its impossibility: the whole as desired but never actually achieved.

For Hegel, the emergence of the unhappy consciousness is a watershed moment when "the concept has become enlivened and enters into existence [*den Begriff des lebendig gewordenen und in die Existenz getretenen*]" (*PhG* §207). The concept is liberated into life from the stone-like stability of formal logical categories on the condition that it becomes two in one, two *and* one, the one and the other, the same and not-the-same, in a veritably negative, irresolvable dialectic. Such doubling, such speculative energizing, holds even more so for the concept of energy: it is at work and in the work, driven outside by its very being at rest. *Its* self-contradictory unity comes to a consciousness of itself when we apprehend the desire for energy as infinitely growing and, in the last instance, unfulfillable. But the consciousness of this self-contradiction is at its sharpest when it finds out, within the conceptual scheme of energy-actuality, that each of its two aspects stands in the way of the other's fulfillment. Phenomenologically, what is at work is not (yet) in the work, and what is in the work is (already) not at work. When we accumulate or possess energy, it is but a resource, as being-in-the-work; when we release energy, it is more or less immediately consumed and depleted, as being-at-work. Insofar as it is self-conscious, our consciousness of energy is unhappy, with the fulfillment of parts preventing the emergence of the whole. In the face of energy, we are all Moses, divided between here and there, the actual and the actualizing, "storage" and "retrieval," containment and release.

The analogy (though this is assuredly more than an analogy) between the unhappy consciousness and energy does not end here. The two participants in a mutually exclusive relation—transcendental and empirical subjectivities—are not on an equal footing: "one of them, namely, is the simple unchangeable [*einfache unwandelbare*], as the *essence*, while the other is the manifoldly changeable [*vielfache wandelbare*], as the *inessential*" (*PhG* §208). The same goes for our default approach to energy: the essential aspect is being-at-work, the ideal of permanent activity, while the inessential is being-in-the-work, the reality of a passive holding (or withholding) of energy in the reserves of potentiality that, at the extreme, include all matter. The struggle for the possession of these reserves, corresponding to empirical subjectivity, is never for the sake of the reserves themselves but for the purpose of "liberating" the energy they contain, and so transcendentalizing the world into pure and total activity. The unhappy consciousness, too, strives "to free itself from the inessential, that is to say, to free itself from itself [*sich von sich selbst zu befreien*]" (*PhG* §208). Neither it nor our notion of energy can tolerate the self-contradictory relation they are locked in, which is why everything is done so as to reduce the relation to one of its terms, to a consciousness (or energy) without itself. What is forgotten in this mad dash to resolve the contradiction is that the inessential is closer to energy-actuality than the untainted, simple, unchangeable essence and that, moreover, the gap of separation—at times, growing to an abyss—is at the heart of relationality. So, energy, like the unhappy consciousness, *is* when it *is not* and *is not* when it *is*.

The lacunae between two or more parties are vital to a relation, but when nothing else comes into view other than this void in-between, the relation disappears. All that remains is a caesura between one consciousness and another, detracting from their coexistence within the same consciousness. In the eyes of the unhappy consciousness, "*this unity be-*

comes at first itself such a unity, *in which differentness* [Verschiedenheit] is still dominant" (*PhG* §210). A relation survives as a play of figure-and-ground—I write "as a play," and, hence, as a matter of force; "a play of forces" is, as we have seen, a redundant expression, since, of force, there is always ever only play—but where the figure melts away and the ground becomes groundless, difference without differends morphs into a black hole. A similar development affects the relation of energy: the difference between its containment in actuality (or being-in-the-work, which is for us the inessential dimension) and its liberation that destroys a given actuality (or being-at-work, taken to be essential) deepens to a chasm, its two sides disconnected from one another. We throw everything and everyone—ourselves included—into this chasm, precipitating a meta-virtualization of the world above and beyond a simple and restricted act of energy release.

An extreme difference between terms, overshadowed by the infinite distance stretching between them, is conceptually equivalent to their sameness. (The "absolute separation" between the I and the other at the outset of Levinas's *Totality and Infinity* gets bogged down in this very quagmire.) If a relation thrives within certain limits, beyond which we run into a non-distinction between distinction and non-distinction, then these limits are not arbitrarily set, but are determined in accord with the mediations articulating (and negating) the independent terms. The problem of the unhappy consciousness is that "it is immediately [*unmittelbar*] itself both, and is, for it, *the relation of both* [die Beziehung beider] as a relation of essence to non-essence" (*PhG* §208). Absent any sort of mediations, it persists as a virtual *possibility* of a relation, not an actual interrelating of opposites. The unhappy consciousness and, for a different reason, the absolute separation of the I from the other forbid the workings of determinate negation and forestall the emergence of a work from their mode of thinking. That is to say: they preclude the flourishing of energy in the non-relations they encapsulate.

No mediations exist between the changeable and the unchangeable, the empirical and the transcendental, within the framework of the unhappy consciousness. Instead of the difference of pure being or the formal equality of "this" I and "this" object, an unmediated combination of the two consciousnesses results in an event, a happening, *ein Geschehen*, "such that the unchangeable receives the shape of individuality [*die Gestalt der Einzelnheit*]" (*PhG* §212). The event is an immediate irruption that substitutes for the patient workings of mediation to produce an unelaborated work—"the shape of individuality," energy in the substantive—forcefully or playfully dispensed to the unchangeable incarnated in the individuality of (transcendental) consciousness. The other consciousness, namely the empirical, is also a happening in the sense that one happens upon it, encounters it as something that "is merely to be *found* [*nur* findet], *by nature*, in opposition to the transcendental" (*PhG* §212). So, for all their differences, disregarding the abyss that stretches between them, the two consciousnesses belong to the first actuality, the merely given rather than the self-given. Or, more exactly, their non-relation (i.e., a dearth of mediations between them) constructs the illusion of mere givenness both in the case of the unchangeable miraculously instantiated in the shape of individuality and in the case of the changeable "naturally" and immediately opposed to it.

The prevalence of the event in contemporary philosophical discourses testifies to the lackluster energy of thinking that eschews patient mediation, repetition, and lingering with actuality. Rather than inhabiting the cleft between the transcendental and the empirical, our fetishized event hardly exits the transcendental domain: through it, the possible momentarily condenses in the singular and, therefore, happens (or fails to happen) as the impossible, in an ether free of workings and works. More often than not, it assumes the shape of what Hegel calls "the absolute contingency," *die absolute Zufälligkeit*, which, despite its apparently ceaseless dynamism, reproduces the "immovable indifference," *unbewegliche Gleichgültigkeit*, of virtual pure being (*PhG* §212). Whether offered in the spirit of a meditation on the conditions of possibility for experience, or on the conditions of *im*possibility, or, indeed, on both at once, the thinking of the event is predicated on a more or less overt rejection of actuality, apriori unplugging itself from every energy supply.

There is, for all that, a semblance of working and of work in the event of transcendental consciousness. The shaping (*Gestaltung*) of the unchangeable produces "the shape of individual actuality [*die Gestalt der einzelnen Wirklichkeit*]" (*PhG* §212), which absorbs into itself the entire energy (in the substantive) of the transcendental domain. Reneging on its task—to mediate between the singular and the universal—this shaping and the shape it produces spawn nothing but formal similitudes to the empirical model. On the point of recognizing itself in the transcendental, the actual individual runs into "the opposition of the impenetrable [*undurchsichtiges*] sensuous *One*, with all the roughness of something actual [*mit der ganzen Sprödigkeit eines* Wirklichen]" (*PhG* §212). The qualities of impenetrability and roughness are those of the first actuality, unrelated to itself and unelaborated with the help of determinate negation. They are consistent with the formalism of evental instantiation, where the unchangeable assumes the shape of individual actuality irrespective of its content. And if form is transcendentally indifferent to content, then it bears allegiance to the virtual at the very threshold of the first actuality.

A smidgeon of energy abiding in the transcendental event is the shape of actuality, "a relation to the *shaped unchangeable* [*den* gestalteten Unwandelbaren]" that supersedes the "relation to the pure *unshaped* unchangeable [*zu dem reinen* ungestalteten *Unwandelbaren*]" (*PhG* §213). In the context of dialectical "mechanics," the unshaped was the wholly virtual empty spatiality, while shapes were the figures delimiting or defining the infinity of this virtual extension. Once it is individuated, transcendental consciousness corresponds to the fixed shapes, objectively governed by the laws of geometry that are untainted by temporal and subjective interferences. The point, however, is to taint this rigid consciousness, to make its pure façade collapse, to impregnate it with subjective law and, above all, with time—in a word, to energize it beyond the shape or the work it has endowed itself with. Time is, in fact, the new shapelessness, a post-shaped self-relation of spatiality, space suffused with energy. Only as time (which is, *nota bene*, different from saying "in time," i.e., in an empirical reality insulated from the transcendental) is "the initially external relation to the shaped unchangeable as an alien actuality [*als einem fremden Wirklichen*] elevated into an absolute becoming-one [*zum absoluten Einswerden*] with it" (*PhG* §213).

The "alien actuality" of transcendental unchangeability is experienced within the non-relation of the unhappy consciousness as a frigid imposition of the law—of necessity—onto the contingent existence of the empirical subject. To be converted into a relation that is no longer merely external, this actuality must be felt as the energy whose source is intimately close to empirical consciousness, though not of one piece with it. It must be handed over to the "absolute becoming-one," a repeated overcoming of the chasm between the two consciousnesses, the absolute being-at-work that aims at the work of "being-one," *Einssein* (*PhG* §214). With this, Hegel proposes to accomplish in actuality what Kant demands in principle: to accept the transcendental law as one's own, to recognize oneself in it and to recognize it in oneself. A subtle insinuation built into this de-alienation of the unchangeable is that Kant denied himself both the means and the end that he so desired, precisely to the extent that he left *Wirklichkeit* in the blind spot of his thinking, or, at best, reduced it to a subset of modal categories—a setback he tried to address with recourse to the teleological apparatus inherited from the Scholastics. Restricting time to a *transcendental* aesthetic and relegating relationality to the categories of *pure* understanding, he fenced his thought in the virtual realm there where it could have brushed upon the actual.

Time is energy en route, on the way to itself and awaiting itself at the end of its peregrinations: interminably on the path toward itself. The same may be said, mutatis mutandis, on the subject of the energy and the time of thinking that do not amount to the effort and the duration it takes to encounter a prefabricated truth. The time of thinking is energy on the way to itself, awaiting and awaited, if neither anticipating nor anticipated in the manner of understanding. The enigma of the unhappy consciousness, which is an apprenticeship in thinking, is not only how it endeavors to forge a temporal relation to the atemporal, but also how it lives through and *is* this contradiction. Thinking, in contrast to understanding that does not in actuality *exist*, is living in and with contradiction. But, at a certain point, this condition becomes viscerally intolerable; it screams for a resolution, which, for the unhappy consciousness, is its own dissolution. Striving for "being-one," the unhappy consciousness abnegates its split essence.

The goal of the unhappy consciousness is no longer to be unhappy, to experience satisfaction in the state of energetic fullness. But what happens is that, all too eager to put its unhappiness behind, it renounces itself as a consciousness and grows unconscious toward its organizing split. Its desperate work is the issue—the issuance—of despair, opting for one of the extremes and so reducing consciousness to a single modality. The work of thinking that used to shuttle between two consciousnesses comes to a grinding halt. Thinking is paralyzed, but its "rest" does not fulfill the *promesse du bonheur* behind aspirations to unity. Instead, in a microcosm of our dichotomous relation to energy, a self-mutilated unhappy consciousness is faced with two choices: *either* complete virtualization and withdrawal into the purity of untouched essence, keeping energy in reserve within the transcendental extreme, *or* indefatigable laboring and desiring activity, its energy beholden to the exteriority of the empirical extreme. In contemporary philosophy, the unthinking alternatives embraced by the unhappy consciousness tally (not with the so-called analytic/Continental divide but) with the predilection for inane metaphysical speculation, on the one hand, and for diehard pragmatism, on the other.

The first solution (resolution, dissolution) sees the "inessential" consciousness identifying wholesale with its "pure" counterpart, such that "the shaped unchangeable seems to become posited [*gezetzt zu werden*] as it is in and for itself" (*PhG* §215). In doing so, the inessential delivers itself to what it sees as an essence, sacrificing its contingent individuality to the virtual, energy-poor universal. An abdication rather than a reconciliation (*Aussöhnung* [*PhG* §216]), this act of shrinking the unhappy consciousness to pure consciousness prevents the former from "relating to *its object* thinkingly [*denkend*]" (*PhG* §217). When being-one is achieved at the expense of tying up the loose ends of consciousness, there is no more time left for thinking. Not because one is addicted to the sham energy of constant doing (or not *just* due to that; after all, work and desire are responsible for another reduction of the unhappy consciousness to a single modality), but because the spacing of time, the non-transcendental and non-empirical interval between the transcendental and the empirical, which Derrida will later on baptize *différance*, is obliterated. A parody of the absolute, the side that effaces all the others in the unmediated oneness of pure consciousness loses contact with energy as well; within its atemporal framework, energy is not en route and it has not arrived (at itself) either. Having delivered itself over to the virtual moment of transcendental subjectivity, the subject is stuck, frozen, or fixated, both temporally and energy-wise.

Hegel dramatically portrays this stuckness of a virtualized consciousness as "the *grave* of its life," *das* Grab *seines Lebens* (*PhG* §217), a life sacrificed together with (and in the shape of) the time and energy proper to finite existence. "This grave itself is, however, an *actuality* [*eine* Wirklichkeit]," he adds in the same paragraph. The crypt of virtual inwardness, within which actuality appears as a grave, contains a consummate perversion of energy into its other, non- or anti-energy, or, to put it curtly, metaphysics. Furthermore, the grave of a life does not necessarily mean that what is entombed there is dead; it could well be that a living life posthumously survives itself in the grave prepared for it, a little as it does in Samuel Beckett's novels (its survival signals the birth of the subject). Or, an actual expression of a life (for instance, in amino acids) could be, at the same time, its grave. Even as it is waved away, self-contradiction comes back with a vengeance, since a *lived* contradiction cannot be done away with in the interiority of *thought*. The sense of being buried alive is a symptom of the cognitive dissonance experienced by, and serving as the phenomenological corollary to, the changeable consciousness that has stepped into the place of the unchangeable. (Lest we take the return of the contradiction lightly, it should be stated that, for Hegel, there is no cognition outside such cognitive dissonance.)

"On the one hand, insofar as it strives to gain access to *itself in the essence*, it merely seizes its own sundered actuality [*die eigne getrennte Wirklichkeit*]; on the other hand, it cannot seize the other *as an individual*, or as an *actual* [*als* einzelnes, *oder als* wirkliches] other" (*PhG* §217). The "either/or" is at its starkest in this formulation: either consciousness embraces itself as an actual individual or bows before an essence indifferent to its existence; either it engages an actual other or the amorphous essence of otherness. The caveat is that, part and parcel of aspirations to being-one, the "either/or" is factored into the "both...and" in the spirit of synergy and true relationality. Energy-actuality is sundered (*getrennt*) at the heart of a project aiming at ideal wholeness: time and energy are regained for thinking.

If consciousness gets "unstuck" in this way, then it abandons its virtual crypt and deduces from the experience of this liberation that "*the grave* of its *actual* unchangeable essence has *no actuality* [*das Grab* seines *wirklichen* unwandelbaren Wesens *keine Wirklichkeit* hat]" (*PhG* §217). In other words, the grave has no effectiveness, no capacity to detain the subject in its interiority; the experienced effect is that of an actuality split, the grave cracked open. Speculative energy erupts from the one—namely, pure consciousness—unable to maintain itself in its integrity.

What lies outside the grave of "the *actual* unchangeable"? Not the unhappy consciousness as it was before the experiment with its reduction to the transcendental aspect, but "an individual that has actuality [*als* Einzelnes Wirklichkeit *hat*] seen from its own perspective" (*PhG* §218). The proof of an individual's actuality has been negative: the subject has surrendered body and soul to pure consciousness, has been encrypted in itself and expelled from this crypt by an impossible act of identification with the outside world. Feeling the bruises of that expulsion on its skin, the individual is privy to self-feeling (*Selbstgefühl*), making it "the actual that exists for itself [*für sich seiendes Wirkliches*]" (*PhG* §218). Through its hard-won self-relation, its synergy with itself newly found after a failed (though in another sense quite successful) traversal of the transcendental-empirical abyss, the "unstuck" consciousness attains actuality—in this case, existent and existential energy. The critical shortcomings of this self-discovery are (1) that the "self" is discovered in a rather mangled state, fractured (*gebrochne*) and estranged (*PhG* §218), and (2) that the individual is actual for itself alone, its *Wirklichkeit* giving no signs to the outside world and accessible only through self-feeling. "The actual that exists for itself" but not for the other is, by and large, virtual—an inner contradiction that recovers the shattered state of the unhappy consciousness, as much as the energy divided between itself and not-itself, the actual and the virtual.

Hence, the second solution: to dedicate oneself entirely to the pursuits of desire and work, valorizing the empirical side of the split, engaging with actual otherness, and leaving the external imprints of actuality (the works) as the outward signs of a self-assured existence. Nevertheless, the substantivation of energy in the products of work and the objects of desire does not heal the wounds of the unhappy consciousness, but merely provides an objective confirmation of "an *actuality broken into two*," *eine* entzweigebrochene Wirklichkeit (*PhG* §219). In the aftermath of an unchangeable shape appearing on the radar of consciousness, nothing is the same as before: actuality is broken down the middle thanks to the realization that, besides the "null" world, negated and molded through labor, there is also a "consecrated world" (*eine geheiligte Welt*), which is literally untouchable (*PhG* §219). Total dedication to attaining the objects of desire through labor does not let the subject come back to itself as whole; in addition to the world one can work upon, an entirely unworkable realm exists that remains resistant to being sublated or digested by the subject (*PhG* §220). The actuality parted into two reiterates the hermeneutical situation of energy, which is divided against itself according to the verbal and the substantive meanings of *ergon*, at-work and in-the-work. Properly understood, all energy-actuality is *entzweigebrochene*, broken into two—a conclusion the unhappy consciousness confirms in practice (i.e., by stumbling upon the limits of practice, of what is practicable) and experiences on its own skin. What is still obscure in its phenomenology is that the unworkable *is* the subject, that which or the one who is at-work.

When the workings of desire and labor culminate in "the annihilation of actuality," *Vernichtung der Wirklichkeit* (*PhG* §220), active consciousness stands for an energy that brings energy to naught. Through these activities, energy negatively relates to itself, works on itself, but in such a manner as to render itself unworkable. Accommodating both energy and anti-energy in its destructive consumption of the world, practical consciousness features a surplus of actuality: itself actual, it is also a "*relation to actuality*," *ein* Verhältnis zur Wirklichkeit (*PhG* §220)—which is what actuality actually is! Between mere reality and absolute actuality, it is the figure of a self-relation that does not know itself as such. A relation to actuality presupposes that the relating term is not identical to the one it relates to, which is to say that consciousness is both actual and non-actual. It is the place where actuality relates to actuality. The working-desiring consciousness does not, however, register this identity in difference and accentuates the hiatus between the relating and the related instead. But even when self-consciously appropriated, the speculative identity of actuality with itself is irreparably virtual: doubled into itself and the other within itself, punctuated by an irreducible spatiotemporal interval, subjectivized, interiorized, de-actualized. As Hegel puts it: "That relation to actuality is the *othering* [*Jenes Verhältnis zur Wirklichkeit ist das* Verändern]" (*PhG* §220) where the becoming-other refers to the virtualization of actuality in excess of itself, its overflow into a relation to what it is not. In its being itself and, in fact, in being more itself than itself, actuality is altered, handed over to virtual alterity, and experiences an inner perversion or conversion that is responsible for all the subsequent dialectical torsions (and distortions).

The otherness of *Wirklichkeit* to itself is the essence of power, which is nothing but pure essence. Within the shattered actuality, power is distributed unevenly: on the objective side of things, actuality is perverted into a powerless, "passive actuality" (*die passive Wirklichkeit*); on the subjective side, it is converted into "an active this-worldliness" (*PhG* §221). Energy comes to be defined with regard to its investment with or divestment of power, despite its dialectical determination (inherited from Aristotle) as not-power, or more-and-otherwise-than-potential. Polarized into extremes, actuality and activity play the roles of a thoroughly substantivized energy and the active force (*die tätige Kraft*) of de-substantivation that, through a perversion of actuality, sublates what it perverts. From the perspective of the absolute, the polarities are the extensiveness and the intensiveness of the same thing, of actuality, which Spinoza chose to designate with the word "substance" (thus, with regard to energy's substantivation). This means that "passive" actuality is never sublated from the outside, but potentiates its own sublation in that it "repels itself from itself [*sich von sich abstößt*] . . . and surrenders the repelled to activity" (*PhG* §221). In the course of its self-repelling routines, it releases speculative energy, which is harnessed in the form of power only because the co-belonging, or the synergy, of passive and active actualities (in sum: of actuality with itself) is overlooked, when not purposefully ignored. Just as the organizing contradiction of the unhappy consciousness was resolved by means of one-dimensional choices and solutions, so energy-actuality lacerated down the middle is dissolved (another possible translation: "dissolves itself") by the power—"die Macht, *worin die Wirklichkeit sich auflöst*" (*PhG* §221)—that emanates from its own self-repulsion.

Inebriated with its power, thought assails *what is* from the apparent position of exteriority, treating materiality as a passive actuality to be forcefully molded into whatever shapes. Powerful thought, which we are still not prepared to part with and which (in affinity to real or mere consciousness) is unaware of its limitations and finitude, presents itself in the form of an intention without extension, whereas the world it toys with is treated as a web of extensions without intention. Not only humility is absent from this attitude but, more significantly, energy, which is replaced by the force of repulsion. This explains why the extremes are "self-degrading" or "self-disintegrating" (*sich zersetzende*), buckling under "the absolute power [*die absolute Macht*]" of thought (*PhG* §221), which deprives both the world and itself of the possibility of self-relatedness, let alone an inner relation to the other extreme. Force, after all, is capable of nothing more than setting up an external relation to the other when power is brought to bear upon actuality. Nothing comes out of it, save for disintegration, the rending-apart of *what is* and of thought in conformity with the condition of the unhappy consciousness.

The arrogance of powerful thought, subverted by its own excess, nonetheless lowers the thinking subject back down to earth. Energy in the substantive—the shape of the unchangeable consciousness and of its individual counterpart—mutates, "relinquished" (*Verzicht*) on both sides as a result of their contact with each other (*PhG* §222). When thought claims for itself "absolute power," it taps directly into the essential, seeing that power is another name for essence, and, consequently, attributes its mastery over the world to something otherworldly, to the ideality of essence interpreted as the "beyond" (*Jenseits*). Having appreciated its dependence on the transcendent, "individual consciousness *gives thanks* [dankt]" to its source (*PhG* §222) and, recovering its humility, begins thinking outside the formal constraints of thought. Before Heidegger, Hegel implies that thinking (*Denken*) is thanking (*Danken*), putting-to-work or actuation by means of the other, who or that is yet to be remove from the piedestal of transcendence. At its origin, thinking affirms energetic powerlessness as the source of its power: in the act of thanking, it gives up the conviction that it is independent, self-enclosed, and purely virtual. It thus exchanges its autistic satisfaction in self-feeling for "the *actual* satisfaction [*die* wirkliche *Befriedigung*]" in desire, work, and enjoyment (*PhG* §222). The unhappy consciousness turns inside out, favoring neither the moment of its retreat deep inside itself nor the deadly virtualizing power it discharges into the world. Its "*actual* satisfaction" is a timeless instant within time (the being-instant of the instant, we might say, rigorously distinguishing it from the now of sense-certainty), the quiescence of energy and the energy of quiescence, the energetic fullness that had been refused to the unhappy consciousness by its schizophrenic splitting against itself.

Two words of caution must be appended to the surprising scenario in which the unhappy consciousness suddenly finds the happiness of fulfillment. First, its thankfulness originates in a self-degrading, self-disintegrating process of virtualization, and the actual giving of thanks is stamped by that entropic development. This is probably why Hegel quips that such acts of thanking are but appearances, *Scheine*, flashes of renunciation (*PhG* §222). (An appearance of renunciation is not to be dismissed out of hand: even if it serves as a smokescreen for something else, what appears is the actualization of energy in the substantive.) Second, and relatedly, the pacification and satisfaction of the unhappy consciousness make it unhappy no longer; in other words, its energetic fullness can be experienced on the condition that it shape-shifts into something else.

That "something" is the third solution to the problem of the split marked as "unhappiness": permeating virtual self-feeling with the energy externalized in a power-laden relation to actuality. The result is the redoubling of energy's work/*Wirk* in "a consciousness that has *experienced* itself as actual and effective [*sich als wirkliches und wirkendes Bewußtsein* erfahren]" (*PhG* §223), one that has circled back to itself with the awareness of its impact on the world. The hopeful undertones of this formulation foretell a more credible transition from mere to actual consciousness than the unhappy consciousness, loaded with the master-servant power imbalances, could guarantee. A genuine experience of the actuality and effectiveness of that consciousness should provoke pain, sorrow, and mourning for everything it has reduced to ash through the exercise of its absolute power, a reckoning that is just commencing today, in the twenty-first century. But a more sinister possibility is also likely: the effectiveness and actuality in question are those of power—hence, of the virtual, virtualizing, world-destroying energy enamored of itself and elevating itself into self-conscious experience. The fulfillment of the unhappy consciousness is the synthesis of the unbound bond (abstract self-feeling) and the bound unbinding (an active relation to actuality) now transparent to themselves. As a consequence, "the enemy is found in its ownmost shape [*der Feind in seiner eigensten Gestalt aufgefunden*]" (*PhG* §223), the shape of *Wirklichkeit* at peace with (and carrying on?) its de-actualizing workings.

The unhappy consciousness is frustrated by its very accomplishment and realization, counteracted by its own enactment, unworked by the workings of its energy. Instead of actuality, it retains a reality, which, unlike mere or real consciousness, it correctly grasps in its truth as nothing—"its *reality* is *immediately a nullity* [*seine* Realität unmittelbar das Nichtige *ist*]"—and adjusts its actions accordingly: "its actual activity becomes the activity of doing nothing [*so wird also sein wirkliches Tun zu einem Tun von nichts*]" (*PhG* §225). No longer simply unhappy, consciousness waxes nihilistic, so that both its workings and its works boil down to nothing, the Nothing that is the immediate (i.e., energy-less) sense of its reality where all mediations have failed. All the same, the workings of this consciousness proceed as "actual activities," knowing themselves—related to themselves—in their being-beholden to nothing. What Hegel points out here are the theoretical (or metaphysical) activities of consciousness, whereby "the immediate annihilation of its actual being [*seines wirklichen Seins*] is *mediated* through the thought of the unchangeable [*durch den Gedanken des Unwandelbaren*]" (*PhG* §226). Mediated into the immediacy of nonbeing, pure theory, nihilism, and metaphysics share the actuality of de-actualization; they are the "actual activities" counteracting "actual being," the energies that de-energize the world cast in the image of nothing—of the Nothing wherein the truth of the real has been intuited. The environmental examples of such an immediate annihilation mediated by the unchangeable abound, ranging from "depleted" uranium to plastics that take centuries to decompose. They are the perverse material embodiments of metaphysical aspirations to eternal being that bring the world to naught.

In a positive twist on nihilism, human self-actualization advances by nothing, for nothing. An exception in the natural teleological order, the human has no proper place, and it is this originary dispossession that distinguishes the human from other animals. One comes to know one's *"actual individuality,"* wirklichen Einzelnen, as a conglomerate of "animal functions," *tierischen Funktionen,* which are henceforth accorded no importance, no "spiritual essentiality" (*PhG* §225). The energy culminating in the human essence comes from nothing natural; it is dispensed by the Nothing forged in a decidedly anti-natural, anti-animal, anti-vegetal nullification of actuality, of the shape in which actual individuality appears. The unhappiness of the unhappy consciousness becomes ingrained in the human condition, provided that "happiness," in the strict sense of the fulfillment of a telos, is reserved exclusively for those who are a part of the teleological order, not for the essentially placeless humanity that prides itself on its being "for nothing." And this is not to mention another positive reading of the Nothing as a hypostasis of the gap between energy and actuality, or between self-consciousness and itself, a focus on mediation at the expense of the mediated terms.

To live up to its task, the de-actualizing, de-naturalizing energy of the anthropic exception must keep on cleansing itself of all determinate figurations, all substantivized energies by which it feels itself "polluted" (*verunreinigt*)—the purity of its power-essence, of its Nothing, compromised by actual existence. It perceives its own animality as an alien figuration, a stubborn substantivation of energy that cannot be shaken off once and for all and that, therefore, requires tenacious de-substantivizing. Its destructive workings do not yield a final work (a nullifying energy results in nothing), to the extent that the animal heritage of actual individuality returns after every bout of de-naturalization and de-substantivation. Though it is set apart from an objective teleological order, the nihilating energy at the heart of the human is not free-floating but is "fixated" (*sich ihn fixiert*) on what it takes to be an irreducible animal threat to the purity of its essence (*PhG* §225). Perversely, this fixation, negatively cathecting the Nothing at work to a despised object, detains that very object in a reaction to the being-in-the-work it aims to undo.

Cardinal as it might be, the animal figuration is not the sole target of the unhappy consciousness. With its eyes set on universal subjectivity imitating the indifference of pure being and nothing, this consciousness is intent on ridding the subject of every shred of individuality discounted as contingent. Grasping universality as working without the works (that is, as *pure* subjectivity), consciousness "frees [*befreit*] itself from activity and enjoyment as *that which is its own*" (*PhG* §228). Activity must be ideally free of acts, let alone the acts proper to a given actor; it must be nothing but thinking, which, as true, does not belong to anyone in particular. This is how nothing is done. The ideal of universal subjectivity is an impersonal I, "poor," *ärmliche* (*PhG* §225), in the actuality of traits that specify every *who* through a series of qualities that correspond to a *what*. As they cling to a pure *who*, Kant and the protagonists of existentialist thought are equally averse to energy in its substantive determination. Although uniqueness and individuality are restored to the subjects of existentialism, thanks to the relation they establish with their mortality, the path toward subjective universality passes through de-personalization (death, of course, also bears with it a de-personalizing force). When that path is blocked halfway, impersonality is taken to be synonymous with universality, and the outcome of the entire movement is bureaucracy, where the workings without works immediately flip over into the works without working. (Kafka explored with unrivaled skill the dialectical co-belonging of bureaucracy and a visceral, proto-existentialist subjectivity.) The point is that objectivity, as a cipher for actuality or for energy in the substantive key, and its attribution to the subject under the heading of "the proper" or "property," are mistaken for particularity, which is to be rejected at all costs.

Still, in what might be dubbed "dialectical justice," the subject inflicts upon itself the same fate it has prepared for the object: when the world is dispossessed of actuality, or of energy in the substantive, so is consciousness, and vice versa. In an effort to do away with everything inessential (apparent, available for-the-other, energetically concretized) in itself, the subject renounces "the *objective* aspects," gegenständliche *Seite*, of its activity outside itself, "namely, the *fruit* of its labor and enjoyment," "the *actuality* they contain [*erhaltene* Wirklichkeit]" (*PhG* §228). With this gesture, it condemns itself to fruitless labor and unfulfillable desire. More subtly, though, it ignores the relational character of property (which Marx will accentuate in virtually all his writings) as the works that *express* the working. The "objective aspects" of activity are seen as objective aspects solely from the vantage point of the absolute, of accomplished energy that revels in the resonances and synergies of being-at-work and being-in-the-work. In the phenomenology of unhappy consciousness, conversely, the externalized actuality of labor and of enjoyment is not taken as the outer *of* the inner but as merely "*external* [äußerliches] *property*" (*PhG* §228), disconnected from the interiority it substantivizes, and, therefore, something to be sacrificed to the formation of the universal.

Far from a limited oversight, the denigration of exteriority blind to its relation to the interior—that is, oblivious to energy's self-relation—is the predicament of much metaphysical and theological thought, starting with the misinterpretation of Plato's writings on the nexus of Ideas and appearances. Indeed, the fetishism of the inner has been a pivotal theoretical and practical problem of energy in the West. Traditionally, being-in-the-work is considered to be exterior and dispensable with regard to being-at-work, the shell of existence subordinated to the kernel of essence. We dream of gaining admission to the realm of essence as that of truth, getting hold of its unlimited power-possibility without having to go through its finite instantiations in actuality. By all means possible we endeavor to guard the purity of essence and, insulating it from contingencies and exposures to exteriority, to procure our energy there. Fossil fuels are the avatars of this logic, of energy conflated with power and sought in physical depths. Despite denuding the bowels of the earth, their extraction skips over, or wishes to annihilate altogether, the level of concrete exteriority; rather than actualized in existent configurations, the extracted energy resources are burned, in a tacit avowal of their affinity to the virtual, and cause the entire livable world to go up in smoke. This is what the sacrifice of exteriority looks like in *our* actuality, which promotes a myriad methods of virtualizing existence and "liberating" energy from whatever is in the work.

The circumscription of actuality to an exteriority, which is both superficial and superfluous as far as the inner essence is concerned, drains consciousness of the energy and of the freedom—of energy-actuality *as* freedom—of self-expression. Surrendering property and enjoyment, the subject "takes away from itself, in truth and entirely, the consciousness of inner and outer freedom, of actuality as its *being-for-itself* [*Bewußtsein der innern und äußern Freiheit, der Wirklichkeit als seines* Für-sich-seins]" (*PhG* §229). The subject stops at the first actuality and its never-ending negation, as though that actuality could be brushed away, instead of undergoing (with the help and across the gap of its virtualization and de-substantivation) changes conducive to its self-relatedness, torn away from itself so as to be tied to itself better. It does nothing to reconstruct actuality as a complex of interiority and exteriority, of being-at-work and being-in-the-work, corresponding to "the consciousness of inner and outer freedom." With this, the subject gives up all too easily on the work of mediation and determinate negation, the *work of and on work* that, with the absolute at its apex, broaches the possibility of transit of the inner into the outer and back again, converting energy-actuality into "being-for-itself" in the synergy of the "self" and the "other" constitutive of it.

Such shortsightedness leading to the "*actual* sacrifice [wirkliche *Aufopferung*]" (*PhG* §229) of actuality is explicable with regard to the fixation of the subject on essence, which now receives more than the token renunciation we encountered at the confluence of thanking and thinking: it receives, as an offering, both property and enjoyment, the body and the world of things collated in the category of exteriority. All this is done in the belief that energy is purified, reenergized, reanimated when released from the structures that detain it in exterior existence back into the domain of its essence. The sacrifice of exteriority as a whole is tantamount to—if we can imagine such a thing—an explosion destroying formed matter and forcing the universe to contract to a point outside space-time and finally imploding into pure inwardness: the Big Bang in reverse ... (Keep in mind that this version of the end of the world is the beginning of thinking.)

Another theoretical fiction of essentialism, which it shares with classical physics, is that nothing of note happens between the moment energy is detained in the actuality of works and the moment it is released from these substantive configurations. Only pure being-at-work matters, while being-in-the-work is just so many ripples on the otherwise smooth surface overlaying deep essence, the ripples that will clear without leaving a trace behind. For Hegel, on the contrary, every negation of actuality preserves the negated not only as a quantum of energy, but also as a qualitative shape that, having appeared, does not leave anything ever the same. The essence of energy is, after all, divided between the non-apparent essence and the apparent non-essence, both of which are indispensable to its conceptualization. This means that, in addition to the essential at-work orchestrating and determinining the non-essential in-the-work, the latter, including its renunciation and disappearance, determines the former. The conditioning of the conditioning by the conditioned is the crux of Hegel's dialectical perversion, especially in themes related to energy-actuality. In this sense, the "actual sacrifice" of actuality does not really accomplish its goal; in effect, it undermines itself to the extent that it retains in itself that which was to be sacrificed, namely the actual. Moreover, it keeps property in the form of "inner" ownness (*Eigenheit*), for instance, "in the consciousness of the decision it itself has taken" (*PhG* §229). A memory of sacrifice functions here as the exteriorization of interiority, its determination through the sacrificial act as that which is spared.

At the limit of de-personalization—an experiment which flounders—the *who* is construed as a *what* that has resisted and renounced the *what*. Essence as the most proper, the deepest interiority tirelessly at work, is neither proper nor pure nor essential enough: differentiated by means of an "inner ownness," it falls short of indifferent being or nothingness and is objectivated, infested with "external" energy: "This emptying out [*Ablassen*] that has happened *in itself* is itself an activity of the other extreme in the syllogism" (*PhG* §230). The pristine domain of essence at work has been chiseled out by non-essence in the work, or, at least, by a negative relation to this non-essence. Therefore, there is no being-at-work that is not also, by the same token, a being-in-the-work: effectiveness without effects is just that—ineffective. Across all the divisions, tears, or crises of energy, the pole that seems to have dropped out returns and, with positive powerlessness, conditions the one that has actively suppressed it.

In our commonplace conception of energy as dynamic force, which is roughly synonymous with power and an incessant working without the works, what is suppressed is energy as substantive actuality, resting in its accomplishments, though not, consequently, passive. It turns out that our situation is identical to the fixation on essence at work depicted by Hegel, and that, by extension, the problems and pitfalls we face are variations on the theme of a suicidal subject eager to purify itself and its world of anything "exterior," to relish its energy reduced to the pole of power or essence at the expense of energy figured, configured in the shape of actual beings. Below the threshold of reason, which is where we find ourselves both at this precise spot in the *Phenomenology* and in our contemporary energy paradigm, this subject engrossed in itself, in the potency of its being-at-work, would have been happy had the world never come into being or had it already ended. That perverse happiness is, in reality, the perversion of the unhappy consciousness, whose "unhappiness is the inverse [*das verkehrte*] only *in itself*: active in itself, it is a self-satisfied activity [*selbstbefriedigendes Tun*]" (*PhG* §230). Having given up enjoyment, the pure being-at-work experiences solipsistic and masturbatory self-satisfaction, a certain self-actualization due to its retreat into the inner from whatever is in the work. The energy switch is again flipped and the quiescence of desire, the energetic rest in itself connoted by *Befriedigung* (indeed: mimicking the cycle and self-relationality of *Wirklichkeit*), is granted to the survivor of a previously sacrificed external actuality.

Henceforth, the actuality of the virtual is not distinct from individual consciousness, but is inculcated in it as "the certainty of being all reality and of being in its individuality absolutely in itself [*der Gewißheit des Bewußtseins, in seiner Einzelnheit absolut an sich, oder alle Realität zu sein*]" (*PhG* §230). That certainty, in Hegel's assessment, is the dawn of reason. After aggravating the split between the two modalities of energy by sacrificing external actuality to inner activity, the absolute emerges from what or from whom was not (and could not) be sacrificed, that is, from individuality in-itself; the absolute is survival (as it will also be in Husserl's phenomenology). What or who survives the sacrifice is the verbal aspect of energy, the working, being-at-work in itself. It follows that this non-sacrificeable essence, this subjective interiority disconnected from the extension, substance, and outcomes that shape being-in-the-work, is for itself the absolute. As such, the interiority at work steps in and represents itself as much as its other, the exteriority of energy's being-in-the-work.

Reason is, therefore, a representation, *Vorstellung* (*PhG* §230), which, as we might recall, mediates between the virtual and the actual, *Energie* and *Wirklichkeit*, pure thought and expressed self-consciousness (see figure 5). Its "certainty of being all reality [*aller Realität*]" is formally true, provided that "reality" is maintained within the semantic confines of the virtual, the isolated, the idiotic and the idiomatic—for instance, the inner willingly exiled from external actuality. Problems begin when representational thinking extends the virtuality of the real to actual existence, which it purports to represent with the blessing of a self-proclaimed absolute, "individuality absolutely in itself." It is then, at the early stages of the mediation provided by *Vorstellung* still under the spell of immediacy, that the actual is rethought on the basis of the virtual, existence is regrounded on the foundation of essence, and *Wirklichkeit* is modeled on *Energie*.

C. Reason and the Self-Limitation of Energy

5. The Certainty and Truth of Reason: Reality Rediscovered

Reason erupts on the dialectical scene with the boastful, immoderate, and totalizing claim that it has "the certainty of being all reality," which is, Hegel adds, how idealism expresses its concept, *so spricht der Idealismus ihren Begriff aus* (*PhG* §232). At first, reason knows no limits, be they external (these have been surpassed thanks to the preceding movements, guaranteeing the freedom of self-consciousness) or internally self-imposed. "Idealism," so often wrongly attributed to Hegel himself, is the truth of this immoderation, this not-knowing of and not-working on the limit.

But this is what happens only at first, at the most abstract and unmediated stage when reason takes its initial steps while still very much under the spell of animism. It does not suspect, for instance, that "all reality" does not embrace everything, or, better, that in embracing everything "real" it misses the actual, which is reality's self-relation. The actual includes "actual self-consciousness," *die wirkliches Bewußtsein* (*PhG* §231), that is, real consciousness related to itself in the form of individuality sublated in the universal. Though sublated, its energy does not diminish; on the contrary, the persistence of individuated actuality compels reason to abandon its delusions of grandeur and to perform the work of mediation, mutually translating the universal and the particular consciousness. Reason is the middle; its truth "appears as the middle [*als die Mitte erscheint*]" (*PhG* §231), which provides it with the energy a pure universal does not have. Even if it takes the shape of representation (*Vorstellung*), reason's middling activity is the basis for that formalized articulation. Representation, we may conclude with broader ramifications than those apparent in Hegel's text, is secondary not to pure presence (itself virtual, abstract, and unmediated) but to the being-at-work of the middle, expressing energetic plenitude. The truth of representation is analogously not the outcome of a perfect fit of the representing and the represented; it is the actualization of the middle in self-expression, in the unity (*Einheit*) of consciousness gathered into the being-in-the-work of what "expresses *itself to itself* [sich selbst *ausspricht*]" (*PhG* §231).

Reason understood as the middle ground has no affinity to foundationalism. In fact, it is conspicuously absent from the hollow groundwork of phenomenology. There is, in a jab thrown at Kant, no such thing as pure reason at home in pure being, just as there are no purely rational beings who are not also finite and embodied. More than that, assuming it were possible, pure reason would be exceptionally unreasonable, readily consenting to the destruction of all actuality, as in Kant's endorsement of the maxim *fiat iustitia, et pereat mundus*, "let justice be done, even if the world perishes." The freedom of negating all actuality in the name of an ideal, which Kant cherishes, is misattributed to reason; it pertains instead to self-consciousness eager to "save and preserve itself for itself at the cost of the *world* or its own actuality [*auf Kosten der* Welt *oder seiner eignen Wirklichkeit*]" (*PhG* §232). The contradiction is glaring: a negatively free self-consciousness wishes to keep itself in being by taking the side of nonbeing, and it aims to garner energy from a renunciation of energy-actuality, including its "own." Kantian philosophy is culpable in passing such unreason for transcendentally purified reason.

The movement of contradiction comes to rest (*Ruhe*) in reason that sustains (*ertragen*) both moments when it "discovers the world as *its* newly actual world [*entdeckt es sie als* seine *neue wirkliche Welt*]" (*PhG* §232). A critique of reason, prioritizing the rupture or the void between terms in a relation, would regress to the split state of the unhappy consciousness that knows no rest. In contrast to this purely negative model of relationality, the rest of the contradiction (above all, of its movement) harkens back to Aristotle and the kind of energy that a free self-consciousness was deprived of. The subject of Hegelian reason no longer needs to posit itself in opposition to actuality, and it is no longer forced to make the tragic choice: "It's either me or the world." Instead, the subject foregrounds the positive terms of the relation and recognizes in the "new world" an actuality modified by contact with reason, the contact that makes it a world *of* reason, without shifting to another world than the one here-below. Upon a certain reading of this world-appropriation, we may tease out from it a colonizing adventure, to which Hegel alludes by using the words "discovers" and "new . . . world," and which, in its turn, points back to the Kantian image of reason as an island in the sea of irrationality. But the relation of appropriation goes both ways: the possessive pronoun "its" (*seine*) draws the new world toward reason, which, for its part, submits to this world, tying its own fate to that of the newly found actuality instead of preserving itself intact and unchanged at the price of existence as a whole.

As I have shown in the "Prolegomena" and have just now reiterated, there is nothing substantially novel in the "new" actuality; it is but the "old" actuality modified, mediated, and therefore energized by reason as the middle or the medium, through which it communes with itself. That is why reason acknowledges *actuality'* as its own in the certainty that "all actuality is nothing but itself [*alle Wirklichkeit nichts anders ist als es*]" (*PhG* §232): it sees in the "newly actual world," which is "all actuality," the work it has carried out—not, to be sure, the labor of an active and abstract form busy with molding passive matter, but the labor of articulating the actual with itself and, in the course of this articulation, rendering it into a world. Inherently impure, the Hegelian reason is nothing in itself. Akin to a middleman, it is a go-between interpreting the subject to itself, the world to the subject, the world to itself. Mediation per se, it already comes charged with energy, ontologically, if not epistemologically, presupposing the actuality it interrelates. The Hegelian reason is social *because and to the extent that* it is mediation, a bridge over what, from the standpoint of the unhappy consciousness, presented itself as an abyss.

At the same time, reason alone, particularly at the precarious level of its self-certainty, is an insufficient, albeit a necessary, condition for experiencing energy in all its plenitude. Although it works as a mediator and hence as the quasi-transcendental means of relating the actual to itself, it is blind to anything but the ends of its activity and deems itself, too, even in Aristotle's version, the highest end. When it asserts that it is certain of "being all reality" and, moreover, that it is conscious "of the *nonbeing* of anything other [Nichtseins *irgendeines Andern*]" to it (*PhG* §233), reason eclipses the path it treaded toward becoming-actual with the destination, in which that very path culminates. In reason "alone" (Kant's preferred condition), being-at-work and being-in-the-work drift apart in the measure that mediated outcomes prevail over the mediating coming-outside-of-itself. As mediation is hypostatized in its results, the mediator forgets her role and place (in the middle) and interjects herself at the end. A dialectical recapitulation of the "forgotten way" (*vergessene Weg*) that reason followed from meaning-making and sense-certainty onward (*PhG* §233) is thus required to repair the broken connection between the substantive and the verbal aspects of energy. Interpreted in this vein, dialectics is the anamnesis of reason's actualization, the absolute making visible the demolished scaffolding of the edifying statement: "reason is all reality and everything other to it is nothing." Or, to put it differently still, dialectics accompanies consciousness in the course of (and, absolutely, after) its transition from the nothingness that quixotically resists the being of unmediated actuality to reason's self-recognition in the actuality it has mediated.

The situation of reason observed from the standpoint of the absolute is simultaneously unprecedented and applicable to every configuration of energy that appears on the dialectical scene. Like other shapes, reason emerges immediately and "expresses an *immediate certainty*," *spricht eine* unmittelbare Gewißheit, of being all of reality (*PhG* §234). In contrast to the other shapes, however, what expresses this immediate certainty is mediation as such. And so, the *how* of the appearance is in immediate conflict with *what* appears, threatening to rob reason not of the energy it *has* but of the energy it *is*. Dialectical repetition comes to the rescue here: it mediates the mediation that has cropped up immediately (hence, abstractly), giving reason a chance to reemerge in a way that befits it and imparting to it the supplemental energy that is nowhere to be found in the first beginning. In this respect, Hegelian dialectics is emphatically different from idealism, which "does not represent the way [*der jenen Weg nicht darstellt*]" (*PhG* §234) and which, therefore, acquiesces with the confusion of means and ends, with the forgetting of actualization in the remembrance of actuality. This, too, is a face of virtualization that takes place not just when the actualizing transitions neglect the actual shapes of energy, but also, in reverse, when the already shaped actuality erases the work of actualizing (logically presupposing a prior de-actualization).

Mediation is, of course, not at all new on the dialectical itinerary: it has been doing all the work well before the formal advent of reason. Nor is the newly actual world of reason entirely new. We would be right, indeed, to be suspicious of *any* qualification of phenomena or modes of thinking as "new," a qualification that is highly fashionable in our contemporaneity with the self-described "new" materialisms, realisms, and even speculativisms mushrooming day by day. At issue is not the tired cynicism of "been there, done that," the fin-de-siècle attitude already present in the biblical Ecclesiastes and still bent on judging novelty based on criteria provided by sense-certainty. The old maxim that the new is the thoroughly forgotten old is correct on condition that the new-old names the one and only finite energy-actuality, filled out, determined, further actualized and released into its own anew, each time we come back to it. Contemplated absolutely, rather than phenomenologically, reason is not a novelty item on the dialectical production line, but another way of retrieving self-consciousness and, through it, "mere" consciousness as related to itself. To say that "reason appeals to the *self*-consciousness of every consciousness [*Die Vernunft beruft sich auf das* Selbst*bewußtsein eines jeden Bewußtseins*]" (*PhG* §234) means (not that Kant's transcendental law is resurrected by Hegel but) that reason brings out and activates the mediations latent in mere consciousness, enabling that consciousness to shed its "mereness" and to metamorphose into self-consciousness. A new shape in the phenomenological show, reason is good old energy, instrumental in binding consciousness to itself.

On the side of the subject, as much as on that of the object, a freshly discovered (*entdeckt*) actuality is an actuality that has been there all along—covered over, unthematized, and overlooked—and one, which, at the right dialectical moment, flashes up and occupies the center of attention. Disrespecting the sequential lighting-up and extinguishing of aspects of actuality, the absolute revisits them so as to highlight the surreptitious workings of the "later" in the "earlier." It precipitates actualization by what phenomenologically corresponds to the future. When reason appeals to the self-consciousness of every consciousness, it indicates an absolute reversal of the phenomenological movement from actuality to *actuality'* to *actuality"*. . . , a reflux from *actuality"* back to the apparently virginal, unmediated, merely given *actuality*. Because in Hegel's text the phenomenological flux and the absolute reflux run side by side, we, this text's conscientious readers, are in a position to piece together the two halves of energy in full awareness of the fractures that keep them apart: being-at-work and being-in-the-work, movement and rest, means and ends, or, in a word, the energy of the middle and the energy of the end.

The mutual identification of reason (certain of being "all reality") and actuality is fragile, as is any affirmation of certainty (*Gewißheit*) in Hegelian dialectics. There is no such thing as "all reality," the thing that would encompass all things and call itself "reason," unless what it refers to is an unmediated universal, the energy-less and "pure *abstraction* of reality [*die reine* Abstraktion *der Realität*]" (*PhG* §235). "All reality" is virtual, an abstraction that signifies separation and unbinding, which goes against the self-relational bonds of the actual and the mediate character of reason itself. Not yet actual, the *all* is none—a "simple *unity*," *einfache* Einheit, not of quantity but of an undifferentiated, indeterminate category in excess of the categorial manifold, which is the essence of reason (*PhG* §235).

The incipient universal one, which has assumed the shape of category, breaks up into many kinds of categories (among them, the categories of quantity *all* and of quality *reality*), replicating the virtual reality of the thing comprised of an infinite addition of multiple properties. It turns out, given this comparison, that "all reality" is, unbeknown to it, already categorially mediated and imbued with energy, its unity far from simple. "All reality" is the virtual doubly actualized; it does not amount to a plurality of things, and "we can no longer genuinely speak of *things* [*von* Dingen] at all, that is, we can no longer speak of what for consciousness would merely be the negative of itself" (*PhG* §236). Though remaining beholden to virtuality, the substitution of *Realität* for *res* suggests that the work of mediation, the enworkment of reason, is underway, and that reality itself—the world according to a category of reason—is one of this work's outcomes. It is this surreptitious substitution that gives consciousness the license to affirm itself together with the world encoded in "all reality," to avow both terms synergetically, above and beyond their participation in the indifferent universality of essence.

Depending on whether reality appears to be the same as reason or its other (be it another term in a relation insulated from, and articulated with, reason by the copula), consciousness reposes in itself, gathered with the other "*in restful . . . unity* [die ruhige Einheit]," or it finds itself in "a restless *to and fro* [*das unruhige* Hin- und Hergehen]" (*PhG* §237). In making this either/or choice, consciousness cheats itself out of energy—movement *in* rest and rest *in* movement, the working in the work and the work in the working—something that entails a blatant repudiation of the principle of noncontradiction with its certainty that rest = rest. Even if consciousness dimly suspects this, it is bereft of the means to express its appropriation by and its belonging to energy. Instead, guided by vulgar idealism, it attributes to itself the energy of appropriation: not of being but of having all reality, or, more precisely, of being all reality by virtue of having it in the full certainty that "everything is *its own* [*alles sein ist*]" (*PhG* §238). Appropriation resolves the formal contradiction of energy-actuality with regard to, on the one hand, the restful unity of the appropriating and the appropriated as a result of successfully executing the task of making-one's-own and, on the other hand, the restless movement of the appropriating drive that has not reached its desired object. But this resolution is itself formal. The label "mine" affixed to "all reality" is empty (*leere*) and pure (*reine*) (*PhG* §238), evincing how the possessive subject swaps the actual for the virtual, energy for essence, dipping back into the logic of sense-certainty. The contradiction, as well as its resolution, put to the test the proficiency with which reason sustains these different levels or juggles them simultaneously.

Deliberately or not, reason omits that it is not only the subject but also the object of appropriation, provided that it has entrusted its fate to the reality wherein it recognizes itself, and that it is speculatively identical to the appropriated *all*. Reason is thus torn between absolute idealism, which yields an empty and abstract essence of identity with the world (a relation reduced to ghostly virtuality), and "an equally absolute empiricism [*zugleich absoluter Empirismus*]," which makes the fulfillment (*Erfüllung*) of a blank categorial form possible on grounds that are alien to it (*PhG* §238). At work, reason is ardent idealism; in the work, it is virulent empiricism. Fulfillment annihilates that which was to be fulfilled (a cognitive schema filled with determinate content); virtual nonfulfillment keeps the world that was to be accepted as one's own at an infinite distance. Kant's adjudication of the dispute between the two competing strands of philosophy is effective only inasmuch as it compartmentalizes energy, severs it from itself, and draws its verbal and substantive dimensions apart, precisely on the pretext of articulating the two.

The formal act of appropriation, treating all reality as though it were an undifferentiated object, is virtualizing, de-actualizing and—I would even say—de-energizing with regard to the appropriating reason and its appropriated object. It utters, "All this is mine" in order to hide the truth, which is the opposite of what it says: "All this is *not* mine; it is alien to me; I do not recognize myself in it; I am not even interested in it—the nondifferentiation of 'all this' is a sign of my indifference toward it." That is why the formal appropriative act needs to be repeated indefinitely, the empty utterance reiterated with growing insistence. Such repetition would go some way toward a recovery of energy, but it stops short of self-appropriation through the appropriation of "all reality." Certain of its identity with the real, reason is not "the actual reason," *die wirkliche Vernunft* (*PhG* §239), sapped as it is of its energy-actuality by (1) merely saying that everything belongs to it, (2) not caring about the determinacies, differences, or distinctions that everything consists of, and (3) not recognizing itself in that undifferentiated "everything" in the very moment of claiming it as the property of reason. In other words, in its certainty of being one with reality (the certainty that constitutes appropriation at the level of knowing), the reason that is frozen in an "abstract concept" (*den* abstrakten Begriff *der Vernunft* [(*PhG* §239]) does not assimilate, digest, or work through the world and is not, in turn, assimilated, digested, or worked through by the world. Its appropriation of the other is a self-expropriation—and probably that of the appropriated other. The difference gaping between ideal and actual reason stands for the evidence of energy squandered. It is this evidentiary difference that instigates the subject to elevate certainty into truth, by filling out the empty category "mine" and, inevitably, by delivering itself to the world.

a. Observing Reason: Becoming-Actual and/as Becoming-Rational

To become actual, reason must grow concerned about actuality by first leaving the virtual enclosure of abstract conceptuality and taking interest in the fine-grained texture of "all reality." This interest in actual being spells out the fascination of reason with the world that appropriates and captivates it before it manages to capture and lay claim to the world. In a typical wordplay, Hegel illuminates the link between "being," *Sein*, and that which is one's own: for consciousness, "*being* has the meaning of *its own* [*das* Sein *die Bedeutung des* Seinen *hat*]" (*PhG* §240). What is its own, however, is not the world of things, the reality of *res*, but the field of experience, "experience itself," *Erfahrung selbst* (*PhG* §240). The actualization of reason depends on its engagement with the being of experience, with the experience of an object and the experience of experience itself: the being-in-the-work and the being-at-work of consciousness. When reason observes (and, hence, experiences) experience, it endows the latter with energetic meaning: contrary to the perception of a thing, experience is not merely given, does not "just *happen*" (*nur* geschehen, *PhG* §240), but is self-given, the first actuality internally modified, tied to itself, and, more to the point, transformed from reality into actuality. Although "mere" or "real" consciousness also deals with the self-given, it is not aware of its actuality. We have already seen how, considered absolutely, consciousness turned out to be self-consciousness; now we can add that it is, at the same time, the observing reason making this very observation about the nature of consciousness from the standpoint of the absolute.

But, to raise a question that contains in a nutshell a persistent vector of Hegel's philosophy, exactly how does reason become actual? By glimpsing itself in "*manifold being* [mannigfaltige Sein], which is to become for the I what is its own [*das seinige*] and wherein the I would view itself as an *actuality* and find itself present as a shape and as a thing [*es sich als die* Wirklichkeit *anschaue, und sich als Gestalt und Ding gegenwärtig finde*]" (*PhG* §241). No longer an empty virtual unity, "manifold being" is differentiated; the being of experience includes, ineluctably, experiences in the plural, testifying to the non-indifference of reason, its interestedness in the world, where it is the in-between (*inter-est*). In addition, reason makes a leap into the substantive dimension of energy, passing from a pure being-at-work (or its essence, at-workness) into being-in-the-work when it becomes "present as a shape [*Gestalt*] and as a thing [*Ding*]." This commitment of reason is, simultaneously, its investment into and limitation by the actuality, in which it takes interest. Whereas, for Kant, the self-limitation of reason was to be accomplished entirely in the virtual domain where it remained transcendentally "pure," for Hegel, such a process cannot commence without the substantivation of limits in determinate shapes or spatio-material figurations. Instead of the ideal limits of the Kantian paradigm, the Hegelian reason changes its point of view, beholding itself in actuality, that is, as delimited by actual shapes and things. Its presence is existential as well as material; it is neither metaphysical nor originary nor *immediately* present.

A mediated—energizing and energized—presence is entwined with absence, bringing us face-to-face with the notion of energy as a trace. Mediations are the archives of negation and loss, even if what is lost through them is, more than anything else, the illusion of immediacy accompanied by faith in fundamental givens (and pre-given ideas) that are valid once and for all. Traces are weak presences with diminished energy only compared to the total and overwhelming presence of metaphysics. But they are energetically vibrant provided that "strong" presence itself is understood as the product of a virtual beginning, which is not ready (in truth, is never ready) to begin: to begin transitioning to the middle, realizing that it has always already been in the middle from the very beginning, delivering itself to the workings and the work of mediation, losing and finding itself again in medias res. In this sense, Hegel forewarns his readers not to embark on a futile search for the essence of reason in "the entrails of things," *Eingeweide der Dinge*, while ignoring the prehistory of its mediation with things. Rather, reason "must have earlier completed [*vollendet*] itself in itself in order to be able to experience its completion [*Vollendung*]" (*PhG* §241). Rotating in the circle of energy, the experience of completion is possible after the workings of reason have been completed, accomplished in its works. The task of reason has been consummated, fulfilled, substantivized in the actuality with which it had suffered through mutual transformations, inversions, and perversions (this "suffering-through" *is* experience). But the completion in question also touches upon something other than reason—the concept and practice of energy consummated and fulfilled in actuality (the ensemble of completed works) that remembers the path of its actualization. The becoming-actual of reason and the becoming-rational of actuality are, again in a circular fashion, the preconditions for energy's movement-rest.

The above interpretation of Hegel could prove useful for an alternative reception of discourses revolving around "the completion of metaphysics," *Vollendung der Metaphysik*—an expression Heidegger coined in his Nietzsche seminars. Lurking behind this expression and its insertion into the context of modern or postmodern nihilism is an unarticulated idea of energy and its exhaustion in light of all the possibilities first indicated in Platonism and depleted with Nietzsche's final inversion of Plato. Assuming, however, that energy grows with every repetition, that it does not move from one possibility to another while depleting the possible in its actualization, the linear narrative of metaphysical completion falters. Given what we have said about the energy of Hegel, the completion of metaphysics—of a fixation on the one essence that claims all actuality for itself—signifies a return to the substantive dimension of energy as actuality-in-the-work now articulated with the verbal-subjective dimension of being-at-work. Energy has two essences, which means that there is no more essence, but only the actualizing and the actualized, the path and the places to which it leads. The Hegelian *Vollendung* does not denote perfection, *Vollkommenheit*, as Heidegger seems to think,[3] but the energizing and energized fulfillment of the finite in its absolute (infinitely reiterated) finitude.

We may find it rather odd that on the course to its completion reason takes the detour of observation, which is usually associated with passive contemplation, ideally detached from the observed object. In fact, that is how the observing reason phenomenologically experiences itself: "concerning itself with things, it supposes that it is taking them in their truth as sensuous things set over and against the I" (*PhG* §242). Something else altogether happens absolutely, demonstrating that "mere observation" is a misnomer, necessary as it may be to the functioning of reason experienced from within, in the midst of its involvements in the world, or in a shorthand, phenomenologically. There, at the level of the absolute, reason's "actual activity [*wirkliches Tun*] . . . knows [erkennt] things and transforms their sensuousness into *concepts*, that is, into a being which is at the same time the I." In this fashion, it discovers itself "as an existing object, as an *actual, sensuously present* mode [*als* wirkliche, sinnlich-gegenwärtige *Weise*]" (*PhG* §242). The actual activity of reason is what makes its actualization possible; its being-at-work in the observing mode, dismissed by reason itself as a kind of non-work or a virtual stance that avoids meddling with *what is*, potentiates its being-in-the-work, a transition toward an "actual, sensuous-present" mode of reason's existence. Quantum physics, too, admits that the observation of quantum phenomena is never detached, that in such an observation the observing subject, or the instrument the subject utilizes, interferes and imparts a portion of its energy to, or receives a portion of energy from, that which is observed. But what quantum theorists are doing is reconciling the phenomenological and the absolute in an immediate way, collapsing the one into the other at a certain level of experience (or non-experience). They stress the instability and indeterminacy of quantum energy, whereas Hegel points out energy's overdetermination, its mediated yet also circular becoming on the basis of energy. The "actual activity" of observing reason thus simultaneously comes to fruition in two "objects": reason's own actual-sensuous presence in the world and the absolute actuality of dialectical energy, retracing (and further actualizing) Aristotle's *energeia*.

i. Observation of Nature: De-Inscription and Organic/Ergonic Life
Let us make another attempt at summarizing Hegel's dialectical approach to energy. Within the process of its *logical* unfolding, energy is

first veiled in its other—a potentiality that has not yet worked itself out, has not yet negatively determined itself, and has not yet been contained "in" the works. It is energy *in potentia* that, in this *in*, is utterly outside of itself. Second, energy is unveiled in the shape of actuality or in the shape of unveiling as such: turned inside out, phenomenally accessible, nothing in itself, existing for the other. But, third, this unveiling is further veiled and obscured insofar as it precludes the memory and the persistent repetition of actualization; what the sheer phenomenality of the actual hides from sight is that energy is an actuality that has arrived at its resting place *and* an actuality still on its way, including this being-on-the-way or being-at-work within the point of arrival, within being-in-the-work. Since it is impossible to elucidate this energy dualism either conceptually or phenomenologically, Hegel resorts to the absolute in his effort to juggle energy's veiled unveiling.

In the process of energy's *historical* unfolding, the first and second stages change places. Energy is thought by the ancients as actuality in the substantive, as that which is (what it is), while potentiality or *dunamis* refers to insufficient actualization, a deficit relative to the default state of energetic plenitude. In the modern conception of energy, what comes to the fore is the possibility, itself seemingly inexhaustible, of activation or potentiation only temporarily detained in forms of substantive reality. From the brilliant, exposed, essentially superficial energy of the Greeks, we have retreated to the dim, hidden, deeply withheld energy of modernity. What Hegel shows is that neither is "false," yet neither is entirely true either; the ancient and modern conceptions and practices of energy are each indexed to a partial truth, which only finds itself at home in dialectical *Wirklichkeit*. Whereas, for the ancients, energy is behind us (and therefore present before us in the shape of *energeia*), for the moderns, it is ahead of us, in its potentially inexhaustible (but actually exhausted) permutations. Hegel, for his part, locates energy between "behind" and "ahead," irreducible either to the one or to the other, resting-vacillating in-between and reiterating this movement-rest along in its every iteration. Such is the portrait of historically mediated absolute spirit as energy.

If one wished to be methodical and meticulous about the divergence, corresponding to the difference between phenomenological and absolute perspectives, then one would need to examine every dialectical stage against the double backdrop of the logical and the historical development of energy. On the one hand, the observation of nature, in line with other points of departure for logical unfolding, is steeped in a multiplicity of the observed that is immediately universal. Not yet actualized in the natural world, the energy of reason is veiled right in the midst of that world's unveiling promised by observation. In a historically mediated approach, on the other hand, it is assumed that everything is already actual independently of the observer. Because nature hides its secrets, our task is to wrest them from it, thus fulfilling the potentiality of knowing in a linear sequence progressing from total ignorance to a complete and accurate image of the entire universe.

What historical reason observing nature is unable to comprehend is that it is co-determined (or, in other words, actualized, filled out, and energized) with the phenomena it observes. The energy of knowing is a synergy of co-actualization, the smelling, tasting, hearing, touching, and seeing determining "the truth" in the same degree as the consciousness that smells, tastes, hears, touches, and sees determines what counts as "the object of this sensation" (*PhG* §244). The mutual outlining of the sensing and the sensed, their becoming-actual in tandem with one another, is also an axiom of Husserlian phenomenology: that is how an "empty" intentionality is "fulfilled" in intuition. Although Husserl himself failed to spot any proximities whatsoever between his thought and Hegel's philosophy, the virtual emptiness and the actual fulfillment of consciousness is one such overlap, largely attributable to the shared Aristotelian background of the two thinkers. The same goes for their common preoccupation with the universality of the sensuous, a preoccupation which nonetheless leads them in different directions: Husserl is convinced that an act of meaning is exhausted in the meant, while Hegel sees in meaning an ongoing mediation: "the perceived should at least have the meaning of a *universal* [*die Bedeutung eines Allgemeinen*], not of a *sensuous 'this'*" (*PhG* §244). I would argue that their implicit philosophies of energy may explain this contrast: Husserl imbues meaning with the energy of the beginning that is gradually spent along the way toward and obviated in the meant; Hegel envisions meaning as the energy of the middle, mediation per se, where reason at work intersects with reason in the work of observation.

On the playing field of observing reason, the mediation of the singular and the universal, of what is separate because encrypted in itself and of what is open to all—this mediation supplants the mediation of the actual and the rational. Modified *actuality'*, *actuality"*, and so on are, from the standpoint of observation, singular universalities or universal singularities. Even before it understands this, the reason that appropriates "all reality" as "mine" "expresses in a universal mode what in actuality [*in der Wirklichkeit*] is at hand only in an individual mode" (*PhG* §245). The phrase "in actuality" here elliptically refers to "in the merely given or not yet modified actuality," where the actual is indistinguishable from the real; by expressing its individuality universally (if only by means of affixing an empty universal label *mine* to *what is*), reason negates, de-actualizes, or virtualizes that first actuality, and so renders it in truth what it already is in itself: virtual. The key is not in what that actuality is but in how it becomes what it is; de-actualized by appropriative reason, it recoils into virtuality in a singularly universal way.

The observing reason initiates its work of mediation with the help of description, into which it pours its naturalistically inclined efforts. Description, *das Beschrieben*, is "a superficial form of universality [*oberflächliche Form der Allgemeinheit*], into which the sensuous is incorporated but without the sensuous itself having become a universal" (*PhG* §245). It operates *as though* it did not mediate the sensuous, did not provide the medium for the universalization of sensuous particularity, did not imbue it with the energy of the actual. The problem with description is that it is blind to its own mediacy and, when aware of the mediating role it plays, attempts to do away with this role, to approximate immediacy as much as possible, to subtract or de-inscribe itself. According to its own ideal, description stands for a pale image of actuality, hopelessly removed by the linguistic intervention from that which it describes.

It is true that description is not actual enough, albeit for another reason altogether: it is too real, chasing as it does after the described (and finally the indescribable) "this." That is to say: description does not do sufficient work on (and with) *what is*, to the extent that it declines the invitation to negate the first actuality of sensuous idiosyncrasy; it refuses to be energized and to energize *what is* and is content, instead, with the self-obliterating act of a cold reflection devoid of reflexivity. This rejection of energy is, for it, energizing, and this is what is considered "objective."

Description subjugates itself to the described object and—in this very subjugation—repeats the object in words, precisely as described. Whether or not it intends this, the repetition is energizing and actualizing, even within narrow descriptive confines. In describing the object, description above all describes itself as a way, valid in its own eyes, of knowing any object: "what allows things *to be known* [*woran die Dinge* erkannt *werden*] is more important for it than the residual range of sensuous properties" (*PhG* §246). Despite its best efforts to delete or de-inscribe itself, to fashion a transparent form that is indifferently receptive to and only externally articulated with the indefinitely variable content that fills it, description shifts the spotlight to itself and, thereby, already moves past the first actuality. In so doing, it effects a doubling that is the signature feature of energy, above all of the speculative variety. Single-mindedly focusing on the known object, it cannot avoid expressing what is at work in knowledge. Hegel calls this description's "doubled essentiality," *diese gedoppelten Wesentlichkeit* (*PhG* §246). If its energy is still rather undeveloped, virtual, shackled to a split in *essence*, that is because description is not self-related, or self-conscious, save for the negative self-relatedness of policing and editing out anything that does not seem to derive from the described object itself. Succinctly stated, it does not touch upon actuality, unlike the dialectical description of description, which, distinct from a meta-description, releases the energy locked in these exertions of observing reason.

The limit of description is also double, with the lower edge of its frame circumscribed by the indescribable "this," too singular and abstract to be put into words, while the upper edge is demarcated by the non-persistence of static determinateness that was to serve as the principle behind differentiation, pointing out "the distinguishing marks," *die Merkmale*, of things. The two self-limitations of description adumbrate the scope of its actuality with the impossibility to descend to pure empiricity, on the one hand, and to ascend to determinateness set in motion, obtained through oppositional relations, on the other (*PhG* §247). Its energy runs out when faced either with an isolated virtuality or with the self-negated actuality of existence. In the latter case, the insufficiency of description becomes palpable in the "instinct of reason," *Vernunftinstinkt*, which, seeking the laws of nature (i.e., the more or less predictable patterns and regularizable arrangements of natural phenomena) with an energy that is itself under the spell of unmediated, unconscious, biological force, consults "the *existing* actuality [seiende *Wirklichkeit*]" of the described objects only as materials to be sublated in the formulation of such laws. The existing actuality of static objective determinations is de-substantivized, dispensed back to the virtual level where it belongs, while the virtual, further virtualized, makes room for the self-given actuality of the law: the dialectically prior actuality "in fact vanishes, and the components of laws become pure moments or abstractions [*diese wird ihm in der Tat verschwinden, und die Seiten des Gesetzes zu reinen Momenten oder Abstraktionen werden*]" (*PhG* §248). Law is the actuality of description, which has outlived its function and which has transferred its energy to the concept.

In the course of this transfer, "sensuous actuality," *sinnliche Wirklichkeit* (treated by Hegel as roughly synonymous with "existing actuality"), loses the countenance of an indifferent and enduring actuality in itself—"*das gleichgültige Bestehen der sinnlichen Wirklichkeit an sich*" (*PhG* §248). Put to work by the law, it does not merely disappear but discovers universality in itself, or finds itself in the universal, in a "rational universality" that reveals itself "as the present and the actual [*als das Gegenwärtige und Wirkliche*]" (*PhG* §249). In other words, the actual and the rational are co-actualized, co-energized, synergized in an observation that surpasses description. Hegel expresses their dialectical identity in strikingly energetic terms when he writes that "what is universally valid is also what is universally effective [*Was allgemein gültig ist, ist auch allgemein geltend*]"

(*PhG* §249), where effectiveness stands for actuality, and validity connotes rationality. There is no validity that is neither at work nor in the work, just as there is no enworkment that is not valid, validated by observing reason. It is a gross misunderstanding of Hegel to impute a normative bent to his equation "is = ought," which is a sine qua non of dialectical ontology as the ontology of energy. I am not even referring to the patently Hegelian way of reading the equation where the "is" says, at the same time, "is not," its speculative non-identity destabilizing every conceivable "ought" that follows. Rather, I am thinking of how the possible, out of which the thin fabric of the "ought" is spun, belongs, along with power and force, to the actual in the form of energy repelled from itself and made other to itself. The possible is actual being or the being of actuality alien to itself and, therefore, dialectically, most fully itself in its otherness.

The perspective on reason's appropriation of all reality as "mine" shifts by 180 degrees when reason defined in terms of "this certainty of having reality [*diese Gewißheit, Realität zu haben*]" (*PhG* §249) is inverted, converted, or perverted into the insight that "the truth of the law is essentially *reality* [*die Wahrheit des Gezetzes wesentlich* Realität *ist*]" (*PhG* §250). Literally, the truth of the law is a thing, a shape of energy, the figuration of an act in the work, whereby reason produces universal effects in the world. Having just laid claim to reality, reason is itself realized or thingified in the valid and effective outcomes of its sweeping movement in and through existence. And the reification of reason is only the start of its energizing self-alienation. "Essentially *reality*," it is a virtual, spectral thing, very much in denial concerning its own thinghood. It is not yet (this "not yet" is a temporal marker within the sequence of dialectical phenomenology) actually *actuality*, which it will be in a different shape, no longer as outwardly observing.

Without yet amounting to a full-fledged actuality of reason, the laws inferred from observation and description combine disparate dimensions of energy-actuality, namely the verbal and the substantive, being-at-work and being-in-the-work. The law "counts as law because it presents itself in appearance [*in der Erscheinung sich darstellt*] and, at the same time, is in itself a concept" (*PhG* §250). As a concept, the law is at work; in its appearances, it is in the work. It exposes itself, handing itself over in a determinate configuration to the observing subject, and, at the same time, it dictates the very determinateness of determination. (The universal exposure of law—its phenomenality and vulnerability, outwardness and being up for grabs—is what makes it universal.) Energy dissipates in the absence of tensions between being, phenomenologically reduced to appearance ("what does not appear . . . is nothing at all [*was nicht erscheint, ist . . . gar nicht*], *PhG* §249), and the concept that comes about from the work of consciousness "purifying" (*reinigen*) the law still "enveloped in individual sensuous being [*umhüllt von einzelnem sinnlichem Sein*]" (*PhG* §251). Besides individual laws, the dialectical unity of concept and appearance, of being-at-work and being-in-the-work, is that of the observing reason as such, insofar as it is, in its turn, "observed" from the platform of the absolute, upon which it appears and is conceived as a shape of energy-actuality as much as a shaping, unshaping, reshaping activity. Only then does it become actually actual, as opposed to essentially real.

Promising as it may be, particularly in comparison to mere description, the pendulum of the laws of nature swings to de-substantivation; it dispossesses the things it embraces of their own actuality, extracting their properties and disposing of them as bodies: "the relation between acid and base and their movement with respect to each other constitute a law where these oppositions appear as bodies. All these isolated things, however, have no actuality [*Allein diese abgesonderten Dinge haben keine Wirklichkeit*]" (*PhG* §251). Under the aegis of the laws of nature, the corporeity of each thing (that is, the shape of its energy) has no meaning. What does acquire significance is the relation of mutually negating qualities, treated as a thing by the scientific rationality that permits such a relation to be the new substantivation of energy-actuality. Absorbed into the law, material things dissolve in it without a chance to be "resurrected" in the universal, to which they have arrogated their properties: "so, too, acid and base are not bound as properties to this or that *actuality* [*so ist Säure und Base nicht als Eigenschaft an diese oder jene* Wirklichkeit *gebunden*]" (*PhG* §251). This is how the modified *actuality'* rolls down the slippery slope of abstraction: by parting ways with the world discernible through phenomenological experience and replacing it with the properties and interactions that furnish another world. This is, also, where the crisis of the sciences originates—in a careless hypostasis that represses the sources of the abstractions it lends a body to.

The actuality of an object inevitably undergoes metamorphosis together with that of the subject, meaning that the energetic shape of observation changes in concert with the observed. Just as the result at which observing reason arrives is "twisted" (is submitted to a *Wendung*) into hypostatized qualities without a body, a materiality without matter, so "a new shape of its observation comes on the scene [*neue Gestalt seines Beobachtens damit auftritt*]" (*PhG* §253). Contrary to what might be expected, the observing and the observed are not detained at the level of pure abstraction; rather, the twisting of actuality dispenses with the body as inert or inorganic and arrives at the object which is "not a *result*," *nicht* Resultat (*PhG* §253), but which "contains in itself the process in the *simplicity* of the concept [*den Prozeß in der* Einfachheit *des Begriffes an ihm hat*]" (*PhG* §254). The concept is "simple" because the two dimensions of energy-actuality are combined in organismic unity where the product *is* the process and the work *is* the working or the enworkment of life. Substantive energy is de-substantivized in itself, and living as such is possible thanks to this ongoing de-substantivizing of substance, this de-inscription of the body related to itself, this self-virtualization of the actual, which has been variously called "the soul" or "the principle of vitality."

The simplicity and apparent sufficiency unto itself of the organic instantiation of energy renders its relation to the inorganic element indifferent, *Gleichgültig*. Actual in itself, the organism is inserted into its milieu, which "cannot be conceived to be internal to the essence" (*PhG* §255), as though that milieu were the plain of virtual pure being. Our global environmental crisis is, in part, due to a historical exacerbation of this attitude. Obviously, Hegel sees in animality a model for organismic life and implicitly dismisses the plant's mode of coexistence with its environment as essential to shaping the plant's living, ever-metamorphosing body. On the condition that one leap over vegetal life, the necessary relation between the organic and the inorganic "ceases to have a sensuous existence, cannot be observed in actuality, and instead takes leave of actuality [*kann nicht mehr an der Wirklichkeit beobachtet werden, sondern ist aus ihr* herausgetreten]" (*PhG* §255). The absorption of actuality and actualization into the organism divests non-organismic existence *and* the space between the two of actuality, as the organic-inorganic nexus falls apart into mutual indifference. The emergence of the organism—that is to say, of the animal—on the dialectical scene denatures nature, siphons energy-actuality from the inorganic world and from its relation to a form of life that negates its own static character. Nature does not thereby vanish; its "taking-leave of actuality" signals that it becomes or remains a reality: non-self-related, abstract, exhibiting a dearth of mediations and self-negations.

The necessity of the organic-inorganic relation will need to be reconstructed starting from the inner necessity of organismic existence. The purpose of an organic being is "merely conserving itself," *erhält sich nur* (*PhG* §256). It projects itself into the future by way of iteration or self-reiteration, repeating and reaffirming its existence, and thus building up its energy-actuality. So, either the absolute is styled after organic being, or this being comes close to the absolute in its own mode of existence. In a properly Aristotelian move, and as a rejoinder to Kant, organismic energy is an autotelic circle, a self-intending purpose concerned with its own preservation. It is there that actuality now lies or moves: the actual is present (*vorhanden*) "not merely as an *external relation* but as its *essence*.

This actual, which is itself purpose, relates purposefully to the other [*Dieses Wirkliche, welches selbst ein Zweck ist, bezieht sich zweckmäßig auf Anderes*]" (*PhG* §257). The autotelic circle of organismic energy is a centripetal force, a self-intending purpose purposefully sucking the purposeless into itself and putting this other at the service of its own conservation. The virtual indifference affecting the relation of the organic and the inorganic is sublated by the non-indifference of an organism toward its fate.

The enworkment of living energy requires putting the world of the elements to work for it within and despite the scheme of abstract freedom, despite, that is, the non-essential belonging or the essential non-belonging of the one and the other in the unity of a dialectical relation. Intending the other, it intends nothing but itself: "What it aims at through the movement of its activity is *it, itself*, and that it aims only at itself is its *self-feeling* [*Was es also durch die Bewegung seines Tuns erreicht, ist es selbst; und daß es nur sich selbst erreicht, ist sein* Selbstgefühl]" (*PhG* §257). A movement that rests in itself—the energy of movement-rest as the self-actualization and the actuality of the self—is formally analogous to thought thinking itself. But formal analogies are insufficient at this stage. In the becoming-actual of the rational, thought is thinking itself in, as, and through organismic existence. There is no end here that is not, strictly speaking, also an end-in-itself achievable by means of the negation of itself (and of the self) and mediated, in turn, by the negation of the other, which is a means, precisely, to the extent that it is incapable of self-negation.

Let us be clear: we have moved past the thinking of life and its living energy when (1) what is at stake is the question of a relation between the organic and the inorganic, or of ends and means, that are already the categories of reason; and (2) the observing reason itself attends to organismic energy, rather than allow consciousness and life to bluntly confront one another. Self-consciousness "finds in the observation of organic nature nothing other than this essence [of itself]," the essence of self-energizing and self-actualizing, of "drawing a difference that is not a difference at all" (*PhG* §257). From the standpoint of the absolute, which repeats in itself the moments or shapes it overviews, organicity and reason appear as shapes of energy-actuality figured in a circle. In Husserlian phenomenology, this compilation of shapes results in sedimentation that suffocates its own animating impulse and needs to be de-sedimented to reanimate the beginning; for Hegel, energy-actuality intensifies in the procession of its shapes, which have to do less with indifferently conjoined mineral sediments and more with organic articulations.

In order to achieve such an effect, reason must admit that, in addition to shaping and unshaping forms of existence, it is also a shape, energy substantivized. "It is a necessity for reason to intuit itself as a thing, its own concept falling outside it [*Ebenso hat die Vernunft die Notwendigkeit, ihren eigenen Begriff als außer ihr fallend, hiemit als Ding anzuschauen*]" (*PhG* §259). Is this idea of a "concept falling outside itself" not similar to the notion of energy, which thrives on the collapse of its self-identity? But doesn't this idea also correspond to the very concept of the concept, its movement and vitality explicable with reference to its ec-static situation? Phenomenologically construed, reason's "own concept" is limited to an active shaping and analysis of existence, to energy's verbal dimension, which includes its actualizing and de-actualizing effectiveness. There is nonetheless also a shadowy, still more proper, "own" concept, which, to observing reason, appears to be radically other and improper: its figuration as a thing. What is most proper to the concept (above all, to the concept of reason) is its distribution between its workings and the works, the activities and their outcomes, neither of which can legitimately lay hold of the concept as such. Beyond a disfiguring representation of *what is* in the ether of abstraction, the concept is also a figure that stabilizes energy in the substantive key. It is, among other things, a thing, that is to say, a figure of the figure, the symbol of shape, a spatial arrangement of qualities over and above an internal ideal.

The perversion of observing reason, given to observation in the form of a thing and therefore as an energetic shape, is indispensable for the appreciation of organic energy beyond the limits of representational thought. When reason supposes that its essence is analytic and synthetic activity, it produces in itself a splitting (in the psychoanalytic sense of the term) whereby its own substantive dimension is externalized and falls by the wayside. It consequently transforms body and life, matter and form, into "the kind of opposition that conforms to its point of view" (*PhG* §261), so that organic being "emerges as a relation between two *existing* and *fixed* moments": "an opposition between the organic *concept of purpose* and *actuality* [*Gegensatz des organischen* Zweckbegriffs *und der* Wirklichkeit]" (*PhG* §262). While energy falls on the side of the concept of purpose, life, activity, and a dynamic form, actuality coincides with the exteriority of the body, matter, the inorganic receptacle for the organic setting-to-work, and passivity. As long as the concept of reason persists in suppressing its thinghood, the concept of *Wirklichkeit* remains similarly skewed and comes to designate all that is outer—"*dem* Äußern *gemeint*" (*PhG* §262)—to the detriment of the tension constitutive of energy-actuality. With nothing but the potentiality to act or "the concept of purpose" for its content, energy winnowed from actuality is a tool from the cache of immature reason that is unprepared to contend with its own figuration as a thing. (Even critical theory is not critical enough in this respect, in that it considers this figuration to be a fetish.)

At this point, de-inscription demands the impossible. Having urged the observing reason on a quest for objectivity to subtract itself from what is observed, de-inscription prohibits the already diminished reason from participating in the objectivity of the object as actuality. To deal with the aporia, Hegel shifts the spotlight onto the *ontological* shape of the inner, of the purely active-conceptual-energetic aspect of organicity: "It is now to be seen what *shape* [Gestalt] the inner and outer have in their being [*in seinem Sein*]" (*PhG* §264). The point of this shift is that, even granting that the inner does not appear in the shape of a thing, it appears before observing reason as an "object . . . that exists and is present at hand for observation [*Gegenstand . . . seiendes und für Beobachtung vorhanden*]" (*PhG* §264). What Hegel does here, of course, is restore the shape, or being-in-the-work, of energy from the standpoint of the absolute, peering over the shoulder of observing reason. In doing so, he resuscitates the dialectical unity of energy-actuality—of the shaping and the shaped—by transposing it onto the difference between the phenomenological and the absolute.

So, then, what is the ontological shape of the inner in organic life as reason observes it? In theology, it is the "soul," *Seele*, the subjective side of universality that "appears as activity," as "the *movement* of *vanishing* actuality [*die* Bewegung *der* verschwindenden Wirklichkeit]" that confronts the objective universality of the outer "existing as the *restful being* of the organic [*in dem* ruhenden Sein *des Organischen besteht*]" (*PhG* §265). In their simplicity, the inner and the outer, the soul and the body, play the roles of the animating and the animated factors within the setting-to-work of organic life. Things are not this simple, though. Energy does not reside in the soul as the animating principle, which, exactly as a principle, is an active abstraction saturated with power rather than energy. Movement and rest are variously indexed to *Wirklichkeit*: the latter is its default state, whereas the former is the negation of restful being. If the soul animates by causing actuality to vanish, by suspending actuality in the movement of vanishing instead of destroying the actual as such, then it procures energy from the vanishing of energy (in the substantive). The ontological shape of the inner is the unfixing of physical shapes, upon which it is obliged to work within the energetic knotting of organic being.

It could not have escaped Hegel that the organic domain is *ergonic*—both etymologically and conceptually tied to the work embodied in the organism and its organs. It is along these lines that shape (i.e., the substantive component of energy) is the "presentation of an actualized essentiality [*Darstellung der verwirklichten Wesenheit*]" (*PhG* §265), the animating principle at work in the work that is a living body. The organs are hybrids of the actualizing and the actualized, the tools into which an organism is differentiated, blurring the distinction between an instrument and its user, the concept of means and that of purpose. Via this differentiation, giving up on a simple opposition between the shape and the shaping, the organism rises to another level of energy-actuality. Essentiality actualized, being sheds its virtuality and purity and is filled out with determinate, self-negated content, which is, in this case, the organismic shape as the expression of the inner principle. The movement of vanishing actuality itself becomes actual; action produces effects in the world (an external actuality surrounding actual corporeity) thanks to the concerted workings of nerves and muscles, at least in animals with a central nervous system. Preparing the mutual enworkment of "body" and "soul," the organs are a fold in actuality, its doubling into the actualizing and the actualized at the apex of living energy.

More so than organs, organic systems (*organische Systeme*) are "the *actual* [wirkliche] and at the same time *universal* [allgemeine] parts" of the whole (*PhG* §267). Actual universals include the nervous system with its "sensibility," the musculature with its "irritability," and the digestive tract, as well as the sexual organs instrumental for reproducing individual existence in itself or in another like it. Ancient philosophers, such as Plato and Aristotle, had an inkling of the convergence of actuality and universality in organic systems when they postulated the correspondence between nutritive, sensitive, and rational souls, on the one hand, and certain bodily loci, such as the stomach, the heart, and the head, on the other. Compared to the animal, the plant is, again for Hegel, virtual existence under the sway of pure being, undifferentiated into distinct organs and organic systems. "The vegetable in fact expresses merely the simple concept of the organism, its *moments undeveloped* [*Der vegetabilische drückt auch in der Tat nur den einfachen Begriff des Organismus aus, der seine Momente* nicht entwickelt]" (*PhG* §265). For this reason, vegetal life is deemed to be poor in energy: the abstract essence of the organic concept is not actualized in the plant and, therefore, endures in the "simplicity" of reproduction, according to Aristotle's conclusions, which Hegel silently accepts. But, though plants obviously do not have muscular and nervous systems, they exhibit all the features of irritability and sensibility, as Schelling and Darwin corroborated already in the nineteenth century. They are, moreover, the living mediations between the organic and the inorganic domains—figures of an organicity that, much like the concept, stands outside itself. Plants brim with energy, which, along with their kind of life, belongs to the in-between.

A possible explanation for this oversight on the part of Hegel is that he underestimated the fluidity of organic determination when it came to the question of vegetal vitality. Generally speaking, the meaning of the organic is twofold: it is, "on the one hand, a part of organic *forma-*

tion [*der organischen* Gestaltung] and, on the other hand, a *universal fluid* determinateness [allgemeine flüssige *Bestimmtheit*]" (*PhG* §268). While "formation," *Gestaltung*, is in itself a synergy of shape and shaping, "universal fluid determinacy" embraces determinacy and indeterminacy, the actual and the virtual aspects of energy. This is why Hegel claims that "the component called *the inner* has its own *outer* component [*Die Seite, welche das* Innere *heißt, hat ihre eigene* äußere Seite]" (*PhG* §268); the shaping has its own shape, the determining has its own concrete determinacy. In the plant, determinacy is so fluid that organic shapes are effectively indistinguishable from shaping—hence, Goethe's suggestion to comprehend vegetal being by way of metamorphosis. Above the threshold of fluidity he finds manageable, Hegel ceases to register living determinations and instead focuses on indeterminacy, virtuality, empty and abstract possibility, the simplicity of the concept. As a result, the dialectical plant flourishes on the barren ground of pure being and is relegated to the territory of nothingness, to the essence of life devoid of actuality.

Why, nonetheless, is the organic realm *ergonic*? What makes it especially hospitable to energy? Hegel's answer is: it elevates life from reality to actuality, gifting vitality with organismic self-relatedness. The move from reality to actuality is accomplished by the synecdoche of organs and organic systems that constitute the entire organism. An organic part is only organic to the extent that it is a part, which, negating its own limits, puts the whole to work—something that does not happen in the inorganic realm. Sensibility, for instance, "goes beyond the nervous system and pervades all the other systems of the organism," prompting its "reflection into itself," *Reflection in sich* (*PhG* §270). Given this conclusion, the plant is real and the animal is actual; distinct from animal organs, plant parts are detachable from the whole, which is not reflected into itself but turned outward. Hegel could not have known about hormonal or calcium networks traversing the extension of the plant or the situational integration of its parts with the help of airborne or below-ground biochemical signaling. What these recent discoveries in plant science reveal, from the philosophical perspective, is a non-organismic (not-totalizing, non-suffocating) modality of integration and self-integration, which holds the promise of energy no less vibrant than that proper to the animal organism. Within the new parameters set by speculative biology, we need not choose between organization and disorganization, order and chaos, enworkment and unworkability. Vegetal life presents us with a determinacy that is not negative, one that does not depend on the negation of itself and the other.

Apropos of organic existence as a whole (which, as we have seen, by and large excludes plants), Hegel imposes a limit on the fluidity of determinacy indexed to the "determinate opposition" (*bestimmte Gegensatz*) of irritability and sensibility, passivity and activity, actualization and actuality. He concedes, moreover, that such oppositions are easily detachable from their physical substratum and betray their logical core: "the empty play of legislation is not tied to the organic moments . . . ; it in general rests on the lack of acquaintance with the logical nature of these oppositions [*mit der logischen Natur dieser Gegensätze*]" (*PhG* §272). Organicity is put to work as a physio-logy, with the oppositional works of organic systems overlaying the workings of logical principles. At the same time, Hegel notes that there is not a straightforward symmetry between sensibility and irritability; their contrast is diluted by a third term, namely "reproduction, which does not stand opposed to these moments that are opposed to each other [*denn Reproduktion steht mit jenen Momenten nicht in einem Gegensatze, wie sie gegeneinander*]" (*PhG* §273). Reproduction, according to Hegel's appropriation of the Aristotelian *to threptikon*, is the principle of vegetal existence and it is not surprising that, like that existence itself, this principle eschews oppositionality. Neither physically nor logically excluding the other, a reproductive organic system overflows both organicity and systematicity. It hints at another energy, which works without pitting the one against the other and without setting the one against itself. And it redirects divergence into diversity, not into a lethal stalemate.

The ambiguity that reproduction injects into the physio-logical construction of organismic energy has long-lasting effects. As soon as Hegel asserts that "organic actuality [*die organische Wirklichkeit*] has in itself such an opposition as its concept expresses, which can be determined as irritability and sensibility," he is forced to add that "both of these once again appear to be at variance with reproduction [*von der Reproduktion verschieden erscheinen*]" (*PhG* §274). Variation, *Verschiedenheit*, not only spoils purely oppositional relations but also belongs, in the dialectical order of things, on the side of an unmediated actuality, of actual difference, and of vegetal ontology. If reproduction introduces variation into organic actuality, then it moderates opposition with non-oppositional energy stemming from exposure to the other. Reproduction is the excluded middle, the alogic part disconnected from, yet vital to, organismic logic, not to mention from its ontological texture, where "the *being* of an organism is essentially universality or reflection into itself [*das* Sein *des Organismus wesentlich Allgemeinheit oder Reflection in sich selbst ist*]" (*PhG* §276). After all, reproduction—especially that of the sexual kind—rather than reflect, deflects the organism, turning it inside out, toward the other and into the third. By virtue of this turning toward and into the other, reproduction breaks with the being of the organism sketched out exclusively on an oppositional energy grid. Even contemplated on its own terms, reproduction is not a simple "faculty" or "system": it is conservative, insofar as it renews the same organism on a daily basis thanks to the digestive tract, and it is revolutionary, insofar as it renews the kind of organism by producing an offspring. Split down the middle, reproduction is the organic seat of speculative energy, the explosion of identity into an identity and a non-identity in the course of attempts at self-preservation.

The way reproduction interferes with the static opposition of irritability and sensibility is characteristic of the organic realm, where actuality—"the actual expression," *der wirkliche Ausdruck*, of the whole—veers closer to the verbal than to the substantive side of energy, "present at hand as a movement that runs through the various parts of the formation [*als eine Bewegung vorhanden, die sich durch die verschiedenen Teile der Gestaltung verlauft*]" (*PhG* §276). Understood in terms of movement, organic energy is present in a mode that, from the point of view of objective observation, amounts to an absence. Irreducible to the parts of its *Gestaltung*, the organism is not a body, but life at work in the works that are its organs and systems. Despite the deplorable practice of vivisection, anatomy can study nothing but corpses, blind to "it [i.e., to actuality] as a process, in which alone anatomical parts have their sense" (*PhG* §276). "Actuality as a process" is the being-at-work of life in the living that eludes the observing reason. In the inorganic world, movement is secondary in relation to the static entities that are put in motion; in the organic realm, seemingly fixed entities are the derivatives of movement. The two components of energy remain the same. What changes is the primacy of the one vis-à-vis the other: organic being evinces a revolution in energy, the upending of its constitution. (One way to imagine such a revolution is with reference to the rotation of the dialectical cycle of energy—figure 1—in the other direction, counter-clockwise.) Considered absolutely, however, it is the inorganic domain that inverts (and perverts) the organic energy of the concept, which is subsequently reinstated in a concrete organic universality.

Hegel takes the fluid determinacy of organicity as evidence that law is powerless to comprehend life. His point is not that life is somehow mysterious or unknowable in itself, but that it exists at a different energetic level than the law. The unity of legal parts, mutually indifferent to one another, is formal and virtual; that of organic entities individuated from the life-process is thoroughly mediated, self-negated, and self-related. Law represents the dead bits of reality caught up and captured in the nets of the system; organic existence expresses its own living actuality: "In this way, the *representational thinking* of a *law* in the organic goes astray. The law wants to grasp and express the opposition as parts at rest [*Das Gesetz will den Gegensatz als ruhende Seiten auffassen und ausdrücken*] . . . , and what lies at the very foundation of the representation of law is that its two parts should have for themselves an indifferent existence [*daß seine beiden Seiten ein für sich seiendes gleichgültiges Bestehen hätten*]" (*PhG* §278). There is no such enduring separation of parts in the physio-logy of the organic, where relations are prior to the related aspects and movement precedes being-at-rest. Although that which is represented by law gives off the appearance of concreteness, durability, stability, and self-sufficiency, it entails truncated mediations and an energy deficit, albeit one that is not as severe as the vacuous virtuality of pure thought. The law is always of the inorganic, an opposition that is literally set in stone and that correlates things with thoughts. Which is why life remains foreign to it.

Hegel's approach to organic being, reconciling the substantive and the verbal dimensions of energy, is mindful at the same time of its works and its workings. Organic being is a unity (*Einheit*) that also produces a unified (*vereinigt*) ensemble of "infinite sublation, that is, of the absolute negation of being with restful being [*das unendliche Aufheben oder die absolute Negation des Seins mit dem ruhigen Sein*]" (*PhG* §279). In its form and in its content, organicity contributes to the doubling of energy-actuality into substance and subject. While the organic form couples substantive unity with the activity of unification, the content combines being at rest with the restless negation of being, the life of an organism irreducible to any of its shapes, organs, or faculties, with which it is at the same time interlaced. Law may indeed also interrelate being and its negation (non-being), but in doing so, it will posit that the terms are initially independent and that being is primary. Organic existence, on the contrary, is at work and in the works starting from the middle (the process, becoming, relationality), from within the rifts of *en*ergy whence the extremes emerge and are individuated. This is what Hegel means by "infinite sublation": the interminable, yet finite, emergence of organic life from, in, and as the middle, between two points that are polarized as a consequence of that very emergence.

Neither law, which is in one way or another always that of noncontradiction, nor understanding with its crystalline structures, is equipped to engage with the middle as such, the site of energy, or "pure transition," *reine Übergehen* (*PhG* §279). Law, including its reflection in understanding, simply does not tolerate fluid determinacy, let alone the scission between being and its negation, between a static embodiment of energy in the work and its disquietude at work. At best, law exhibits a snapshot of the world, a frozen frame of actuality "in the mode of fixed determinateness, the form of an immediate property, or a restful appearance [*die Weise einer festen Bestimmtheit, die Form einer unmittelbaren Eigenschaft oder einer ruhenden Erscheinung*]" (*PhG* §281). Given the choice between "process" and "product," law opts for the latter, foregoing organic fluidity and energetic mediations—energy *as* mediation. The "restful appearance" of organic being it demonstrates is, then, for all intents and purposes, the identical twin of inorganic reality, of the outer without the inner. Focusing on the shape of appearances, law and the perceptual understanding that supports it cling to the phenomenality of what is in being at the expense of organismic self-reflectedness; they view the organism "as it is *for another* [für ein Anderes]" (*PhG* §284) and objectify it as a result. Law and understanding re-create the organism in their own image, reproducing the deficient modality of their conceptual energy (its partiality, the propensity to deal exclusively with substantive works) in actual existence.

For Hegel, "the *actual* organic being is the middle [*das* wirkliche *organische Wesen ist die Mitte*], which aligns the *being-for-itself* of life with the *outer* as such, or with *being-in-itself*" (*PhG* §285). The energy-actuality of this being arises from the middle excluded from the purview of law and understanding that, having reduced everything determinate to the fixity of shape, surrender the half of *Wirklichkeit*, which dovetails with the freedom of "being-for-itself." Instead of the middle, an objectifying grasp of the organic begins and ends at the end, with its "being-in-itself" modeled on the inorganic domain and equivalent to sheer "being-for-another." Shaping up here is a circle that has little in common with dialectical circularity: in the eyes of law and understanding, life is absolute exposure—its "in-itself" immediately available "for-another"—and, above all, exposure to the objectifying violence of law and understanding. Biopolitics is predicated on this thesis.

Perhaps the only track leading to the middle place of actual organic existence from the rarefied categories of understanding is number. Hegel is at his most Platonic when he writes that number "is the middle term of the shape [*die Mitte der Gestalt*], wherein indeterminate life is linked to actual life; it is simple like the former and determinate like the latter" (*PhG* §285). Presumably concrete, the "middle" of shape is sheer abstraction: number *in* life as the DNA code, formulas of molecular composition, and everything that establishes differentiations within the sweeping movement of indifferent life, transformed into a "multiformed actuality," *vielförmige Wirklichkeit* (*PhG* §285). Beyond the phenomenality of appearance anchored to perceptual understanding, numbers shape the organic shape of energy, if in a wholly exterior, measurable manner. They are indifferent differentiators, actualized in a "multiformed" diversity that is likewise indifferent, a real actuality bordering on the virtual. But at the same time, they are the inner aspect of outer organismic constitution—what is at work in the work of a living shape.

When Hegel locates in the inner and the outer (in the shaping and the shape, the workings and the works) their own interiority and exteriority, he deconstructs a simple spatial, metaphysical, and energetic binary. If the inner is the energizing and the outer is the energized, then both the shaping and the shaped moments of organic being draw their actuality from two different sources. To the interiority of the first, Hegel attributes "the concept as the restlessness of *abstraction* [*Begriff als die Unruhe der* Abstraktion]; the inner of the second has number's "universality at rest [*die ruhende Allgemeinheit*]" (*PhG* §286). Both concepts and numbers are universals representing the opposite sides of energy, the one in flux and the other static. Today, numbers and calculation impinge on the terrain of conceptuality and thinking: the inner of the outer usurps the place of the inner of the inner, and numerical universality comes to constitute reality. Life, physical, and social sciences rarely note anything aside from numbers, and, with that "universality at rest" exacerbated—inflated beyond the confines of energy's shapes—thinking wanes and reality does not make the leap toward actuality. The world becomes digital, shrunk to its objective universal essence, while the thought of this essence is identified with thought as such, stripped down to the bare bones of calculation and algorithmic programming.

  As the energy of thinking dwindles, so do the possibilities of organic existence, which, despite exercises in gene editing and recombination, cannot develop from the inner of the outer (the universality of numbers) alone. Organismic enworkment is double: conceptual, when theorized absolutely; numerical, when reduced to the biological determinism of the genetic code. Without the first element, we are locked in digital (virtual) reality—thoughtless, non-actual, and with no room for organicity. According to Hegel, efforts to grasp the organic through numbers are futile: "This treatment of the *shape* of the organic as such [Gestalt *des Organischen als solcher*] and of the inner as inner merely of shape is in fact no longer a treatment of the organic" (*PhG* §287). One cannot transfer methods and procedures from the physical to the life sciences; were one to undertake this transfer, one would be blinded to organismic self-reflectedness and non-indifference, which are, incidentally, crucial facets of energy-actuality. It is no wonder that, in a self-fulfilling prophecy, an organism studied and analyzed by means of numerical operations is but a complex machine. Under the spell of mathematical universality at rest, we live in a world hostile to life, to life's comprehension and actual flourishing. We undercut a vital energy (our own included) by tying it entirely to the measurable, the calculable, and the objectively determinable.

  In mathematical universality, law finds its desired object free of the "movement of process [*Bewegung des Prozesses*]" and immured in a "*quelled* unity [beruhigte *Einheit*]" (*PhG* §289). For it, everything is in the work, sedimented in unity at rest, available for examination or extraction in the form of stored energy. That organic entities are subsumed under the same logic as their inorganic counterparts, whose materiality they bear and commemorate in their physical makeup and outward shapes, is a sign that, reduced to this dimension of their being, they are immediately ready for counting, accounting, and manipulation as a set of energy resources. Their own energy, their setting-to-work as self-reflected and non-indifferent, drops out of the universal bookkeeping, because that energy is untranslatable into numerical figures. The quantifiable aspect of organicity is, to be sure, always present in a living shape, but the shaping is nonquantifiable, even when its guiding factor is a number. What "the inner of the outer" isolates as the essential condition of possibility for organic being is merely one category—quantity—postulated as the determination of specific qualities or properties. Leaving the "inner of the inner" outside this frame of reference, scientific reductionism skips over all the other categories comprising a complex organismic unity. For its part, the fluid determinacy of the concept at work gathers into itself the rest of the categories (or, from the indifferent perspective of calculation, the rests) on the dynamic underside of living energy, which overflows a static "table" of categories. It holds the key to something without which an organism (or any other entity, for that matter) would fall apart, namely relations that, in the case of organismic existence, belong in the fold of self-reflectedness grounded in a self-negation. The relation between numbers and qualities, too, requires the intervention of this repressed side of energy, since the number as such "has no necessary relation but instead demonstrates the abolition of all lawfulness [*keine notwendige Beziehung zu haben, sondern die Vertilgung aller Gesetzmäßigkeit darzustellen*]" (*PhG* §290). A quelled unity preceding its relations is, simultaneously, the only thing that law can relate to and work with and the very thing that, precluding relationality, inverts lawfulness into sheer lawlessness and the chaos of indifference. It follows that no sooner does law find its desired object than it itself is negated, allying itself to the impoverished energy in the work of fixed quantities and qualities.

A jump from the numerical to the genetic determination of living universality does little to remedy the situation. Adjoining genus to number, Hegel is undoubtedly evoking the Platonic *eidos*, a prototype of the universal forever frozen in the (unproduced and indestructible) work. "The organic that is, in itself, universal is *genus* [Gattung]"; its universality, however, is a "freedom vis-à-vis its actuality [*Wirklichkeit*], which is none other than a freedom . . . over and against the shape [*Gestalt*]" (*PhG* §291). The freedom of the genus indifferent to its specific variations, to differences in the concrete forms it assumes in its specimens, is the instantiation of a concept acceptable to calculative rationality. It is, then, situated between a biologically determinist (biologicist) and an absolute mode of theorizing. Free of a necessary relation to the actual, the genus—though it substitutes for the previously missing distinction of kind (or quality)—is as virtual as the number. That the actuality of living shapes and the genus meant to express their universality persist in a state of mutual indifference is attributable to the fact that the two dimensions of energy have not been reconciled. Here, the "inner of the inner" no longer falls by the wayside but is objectified in a general shape, and so detained in "restful simplicity [*ruhender Einfachheit*]" (*PhG* §292). Formally, the outcome is the same as in the numerical determination of organicity: a work chopped off from the being-at-work of life itself. But the process through which this outcome is attained is drastically different: the universality of the genus is not that of a contentless numerical abstraction, but of what organic existence is in itself. Therefore, the energy of the genus is more developed than that of arithmetical virtuality, in that the former, unlike the latter, irradiates from the self-relation of actuality, which immediately suppresses its own source and grows indifferent to the living content it has determinately negated.

As Hegel construes it, genus is a deficient hinge for the entire project of interlacing energy with itself, of the rational becoming actual and vice versa. The universality of genus only holds in itself; were it also universal for itself, it would have intruded into the territory of self-consciousness. If the moments of this rational term "were actual, organic genus would have been consciousness [*die als solche Momente hier wirklich wären, so wäre die organische Gattung Bewußtsein*]" (*PhG* §292). I wonder to what extent organic genus, reconstructed after the fact in evolutionary theory, *is* consciousness. Bracketing this possibility, the universality of genus is not self-grasped, and the dialectical energy-actuality proper to it is inferior to that of self-consciousness, even though it is, as I have just mentioned, superior to numerical abstraction.

Nonetheless, in the spirit of Hegel's philosophy, shortcomings vaunt an unexpected strength: the position of organic genus in the middle, between arithmetical virtuality and self-conscious actuality, grants it the authority of mediation, harboring more energy than we think. For this reason, "actuality begins with it [i.e., with the genus], though what enters actuality is not genus as such, i.e., not something generally thought [*die Wirklichkeit fängt von ihr an, oder was in die Wirklichkeit tritt, ist nicht die Gattung als solche, d.h. überhaupt nicht der Gedanke*]" (*PhG* §292). Actuality itself is broken down the middle in the place of genus: while it begins (*fängt*) with the genus, it does not make an entrance (*tritt*), as on a theatrical stage, in "genus as such." This fracture between the conceptual beginning and a dramatic-phenomenological entrance of actuality not only remarks the difference between *actuality* and *actuality'* but also demarcates a disjunctive articulation, the crease, the hinge, or the joint of the Hegelian project. What enters into actuality without actually beginning is individual life; what begins without really entering into actuality is the universal life of a species.

A living energy, or what I am calling here *the ergonic nature of the organic*, unravels as a dialectic of universal life and singular existence, of the genus and "that same life as individual" (*PhG* §293). Taken together, the two moments amount to the ergonics of organicity—the energy where what is at work belongs to the extreme of the genus and what is in the work falls on the side of an organism as the singular embodiment of the universal. It is thanks to the ergonic processes taking place in the organic world that genus can quit its "simple essence," *einfache Wesen*, and, parting against itself, receive "simple determinatenesses," *einfachen Bestimmtheiten*, in the world (*PhG* §294), while a singular and no less abstract individuality can open itself up to the shaping effects of the genus. Organic ergonics cannot take off the ground unless both renunciations of a simple—virtual, unmediated, self-enclosed—identity happen in parallel, marrying the rational idea of a living being to the actual matter of life itself. Hegel's ergonics is a reworking of Aristotelian hylomorphism, of existence prefigured in clusters of formed matter (or mattered form) constituting every being. This "prefiguration," in Hegel's rendition, is itself a work, an outcome of the labor of the negative, through which beings are produced after having been thoroughly permeated by nothing.

The shapes of hylomorphic formations, being-in-the-work handed over to observation, show that "only reason can become *life in general* [*nur die Vernunft* als Leben überhaupt *werden kann*]" (*PhG* §295). The rational becomes actual *in general*, that is, as a virtual abstraction, as a concept of life that, thanks to its conceptualization, is compatible with reason. The generality of the process dampens celebrations of its idealist tinges. "Shaped existence," *gestalteten Dasein*, or the hylomorphic formation of living beings, adds a substantive element to the energy at work in the commerce of reason and life. But an intermediate element is still missing between *hulé* and *morphé*, the living and reason/life, being-in-the-work and the at-work of organicity (hence, the composite term "hylomorphism"). Whereas "consciousness [is] in-between universal spirit and its individuality [*zwischen dem allgemeinen Geiste und zwischen seiner Einzelnheit*]," such that "this middle term [*Mitte*] would have in the *movement* of its actuality [*an der* Bewegung *ihrer Wirklichkeit*] the expression and the nature of universality" (*PhG* §295), life and the living have no such middle term (despite genus—the rational wrapping of life—standing between the universality of pure number and self-consciousness, and perhaps forming a consciousness of its own over long evolutionary periods). It is in this context that we ought to comprehend Hegel's statement that "organic nature has no history [*die organische Natur hat keine Geschichte*]" (*PhG* §295); history, always and necessarily, retraces the movement of actuality preserved in the shapes of consciousness—not because the latter has some privileged anthropocentric status, but because it is the middle par excellence. And history can be only of the middle, of energetic intermittencies freed from the stasis of origin and destination.

The preceding raises a curious problem: does energy have a history? In keeping with the first law of thermodynamics, we must answer in the negative: energy is ahistorical because its quantity is preserved across all alterations, which means that it is essentially unaffected by the passage of time. So, Hegel seems to drive a wedge between different types of energy. That of organic and inorganic nature has no history; that of consciousness and its multifarious shapes is historical through and through. From the standpoint of the dialectical absolute, moreover, ahistorical energy is ensconced within the history of spirit. If nature is spirit out of touch with itself—unmediated, unrelated to itself, poorly energized—then the more mediations actuality accrues, as it struggles to extricate itself from being straitjacketed in (virtual) reality, the more historical it becomes. The limit of history coincides with the border between reality and actuality; as soon as the real gets in touch with itself, attaining actuality, it is historicized. The fullest, most robust energy interrelated with itself is the most historical (yes, dialectical historicity admits of degrees!). The history of energy is a story of its transition from an ahistorical to a historical form, narrated from the vantage of the energetic apex, a reiteration of its itinerary *after* the end of history.

ii. Observation of Self-Consciousness: The Perversions of Natural Energy

In a signature gesture of dialectical perversion, observation can coil onto itself, passing into self-observation. This U-turn bends energy-actuality, interrelating it with itself, so that "when observation now turns into itself and directs itself to the actual concept as free concept [*indem sie sich nun in sich selbst kehrt, und auf den als freien Begriff wirklichen Begriff richtet*], it encounters in the first place the *laws of thought*" (*PhG* §299). Related to itself, the concept is both actual and free, and it is from this new starting point of energetic freedom that it can venture back into the outside world via a double, redoubled consideration of itself and its other. All the same, we should not ignore the twists and turns thanks to which a free actuality is finally possible: logic and psychology accrete around a perverse energy of nature, its laws comprised of relations among static elements warped into the laws of thought that are the first targets of self-observation. As in any twist, the lines before and after the bend part ways: on the one hand, the formal truth of logical stipulations is a throwback to energetic impoverishment, the purely virtual play of a thought-thing (*Gedankending*); on the other hand, the universality of thought thinking itself is, more than an abstraction, a concrete and energetically vibrant self-relation that "immediately has being and all reality in it [*unmittelbar das Sein und darin alle Realität an ihm hat*]" (*PhG* §299). With observation for its activity, such thought observes itself along with its other—after all, observation as such, *Beobachtung*, implies a certain coming-outside-itself, even when ostensibly directed inwards.

The importance of the fact that observation persists across the perversions of the dialectical gaze cannot be overestimated. In the context of self-consciousness, this persistence signifies a break between "self" and "givenness" in "self-givenness." In spite of thought receiving its law from nowhere else but itself, the observation of what is received "obtains the determination of a *found*, given, i.e., *merely existing* content [*erhält sie die Bestimmung eines* gefundenen, gegebenen, d.i. nur seienden *Inhalts*]" (*PhG* §300). Self-observing consciousness stumbles across itself, and the outcome of this run-in with itself is both this very "self" and the formal domain of logic. The laws of thought are the moment of mere givenness within self-givenness, which explains why they cannot extend to anything other than "the *motionless being* of relations [ruhiges Sein *von Beziehungen*]" (*PhG* §300), mental energy captured in the work upon having been abstracted from the workings of consciousness. The perversion built into self-conscious observation results from its fidelity to "law" and to "nature," leading it to transpose the procedures and apparatus of naturalistic observation to the life of the mind and its spinoffs, be they logic or psychology. It is this fidelity that blinds self-observation to the full extent of self-givenness, and, correlatively, denies it access to both dimensions of energy. What self-observation finds in the shape of "the motionless being of relations" is but nature, now qualified as "inner" or "second" and extracted from the entire "context of movement [*Zusammenhang der Bewegung*]" (*PhG* §300), which comprises the life of self-consciousness. That is to say: self-observation is out of touch with the verbal side of energy, the being-at-work of thinking, from which issue stable thought unities, enunciated as laws.

And yet, despite everything, regardless of all its blind spots, self-observation proceeds from the life of the mind and *is* this very life. Forgetful of the context of movement as it is, the milieu where the laws of thought coagulate does not cease to be movement and alteration. By virtue of its own failures and oversights, self-observation twists knowledge into being, the rational into the actual, or, more precisely, "perverts its nature into the shape of *being* [*verkehrt seine Natur in die Gestalt des Seins*]" (*PhG* §300). In the sphere of self-consciousness regarding itself, perversion is not an exception to the law but the law's essence. The doubling of the subject and the object of observation in the same agent departs from the thinking activity—the being-at-work of thought—only to return to this point of departure as a substantialized, hypostatized ontological shape—a being-in-the-work that is seemingly independent from the operations of thinking. Thanks to this machination, the central Parmenidean thesis concerning the sameness of what is for thinking and for being is confirmed at the expense of the movement of thought, mesmerized by its own perverse shape.

With the synergy (*Zusammenhang*: a hanging-together, also translated as "context") of energy's movement and rest shattered, a self-observing consciousness accepts the scheme of things according to which it is divided into an impassive observer and an acting consciousness subjected to uncompromising scrutiny by its virtual double. Here, too, inversions abound: the subject is the observer who cannot act; the active consciousness is its object (*Gegenstand*), "which is for itself in such a way that it sublates its otherness" (*PhG* §301). In this veritable carnival of self-observation, in this mad dance of energy, being-at-work and being-in-the-work switch places; subject appears to be substance and substance dons the mask of subject without channeling these oscillations into the actuality (the being) of becoming.

At home in its otherness to itself (i.e., never at home and never "in itself"), the observing self-consciousness "has its actuality in this intuition of itself as negative [*in dieser Anschauung seiner selbst als des Negativen seine Wirklichkeit hat*]" (*PhG* §301). It draws its energy from its noncoincidence with itself across the divide between the observing and the observed "self"—the noncoincidence it treats as a model for relating to the outside world it revisits with its virtual luggage. More than that, just as the laws of thought are but versions, or perversions, of the laws of nature, so the world rediscovered by the Janus-faced observing/observed self-consciousness and made up of "diverse modes of its actuality [*die verschiedenen Weisen seiner Wirklichkeit*]" is one of "a *previously found otherness* [*eines* vorgefundenen *Andersseins*]" (*PhG* §302). (Of course, from the standpoint of dialectical completion, it is nature that stands for the perversion of spirit, still unrelated to itself.) Even when bathed in its proper element, the observing self-consciousness perceives its surroundings as other to it because it remains, in itself, other to itself. Due to its total reliance on the act of observation, distancing the observer from and externalizing the object (however intimate), self-consciousness is alienated from its own energy and from the concomitant possibility of absolute self-givenness. The ancient injunction "Know thyself!" does not mandate the same thing as "Observe thyself!" There is a specific name for the self-alienation of self-consciousness in observation: psychology (*PhG* §302).

Modern psychology contains the truth of self-observing consciousness that studies itself as though it were confronted with natural phenomena. Since its inception, this discipline has desperately wanted to be counted among the sciences, from which it borrowed the empirical methodology. As a bonus, it receives from the desired methodology a haphazard view of its subject matter, modes of spiritual existence presented as "heterogeneous and contingent things that can be brought together as in a sack [*wie in einem Sacke, so vielerlei und solche heterogene einander zufällige Dinge beisammen sein können*]" (*PhG* §303). The more fidelity modern psychology has to the natural sciences, the more perverse its field: its energy is curtailed, un- or disarticulated from itself in the unity of psychic existence, and is narrowed down to mental works—randomly collected "dead things at rest [*als tote ruhende Dinge*]"—to the exclusion of what is at work in the mind's "restless movements [*als unruhige Bewegungen*]" (*PhG* §303). It is not difficult to spot the extreme substantivation of energy in this description of psychology, which, for a lack of better terms, loses sight of both *psykhé* and *logos* in its pursuit of scientific legitimacy.

Things hardly improve when the observing self-consciousness zooms onto the individual. "*Actual* individuality," *die* wirkliche Individualität, is taken "spiritlessly as an individual existing phenomenon [*geistlos als einzelne seiende Erscheinung*]" as soon as we apply to it the universal psychological method and enumerate this or that person's inclinations, talents, and so on (*PhG* §304). In other words, psychic life in its singular actuality is fashioned into an object for classification, a point of intersection for multiple mental works. So understood, an actual individuality exhaustively captured by its objective determinations is sapped of its energy-actuality, which presupposes a psychic self-relation beyond a phenomenalization (or substantivation) of the individual. It is not that the subject is an impenetrable mystery of singularity; rather, it is an energetic concert of phenomenal works and that which is at work in thinking, intending, desiring, and so on. The "face" is the interface of the two dimensions of energy in mental life. Therefore, instead of standing opposed to universality, "its [the individual's] essence is the universal of spirit [*ihr Wesen das Allgemeine des Geistes ist*]" (*PhG* §304).

Under the influence of scientific observational psychology, the energetic interface of psychic life, too, is perverted: being-at-work now belongs to the cultural context wherein individuality is concretized as the being-in-the-work of cultural energies (*PhG* §305). But the perverse truth of this perversion—the truth upon which Nietzsche also chanced—is that energy grows stronger the weaker it becomes. The "law of individuality" is the anarchy of universality: the individual is both the quelled work of the universal context and someone who perverts (*und sie vielmehr zu verkehren*) that universality by being opposed to it (*PhG* §306). The individual works with and against the universal milieu of cultural life, so much so that the energy of individuality comes to be defined by this "with-against," a self-subverting synergy with the surroundings that are not allowed to influence it in the manner of natural causality, in the way a rock on a beach is polished by the relentless power of the waves. This other energy is that of a determined and determining determination, its determining moment achieved on condition that it render the context, which envelops it, unstable and indeterminate. Individuals are only individuals to the extent that they unconsciously receive and pervert the universality that their very existence expresses—to the extent, that is, that they both hypostatize and de-substantivize their universal milieu.

There is, consequently, a split or a doubling in actuality, translated into the twofold sense of "world" as a "*world existing in and for itself* [*an und für sich seiende Welt*]" and as the "*world of the individual*," Welt des Individuums (*PhG* §307). This duality recalls the atomic fission of meaning in energy, in *ergon* that denotes the workings and the work, the virtualizing–de-substantivizing activity and a completed, substantivized act. An ostensibly superfluous addition to the plane of natural forces, individuality divides this plane in two and perverts it ("the present-at-hand becomes *perverted* by it [*das Vorhandene von ihm verkehrt worden ist*]" *PhG* §307). This perversion is the inner torsion of energy-actuality that remains incomplete without its own emptying-out into the void of the subject, without the de-actualizing instant that makes what was evidently present absent. Instead of "the world," there are now world*s* within actuality, at times disrupted and at other times seamlessly expressed by the individual, who acts as their lever; the individual chooses whether to "let the stream of influencing actuality flow unimpeded or to break off and pervert it [*daß es entweder den Strom der einfließenden Wirklichkeit an ihm gewähren läßt, oder daß es ihn abbricht und verkehrt*]" (*PhG* §307). A split—a discontinuity—is finally established between the continuity and discontinuity of energy flows, regulated by individual activity that creates the individual as such (performativity) and supplements actuality to make it what it is by incorporating a perverse negation and negativity into it.

Here, we have yet another intimation that energy-actuality is never pure: if it were to be so, presence, the world, and being itself would not have been divided against themselves, redoubled, and infused with their opposites. Perversion is not a marginal deviation, but the essence of *Wirklichkeit*, interrupted and channeled (i.e., mediated) by individuality, which, as it turns out, mediates itself in the wake of Aristotle's *energeia*: "Individuality itself is the circle of its own activity, within which it has represented itself as actuality [*worin sie sich als Wirklichkeit dargestellt hat*]" (*PhG* §308). The negation of the world in and for itself, of actuality as objectively present, re-presents itself in a self-sufficient shape of actuality, condensed into a circle. Well before Heidegger, Hegel realized that the world of the individual *is* the world from that individual's perspective and, vice versa, that "individuality is what *its* world is as *its own*" (*PhG* §308). The proper of the individual is the perverse of the world as such and in itself; the world's private appropriation is the expropriation of the world shared, present, and available to all. A break in actuality is—actually—what cuts phenomenally accessible energy off from energy withdrawn into itself, at work in individual self-creation. Could it be that communist dreams are grounded in a desire to do away with private perversion altogether and to reconcile the two dimensions of energy under the aegis of the common world?

iii. Observation of the Relation between Self-Consciousness
and Its Immediate Actuality: The Body at Work

The buildup of dialectical energy has reached its apex and, having crumbled, needs to be reinitiated at another level of the complex spiral that is the *Phenomenology*. Among the ruins of the previous stage, the one that predominates is a cleft in the world that segregates the world as such from the universe of the individual. At first, the relation between these worlds, or between self-consciousness that is and that enacts its own world on the one hand and the immediate actuality external to it on the other, is itself immediate, which is why they stand in "mutual indifference to one another [*die Gleichgültigkeit beider*]" (*PhG* §309). Expressed otherwise, the space between them is purely virtual, and there is no (or very little) energy circulating in it. To fill out and actualize this space, it is necessary to introduce into it a transitional figure that spans the two worlds—the figure of the body.

Closely allied with Aristotle's notion of entelechy, dialectical energetics construes the living body as a place wherein "his [the individual's] nature is originarily put to work [*seine ursprüngliche Natur ins Werk richtet*]" (*PhG* §310). In a further refinement of what I have termed "the ergonic paradigm," the body is the *ergon*-organ-instrument of self-conscious individuality and, therefore, a work that is already at work on the behest of the individual to whom it belongs. What is undeniably modern about the Hegelian theory of the body is that he treats it as a sign, *ein Zeichen*, *through which* self-consciousness acts and expresses itself. In the sphere of self-consciousness, a sign entails no disconnect between the signifier and the signified, or, if you will, between the soul and the body, but is, rather, the expression of the former in the latter.

Granted: the body is an unchosen instrument; it is what has been received prior to and in excess of the individual's capacity to decide or to receive, the immediate givenness without self-givenness, "what-has-not-been-done," *Nicht-getan-haben* (*PhG* §310). As such, it belongs to the real rather than to the actual and does not signify much outside itself. If that is so, then, despite its capacity for movement and indeed self-movement, a living body falls on the side of energy at rest, "the fixed being of a phenomenal actuality [*das feste Sein einer erscheinenden Wirklichkeit*]," externally tackled by energy-as-movement, "the movement of consciousness [*Bewegung des Bewußtseins*]" (*PhG* §310). But only at birth and shortly thereafter does such a relation between the subject and its body (and, by implication, between the signifier and the signified) as a "found" entity hold. Leading self-conscious existence means nothing other than assuming even the merely given as self-given, throwing everything one is and has into the circle of individual self-creation. In this context, the body of an individual is not a brute fact but an act in the substantive: "his body is an expression of himself, *brought about* by him [*ist sein Leib auch der von ihm* hervorgebrachte *Ausdruck seiner selbst*]" (*PhG* §310). The body is a work to be interpreted, and, in the course of this interpretation, the hidden workings of self-consciousness will emerge to the light of presence, that is to say, they will be indicated, they will come through as meaning does in a sign. From the standpoint of the absolute, then, the immediate actuality of corporeality, the body's deficient (because unmediated) energy, is already mediated unbeknown to mere consciousness. The point is to recapture this mediation by means of a self-conscious interpretation—itself a kind of mediation—that links mere consciousness to the absolute.

A figuration of the individual, the body is energy substantivized in a human shape (*eine menschliche Gestalt*), as "the expression of the individual's own actualizing posited by himself [*als Ausdruck seiner durch es selbst gesetzten Verwirklichung*]" (*PhG* §311). Through the shape of the body, which is a work in progress, individuality at work speaks silently, giving signs of its dietary practices, physical activity, cultural molding, and so forth. The body, in effect, is a never-completed construction site, a crossroads of "cultured and uncultured being and the actuality of an individual suffused with being-for-itself [*ungebildeten und des gebildeten Seins, und die von dem Fürsich-sein durchdrungne Wirklichkeit des Individuums*]" (*PhG* §311). It is the already given and the yet to be received, a mediation between the immediate and the mediate, the actuality and the actualization of individuality. The energy of the body, in turn, is not only a static repository of caloric resources necessary for my activity in the world but also, inasmuch as it expresses individuality, the movement of the inner turning inside out and a zero-point for the inscription of the otherwise hidden subjective intentions, wishes, and aspirations onto the living-breathing superficies of actuality. Far from being a mere vessel for spirit, which may be easily discarded without any serious consequences to what truly matters, the body is an energetic link (or, better, energy *as* a link) between the world in and for itself and the world for an individual. And its organs are, no doubt, the very things, whose workings make possible a piecemeal transformation of the first world into the second.

Unlike its theo-metaphysical double, the Hegelian spirit cannot survive in isolation from sensuous actuality, for instance by retreating into the security of substance from the empirical plane of accidents. Because, at work and in the work, spirit *is* energy, it does not tolerate a prolonged stagnation in the pure virtuality of self-identity above, beneath, or behind the world. The same goes for individuality or, in everyday parlance, personality: speculations about individual tendencies or dispositions are useless, unless they are concretized in actual deeds bearing fruit in the external actuality of the world. In and of itself, personality is a gutted concept, just as behaviorism is an exiguous form of explaining individual conduct, since each focuses exclusively on the inner or the outer without making an effort to transition from the one to the other. While the body is the initial thread used for making this transition in Hegel's thought, its organs are, at the same time, the means and the medium, the works and the workings, for imprinting individuality onto the public world, shared with many others. So, "the speaking mouth, the laboring hand, and, if one so wishes, the legs as well as the organs of actualization and fulfillment [*verwirklichenden und vollbringenden Organe*] . . . have activity *as activity*, that is, the inner as such, in them" (*PhG* §311). They are the actualizing and actualized energy carriers that traffic bits of interiority, in the guise of accomplished intentions, across the boundaries that separate the inner from the outer. Interior, and yet on the outside, the mouth, the hand, and the legs sift individual interiority through them until it, too, enters the recognizable shape of a work.

Speaking of organs, we might experience a sense of déjà vu, of being transported back to the ergonics of the organic sphere. Much in dialectics happens as a replay and a replay of the replay, but there is always a difference factored into the repetition, which is, as we recall, energizing. In this case, what is different is that, rather than life setting itself to work in the organic sphere, it is individuality that sets itself to work in an organic body. When it comes to the ergonics/organics of life, there isn't really much sense in invoking deeds—its workings are not yet deeds. The deed is attributable strictly to an individual, who, thanks to the activities of the organs, acts in such a way that "actuality is sundered from the individual [*von dem Individuum abgetrennte Wirklichkeit*]" (*PhG* §312). Whereas the workings of life are one with its works, individual acts leave their works behind, unglued from the actor. In contrast to the seamless, continuous, and contiguous energy-actuality of life itself, individually inhabited and created actuality is predicated on a void, a spatiotemporal rift between the actor and the accomplished act.

Counterintuitive as this may appear, the basic alienation of individuality is more energetically supple than the manifestations of a purely natural energy: in the last instance, the two sides of a splintered actuality comprised of the individual and a freestanding work get at the doubling, constitutive of energy "itself," of its meaning, and of meaningfulness in general. Expression is the most appropriate mode of conveying the actual, but it is not at all semantically straightforward; if anything, it is more ambiguous than representation or pure thinking, due to the expressing and the expressed inevitably falling apart. As Hegel puts it, expressions express the inner both too much and too little—too much, because the inner is presented, rather than represented in them; too little, because the inner presents itself as its other (the outer), and so, resisting presentation, slips away (*PhG* §312). What if an intensifying ambiguity (not confusion, but ambiguity within clearly set parameters, or what we might call "amphibology") were to indicate proximity to energy-actuality? If so, then every philosophical appeal to "clear and distinct ideas," to certainty (including sense-certainty, situated at the lower rungs of dialectics), or to indubitable foundations is locked in the ivory tower of the virtual, its intellectual energy undercut.

Hegel brings this insight to bear upon his reflection on energy in the substantive, or, in his words, "the accomplished work," *vollbrachte Werk*. Eminently ambiguous, "the act as an accomplished work has a double and opposite meaning [*hat die doppelte entgegengesetzte Bedeutung*]: it is either the *inner* of individuality and *not* its expression, or, as the outer, an actuality *free* from the inner [*eine von dem Innern* freie *Wirklichkeit*]" (*PhG* §312). The duality persists so long as we are roaming the trails of phenomenology, where a quasi-transcendental slit between what appears and the (non-apparent) appearing of what appears (in Hegel's simplification: the outer and the inner) cannot be sutured. Uniting—the one *as* the other—the act and the accomplished work that channel the two senses of energy's *ergon* is bound to split the atom of meaning, rendering it "double and opposite" to itself. The act, after all, never passes into the work without remainder; the objectification of the process in the product says nothing about the work as experienced by the individual. Similar to the body, the experiential layer of energy's transformations is not a disposable epiphenomenon, but the inner, without which the complex of energy-actuality crumbles. Free from the inner, as much from ambiguity, actuality shrinks to an accomplished work that obfuscates its own accomplishment, a work disengaged from the act that had called it forth, a sign no longer pointing toward what it signifies.

What interests Hegel in the inoperativity of the sign is the failure of signification in the midst of the otherwise efficacious acts expressing the inner in the outer. A successful expression fails because the expressing externality expresses the expressed interiority in a wholly external way, entombing the movement of individuality in "a restful whole." The atom of energy's meaning (and of meaning as such) will remain split, for, despite serving as a sign for the inner, the outer has "an *actual* aspect that is, for itself, meaningless [*dessen* wirkliche *Seite für sich bedeutungslos*]" (*PhG* §313). Along with mere consciousness, a self-consciousness that relates to immediate actuality falls into the trap of Saussurean signification: the actuality of the expressing is, in and of itself, meaningless so long as it is not intrinsically mediated with the expressed; the tie between the inner and the outer, the working and the work of signification, is virtual: "arbitrary," *zufällig*, "a free caprice," *die freie Willkür* (*PhG* §313). The outer as outer cannot express the inner. A series of mediations must precede the moment of meaningful expression, in which the inner of the outer would intersect with the outer of the inner. Without this, the actuality of expression would not cross the threshold of *actuality'*, its energy dissipating in the loose, virtual links of signification.

Vicariously, the problem of signification addresses a deeper issue of the Cartesian mind-body split. How is my body—that most immediate and most intimate of actualities—to receive the principle of individuality if it is not already a working and a work, an interiority turned inside out and an exteriority interiorized? The body cannot be a passive substratum for the mind; it must already have (and it must already be) energy-actuality in order to welcome, set to work, and express that which consciousness and self-consciousness intend for it. Once the body and the mind have been separated, attempts to rearticulate them are as hilarious as those in astrology, palmistry, physiognomy, and phrenology. At least physiognomy, Hegel quips, examines character as subject and substance, as "conscious essence" and "existing shape," locked in the opposition of the inner and the outer. Palmistry and astrology, for their part, lump externality with externality (*PhG* §314), and so express the truth of a wholly arbitrary signification. To avoid this absurdity, self-consciousness must debunk the myth of the immediate (virtual) actuality of the body and acknowledge the energetic mediations of corporeality: the unconscious as the outer of the inner and bodily awareness as the inner of the outer. The body at work is not inert materiality that takes the mind in as something alien, but is itself a thinking-feeling-intending actuality.

While reflecting on the corporeal moments of signification and expression, Hegel seems unable to leave the behind. He keeps circling around the hand, driven to it by his own and experimenting with various orbital approaches to it. The main premise of palmistry is, in a sense, right: one's fate is in one's hands. Both the instrument and the outcome of hominization, the hand—the bodily being-at-work and the being-in-the-work of the human—clasps both sides of energy. "After the organ of speech, it is by and large the hand, by which one brings oneself to appearance and to actualization [*sich zur Erscheinung und Verwirklichung bringt*]" (*PhG* §315). The hand is the quintessence of the human organ/ *ergon:* it is substantivized organic energy that further energizes, actualizing the one to whom it pertains and bringing the human to appearance (*Erscheinung*) through the works (literally, the handiwork) produced. In doing so, the hand draws together the inner world of the individual and the outside world reworked into "its actuality," *seiner Wirklichkeit* (*PhG* §316). It can accomplish this energizing work of mediation only because it, along with the other parts of the organic interface that is the body, is the middle term between individual interiority and the exteriority of the world.

As we've already noted, all mediations of the inner and the outer that are not already, *beforehand*, mediated are doomed. The interface of bodily energy must interrelate the inner of the outer and the outer of the inner, if it is to facilitate the convergence of two worlds and two modes of energy. It is against this backdrop that Hegel returns to the hand, as much as to the face as such an interface, that is, as the exteriorization of the inner relation to the outer.

The face speaks beyond words; it is never silent since it is "*expression as reflection upon* the actual expression [*Äußerung als* Reflection über *die wirkliche Äußerung*]" (*PhG* §317). In the face, on the face of it, actuality communes with actuality, even as it perpetually flows through the interiorizing-virtualizing moment of reflection. The face permits energy to circulate on the surface, or, to go back to the hand, to wear the soul on one's sleeve. The Aristotelian notion of the soul as inner discourse, hearing-oneself-speak, "theoretical activity [*theoretische Tun*]," or "the speaking of the individual with himself [*die Sprache des Individuums mit sich selbst*]" (*PhG* §317), which will persist in Western philosophy all the way to Husserlian phenomenology, is thus freed from its virtual corralling and is injected with a healthy dose of energy-actuality. The face with its grimaces and expressions, including its forced neutrality colloquially referred to as a "poker face," is more than a series of external signs for the soul; it *is* the soul as actuality, or, more exactly, it is a series of external signs for the soul *as* the soul's actuality. The soul, if we are still willing to hold onto this paleonym, is nothing but the body at work and in the work. It is, therefore, phenomenally available to others, who, by looking at the face, can overhear the individual's discourse with her- or himself, just as plants can eavesdrop on the biochemical signaling of their neighbors intended for the distal parts of the signal-emitting plant itself.

A self-conscious relation to the immediate actuality of the body is theoretically free for the taking by other self-conscious existences, who observe this immediate actuality "from the outside," that is, from the very exteriority where the soul is eventuated. Still, the problematic of the sign obtrudes on the observation of "the individual's *being*-reflected out of his actuality [*das Reflektiertsein des Individuums aus seiner Wirklichkeit*]" (*PhG* §318). The link between the reflecting and the reflected is not secure, and it is highly doubtful, as deconstruction has taught us, that it will ever be—not least, for the individuality that is so reflected. Rather than abolished in expression, the sign is sublated: canceled, as well as preserved and elevated. So long as there is no simple unity (and there never is; the unmediated first principle is a virtual negation of the actual), the constituent parts of the provisional whole, whether it is the structure of the sign or energy, disintegrate. The individual's "being-reflected out" detains reflection in substantive being, in *ergon* in the shape of a work, which, taken in isolation, may not be expressing anything at all. A complete, actualized expression is indeterminate (and, thus, virtual) in its relation to that which it expresses. Are its bonds to the inner merely obfuscated or are they nonexistent? Observation is unable to respond to this question, since it is incapable of distinguishing the substantive outcomes of expression from those of signification, expression's "being-reflected out of actuality" from a sign "indifferent to the signified [*das gleichgültig gegen das Bezeichnete*]," a face from a mask (*PhG* §318). Though exposed and superficial, bodily exteriority is a mystery not because it is unclear what it signifies or expresses, but because we do not know *if* it signifies *or* expresses, if it projects a virtual disconnect between the animating and the animated or an actual bonding of the two.

In the face of bodily indeterminacy, observation falls out of touch with individuality. Individuality "*puts its essence in the work* [legt ihr Wesen in das Werk]," without which it cannot move past the virtuality of traits and capacities, whereas observation, having learned that the work does not reveal whether it is produced in a process of signification or expressing, counts the work, "be it speech or a hardened actuality [*es sei der Sprache oder einer befestigtem Wirklichkeit*]," as the opposite of essence—"the *inessential outer,*" unwesentliche Äußere (*PhG* §319). However empirically grounded, observation joins forces with the theological and metaphysical paradigms that have predominated in the West, favoring the unapparent and, indeed, the unobservable. It may sound tautological to say that energy-actuality is weakened when its "hardened," substantivized aspect is dismissed as inessential, but this tautology has been setting the agenda for belief and for thought alike over millennia. In a patent metaphysical inversion, the weakness of pure virtuality shorn of concretized actuality has been taken for strength, which in Christianity corresponds to the interiority of the soul, the soul as pure interiority. Between the interiority of the intention (*Absicht*) and the exteriority of an accomplished work, the body disappears: energy is drained from work's substantive actuality and from the corporeal interface of interior outwardness and exterior inwardness. The valorization of intentions over acts, of meaning-to-set-to-work over workings and works, retreats into the virtual domain of power devoid of actuality—a situation abhorrent to Hegelian dialectics. The merely meant or intended (*Meinen*) turns out to be "fancied existence [*gemeintes Dasein*]," itself the proper object of observation that has capitulated before signification (*PhG* §319). Henceforth, observation will have lost its way: the intended (*Meinen*), as the essence indifferent to its outward actualizations, is but something fancied (*gemeintes*), unobservable, yet believed to exist.

Preoccupied with individual capacities, in lieu of behavioral evidence, observation shifts into the gear of a "presumed actuality," *vermeinte Wirklichkeit* (*PhG* §320), into which an outward actuality is dissolved. The qualifier "presumed" (*vermeint*) adds to the wordplays peppering these paragraphs in the *Phenomenology* around "the intended," *Meinen*, which is perverted by the addition of various prefixes, such as *ver-* or *ge-*. The perversion in question is not at all extraneous to the intended, but is characteristic of its pure form: the merely intended that is not realized in the world is, as such, perverse—fancied, presumed, groundlessly inferred, above all by the intending agent. In fact, the inference of pure capacities, standing—at the level of the individual—for the energy-poor virtuality, or else for the noumenal idea of the soul, must necessarily be groundless, in that it leaves no room for expression and hands itself over to arbitrary signification. To the hermetic interiority of virtual, "presumed" actuality corresponds the immediate exteriority of facial features, singled out in the study of physiognomy. Given the desaturation of actuality in fancied existence, the relation between these extremes is indifferent and contingent, since neither of them is self-negated, mediated (as the inner of the outer, etc.), and energized. It follows that physiognomy, palm reading, and other such "esoteric" practices still popular nowadays are more than absurd anachronisms; they have their raison d'être as splashes of despair provoked by energy's dissipation and as attempts to cover over the widening gap between the inner and the outer in a totally outward fashion.

Hegel juxtaposes the accomplished deed to possible intention and concludes that "the *true being* of human beings is rather the *acts*, in which individuality is *actual* [*Das* wahre Sein *des Menschen ist vielmehr seine Tat; in ihr ist die Individualität* wirklich]" (*PhG* §322). Akin to plants, our true being is on the surface, in the actuality of acts, thanks to which we become who or what we are. Performatively, individuals make themselves through their ways of behaving, so that, in a classical Aristotelian circle, individual actuality comes out of actual individual acts. This circle holds in itself being and truth, "true being," *das wahre Sein*, as *energeia*: it is where the *en-* of *energy* dwells. Hegel even pays tribute to the etymology of *Wirklichkeit*—its provenance from *Wirk/Werk*—writing that the individual's "work [*Werk*]" alone "is to be regarded as his true actuality [*seine wahre Wirklichkeit*]" (*PhG* §322), harking back to the *ergon* at the heart of *energeia*.

What is the lesson to be drawn from this valorization of work, of the acts' being-at-work that adds up to the being-in-the-work of individual actuality? Hegel leaves us with the choice between false and true perversions: energy's frittering away in dead-end virtuality or its twisting into *actuality'*. For, while "true being" encompasses individual acts, the works these spawn constitute "true actuality" without any assurances that individuality would not be "altered and perverted," *verändert und verkehrt*, by how they are eventually interpreted (*PhG* §322). The second perversion is decisive to energy itself, which, faithfully corresponding to itself, alternating between the substantive and verbal senses of work, betrays itself, regardless of the side it switches to at the moment.

The particular shape of external actuality (its unique mode of stabilizing or substantivizing energy) matters as far as the extent and the effects of its perversion are concerned. Is this shape molded from words, works, or the body itself? From a mix of these? In the objective vestiges of my acts, traces of my specific intentions responsible for the works may be detected—needless to say, at the risk of over-, under-, or misinterpretation. In a subset of these traces that are my words, which are likewise always open to misinterpretation, there is a near simultaneity of the expressing and the expressed, the workings and the works that Hegel groups under the heading of "psychology." In the bodily immediacy that excites a physiognomist, the movement of intending and expressing is erased and what comes to the fore is "a totally *restful* actuality, which is not in itself a speaking sign [*eine ganz* ruhende *Wirklichkeit, welche nicht an ihr selbst redendes Zeichen ist*]" (*PhG* §323). It is not that the body in its sheer materiality is dumb and mute, meaningless and non-signifying; rather, its actuality signifies something other than the fancied universe of an abstract personality with its propensities and capacities. The body speaks not only by way of the mouth, but throughout its extension, and it conveys a living energy, as opposed to the fiction of a virtual, disembodied mind. At any rate, the contrast between the works, with which psychology deals, and the works that fascinate physiognomy unexpectedly vindicates Christianity. Even if, between the lines of Hegel's ironic take on pseudo-science, we discern a tacit critique of how post-Augustinian Christianity construes the soul as the hidden realm of pure interiority, the saving grace is in the point of access to the Christian psyche—by means of the confession and its words. The confession is, in effect, an act of stating (and so bringing forth) the non-actual without making it actual, *except in speech*. It is an act that ensures the persistence of the soul as entirely non-actual before and after its confessional shaping in words.

The rigor of the Hegelian approach to *Wirklichkeit* at the confluence of energy and actuality, where Aristotle's *energeia* posthumously (dialectically) comes back to life, is evinced in the imbrication of work (*Werk*) and effectiveness (*Wirkung*). On the one hand, in the interface of the inner and the outer that are crudely labeled "soul" and "body," the "spiritual individuality" of the former must boast an embodied extension in order to have an effect on the latter (*PhG* §325). The brain will be nominated as a candidate for such an embodiment of the disembodied shortly. On the other hand, the individual's "being-reflected-into-himself is itself *efficacious [dies In-sich-reflektiert-sein selbst wirkend ist]*" (*PhG* §325), which means that the virtual has an actuality-energy-effectiveness of its own. Opting for internal effectiveness and sacrificing external actuality to that effectiveness is the birthright of metaphysics. Hegel does not necessarily reject virtual efficaciousness, nor does he deny the power of the intentions we impute to others and to ourselves, contrived as they may be. All he tries to do is address the imbalance between reflection and expression, the virtual and the actual, and to configure *Wirklichkeit* as a back-and-forth of their incommensurable kinds of efficaciousness.

Hegel's notes on efficaciousness are interspersed with the continuing philosophical narrative that frames organs, the organism, and organic being as the *ergonic* elements of life. Seeking the bodily extension of what is presumably non-extended requires us to isolate an organ that would not be instrumentalized for a determinate task. A vast majority of organs, Hegel concedes, are "work equipment," *Werkzeuge*: the hand is the organ of work (*Organ der Arbeit*) as such; the genitalia are the organs of the sexual drive (*das Organ der Geschlechtstriebes*), and so on (*PhG* §325). Although, as parts of the bodily interface, they span the working and the work, these organs follow the model of causality that holds for natural energy and are exempt from the movement of self-reflectedness (*PhG* §326) with its virtual efficaciousness. Wide as the range of laboring activities the hand performs may be, it does not escape the teleological *for-what* that deploys the working and the work for the purposes of objective organicity. Already the specialization of the "work-equipment" organs gives us a clue as to their harnessing for substantive ends and the concomitant impossibility of de-substantivation. Conversely, the bodily extension of the non-extended can only be an organ of determinate indeterminacy, that is, the brain. (Let it be stated in passing that Hegel himself problematizes the specialization of all other organs in his *Philosophy of Nature*. There, speculative energy is embodied in organs such as the mouth [used for speaking and kissing, as much as for spitting and eating] and genitalia [for sexual reproduction and urination]. This self-correction implies that most, if not all, of the organs in the body have a lot in common with the brain, as seats of determinate indeterminacy.)

Quite understandably, the energy of the central nervous system is self-contradictory from the perspective of formal logic: it is the same as and different from that of other physiological mechanisms. Despite its continuity with the rest of the body, the central nervous system is the one and only organic network that displays the virtualizing tendency of organismic reflectedness into itself. (Perhaps a physio-anatomical expression of its exceptional nature is to be found in the blood-brain barrier.) Partaking of distinct energy regimes, that of being and that of the concept, the central nervous system befits a "spiritually-organic being [*geistig-organische Sein*]" (*PhG* §328) and is reflected into itself even as it is oriented toward exteriority. This synergy propels it to the vanguard of dialectical energy, mediating movement and rest in the immediate actuality of the body (whereas self-consciousness is this mediation in the *mediacy* of conscious existence): "The *nervous system* is the immediate rest of the organic in its movement [*Das* Nervensystem *hingegen ist die unmittelbare Ruhe des Organischen in seiner Bewegung*]" (*PhG* §327). The nervous system is the infrastructure for substantivized organic workings. In it, organic movement sets itself to work. Stating this is not sufficient, however: it remains to be seen how such substantivation differs from other organic structures and even from the part of the living body that has the most in common with the inorganic world. I am referring, of course, to the skeleton.

The kernel of truth in phrenology is that, as substantive structures, as the body's being-in-the-work, the nervous and the skeletal systems appear to be objects of the same type from the perspective of outside observation. As participants in the immediate actuality of the corporeal, the brain and the skull are on a par and are barely distinguishable from one another. For this reason, protrusions and depressions in the latter are treated as momentous for individual propensities. The contrast between the brain and the skull is clear only where one is deemed "the bodily *being-for-itself* of spirit [*körperliche* Für-sich-sein *des Geistes*]" and the other is thought of as "a fixed, restful thing [*das feste ruhende Ding*]" (*PhG* §328). As opposed to the skull, the brain is external actuality turned inward, substantivized energy that makes the de-substantivizing movement of reflection possible. At the limit between the inner and the outer, the brain is the perfect locus of energy, in the work within the body and at work in spirit. This commonsense conclusion seems to invalidate any claim of phrenology to truth. Yet, in a gesture worthy of deconstructive applause, Hegel shows that the outer of the outer determines (or de-termines) the inner: the skull "presses on the brain and so sets its outward boundary [*das Gehirn drükt und dessen äußere Beschränkung setzt*]" (*PhG* §329). The thing at rest regulates the limits of self-reflected movement; exteriority invests interiority with meaning and, indeed, with energy, which, continuing the line of vegetal thinking, emanates from and is received on the outside. The skull is not a mere casing of the brain, just as the body as a whole is not a discardable sheath of the soul. The existent shape, or the external actuality, of energy is as important as the movement of shaping, unshaping, or reshaping. The fate of expression (*Ausdruck*) is linked to the physical pressure (*Druck*) that, allegedly trivial, haunts the relation of the skull and the brain. Hegel's unspoken ironic inference from the above is this: confessional acts aside, phrenology holds more truth than Christianity.

What ensues is a long, and no less ironic, discussion of how the skull anchors the human, culminating in the scandalous speculative declaration "the being of spirit is a bone [*das Sein des Geistes ein Knochen ist*]" (*PhG* §343). Not to be easily dismissed, this line of argumentation is vital to our understanding of Hegel's energy-actuality, which is committed to the exteriority of material existence as much as to the virtualizing movement of self-reflection. As energy, Hegel's spirit is far removed from the noumenal, the phantasmatic, the ghostly; it is nothing but a parade of existing shapes and their conversions or perversions. The statement "*the actuality and existence of humans is their skull-bone* [die Wirklichkeit und Dasein des Menschen ist sein Schädelknochen]" (*PhG* §331) means that the actual, substantive figuration of human being determines this being's virtual essence in the same degree that the latter determines the former, genetically if not conceptually. A mistake of phrenology is to have individuated the figuration, which, in Hegel's text, refers to all "humans," to the human species. In addition to serving as an outer envelope, negatively delimiting the evolutionary increase in brain size, the skull is also a positive phenomenalization of a specifically human shape, the energy of humanization embedded in this work. With the emphasis of "the actuality and existence of humans"—that is, on the substantive aspect of their energy—the skull-bone is no different from the political state, and the statement I have just cited is commensurate with saying that the actual being of spirit is a state (something Hegel actually asserts in his *Philosophy of Right*). Both are the visible works of spirit that determine, whether biologically or culturally-politically, how it will be put into work in the future.

The point Hegel disregards is that there is a still more outward limit on the size of the brain, namely the diameter of the dilated birth canal in preparation for birth. He remains oblivious to the gynecology of spirit in its immediate actuality, the energy of a woman's body that, within the limits of its pain-suffused generosity, determines the objective aspect of the human (the head) and, more fundamentally, the very "being of spirit." The female body at work or in labor brings about as an accomplished work the possibility of the human as human—the "actuality and existence" of a newborn body, as much as the outer delimitation of the outward expression of its self-consciousness. In the dialectic of the brain and the skull, of plasticity and rigidity, of organic movement beyond itself and a reminder of inorganic nature, the third element that recedes from view is the energetic mediation between the two commencing in the maternal other. In other words, Hegel neglects to mention that the being of spirit is the mother's pelvic bone.

The subsequent treatment of the skull in the *Phenomenology* is an apt and colorful illustration of the Hegelian energy-actuality paradigm. As an "indifferent, unencumbered thing [*gleichgültiges, unbefangenes Ding*]" (*PhG* §333), the skull in its osseous mereness is virtual existence, the apogee of virtual reality detached from what it is supposed to contain, from the rest of the body, and, in the first place, from itself. Moreover, its empty virtuality theoretically presages the de-actualizing movement of the French Revolutionary Terror and the heads that rolled off the shoulders of its victims. Taken in isolation, the skull is cut off from the rest of the body, wrought from the organic/ergonic arrangement it is a part of ("The skull-bone is not an organ of activity [*kein Organ der Tätigkeit*], nor even a speaking movement [*eine sprechende Bewegung*]" *PhG* §333). In a thinly veiled rejoinder to Shakespeare's Hamlet, Hegel deems the skull mute: it does not have enough energy-actuality either for expression or for signification, although it does tend to evoke the thought of mortality. Incapable of speaking for itself, it has no "value of a sign [*Wert eines Zeichens*]" (*PhG* §333), which means that the hermeneutical energy for saying anything about it must be derived elsewhere, destining its interpretation to persistent arbitrariness. Like the indeterminate "this," the skull-bone borders on the inexpressible, and the determinations ascribed to it will disclose nothing more than the contingency of their relation to the determined indeterminate object.

Nonetheless, the skull is, and the fact of its sheer being inscribes it, along with everything "real," within the matrix of energy-actuality under the sign of deficiency. Hegel proceeds to define the skull as "*spiritless actuality, a mere thing* [geistlose Wirklichkeit, bloßes Ding]" (*PhG* §335), or, in our terms, as energy without energy, a work set loose from the bio-spiritual workings of the organism. The skull is irreducible to an organ without a body, to paraphrase Deleuze and Guattari; it is a body part that is not an organ at all, but a bone put to the work of procuring meaning from the position of its own meaninglessness, vacuity, detachment, disarticulation. However immediate the actuality of the bone in an organism, it points beyond itself at the ensemble of life it participates in, at the synergy of cells, tissues, anatomical structures, and physiological systems that obtain their energy and their sense from their co-belonging in a shared context. Without such a context of living and signifying, the body and its parts are moved externally in a way that is no different from a stone. Their determinations and articulations are ossified, becoming literally osseous—*Knochenbestimmungen* (*PhG* §335)—as they also are in a body of thought that scoffs at synergy.

Essentially intermediate and highly mediated, energy is neither movement nor rest, but rest in movement and movement in rest. Total pliability is as detrimental to it as absolute immobility; an isolated subject and an independent substance are equally divested of energy. And, in fact, such a subject and such a substance go hand in hand. When the object is impenetrably dense, its mediations removed, the subject with all the arbitrariness of abstract freedom takes it upon itself to supply what is wanting in the object. To contend with the ossified determinations of the skull-bone, the phrenologist is an "observer who sets himself to work to determine these relations [*der Beobachter jedoch ans Werk, Beziehungen zu bestimmen*]" (*PhG* §337). The observer supplants the energy (being-in-the-work and being-at-work) of the observed, slipping purely subjective projections and interpretations in the place of the object. This is the only method for animating the static reality of the virtual, so much so that it appears to be the most vibrant level of existence, where everything is possible. Aleatory possibilities substituting for "an *actuality* that is not present [*die* Wirklichkeit *nicht vorhanden*]" are entirely appropriate to the virtual reality of a separate skull-bone *and* to the freedom of the individual "indifferent to being as such" (*PhG* §337). Anything whatsoever can be stated about the significance of the skull that is beyond the pale of signification and expression. Baseless chatter pretends to be speaking for and representing the mute thing. Can we not recognize some of our current political authorities in this dialectical account of phrenology?

A purely subjective determination and the empty chatter that conveys it both say and unsay (contradict) themselves. Singled out for scrutiny, physical marks on the skull "indicate something actual and a mere *disposition . . .* or something non-actual [*etwas wirkliches als auch nur eine* Anlage . . . *daß er etwas Nichtwirkliches*]" (*PhG* §338). How is this contradiction different from that of energy, which is similarly actual and non-actual (de-actualizing or de-substantivizing)? First, the non-actual moment of energy is not a disposition, a passive "maybe," but movement away or toward actuality. Second, and more importantly, we would be making a crude mistake were we to confound dialectical contradiction with that built into sheer possibility. On the virtual plane of phrenology, where the sign and what is signified are mutually indifferent, everything is concomitantly possible and impossible; without its interlocking with impossibility, possibility itself is not possible, as Derrida confirmed time and time again. A dialectical contradiction is, conversely, a *self*-contradiction, creating that very "self" and negatively mediating the real on the way to the actual. Rather than drown in pure possibility, which is immediately or non-mediately *im*possible, the contradiction that impels dialectics emanates from the speculative energy of actuality, its splitting into the actual and the non-actual. In turn, the actual marks on a skull-bone and the potential dispositions they are supposed to allude to cannot be traced back to this speculative fission of the same and its explosion into an identity and a non-identity. There is no energy whatsoever in phrenology's static opposition of the actual and the non-actual, the opposition always ready to flip into an immediate identity.

That said, phrenology obliquely teaches us a lesson regarding two principal modes of actuality it immediately lumps into one in its own interpretative activity. Its take-home message is that external "*being* as such is not the truth of spirit in general [*das* Sein *als solches überhaupt nicht die Wahrheit des Geistes ist*]" (*PhG* §339). A phrenologist's conscious conjecture must straddle, if only haphazardly, the skull's external being with the meaning it holds regarding the dispositions of its owner. By virtue of this mediation, which does not quite reach the subject's self-consciousness, the exteriority of the bone is overwritten with the interiority of sense, and "consciousness is only *actual* for itself through the negation and abolition of such [external] being [*das Bewußtsein sich allein* wirklich *ist, durch die Negation und Vertilgung eines solchen Seins*]" (*PhG* §339). Consciousness attains to actuality, is energized and interrelated with itself and its other, when it de-actualizes external actuality, proving that pure substance is nothing substantial, that it is no more than virtual reality. Conscious activity replaces the opposition of the actual and the non-actual with a contrast between interior and exterior actualities, the actuality that *"thinks itself* [der sich denkenden]*"* and the "existing actuality [*der seienden Wirklichkeit*]" (*PhG* §339). Phenomenologically, an inner actuality is primary, whereas, for the dialectical absolute, the movements *between* the two actualities—amounting to the so-called "truth of spirit"—are of paramount significance. The momentum of de-actualization enables a swaying from one actuality to another without ever sliding into the non-actuality of mere possibility.

The actuality of consciousness achieved through a negation of external being is, admittedly, redolent of violence. As far as Hegel is concerned, an appropriate response to a physiognomist is a slap in the face, and to a phrenologist—smashing the skull (*PhG* §339). In both cases, the object charged with the excess of meaning is nullified, be it by destroying its integrity or by humbling and humiliating it. This nullification does not, for all that, add or subtract anything from the object, but simply reveals its inherent nullity and untruth. The negation of external being is, itself, not external, not arbitrary; it accelerates or recollects the self-negation proper to existing actuality. Genuine violence lies in the assertion that the (potential and actual) being of a human (or of any other being, for that matter) boils down to a bone, and it is *this* violence that is foregrounded and negated when the bone is smashed, shown to be "nothing *in-itself* [*nichts* An-sich]," and refused the status of "true actuality [*wahre Wirklichkeit*]" (*PhG* §339).

Now, the truth of actuality does not lean on the side of interiority, either. Instead, it is at work and in the work in the middle, in the movement-rest of the existing and self-reflected actualities. Assuming that the inner actuality is conscious and the outer is unconscious, energy is sparked off in the "contingent relations between conscious and unconscious actuality [*des zufälligen Verhältnisses von bewußter Wirklichkeit auf unbewußte*]," between the inner and the outer, in the mediation of thinking mediacy and bodily immediacy (*PhG* §342). If spirit "is the necessity of this relation [*die Notwendigkeit dieser Beziehung*]" (*PhG* §342), i.e., the necessity of contingency, then, its designation as "absolute" notwithstanding, it remains true to the middle as the space-time of energy at its most intense, both energizing and energized.

On the one hand, the body at work is already an intersection of conscious and unconscious existence, an energetic site with a thingly extension and living intentionalities, some of them rolled into themselves, interiorized, unknown even to the subject in whom they are lodged. On the other hand, for phrenology, physiognomy, palmistry, and so on—

endeavors that bear a striking resemblance to our contemporary "scientific" psychology, in which statistical data take the place of objective corporeal markers—the body is an arbitrary sign, a surface of inscription, a substratum for conscious personality. Yet, consciousness is not at work on the construction site the body has been transformed into: it cedes this role to the abstract tendencies for action that, beyond individual control, put individuality to work. There is no middling position between the extremes of dispositions and the bone markers they supposedly correspond to. Extricated from the relation of consciousness and the unconscious, energy dissipates, entropying into the nonconscious "dead thing [*totes Ding*]" to which the "outer and immediate actuality of spirit [*die äußere und unmittelbare Wirklichkeit des Geistes*]" has been restricted (*PhG* §343). In exchange for the necessity of contingency, we get the contingency of petrified necessity in a non-relation of two externalities.

Obviously, energy wanes both on the side of the observed object and on the side of the observing subject. Binding itself to a thing and committing to a reified augury of self-consciousness, self-conscious observation itself becomes thing-like. Suspended between mediation and a relapse into immediacy, this development holds out a promise as well as a threat. Since self-consciousness delivers itself to thinghood, it rediscovers itself as a form of mediation (and, hence, of energy) in "the unity of I and of being [*die Einheit des Ich und des Seins*]," which is the category (*PhG* §344). At the junction of the Aristotelian and the Kantian notions of the category, Hegel situates thingified self-consciousness in the excluded middle of substance and de-substantivation, in the very spot of energy that has been debarred. But this mediacy is not available to the observing self-consciousness itself—only to its being recollected from the standpoint of the absolute. As the de-actualizing moment of the I is forgotten, "*pure* category" collapses into one of the dimensions that comprised it, namely "a form of *being* [*der Form des* Seins]," as an unmediated object matched by an unmediated consciousness (*PhG* §344).

With the essential ambiguity of energy resolved in favor of impenetrable substance, of a detached being-in-the-work, what emerges is "conceptless naked thought, which takes the bone to be the actuality of self-consciousness [*begrifflosen nackten Gedankens, für die Wirklichkeit des Selbstbewußtseins einen Knochen zu nehmen*]" (*PhG* §345). When the body is not at work, neither is the mind. Conceptless thought is naked because it strips energy-actuality down to brute products (to the bone), the works at rest that are amenable to the power of observation. Alongside the skull, the observer's brain and self-consciousness are also naked: they are resigned to immediacy in the midst of the mysterious mediations that they are *in themselves*. A reactivation of self-conscious reason will have to commence from the depths of its abjection, its tethering, together with the body it resides in, to objective actuality.

b. The Self-Actualization of Rational Self-Consciousness: Becoming-Rational and/as Becoming-Actual

The initial movement of observing reason is, thereby, inverted. Having abandoned the virtual enclosure of abstract conceptuality, self-consciousness is not satisfied with its acute interest in "all reality"; it takes this reality upon itself, consigning itself without remainder to a thing. To complete this rotation of energy-actuality, self-consciousness needs to take leave once again of the objective actuality, to which it has limited itself, on the path to a fresh process of de-substantivation. In keeping with speculative energy, naked self-consciousness demands no outside assistance to clothe itself in another layer of meaning; it turns its skin inside out and so fashions its attire from an immanent negation of its own nudity.

Truth be told, self-consciousness is never absolutely naked, covered as it is at the very least by its own doubling, its splitting against itself. The moment of speculative fission is when "*it is for itself* that self-consciousness is *in itself* objective actuality [es ist für es *daß es* an sich *die gegenständliche Wirklichkeit ist*]" (*PhG* §347). If self-consciousness lurks behind itself and registers "for itself" its reduction to objective actuality "in itself," then it implicitly mediates all appearances of immediacy, leaving its energetic imprint on them. What is immediate for self-consciousness "has the form of what has been sublated [*die Form eines aufgehobenen hat*]" (*PhG* §347). The shape of self-conscious immediacy is the shaping of previous mediations. In this way the thing is un-thinged, and the physical limits of the skull, the brain, and even individual self-consciousness are breached. Coming to visibility beyond or beneath them is their organismic and communal ground, upon which energy comes into its own as *syn*ergy.

In its emergence from the dead actuality of a thing, reason undergoes de-substantivation in the other, who restitutes to it the verbal modality of energy it had sacrificed in order to have a body. The vehicle for reason's de-substantivation is no longer the individual other, but the precepts, laws, customs, and other works of a community, in which a universal subject is discernible. Such works form "the real substance" (*reale Substanz*) "into which the earlier forms [of consciousness] return as to their ground [*als in ihren Grund zurückgehen*]" (*PhG* §348), and which is comparable to the substantive dimension of embodiment that apportions physical energy in a much more limited and privatized fashion to each.

Instead of an isolated confrontation of an individual subject with an object, the pairing of universal reason and the historical ensemble of self-consciousnesses weaving a culture creates the materal and spiritual conditions for becoming-rational *as* becoming-actual. Individual subjectivity itself is only possible to the extent that it flourishes on the ground of the communal works, which comprise substantive rationality. Going back as far as "mere" consciousness, we must avow this ground as the precondition for individuation, previously obscured by the isolated and isolating approach to the I and the objects I occupy myself with. All energy is individuated from the synergy grounding it, only to melt back—in the form of works—into the synergic milieu from which it had condensed. That is why all individual moments only "have their *existence* and *actuality* [Dasein *und* Wirklichkeit] when they are sustained by that ground" (*PhG* §348).

Seeing that there is no energy without synergy, energy dialectically appears here for the first time in its *truth*—a word Hegel uses insistently on these pages. The realm where energy-as-synergy shows itself in its truth is *Sittlichkeit*, or ethical life (*PhG* §349), which is also the highest development in the *Philosophy of Right*. The value of Hegel's contribution to the thinking of energy cannot be overestimated: it is pointless to postulate the truth of energy-as-synergy abstractly, in the form of a principle for thought or for action. That truth, which is incommensurate with theoretically determined veridicality, needs to be worked out and worked through; it demands time for its activation and actualization. Truth *is*, insofar as it acts—insofar as it is actual and effective. The energy *of* truth, its actuality and effectivity, is the outcome of the immediate coincidence, the subterranean synergy, of "the *thought-out* law," *das* gedachte *Gesetz*, and "the equally immediate actual *self-consciousness*," *ebensosehr unmittelbar wirkliches* Selbstbewußtsein (*PhG* §349). If Hegel implicitly calls upon us to move past the final stages of his *Philosophy of Right* in these lines, this is because the unity of the two making up *ethos* is yet to be mediated, their synergy still to be envisioned. Customary or ethical life (*Sittlichkeit*) is, after all, the unconscious synthesis of individual self-consciousness with the ensemble of self-consciousnesses that has decomposed into universal subjectivity and culture. We must await the de-substantivation and virtualization of ethics that would break its suffocating ties, while safeguarding the energy consciously threaded out of these linkages.

The political consequences of Hegel's argument are momentous. Synonymous with the fulfillment of synergy, the *Volk* is no longer the crowning achievement of spirit, but the background from which more individuated figures will stand out. Its energy-actuality is biased toward the substantive work of reason present in the shape of "fluid universal *substance*, as the unchangeable simple *thinghood*" (*PhG* §350). When Hegel writes that "in the life of a people [*in dem Leben eines Volks*], the concept of the self-actualization of self-conscious reason has in fact its complete reality [*seine vollendete Realität*]" (*PhG* §350), he is insinuating that that concept itself is not yet actual, not yet interrelated with itself, but is *merely* real, thing-like, even if the completion, or the accomplishment, of its reality already borrows a signature feature of actuality. In the life of a people, the self-actualization of reason is still not actual, but only real—virtual, disjoined, independently substantive. To attain actuality, that life must be immanently disrupted by individual action and become either no longer an immediate *life* or a life that no longer characterizes the *people* as a whole.

Hegelian ethics is, we might say, energized by a conduct that is decidedly (and, indeed, self-consciously) nonethical, even if it stays rooted in the realm of *Sittlichkeit*, of substantive reason that grounds individual subjectivity, regardless of whether the latter is opposed to it. A people exists, just as a table exists, but it is not the full actuality of self-relatedness without the negative mediations that cut through the iron shield of its identity. It is, in other words, incomplete without the ostensibly superfluous energy emanating from individual activity anchored in, nourished by, but also breaking off from, the work (*Werk-ergon*) of singular agents "which is brought forth by themselves [*das von ihnen hervorgebrachte Werk*]" (*PhG* §350).

Lest we be under the impression that Hegel romanticizes individual action, his position is clear-cut: our "purely singular" activities are within the purview of biology, rather than culture, related as they are to needs and our "natural being," *Naturwesen* (*PhG* §351). (Nothing is more real and, therefore, more virtual than need!) While they break through the substantive work of self-actualized reason, singular individual acts are, at bottom, as real as the thing they negate. This is a classical case of speculative energy: the real divides into real and non- or irreal, procuring energy-actuality from the depths of the virtual. Such a scenario should not be surprising, given that pure singularity (for instance, of individual acts) is by definition set apart, unmediated, virtual and virtualizing. The most basic of our needs, Hegel relates, echoing Adam Smith, "have actuality . . . through the universal sustaining medium, through the *power* of the whole people [*Wirklichkeit haben . . . durch das allgemeine erhaltende Medium, durch die* Macht *des ganzen Volks*]" (*PhG* §351). Stated otherwise, our needs receive their energy-actuality and the possibility to be satisfied from the very life of the whole, from which they break off, but the whole itself ("the power of the whole people") has no actuality without this virtual remainder of independent individuality. The existence of a people is, itself, virtual—a matter of power, *Macht*—before it bestows actuality on a single person. Actuality germinates in the fission of the virtual, divided into the power of the whole and the powerlessness (unfulfilled needs) of singular existence, with the one brought to bear on the other.

If actuality is reality's self-relatedness, then at the level of coexistence there is no better way to forge its mediations than by interrelating the subject in need with all other subjects of need. This is the Smithian basis of Hegel's position that proclaims: "In his actuality, the individual is entangled with the activity of all [*ist in seiner Wirklichkeit in das Tun aller verschränkt*]" (*PhG* §351). The entanglement is dialectical synergy, which lends energy its meaning. A totally stand-alone individual is the paradigm case of the virtual, which is but actuality oblivious to itself, forgetting its own beginnings as much as its end. To a certain extent, this forgetting is unavoidable in individual existence viewed from the phenomenological perspective of an individual, rather than the absolute. "The individual in its *individual* labor *unconsciously* performs *universal* labor [*der Einzelne in seiner einzelnen Arbeit schon eine* allgemeine *Arbeit* bewußtlos *vollbringt*]" (*PhG* §351). A work brought to fruition in individual activity is the *ergon* of the universal, the en-ergy of the whole, which, at the same time, nourishes and sustains the activity that stands out from it and which awaits its decaying return to the bosom of the whole. But what is still unresolved here in the enworkment, activation, or actualization of need is the fact that the connections between the individual and the universal levels are unconscious, that is, immediate, unselfconscious, void of an energy of their own. The bond between individual activity and the activity of all is essentially unbound, because not yet tied to itself. A mediate relation between the universal and the singular—the relation pulsating with the energy that fulfills the work of the universal in singular *self-reflected* workings—has not yet been discovered at this point.

An alluring resolution of this dilemma is the no less immediate identification of the individual with the ethical milieu, so that "in a free people, reason is in truth actualized [*In einem freien Volke ist darum in Wahrheit die Vernunft verwirklicht*]" (*PhG* §352). The question, of course, is what Hegel means by "a free people." Is he referring to the political freedom of a people that governs itself? If so, is its energy-actuality achieved thanks to this universal self-relatedness expressed in autonomous state institutions? Alternatively, does he have economic freedom (the epitomy of bourgeois freedom) in mind, where the work of the whole comprises the micro-operations of the market, reflecting the productive activities of each? Or, again, is he alluding to freedom of speech, of the press, of religion, and so on, those liberal safeguards against the brutal imposition of a substantive *ethos* on individuals?

Whatever the interpretation of *das freie Volk*, the self-actualization of the rational via a direct identification of an individual with the work of the people, however free, is highly suspect, in the first place for Hegel himself. For the energy of the whole to become that of the individual, and vice versa, there needs to be tension, friction, and opposition between the extremes that are prematurely reconciled in an immediate recognition of the individual in the universal. The bliss (*Glück*) of reason is short-lived, and the truth of its actuality is revealed for the falsehood it is when we come back down to earth, to "real *ethical life*," *die* reale Sittlichkeit (*PhG* §354), which substantivizes the work of universality without leaving any space for the subject position thought to be identical to it. For the reality of *Sittlichkeit* (condensed, for instance, in the "power of the people") to exit from its virtual enclosure, the subjective supplement, both negating and relating it to itself, is in order.

Surely, the subject opposing the laws, customs, and conventions of her culture saws off the branch on which she is sitting, or loses her footing. But this loss, brimming with energy, is already a repetition of the initial loss of trust—*sein Vertrauen verloren* (*PhG* §355)—provoked by those conventions, customs, and laws that militate against concrete individuality, say, by discriminating against women. The energy of subjectivity presents itself as the energy of rebellion and negativity that de-substantivizes *ethos*, vacates it of the substantive works that went into its composition, and transforms it into "a mere thought without absolute essentiality, an abstract theory without actuality [*nur ein Gedanke ohne absolute Wesenheit, eine abstrakte Theorie ohne Wirklichkeit*]" (*PhG* §355). The subject *un*works the law, be it written or unwritten, and along the way undoes itself, assuming that even the satisfaction of basic needs is possible solely in the universal context, which dissolves into a virtual abstraction. The self-actualization of rational self-consciousness invariably goes through the phase of de-realizing both its subject and substance.

Ethical life is drained of its vitality and appears to be a series of hollow shapes, the substantivations of energy, which, already brittle in themselves, can be smashed by a living subject like so many clay idols. It is shorn of energy as manifestation, bereft of the mediated unity of the manifested world, or actuality, and the manifesting, actualizing movement. In ethical life past its prime, energy is apportioned asymmetrically between individual workings and collective works that are perceived as nothing but obstacles, resulting in a situation where "ethical substance has sunk to the level of a selfless predicate [*die sittliche Substanz ist zum selbstlosen Prädikate herabgesunken*]" (*PhG* §357). But, since energy is unviable without synergy, since there is no existence without coexistence, another mode of subjective co-imbrication comes into play, this time spun out of the subject's opposition to ethical life. Its origins steeped in the interpretation of the law as an "abstract theory without actuality," this congenitally negative mode of synergy is morality.

Regulating the conduct of two or more isolated persons abstracted from the thick contexts of their lives, morality is the doctrine of subjects without substance, of interpersonal workings without works. Its synergy is like bonds tied in a void, which is why, essentially non-manifest, it absconds from actuality and nestles in the dark recesses of the inner world. Morality is "a higher shape [*einer höhern Gestalt*]" than ethical life (*PhG* §357) within the phenomenology of individuality it elevates; within the world of spiritual substance explored in the *Philosophy of Right*, however, it is a step lower than *Sittlichkeit*. A shape of energy that abhors the substantive actuality of social and political institutions, including written laws, morality is exceptionally suitable to pure individuality, unshaping and reshaping itself without a final figuration in sight. Individuals feel that they have rid themselves of external determinations and are ready to receive energy-actuality from nowhere but themselves: self-consciousness aims "to give itself actualization as an individual and to derive enjoyment from this self-giving [*sich als einzelnes die Verwirklichung zu geben und als dieses in ihr sich zu genießen*]" (*PhG* §358). Self-actualizing, they abut the ideal of drawing energy only from themselves, the ideal which is behind the political slogan of "energy independence" in the United States. Hegel would retort that the pleasure experienced in receiving only the self-given is rational delight, the quasi-masturbatory self-enjoyment of reason full of and in itself.

In the self-actualizing operations of rational self-consciousness, a massive energy-actuality swap takes place, effecting a transition from the immediately given *actuality* to a self-given *actuality'*. So much so that this localized transfer emblematically concentrates in itself the entire chain of energy transformations that traverses the *Phenomenology*: "consciousness appears divided into this previously found actuality and a *purpose*, which it attains by sublating the latter. In place of the first actuality, it now makes its purpose into actuality itself [*das Bewußtsein erscheint entzweit in diese vorgefundene Wirklichkeit und in den Zweck, den es durch Aufheben derselben vollbringt, und statt jener vielmehr zur Wirklichkeit macht*]" (*PhG* §359).

I insist on reading these lines attentively: it is not that the actualized purpose supplants the first, merely given actuality, curing along the way a wounded consciousness. Instead, self-actualizing self-consciousness furtively slips its purpose into the place of the first actuality. Self-givenness is still only a sleight-of-hand, a shift from immediacy to mediation, which is itself immediate to the extent that it ends with the inward and interiorizing movement of idealism. Mediation itself has to be mediated, energy energized. If the purpose is what is truly actual, then that which is worked toward replaces the workings as well as the works, suffusing dialectical energy with more vacuity. A purpose made actual is (actually) virtual; it belongs to a self-consciousness that "is for itself, therefore, reality as immediately self-expressing individuality, which no longer finds any resistance to an actuality that is opposed to it [*ist es sich also Realität als unmittelbar sich aussprechende Individualität, die keinen Widerstand an einer entgegengesetzten Wirklichkeit mehr findet*]" (*PhG* §359). Frictionless, it wastes the energy that it presumably gifts itself with. The immediacy of its self-expression provides an important clue to the wanting nature of the mediation, which rational self-givenness dictates. The absence of resistance between a posited purpose and a pre-given actuality is, itself, to be overcome.

i. Pleasure and Necessity: The By-Products of Energy Conversion

The curtain falls. There is nothing to be observed in the dynamics of rational self-actualization, though this "nothing" is only what it is based on the standards of empirical observation. But a great deal happens in the de-substantivation of actuality carried out by rational self-consciousness. That self-consciousness is "for itself, *reality* in general [*sich überhaupt die Realität ist*]," but a reality that "does not yet exist [*der noch nicht seiend ist*]," one that is confronted by "*being* . . . as another actuality [*das Sein . . . als eine andere Wirklichkeit*]" (*PhG* §360). The works and the world of substantive energy-actuality appear alien to the virtual reality of rational self-consciousness, which is eager to "make this other into itself [*dies Andre zu sich selbst zu machen*]" (*PhG* §360), all the while energizing itself by repeatedly overcoming the resistance of otherness. Those who attribute "idealism" to Hegel are convinced that the process of assimilating the other to a virtual identity exhaustively describes dialectical movement. They turn a blind eye to the fact that he qualifies the appropriation of the other as "*the first purpose*," erste Zweck (*PhG* §360), which is, therefore, the emptiest and most abstract form of mediation. There is, after all, no energy conversion without a back-and-forth of affecting and being affected between immediate actuality and virtual reality, between "materialism" and "idealism," alterity and self-identity.

Rational pleasure is the by-product of making the other into the same, that is, of negating an alien actuality and subsuming it to the reality of self-consciousness. Were this the end-all and be-all of dialectical energy conversions (of the transition from *actuality* to *actuality'*), Hegelian spirit would be living in a world of pure rational pleasure. But this is not the case: rational necessity obtrudes as a limit to the domestication of otherness set by residual resistance to harnessing the energy-actuality of the outside. Negative dialectics—the dialectics of the remainder, which cannot be incorporated into the energy regime of the same—is, far from the rejoinder to Hegel that Adorno makes it into, the sine qua non of Hegel's *Phenomenology*. At the very least, the domestication of otherness provokes the alienation of sameness and renders unviable the preservation of virtual identity and its ideal purpose. The self-actualizing dynamic unravels, as the initial "self" is marooned along with the actuality it has first contended with. The purpose itself suffers alterations as it remakes a merely found actuality, leading to a mutual contamination of the energies pertaining to the externally given and the self-given until the latter is acknowledged as the former, irrespective of the foisting of the former onto the latter. (This contamination, combined with this acknowledgment, is at the heart of the absolute.) Taken in combination, the two alterations—of the self and of the purpose—signal that a self-actualizing self-consciousness is unable to persist in a state of bliss, of the unending pleasure it seeks from the act of making the other into the same.

While it can, rational self-consciousness draws enjoyment from life, "plucked as a ripe fruit [*wie eine reife Frucht gepflückt*]" (*PhG* §361) in the course of its self-actualization. It is neither living entities nor life itself that self-consciousness takes pleasure in, but the conversion of life's immediate actuality into the mediacy of self-consciousness. The object of enjoyment is alterity—not the principle of vitality, not this or that living being, but life as a synthesis of these two moments—devoured by sameness. In the process of its self-actualization, self-consciousness draws not just pleasure but its energy from the act of plucking the fruit, which is no longer only vegetal. Physical digestion, converting chemical into mechanical and thermal energy, as well as mental digestion, transforming immediate being into a represented one through the categories of understanding, are superseded by self-consciousness devouring the alterity of life, which amounts to its own self-devouring. Self-consciousness enjoys itself in enjoying its other and procures its energy from itself-neutralizing-the-other. From the de-substantivation of the other, this self-consciousness, "which knows the other as its *own selfhood* [*welches als* seine eigne Selbstheit *das andre weiß*]" (*PhG* §362), extracts the substantive dimension of energy-actuality and is actualized as the object of its own enjoyment—a rational affect feeding on the assimilation of otherness. It builds itself up by destroying the otherness of the other.

Hegel is convinced that the energy occasionally ascribed to dialectics as such (and, we might add, representative of contemporary humanity in *our* relation to life in its different human and nonhuman modalities) is unsustainable. The mediated actuality of rational self-consciousness is de-actualizing: "the achieved actuality of its individuality sees itself annihilated by the negative *essence*, which opposes it as empty and shorn of actuality and which, all the same, is a consuming power [*die erreichte Wirklichkeit seiner Einzelnheit sich von dem negativen* Wesen *vernichtet werden sieht, das wirklichkeitslos jener leer gegenübersteht und doch die verzehrende*

Macht desselben ist]" (*PhG* §363). Rational self-consciousness pleased with the assimilation of the other to the same is a sublation of actuality that is virtual and virtualizing, in that it assumes the amorphous shape of a "consuming power," potency "shorn of actuality," *wirklichkeitslos*. Its energy is anti-energy—and it *knows that* ("its experience is intuited by its consciousness as a contradiction" [*PhG* §363]).

The passage from pleasure to necessity reduplicates the plunge of various kinds of certainty into the unhappy consciousness divided against itself. Necessity is the self-consciousness of rational self-consciousness, its disenchantment with enjoyment in the awareness that, in de-substantivizing otherness, it de-substantivizes sameness as well. The "plunge into life" turns into "the consciousness of its own lifelessness," "an empty and alien necessity as *dead* actuality [*die leere und fremde Notwendigkeit, als die* tote *Wirklichkeit*]" (*PhG* §363). It is not that the obstacles of necessity are externally opposed to the self-expanding pleasure of self-consciousness; rather, in the clarity of the lived contradiction "energy = anti-energy," necessity is soberly appraised as the dead actuality of enjoyment itself. Demanded to no end by the virtual-virtualizing interiority of all-consuming power, which discerns in itself the only true reality, rational enjoyment aware of itself is, by the same token, mindful of its dependence on the deadening de-substantivation of otherness. How does this exceedingly serious play of life-and-death, enacted on the stage set by rational self-conscious existence and no longer on the biological plane, pertain to the question of energy-actuality?

One stubborn supposition ingrained in philosophical idealism is that life—and, above all, infinite, pure, and absolute vitality—is tireless activity, whatever its outcomes. The Thomist reception of Aristotle, whose *energeia* is translated into divine *actus purus*, is but the most prominent instance of this harmful assumption. Indifferent to the works they spawn, the workings of ideal life are essentially de-substantivizing, as opposed to "creative" or "productive," and rational self-consciousness is not an exception to this rule. Its operations yielding rational pleasure consist in making an object out of the transformation of the other into the same: stripping away its substantive dimension and rendering it consistent with the being-at-work of self-consciousness. But, in the absence of existing otherness, the machinations of pure life would be impossible. There needs to be "hard," substantive actuality, energy hardened into determinate forms, for life to go on living (or surviving). As a result, "the individual is led to ruin and the absolute brittleness of individuality is pulverized on an equally hard, albeit continuous, actuality [*das Individuum nur zugrunde gegangen, und die absolute Sprödigkeit der Einzelnheit an der ebenso harten, aber kontinuierlichen Wirklichkeit zerstäubt ist*]" (*PhG* §364).

What shatters on the hard and continuous surface of actuality is, more than anything, the illusion that life and energy can (and should) do without substance, helping themselves to works in the substantive as no more than fuel for de-substantivizing routines. The "transition" (*Übergang*) of self-conscious "living being" to "lifeless necessity" (*PhG* §365) is, therefore, seen absolutely as the discovery of how necessary lifeless necessity is to the living of a life or to the enworkment of energy. The transition is a change in perspective more than the actual dying and interment of self-consciousness, which had been already wedded to "dead" substance without knowing it.

The shadowing of rational pleasure by necessity is explicable with reference to the irreducible duality of energy, its being-at-work inseparable from being-in-the-work. An outside compulsion intervenes even in acts of devastating exteriority as exteriority—by assimilating it to the same—and that is the source of a painful experience of necessity, whereby self-consciousness "becomes even more a riddle [*ein Rätsel*] to itself" (*PhG* §365). In the shape of necessity, exteriority (and, hence, the question of shape as energy's substantivation) makes its traumatic comeback. The negation of self-givenness, necessity is given without the receiver having chosen it or as much as having suspected that it has been dispensed. Necessity is a gift, or maybe even *the* gift: terrible, unexpected, destabilizing. It is, at the same time, a moment of truth for the virtual and virtualizing self-consciousness, which meets in it a crushing counterpart to its own power: "*Abstract necessity* thus stands for the merely negative, unconceived *power of universality*, in which individuality is shattered [Die abstrakte Notwendigkeit *gilt also für die nur negative, unbegriffene* Macht der Allgemeinheit, *an welcher die Individualität zerschmettert wird*]" (*PhG* §365). The residual actuality of individual self-consciousness succumbs to the virtuality of necessity that finishes the work of "pulverization" begun in the encounter with "hard and continuous" external actuality. After this encounter, subjective interiority will always be that of a shattered individuality, its fate pre-delineated in the rise of the unhappy consciousness.

ii. The Law of the Heart and the Madness of Self-Conceit:
Energy and the Principle of Noncontradiction

However unconscious in its provenance from the outside, the Hegelian gift must become self-given. The absolute demands that, contrary to my first impressions, I receive the world and myself from myself. Only if this statement is understood as an abstract apriori principle will it be redolent of idealism. Time, mediating negations, energy conversions, the entire dialectical apparatus with its works and workings—all this needs to be activated, actualized, put to work for the merely given to be accepted as self-given. Necessity does not escape the same fate, which is no longer fate in the sense of blind submission to the law of the unconscious; reflected into itself, consciousness knows necessity as *itself* (*als* sich), such that it retains in itself necessity's "essence absolutely *alien* to it [sich absolut *fremden* Wesens]" (*PhG* §366). In this, self-consciousness corroborates, once again, that it has instantiated a discontinuous, broken actuality, when compared to the uninterrupted actuality of the outside. Its discontinuity is, in effect, the feature which gives it the edge by letting it approximate the "structure" of energy-actuality, crisscrossed by fault lines between its two modalities. Interiority is no longer the black hole of virtuality but a split in actuality, which is initially conflated with actuality's virtual negation. Through it, the *en-* of energy embarks on a protracted journey toward actuality, that is to say, toward itself.

The objectively universal, empty, and virtual law is at a further remove from energy-actuality than the subjective law "of the heart." Guarding the memory of its having been pulverized by necessity, this second kind of law is rooted in an originary trauma, or, ontologically, in the caesura between the two modalities of energy repeated in the "self" of self-consciousness. That self-consciousness "knows *immediately* the *universal*, or the *law* it has in itself [*weiß* unmittelbar *das* Allgemeine, *oder das* Gesetz *in sich zu haben*]" (*PhG* §367) is an achievement, despite the presumed immediacy of such knowledge. It knows this thanks to the blow that made it part against itself and accommodate the previously external necessity in itself. No such negation (experienced by self-consciousness as the opposite of rational pleasure) was required of the objectively universal law, which, lagging behind the law of the heart in the degree of its mediateness, sides with virtuality. It is worth keeping this ellipsis in mind: the Hegelian law of the heart is the law of a *broken* heart, which, by virtue of its brokenness, channels energy-actuality.

A broken heart is the metaphoric side effect of an ill-starred love affair. The Hegelian inner law seems to have nothing to do with such matters, however; it dwells in a heart literally broken, shattered in its pulsating energy-actuality by the power of internalized necessity. Yet, this objective crush does not preclude a "subjective" interpretation tinged by the rhetoric of amorous failure: the law of the heart is required because love cannot dictate the law, but is relegated to exceptional interpersonal situations, and also because the law as such is the upshot of a broken heart, of love frustrated. A loving heart, for its part, is broken *even if* its isolated love life is satisfactory; it cannot contain a libidinal bond for the energy-actuality of all (synergy), leaving it up to the self-consciousness that interiorizes the law to fulfill its own universal purpose: "the heart that nonetheless has the law in itself is the *purpose*, which it intends to actualize [*ein Herz, das aber ein Gesetz an ihm hat, ist der Zweck, den es zu verwirklichen geht*]" (*PhG* §368). That the purpose is still to be realized implies that the law of the heart is mired in virtuality, which "stands opposed to actuality [*steht eine Wirklichkeit gegenüber*]" as alien to it. "Not yet actualized [*noch nicht verwirklicht*]," it is "something *other* than the concept [*etwas* Anderes, als der Begriff ist]" (*PhG* §369).

Despite housing the universality of the law, the heart enables a retreat of self-consciousness into itself and, therefore, its return to a condition where external actuality is temporally partitioned into the past and the future. On the one hand, there is the actuality that is pre-given, to which the purpose is opposed; on the other hand, there is the actuality to be achieved according to the purpose, so that the law of the heart would become identical to the concept. It follows that the law of the heart is distinct from a simple escape from actuality. It announces, rather, a confrontation between one actuality and another, the "not yet actualized [*noch nicht verwirklicht*]" self-given universality of the law and the always-already actual, purely given, "alien necessity [*einer fremden Notwendigkeit*]," which is an outcome of the subject's alienation from truth (*PhG* §369). Both the not-yet and the always-already stand out against the horizon of a third, properly dialectical actuality that negates (and, in negating, preserves and elevates) them: the energy-actuality of the heart worn on the sleeve, the inner made outer and exteriority fully internalized.

Dialectical movement *actually* unfolds on the basis of the third moment as an absolute. Phenomenologically, though, the law of the heart sets itself to work in being counter-worked, in a clash of actuality with itself as other—a still feeble actuality of the inner smashing against the walls of the rock-hard "outwardly necessary" actuality that, with its mediations out of sight due to the subjective estrangement that brings it into being, is even weaker than a merely external actuality. Consequently, the law of the heart is energy *and* anti-energy, a setting-to-work and a de-activation or a de-actualization, at one and the same time. It is operative only to the extent that it works against the principle of noncontradiction, in which X and not-X are treated as mutually exclusive. And in this, in its partiality as a dialectical moment, it encapsulates the universal essence of speculative energy and of dialectical energy in toto.

"The law of the heart" is, furthermore, the way Hegel encrypts Kant's moral philosophy. A twisted substitution we encounter in Kant is the following: the universality of the goal (namely, "bringing about *the welfare of humanity* [*Hervorbringung* des Wohls der Menschheit]," *PhG* §370) immediately confers universality on the subject desiring or aspiring toward that goal. The moral subject imagines itself occupying the empty spot of a virtual universal, which is never to be actualized, never to be accomplished, and which persists solely in the shape of an ideal. It acts as though energy-actuality were not divided, above all against itself. The hard work of mediation, of working on, with, and against actuality, fracturing and fractured against itself, is abandoned. Kant's moral subject contents itself with dwelling in the "unbridgeable" principle of noncontradiction, which at the same time it (contradictorily) bridges by means of the transcendental *as if* at the heart of the law of the heart. Consequently, "what it actualizes is the law itself, and its pleasure is at the same time universal for all hearts [*Was sie verwirklicht, ist selbst das Gesetz, und ihre Lust daher zugleich die allgemeine aller Herzen*]" (*PhG* §370). The dialectical meaning of the Kantian *as if* is that of a virtual synergy, the coincidence of pleasure and the law in the substitution of the law of the heart for law as such.

To be sure, an adherent of the law of the heart realizes that external law and necessity exist, provoking not pleasure but the sense of an imposition. This realization is combined with the demand to transform or reform such a law, which is but a "semblance" (*ein Schein*) of lawfulness, by stripping it of the associated "violence and actuality," *welcher das verlieren soll, was ihm noch zugesellt ist, nämlich die Gewalt und die Wirklichkeit* (*PhG* §371). The inauthentic energy captured in external law *is* violence itself; it stands for a merely stumbled-upon actuality, which the subject experiences as jarring and inconsistent with universal pleasure. To divest the outwardly necessary actuality of its right and to cut its ties to violence, one needs to turn it into *actuality'* given to oneself in the subject's innermost core, the heart.

Continuing the twisted substitution we have seen the subject engage in, what actually happens is a certain mix-up: the transformed and self-given *actuality'* is mistaken for the virtual enclosure of the subject, which is instrumental for the movement of that same transformation. In the aftermath of this confusion, which is crucial for the formation of the Kantian transcendental subject, the fissuring of energy-actuality and the tensions between *actuality* and *actuality'* are misrecognized and translated into an opposition between the actual and the virtual. At the height of virtuality, the law of the heart becomes synonymous with the self-actualization of law and the condition of possibility for "the consciousness *of itself* that has therein pacified or satisfied *itself* [*das Bewußtsein* seiner selbst, *daß es sich darin befriedigt habe*]" (*PhG* §371). Energy-actuality totally virtualized is the modern, topsy-turvy stand-in for the fullness and self-fulfillment of Aristotelian *energeia*. Hence, also, the language of the subjective accomplishment—or literally, the bringing-to-fullness—of the law: "The individual thus *accomplishes* [vollbringt] the law of its heart" (*PhG* §372).

Instead of nursing a broken heart, the subject of the new law indulges in masturbatory pleasure. But it is this very pleasure that breaks through the virtual enclosure of the heart and gives rise to an alternative order of being, "an actuality that is in and for itself lawful [*einer an und für sich gesetzmäßigen Wirklichkeit*]" (*PhG* §372). As always, a virtual niche cannot hold anything in itself for too long; it cannot, in its carrying or holding capacity, withhold actuality. The further into itself the subject retreats, the more it gravitates toward the other in a speculative split with itself that (internally) converts its self-satisfaction into something alien to it. In its pursuit of pleasure, the subject stumbles upon the actuality of the virtual. Although "*universal power*" (allgemeine Macht), "the indifferent" (*gleichgültig*), and "a form of *being*" (*die Form des* Seins) (*PhG* §372) are expressions synonymous with virtuality, they come to denote the actuality of the transcendental domain experienced via the disinterested, universal pleasure that gushes forth from the law of the heart. The acts of judging and deciding on the basis of that law clothe the pronouncement, let alone its attendant affect, in the mantle of the actual. While virtuality is actualized by carrying out this judgment and making this decision, actuality is, in turn, virtualized, "for his act means that he posits his essence as a *free actuality* [*das Tun hat den Sinn, sein Wesen als* freie Wirklichkeit *zu setzen*]" (*PhG* §372).

How can an essence—the virtual per se—be an actuality, and a free one at that? We need to reflect on what Hegel means by "*free actuality.*" At the most obvious level, its freedom is due to a departure from external necessity and the ostensibly independent actualization of the inner law, the law of the heart, in the universality of transcendental moral judgments. There is also a deeper sense of being-free: the actuality of Kantian law is liberated from actuality itself, conceived in the shape of factical existence; it is an actuality free of actuality, the release of energy immediately virtualized. Set loose from the constraints of self-identity as much as from the principle of noncontradiction, the free actuality of the law of the heart is, at the same time and in the same manner, actual and non-actual, an effective (external) act and inner essence. But, because it is unbound from itself, because it does not comprehend its judgments as *acts*, this actual virtuality emulates virtual reality and wastes whatever energy it has managed to muster. It is not that the subject's escape from finite existence has been incomplete; rather, it is that, having cut the last shreds tying it to outward necessity, the subject forgot that the act of cutting is, itself, the strongest bond holding it fast to actuality.

Ambiguity does not cease here, and for good reasons: once postulated, the law of the heart is ambiguity incarnate—the actual and the non-actual—expressing, above and beyond its isolated intention, the character of dialectical energy-actuality. Far from melting into universality with transcendental moral judgments for catalysts, the subject stands divided between the form and the content of the act: "His act belongs to the universal *as actuality*, but its content is his own individuality [*Seine Tat gehört als Wirklichkeit dem Allgemeinen an; ihr Inhalt aber ist die eigene Individualität*]" (*PhG* §373). The shape of actuality and that which fills it are parts of two different energy regimes: the former has already crossed over to *actuality'*, whereas the latter stays locked in immediate *actuality*. Furthermore, the desired shape of energy-actuality is ideally virtual (drained of energy)—something that contributes to its suspension on the threshold, between two distinct stages or regimes. The true energy of the law of the heart does not irrupt from its content or from the form, but from the frictions between them, the edges of one actuality colliding with, rubbing against, and resisting those of another.

It is possible to read the complications of the law of the heart, which sweeps the principle of noncontradiction aside, as a heuristic device illuminating the general dynamics of energy in the Hegelian dialectics. The precept it leads us toward is that energy is enworked in and through its counter-enworkments, while its work and workings are inextricable from a certain "delaboration," a playful word I would like to coin, a word that negates elaboration and puts the actuality of "labor" at the mercy of deliberation. The collision of one actuality with another (which it both is and is not) does not shatter the legislating heart. Like an adrenaline shot, the collision enlivens the heart, forces it to beat faster in its non-self-coincidence, which *is* its being: "Instead of achieving *its own being*, it achieves within this being the alienation *of itself from itself* [*statt dieses seines Seins erlangt es also in dem Sein die Entfremdung seiner selbst*]" (*PhG* §374). It turns out that a purely inner necessity is no more alive than the "objective" outer necessity; a pre-given actuality is no better or worse than the arrested movement of its virtualization. The *en-* of *energy*, a prefix denoting interiority, does not boil down to subjective interiority, but belongs in the circle formed as a consequence of perennially transgressing the boundaries between inner and outer necessities—the circle in which dialectical necessity gyrates. Every such transgression is an energy grab at the expense of static identity and an affirmation of life compatible with the actual. "Actuality is an enlivened order [*die Wirklichkeit belebte Ordnung ist*]" (*PhG* §374), the law of the heart surmises, equating life with the ordering and disordering of a pre-given "reality" and with the universal edicts this law proclaims.

We ought not to be under the impression that the energy exchanges and conversions, which contribute to dialectical circularity, are smooth and trouble-free. On the contrary, if delaboration is part and parcel of every elaboration—if energetic enworkment inevitably runs into its own counter-work—then the cycle of energy-actuality is drawn around and within constant disruption. (One might say, along these lines, that disorder is ingrained both in order and in the act of ordering.) Similar to other virtualizing techniques, the law of the heart is delaborative: it is capable of both gaining the time for deliberation and of devastating actual works along with "external" actuality in its entirety.

Hegel signals the affinities of the law of the heart to what I term "delaboration" when he writes that "the nature of actualization and that of effectiveness are unknown to it [*ist ihm die Natur der Verwirklichung und der Wirksamkeit unbekannt*]" (*PhG* §374), which is nearly the same as concluding that the law of the heart does not know itself, does not recognize itself in its outcomes. While judging, it does not judge its own actions or judgments, and so contains a rift between the verbal and the substantive aspects of energy-actuality. It works without being aware of the meaning of work, as indicated in the common root *Wirk* shared by *Verwirklichung* (actualization) and *Wirksamheit* (effectiveness). Unbound from itself, it satisfies the definition of virtual reality and is prevented from rising to actuality not because it rejects mere exteriority, but because it has no inkling of the repercussions that, not at all contingent or external, are integral to its own nature.

The two halves of energy are unfastened from one another in the guise of the non-correspondence of content and form: that is the fulcrum of delaboration. The law of the heart is not an exception. The form of universality, its applicability to all hearts, is not borne out by experience—many hearts reject it, so that, "for this shape of self-consciousness, what emerges from its experience as the truth *contradicts* what it is *for itself*" (*PhG* §375). Delaboration sets itself to work: the law of the heart becomes unworkable, negated or de-elaborated by the experience of its frustrated actualization, even as it makes deliberation—and, indeed, thinking itself—possible in the gap of self-contradiction. At the same time, dialectical failure is a badge of success, if we remember, as Hegel does not fail to mention, that this gap and this essential contradiction make up self-consciousness, a shape of energy-actuality that is hopelessly (or hopefully) delaborative. In coming off its hinges affixed to content, the form of inner law recovers the absolutely unhinged form of self-consciousness itself, the liveliness of energy in its non-self-coincidence, in the unending flight of its verbal from its substantive dimensions.

When Hegel writes that "through the actualization of that law, the universally valid order has equally become [for self-consciousness] its own *essence* and its own *actuality* [*die allgemeine gültige Ordnung ist durch die Verwirklichung jenes Gesetzes, ebenso ihm sein eigenes* Wesen *und seine eigene* Wirklichkeit *geworden*]" (*PhG* §375), what he is really saying is that it has become its own through the *non*-actualization of that law, or, better yet, through a non-actualization that betokens a higher actualization still than the seamless, positive, and affirmative actualization of an abstract potentiality in a piece of work. Secure ownership is achieved by means of alienating that which is straightforwardly one's own. De-substantivation and virtualization involve the self-repulsion of *Wirklichkeit* that makes it, in all its self-contradictoriness and non-self-coincidence, all the more *itself*.

In the following paragraph, we can glimpse Hegel rejoicing like a child at his own ingenuity. He has basically discovered the perversity of perversion, "this inner perversion of its own self [*diese innere Verkehrung seiner Selbst*]" (*PhG* §376), the negation that turns the negated term around in such a way that it is reaffirmed, with renewed strength and with the explosive charge of speculative energy, as itself and not-itself. Pure madness, *Verrücktheit*, the essence of self-consciousness "is immediately a non-essence, its actuality—immediately a non-actuality [*sein Wesen unmittelbar Unwesen, seine Wirklichkeit unmittelbar Unwirklichkeit ist*]" (*PhG* §376). Translated into our terms: its virtuality is immediately non-virtual, and its energy is immediately non-energy. Madness is holding mutually exclusive elements as valid at the same time, in one and the same heart, in blatant violation of the principle of noncontradiction. The word "madness" no longer names a deviation from the norm of sanity that is in force for the vast majority of reasonable people, most of the time. Rather, madness is the essence/non-essence, the energy/non-energy of self-consciousness and, more than that, *the energy/non-energy of energy*. Self-consciousness is unhinged and delaborative, seeing that it works by not working and doesn't work by working. What it perverts is its self; the "self-" of self-consciousness is produced in and as this perversion, the desaturation of energy-actuality that is responsible for *its* kind of energy-actuality.

The madness of self-consciousness is, of course, also that of dialectical phenomenology. Fundamental, foundational unhinging explains the divergence between the phenomenological perspective, the lens under which shapes of energy-actuality construct their worlds, and the perspective without perspective (or with *all* the finite perspectives infinitely repeated) of the absolute. Madness writ large, partly overlapping with what I have been calling "delaboration," is the engine powering the Hegelian project, as he himself confirms with lucid self-awareness: "consciousness knows *itself* in its law as this actual and, at the same time, because it is this very essentiality, its actuality is *alienated*, both as self-consciousness and as absolute actuality that knows its own non-actuality [*ist aber das Bewußtsein in seinem Gesetze sich seiner selbst als dieses Wirklichen bewußt; und zugleich, indem ihm ebendieselbe Wesenheit, dieselbe Wirklichkeit entfremdet ist, ist es als Selbstbewußtsein, als absolute Wirklichkeit sich seiner Unwirklichkeit bewußt*]" (*PhG* §376).

Consciousness knows itself as actual in something—the law of the heart—that does not and cannot have any actuality or awareness of external effectiveness. Perversely, it attains its "self," rising to self-consciousness, in and as a failure to retrieve itself, the necessary failure of coordinating absolute actuality and the stages of spirit, appearing, from its standpoint, as non-actual. Yet, because absolute actuality is *both* absolutely different from *and* the same as the so-called intermediate actualities, it realizes its own non-actuality in contemplating them. The self that comes to fruition by way of alienation from itself is, thus, dialectics, madness, and energy-actuality—*Wirklichkeit*, which we cannot translate with a single word in English and which, in the language of Hegel (I do not mean only German here, but also the language of Hegel's *philosophy*), sparkles with multiple meanings, sending us back to work, effectiveness, *actualitas*, Aristotelian *energeia* . . . This non-identity is madness, from the depths of which dialectical reason wishes to surface only to dive back into it time and again, not resolving but intensifying it thanks to the ongoing repetition of everything that goes on in the absolute. Absolute form and absolute content are, on the hither side of pure reason, absolutely unhinged, madness absolutized, energy-actuality at odds with itself in the closest proximity to itself.

To go back to perversion: a properly (that is, a perversely) dialectical question would be not what it is but what it does. We would need to deduce the being of perversion from its doing, its work from its workings. What does perversion do? It perverts, and to maintain itself it must keep perverting further. As for the absolute, it is the greatest perversion of them all, the belonging-together—which Hegel eventually diagnoses in the law of the heart—of the perverting (*das Verkehrende*) and the perverted (*das Verkehrte*) in a play on energy's workings and its works (*PhG* §377). The perversity of perversion, the law of the heart, has to keep doing what it does best: to pervert, and especially, to pervert *itself*, which is how the pursuit of a universally valid order flips into its opposite, into "self-conceit" as an extreme consequence of the voiding of actuality.

On the one hand, for the law of the heart, "*actuality* as a *valid order* is void [*die* Wirklichkeit, *eben das Gesetz als* geltende Ordnung, *vielmehr das Nichtige*]"; on the other hand, "its *own* actuality, itself as the individuality of consciousness, is *for it* the essence [*seine eigne Wirklichkeit, es selbst als Einzelnheit des Bewußtseins ist* sich *das Wesen*]" (*PhG* §377). The madness of the inner law mutates into self-conceit when self-consciousness is torn between two actualities, neither of them fully actual for it—the former *already not actual*, the latter *not yet actual.* Having abandoned an externally valid order, having nullified its validity, self-consciousness is still on the verge of discovering a transformed actuality as something effective and self-related. In a limbo, its madness consists in a seemingly interminable wandering in a desert, a protracted delay; having left the land of slavery behind, it still has the realm of freedom ahead of it. This, too, is delaboration: the continual twists of perversion and perversion's perversion, on the one hand, and the suspension of transition in a quasi-frozen in-between, on the other: the enworkment of energy in the simultaneity of movement and stoppage, with which Aristotle was acquainted all too well.

Given the universalist aspirations of the law of the heart, supposedly held to be true by all hearts, the madness that afflicts it (or, we should say with Hegel, the madness that it is) strikes the sociopolitical sphere in a regime we label "liberal." This regime draws its legitimacy—its "actuality and power," *Wirklichkeit und Macht*, as Hegel puts it, recruiting both actuality and potentiality—from the insane act of elevating individuality to the form of the order: "*die Individualität als die Form derselben*" (*PhG* §378). The singular becomes the form of the universal, just as the inner law commanded, while the content is supplied by an external actuality that is de-actualized, deactivated, de-substantivized, sublimated, and virtualized into the actuality of the individual, yielding "spiritual universality and substance [*geistige Allgemeinheit und Substanz*]" (*PhG* §378). The form now adequate to the content, it seems that the broken heart is mended, that its law is virtually the same as love, that the unhinged content-form relation is set aright, and delaboration is surpassed.

But Hegel gives us a cue to the contrary: we are not dealing here with shapes of energy expressed dialectically through the mediations and determinate negations of their content, but with a hollow form, one indifferently stuffed with any content whatsoever. It is for this reason that Hegel uses the Latinate word *Form*, not *Gestalt*, to depict the contribution of individuality to the new order it invests with meaning. There can be no emergence of *Gestalt*, in fact, where mediations are nonexistent, where "all individuals are immediately this universal [*alle Individuen unmittelbar dieses Allgemeine sind*]" (*PhG* §379). Liberal society resolves the crisis of energy and madness itself in a mad fashion: by foregoing energy-actuality altogether and lumping the singular and the universal in a unity of content and form that has not been, dialectically *and* psychoanalytically speaking, worked through but merely acted out. In so doing, it raises the stakes of delaboration.

Although we are, perhaps, even more apprised of liberal formalism than Hegel was in the nineteenth century, his inferences are profound and far-reaching. One such inference is that liberal formalism and the Hobbesian war of all against all are two sides of the same coin, or, otherwise put, that Kant is a continuation of Hobbes by other means. Fending mediations off, foregoing an energetic solution to the energy crisis of the inner law, the universal shatters (as did, for instance, the thing with its multifaceted dimensions and qualities before it) into individual universalities, each of them wielding an equal claim to validity: "The universal, which is present here, is hence merely universal resistance and the combat of all against all [*Das Allgemeine, das vorhanden ist, ist daher nu rein allgemeiner Widerstand und Bekämpfung aller gegeneinande*]" (*PhG* §379). With insufficient mediations, energy falls back into a mechanistic modality, a physics of the social and political arena (the proverbial billiard table), which is rife with frictions and collisions at worst and non-contact at best between the individuals isolated each in their virtual actuality.

Resistance to the other can be politically organized, streamlined, made efficient and set to work for the purpose of waging war. But, by and large, political reality is the arena of *Realpolitik*, or what Lenin used to refer to, derogatorily, as "the politics of small tricks." The political reality of "business as usual" is virtual, and this is what Hegel means by *the way of the world*, *Weltlauf*, which corresponds to the verbal facet of energy; being incessantly at work, devising strategies to navigate the system and take advantage of it, a "restless individuality," in another assault on the principle of noncontradiction, concludes that "the actual is non-actual and the non-actual actual [*das Wirkliche unwirklich und das Unwirkliche das Wirkliche ist*]" (*PhG* §380). The substantive facet of the same energy belongs to the subject who estranges itself from the rat race to the abyss of the *Weltlauf* and who represents virtue, the "motionless essence . . . which is not nothing but also not actuality [*das nicht gar nicht, aber doch keine Wirklichkeit ist*]" (*PhG* §380). The consciousness of virtue is not nothing, because it is a stable being-in-the-work of the inner principle, but it is also not actuality, because it leaves the workings of the actual outside itself.

Slotted between being and nothing without instigating (in keeping with Hegel's *Logic*) the dialectics of becoming, the pole of virtue bears witness to the fracturing of energy-actuality. While, guided by its stable principles, it feels disgusted by the wheeling and dealing that takes place in the way of the world, this way itself, falling back on its dynamism as the absolute standard, makes a laughingstock of the virtuous subject. Energy-actuality splinters into power and a powerlessness that aims, through its act of taking exception to the way of the world, to be higher than worldly power.

iii. Virtue and the Way of the World: Adventures in Power, Powerlessness, and Virtuality

Although we are still examining energy-actuality, the contrast between virtue and the way of the world, between power and powerlessness—that is to say: between potency and impotence—has plunged the dialectic into virtuality of varying degrees. As a rule, the more fractured actuality is, the more it passes for and into its other. Tremendous discharges of speculative energy accompany this passage. Virtue is here an attempt to master virtuality, while renouncing the mastery proper to power.

"Virtue" names the escape of the subject from a constant struggle for power in the outside world to the virtual domain of its own uprightness, of inner strength. The movement of de-substantivizing the way of the world, which refers to external actuality, rounds off the complex of virtuality-virtue-power-essence. But, because that shape of external actuality is already de-substantivized in itself—its energy sapped by lopsided restlessness, workings without works, and conflict—the repetition and escalation of de-substantivation in the insistence on virtue achieves the opposite effect of recalling actuality back to itself. Therefore, consciousness finds order not in the "*existing actuality*," seiende Wirklichkeit, of the way of the world, but in this way's "essence," which is but "the universal *perverted* through *individuality* [*durch die* Individualität verkehrte *Allgemeine*]" (PhG §381).

For dialectics, virtue is, rather than the principle of moral uprightness, the perversion of a perversion, a radical move of replacing power games with a certain powerlessness, which, by intensifying the dynamics of virtualization, swerves back to actuality. It is from Hegel that Nietzsche derives his notion of slave morality, drawing on the relation of mastery and servitude, as well as on the desaturation of power in virtue, which, as powerless, arrogates to itself a higher power. In our terms, this is the work of counter-work, or the energy of anti-energy: virtue rejects the outer energy-actuality of the way of the world and converts this rejection into an energy outlet, on the basis of which it then constructs another (virtual and virtuous) actuality of a truly perverted perversion.

Why is the way of the world perverse? Hegel's judgment is not at all normative, or moralizing. What he brings into relief are the internal contradictions of the energy-actuality, out of which the way of the world is spun. Let us decelerate further and run the film of the *Phenomenology* frame by frame, so as to follow the subtler movements of Hegel's thought. We will then keep abreast of *Wirklichkeit*, well beyond the horizons of virtue and what it reacts against.

The way of the world is focused on "singular individuality," seeking "pleasure and gratification [*Lust und Genuß*]." There is nothing to energy-actuality within this framework of a single-minded motivation and its fulfillment, save for this very pleasure and its satisfaction: "actuality is merely the singularity of pleasure and gratification [*Die Wirklichkeit ist nur die Einzelnheit der Lust und des Genusses*]" (PhG §382). Yet, pleasure has a law peculiar to it, namely the assimilation of the other to the same, the incorporation of a previously alien actuality to that of the subject, who is satisfied by, and obtains power from, the becoming-same of the other.

Dictating the law, pleasure is universalizable in (and despite) its opposition to universality—something that produces "an absolutely contradictory actuality [*absolut widersprechenden Wirklichkeit*]" (*PhG* §382). The absoluteness of the contradiction has to do with the fact that it is a profound *self*-contradiction, a speculative reflection yielding the inverse image of what is reflected. Not just perverse, it is perversion (*Verkehrung*), surveyed under the lens of "*objective* actuality [*gegenständliche Wirklichkeit*]," and madness (*Verrücktheit*), seen from the standpoint of subjective actuality (*PhG* §382). Where this state of affairs overreaches the predicament of the way of the world is in the internalization of the contradiction, as self-contradiction, and in its adaptation to energy-actuality. Still ongoing and already accomplished, "dynamic" and "static," effective and ineffective, a self-identity and absolute otherness to itself—energy-actuality is cobbled together from numerous contradictions bundled into a whole that is always on the verge of falling apart.

Subjectively speaking, energy-actuality is mad, deranged, unhinged, and our quest after it acquires the traits of the desired object, which is more-and-other-than-object. Objectively speaking, energy-actuality is the inversion (or perversion) of itself into its other: a lapse from the positive powerlessness of fulfillment, of a work already accomplished, to the power of working (and unworking) *what is*. The power it commands stems from oscillations *between* power and powerlessness: "the universal thus exhibits itself in the two aspects as the power of their movement, but the *existence* of this power is merely a universal perversion [*Das Allgemeine stellt sich also wohl in beiden Seiten als die Macht ihrer Bewegung dar, aber die* Existenz *dieser Macht ist nur die allgemeine Verkehrung*]" (*PhG* §382). The same goes for the universal as for energy-actuality itself: the "phenomenon" of *Wirklichkeit* is exhibited in the power of movement between its two aspects (the working and the work; "energy" and "actuality"), but the existence of energy-actuality as power is its universal perversion into its constitutive negative moment, that is, into what it is not.

The movement—or the setting-in-motion—of movement and rest gradually sheds the latter element it mobilizes. The enworkment of movement in modernity, dismissing ancient insights into the dialectics of movement and rest, falls into the trap of bad infinity applied to the dynamics of motility. Power is separated from its source, unplugged from the outlet of speculative self-contradiction upon which it feeds, and mired in a hyperinflation of a single aspect out of the two that set it to work. That is why its *existence* is either impossible or perverse, for what remains of an actual power that rejects its own actuality? Of an energy that dispenses with, rather than determinately negates, the substantive *ergon* responsible for the productive friction with the verbal dimension of work?

We now have a clearer reason for deeming virtue to be the perversion of a perversion: virtue renders explicit the subjective universality latent in the way of the world and, therefore, dispenses to the universal "its true actuality [*seine wahrhafte Wirklichkeit*]" (*PhG* §383). The truth of virtue is the untruth of the way of the world faced with a true image of its universal inner lawfulness. Yet, the "true actuality" of virtue is, itself, not actual: "this true essence is . . . not yet actual, and so virtue merely *believes* in it [*Dies wahre Wesen . . . ist noch nicht wirklich; und die Tugend* glaubt *es daher nur*]" (*PhG* §383). If virtue contributes to a veritable virtualization of the virtual, its truth is the demonstrated perversion of power: power is consolidated with the help of powerlessness that leaves behind any and all footholds in actuality and that invests faith with meaning. Reconstructed from the vantage of the absolute, faith endeavors to mend the detachment of energy converted into mere power from actuality, whereby the actual is essential yet non-apparent and inaccessible—hence, one can only believe in it. On this view, faith supplants and supplements (and supplements in supplanting) the actuality missing from the pure power of subjectivation, de-substantivation, and virtualization. In doing so, it gives off the impression that an authentic actuality can come about without the efforts of individual activity, if not by suppressing, negating, and denouncing the work involved in such efforts.

While virtue strives to occupy the place of the highest powerlessness, experienced both in itself and for itself, it ends up mutilating the essence of actuality, not to mention the energy entwined with the actual. For a virtuous consciousness, the core of actuality is no longer active, and it is dependent neither on an act nor on work but on a retreat from them: "the existence of an effectuated good is thereby the cessation of its [the subject's] *activity* [*dadurch bewirkte Existenz des Guten ist hiemit das Aufhören ihres* Tuns]" (*PhG* §383). The dream of virtue is an energy that would be in effect without the effectiveness of an action, which a virtuous subject perceives as whatever happens in the way of the world. In addition to the workings that go into energy-actuality, its works are refused, as virtue renounces "the enjoyment of the fruit of its labor and sacrifice [*ohne aber der Früchte ihrer Arbeit und Aufopferung zu genießen*]" (*PhG* §383). The cause behind this refusal is fundamentally the same as that behind the relinquishment of action: the objectivation of acts and the subject's pleasure-driven relation to them are, for virtue, indicative of the way of the world, in which it sees itself betrayed. Virtue thus aspires to keep the sphere of subjectivity pure, free of objective expressions and modes of behavior that must contend with the world's imperfections and impositions.

A double negation of the "external" being-at-work and being-in-the-work in virtue gives us to understand that the sense of a *perverted perversion* depends, simultaneously, on setting perversion aright and intensifying it. Setting aright, because the subject is recalled from its addictive search for pure potentiality back to the supreme powerlessness that feigns to be beyond activity and passivity, power and powerlessness. Intensifying, because the rift in energy-actuality that was felt in the way of the world deepens, to the degree that faith in an invisible essence steps in and disguises the contradictions of effectiveness without effecting and without effects, of the actuality of the good stripped of acts and works alike.

In the semantic field of the Hegelian system, virtue is explicable as a regression to the abstract, virtual, and hollow universality of what in *Philosophy of Right* corresponds to a "free," not-yet-embodied will. "While virtue *wills* to implement the good, it does not give the good its actuality [*denn sie* will *das Gute erst ausführen, und gibt selbst es noch nicht für Wirklichkeit aus*]" (*PhG* §384). Like an abstractly universal will, whither it returns, virtue's powerlessness brandishes the universal power to do everything without actually—in acting, in the acts, in actuality—committing to anything. The amorphous shape of energy, as we tend to figure it for ourselves in the twenty-first century, bears strong resemblances to the universal power of an abstract will, subtracted from material existence. We mistake its resolute noncommitment for freedom: first of all, freedom from actuality. The circuits of global financial capital and the virtual space of the Internet are mutually reinforcing in the formal message "*Everything is possible*" that they transmit. Their energy, analogous to the energy of virtue, is an anti-energy, the counter-work of actuality.

Nevertheless, the analogical alignment I have just presented comes up against its structural-logical limits. Virtue is not the starting point of the phenomenological process; already energy-intensive, it is dogged by an inner contradiction that is inapplicable to the initial element of the *Philosophy of Right*, namely the difference between its abstract indifference (as virtual) and the good it is meant to promote. This contradiction, in line with Hegel's thinking, will provide an impetus for the expulsion of virtue from its sheltering in pure potentiality and for its reconnection, in the shape of moral action, with the energy-actuality it has deviated from.

Before the inner contradiction of virtue explodes, "the good or the universal, as it comes on the scene here, exists as what are called *gifts, capacities, or powers* [*Das Gute oder Allgemeine, wie es also hier auftritt, ist dasjenige, was die* Gaben, Fähigkeiten, Kräfte *genannt wird*]" (*PhG* §385). It exists, therefore, in the mode of *actual inexistence*, perverting *Wirklichkeit* into its exact opposite and nourishing itself with the movement of this perversion. The truth is supposed to reside in the sphere of subjectivity and away from the world, not in the substance that activity modifies: in the person, not in the act. The bastions of the virtual, truth and the good, are jealously guarded against their own expressions in *what is*. They are transcendentally indifferent to empirical occurrences. A person, as a pure potentiality, remains fundamentally good, despite killing or raping, and so the concept of goodness becomes utterly meaningless. As though the work of the hand or another organ, its energy or enworkment, had nothing to do with the virtuality of thought, desire, or intention. As though, to maintain their essential purity, truth and goodness had to be kept rigorously apart from "external" actuality, upon which their effects could be imprinted, with unavoidable alterations, and which is but an intricate network of their imprints.

A fixation on "gifts, capacities, or powers" is infantile, its immaturity conditioned by faith in a perpetual promise of the good and by dissatisfaction with the very idea of realization or self-realization in the ever-so-imperfect actuality. This fixation, too, operates with a barefaced self-contradiction: the "powers," *Kräfte*, of and for the good are quite powerless when it comes to *Wirklichkeit*, since they cannot be expressed in substance. As non-actualized and non-actualizable potentialities, they ontologically refute the Spinozan notion of power as the power-to-be, to persist in being, and to give a body and voice to as many substantive modalities as possible. The powers of the good are, *au contraire*, the powers not to be, to excuse subjective virtuality from the being-in-the-work of actuality, and, by taking such exception, to get hold of "the spiritual represented as a universal [*des Geistigen . . . als ein Allgemeines vorgestellt*]" (*PhG* §385). But, for Hegel, spirit is not (only) spiritual, and its effectiveness—the energy of its being-at-work—is fragmentary without the substantive actuality of being-in-the-work. The universal is not universal enough, unless it commits and delivers itself to finite particularity. Energy is not energetic, if it stops at the dynamism of powers and refuses the respite of the actual. The good is not good (and no good), when limited to a capacity to be good.

Imprisoned in itself, in a virtual domain of pure potentiality, virtue recognizes the existent good in its other, in moments of the way of the world where "the universal is not an abstraction but is enlivened by individuality and is for the other, that is to say, it is *the actual good* [*ist das Allgemeine, nicht nur als abstraktes Allgemeines, sondern als ein von der Individualität belebtes und für ein Anderes seiendes, oder das* wirkliche Gute]" (*PhG* §386). The substantive dimension of energy-actuality is phenomenally available, discernible, turned outward, and so exists for the other in contrast to the withdrawal of the virtual domain. The power supply feeding the powers of the good lies outside virtue and virtuality; moreover, it is to be found in their other—in appearance, act, the work already carried out. Although virtuous consciousness disparages the way of the world, it discovers the concretization of its own designs only in its enemy, in universality animated by phenomenal individuality.

Energy is put to work as anti-energy, mobilized by that which is other to it, or by frictions with that otherness. It is the place where phenomenology and ethics merge in being-for-the-other, that is, in providing the universal with an actual shape (exposed to the senses and to sense-making) and in acting for the good of the other. That the actual good "has its existence in the actuality of the way of the world [*in der Wirklichkeit desselben auch sein Dasein hat*]" (*PhG* §386) means that betrayal (as expression *and* sacrifice) is inexorable and that the betrayal of essence (in this case, of virtue) is how one keeps fidelity to it. Whether latently or overtly, the onto-phenomeno-ethical thought and practice of being-for-the-other base themselves on the cornerstone of betrayal in their attempts to de-virtualize essence, to bring it back from its retreat from the world while holding onto a figure of subjectivity. Energy-actuality itself is a concept that betrays itself, that expresses and violates its self-identity, procuring its own energy-actuality from this betrayal, which we know as Hegel's dialectics.

Virtue sees in externalization a waste of its innermost energy reserve and potential, not to mention that, like logical and colloquial modes of thinking, it believes betrayal to be entirely inconsistent with fidelity. As a result, its fidelity to a static identity produces the greatest betrayal, more severe than the expressive sacrifice of essence in existence. The goodness of virtue in itself is absolutely not itself; it is not-good. "Insofar as it is *in itself*," the good is "a passive instrument of gifts and capacities, matter devoid of actuality [*ist es das passive Werkzeug der Gaben und Fähigkeiten, die wirklichkeitslose Materie*]" (*PhG* §388). Devoid of finality, which is only conceivable as the culmination of a series of mediations, the good becomes a means without an end, its energy drastically reduced, its work encapsulated in a piece of equipment (*Werkzeug*) at the behest of mere potentiality. Having cracked and discarded the shells of the act and its outcomes, separated from the kernel of the good, virtuous consciousness keeps for itself the passivity of essence, consisting of power and powers that, without the influx of actuality, are the identical twins of powerlessness. This consciousness throws the proverbial baby out with the bathwater: it rejects the good together with phenomenality, both of them intersecting in the region of being for-the-other.

The insistence on isolating essence from existence translates into the classical (pre-Einsteinian) disengagement of matter from energy, such that the former is assigned the quality of passivity and the latter is imbued with sheer activity. "Matter shorn of energy-actuality," *die wirklichkeitslose Materie*, is, without a doubt, the commonsense concept of matter. When this bankrupt view predominates, the thinking of energy suffers as well: energy-less matter and matterless energy, materialism and idealism complement one another as the remainders of one and the same process, which I have just referred to as the "disengagement" of matter from energy and of both from the speculative energy of dialectics.

The perversions that virtue (the presumably unperverted and incorruptible) instigates are multiple: the good becomes not-good; essence passes into its other and turns out to be inessential; powers amount to powerlessness, impotence, and the passivity of matter. In light of virtue, the finality of the good also dissipates and "its purpose is in fact the abstract non-actual essence [*das abstrakte, unwirkliche Wesen in der Tat ihr Zweck ist*]" (*PhG* §389). The end of virtue is an endlessly hollow virtuality that has no foothold in the world and that is divested of the energy of the good guided by the thinking and attainment of ends. The end of the good is thus perverted into the means, oblivious to the substantivation of energy's work. It follows that Hegelian virtue is an exquisitely perverse, perverted, and perverting thing, if there ever was one. However, since perversion provides dialectics with an engine of sorts, this means that, in disengaging from dialectical relationality, virtue goads dialectical movement on. The energy desaturation it triggers, the powerlessness of potentiality it glorifies, energizes the process whereby energy-actuality communes with itself.

In keeping with the perverse and perverting power of virtue, the actuality it desires is the extinguishing of the actual in self-contradiction: virtue "wanted to consist in bringing the good to *actuality* through the *sacrifice of inidivduality*, but the aspect of *actuality* is itself nothing other than the aspect of *individuality* [*wollte darin bestehen, durch* Aufopferung der Individualität *das Gute zur* Wirklichkeit *zu bringen, aber die Seite der* Wirklichkeit *ist selbst nichts anders als die Seite der* Individualität]" (*PhG* §389). A virtuous actualization of the good hinges on the negation of actuality indexed to the individual who acts, or even simply intends to act. Virtue has already dispensed with the world of substance, with objective "works" read as irrelevant to the essence of goodness; now, sacrificing individuality, it gives up on its subjective workings. What virtue really wants is energy-actuality without energy-actuality, its two constitutive aspects done away with and only the space between them (graphically represented by a hyphen) retained. By means of this major self-contradiction, virtue strains to "bring the good to actuality," which it has in the meantime doubly undercut. Unconditionally virtualized, it eventually brings the good to naught, to nothing really.

Hegel takes it for granted that virtualized virtue is quintessentially modern; in its ancient iteration, the concept and its corresponding practice were "grounded in the *substance* of the people [*der* Substanz *des Volks*]" and "had an actual, already existing good for their purpose [ein *wirkliches schon existierendes Gutes zu ihrem Zwecke*]" (*PhG* §390). In a circular mode of reasoning, ancient virtue aimed at what already was—at the existent actuality of the good—and this aspiration served as its energy source. It banked heavily, if not exclusively, on the substantiveness of *ergon*, the solidity of existent actuality, of the ground, of the people, of the good itself. Modern virtue rebels against what used to be virtue; it recasts "actuality as *universal perversity* [*Wirklichkeit als eine* allgemeine Verkehrtheit]" void of any and all content (*PhG* §390). This emptying-out is necessary for unmooring from a stiflingly substantive energy-actuality and embarking on a search for its active underside. But, while necessary, the virtualization of virtue is insufficient unless, through the winding detours of its perversions, it arrives at the shores of *actuality'*. Here, we might ask, however: does the newly gained *Wirklichkeit*, scarred by the substantive attachments of the past and their perversions, still live up to the definition of virtue? Is it not, just like energy-actuality itself, beyond power and powerlessness?

One outcome of the dialectic of virtue in Hegel is an individuality that, having passed through the grinder of sacrifice, is realized in its *self-realization*. This is where extremes meet: motion and rest are articulated in self-movement; the workings and the work of the universal cross in the individual: "the setting in motion of individuality is the reality of the universal [*die Bewegung der Individualität ist die Realität des Allgemeinen*]" (*PhG* §391). Static universality is, experienced in and for itself, dynamic individuality. At arm's length from the ideal movement of self-creation, the energy-actuality of this self-realized individuality hinges on the realization that the "external" way of the world is not independent, accidentally stumbled-upon reality, but a work, left behind by universality itself. One learns that "the way of the world is not as vicious as it appeared, for its actuality is the actuality of the universal [*denn seine Wirklichkeit ist die Wirklichkeit des Allgemeinen*]" (*PhG* §391). Spinoza had a flicker of this insight when he heeded the ancients and concluded that what was in being (or in substance) was already good. Hegel rounds off the substantive being-in-the-work of this ethical ontology with the being-at-work of universality localized in active individuality. After the tide of virtualizing and virtualized virtue recedes, the way of the world discloses, like the denuded bottom of a sea, its universal grounds, means, and ends.

More so than Spinoza, Aristotle and Adam Smith preside over the Hegelian energy-actuality *after virtue*. The motion-rest of the universal is a reflection of the unmoved mover, whereas the actualization of universality in the pursuit of particular individual interests is a shadow of the invisible hand. Individual "actuality in a non-sundered unity with the universal [*die Wirklichkeit in ungetrennter Einheit mit dem Allgemeinen*]" is the "individuality of the way of the world that thinks it is acting merely for itself, or in its self-interest, but is better than it thinks," for it accomplishes the common good (*PhG* §392). Here, power and powerlessness are diverted from virtue to the arena of spirit itself, which, like transcendental reason, works (universally) behind the backs of those who work toward the attainment of their narrow private ends. The actuality of individuality "in a non-sundered unity with the universal" is the world seen from the perspective of the absolute, reminiscent of Smith's and Kant's approaches.

The post-virtuous energy-actuality of selfish actors unwittingly contributing to the attainment of unselfish goals is nowhere near the dialectical crest. Contrary to the invisible hand and transcendental reason pulling history forward, the Hegelian absolute cannot move behind the backs of actual individuals—or, at least, not for long. *Its* self-realization demands the recollection of actual individuals just as they are, neither better nor worse in their own actuality, which is as universal as it is singular. The gap between its *Wirklichkeit* and theirs must narrow to an infinitesimal interval in the remembered repetition of their workings and works. Only then will the "non-sundered unity with the universal" appear, de jure and de facto, in its truth as the acting individuals' non-sundered unity with themselves.

The indivisible oneness of *Wirklichkeit* with anything or anyone is complicated by the fact that—split between the substantive and verbal senses of *ergon*, *actus*, or *Werk-Wirk*—it is not one with itself. The stubborn persistence of a gap in the absolute is due (from the absolute, rather than a phenomenological perspective) to the genetic non-self-coincidence of energy-actuality. That said, the noncoincidence in question turns out to be anathema to all metaphysical analyses: in *Wirklichkeit*, there is no segregated, reserved, and, therefore, consecrated deep essence set over and against actual appearances; it simply gives birth to its other in the processes of its own energizing actualization. In other words, its truth is its perversion.

The unity of individual actuality and the universal can be readily deduced from the essential demonstration of essence in appearance, or, more exactly, in the appearing of appearances. In metaphysical thought, an inaccessible, inexhaustible, and untainted inner source spawns the ephemeral epiphenomena that occlude it. For the perversion of metaphysics to be dialectically perverted, the outer must "give life," *Leben gibt*, to the inner, to the in-itself which "is immediately this presence and actuality of the processes of individuality [*ist unmittelbar diese Gegenwart und Wirklichkeit des Prozesses der Individualität*]" (*PhG* §393). The problem of an energy deficit (read: of insufficient mediate repetitions) lingers in the immediacy of conjugating the interiority of what is in itself with the exteriority of what is for the other. But the gift of life received from the outer "shell" of appearance, from the body, actual being, and so on, is remarkable, when framed in the context of the model of animation spreading centrifugally from the innermost "kernel." The process of individuality and its actual product, the workings and the work of individual self-production, are dynamically arranged in such a way that the process is produced by the product, the workings by the work. This is what "individuality real in and for itself" looks and feels like.

c. Individuality Real in and for Itself: A Recircuiting of Energy

A self-consciousness of self-consciousness does not, in Hegel's *Phenomenology*, exponentially multiply the meta-levels of individual awareness, just as self-consciousness is not a meta-level of consciousness. It is, rather, an adaptation of the Aristotelian unmoved mover to the world of finitude and to the modern philosophy of subjectivity. A self-consciousness that "has secured the concept of itself" is "the self-moving permeation of the universal—of its gifts and capacities—and of individuality [*die sich bewegende Durchdringung des Allgemeinen—der Gaben und Fähigkeiten—und der Individualität*]" (*PhG* §394). Besides indirectly invoking Aristotle in the expression "self-moving [*sich bewegende*] permeation," Hegel implies that the self-consciousness of self-consciousness is the suffusion of the actual (existent individual) with the virtual (universality and its potentialities)—of the work that is none other than the "working" subject itself with the workings that unsettle, de-substantivize, and grant universal actuality to the particular. How does this suffusion happen? Analogous to the alternating current in an electrical circuit, it depends on an alteration of the direction of negative charge in the relation of self-consciousness to energy-actuality.

At first, the vector of virtualization required self-consciousness to treat actuality with utmost suspicion, as something in itself dead, something to be energized only by means of a determinate negation. It "*stumbled upon* an *actuality* that would be its negative, through the sublation of which it could actualize its own *purpose* [*es fand eine* Wirklichkeit *vor, die das Negative seiner wäre und durch deren Aufheben es erst sich seinen* Zweck *verwirklichte*]" (*PhG* §394). Not only did self-consciousness see in itself the one and only energy supply for actuality, but it also attempted to discharge this energy by overcoming the resistance it perceived as emanating from the outside, from a powerful negation of itself that was to be energetically negated. The two negative charges—that of actual being and that of self-consciousness—yielded a quasi-vacuum of subjective interiority, a virtual niche housing the law of the heart and virtue that, having withdrawn from the world, devalued activity along with the merely given actuality.

A dialectical alteration of the negative charge consists more in showing how the accidents of existence defined the essence than in the actual passage of essence subtracted from the world into existence. It demonstrates how the phenomenologization of the subject in the act and of potential energy in actuality *constituted the subject and potentiality to begin with.* A sweeping movement of perversion revels in the outward determinations of the subject, reinforced by turning subjective interiority inside out. What it is "in itself"—thoughts, aspirations, dreams, and desires—pours out into a being accessible to others: "however, the *purpose* and *being-in-itself* have emerged as *being-for-the-other* and a *previously found actuality* [*aber* Zweck *und* Ansichsein *als dasselbe sich ergeben hat, was das Sein für Anderes und die vorgefundene Wirklichkeit ist*]" (*PhG* §394). The end and the beginning meet in the circle of an interiorized energy-actuality and an exteriorized subjective virtuality, for which *Wirklichkeit* is no longer "its negative"; it is *actuality'*.

In a transition from the energy of being to that of the concept, the meaning of *Wirklichkeit* undergoes a ground-shift: whereas the negated actuality belonged under the umbrella of immediate being and subjective interiority fell under the category of pure (virtual) being, the "new" recircuited actuality is part of the concept that has given itself a body and an external reality in the process of becoming, mediating being and nothing. The perspective of the absolute instructs us, moreover, that the energy of (immediate) being was actually the energy of the *idea* of such being. The energy of the concept is the realization of this idea, sifted through the self-realization of individuality, of the self-consciousness mediated with itself and with its other, synergized and energized to the brim.

A perverting catalyst for the rewiring of the circuit is the act, which expresses the subject, literally pressing it outside of itself, into a being-for-the-other. With regard to self-conscious self-realization, "activity [*das Tun*] is in itself its truth and actuality [*seine Wahrheit und Wirklichkeit*], and the representation or the expression of individuality is its purpose in and for itself" (*PhG* §394). Energy and truth, the purpose and actuality, cease to negate each other in the act that betrays—expresses and perverts: perverts in expressing and expresses in perverting—individuality. The crux of activity is the translation of gifts, capacities, and, more broadly, of everything to do with potentiality and power into an actuality that is acknowledged to be a work of the acting subject. This translation is obviously going to be incomplete and will involve a mistranslation (hence, the betrayal) of subjective potencies and potentialities that, as they touch *what is,* mutate together with *what is.*

And Hegel goes further than this: the masterpiece, the substantive aspect of active energy, is the acting individual herself, seeing that the purpose is her representation or expression, *Darstellung oder Aussprechen.* Here, the expressed *is* the expressing, which is why the act is "truth and actuality" in a simultaneous folding or unfolding of the two dimensions of energy, the work and the working. A shift from the energy of being to the energy of the concept takes place in this crease, where actuality is no longer thought of as external and subjectivity no longer stands for an interior remainder subtracted from that exteriority. Expression in activity offers us, so to speak, a "two-for-the-price-of-one" tarif of energy production (and consumption).

The paradox built into the alternating circuits of dialectical energy is that the qualities "active" and "passive" are inapplicable to that activity which has its end in itself as the working work of individual self-realization. Such an activity "alters nothing and goes against nothing; it is a pure form of translation of the *yet-unseen* into the *already-seen* [*verändert nichts, und geht gegen nichts; es ist die reine Form des Übersetzens aus dem* Nicht-gesehenwerden *in das* Gesehenwerden]" (*PhG* §396). Non-oppositional and non-destructive, verging on the quiet workings of vegetal life, this activity brings energy into its own, guiding it from invisible potentiality to visible actuality, letting it emerge to the light, grow, and flourish, while staying rooted in nourishing, moist darkness. The phenomenological translation of what has not yet been seen into having-been-seen facilitates the backflow of energy to itself, which is the otherness proper to it as actuality. As actual, energy comes to visibility, presents itself as what it is, turns out to be a phenomenon or a set of phenomena, while the act of its self-presentation occasions the realization of individuality "in and for itself." It is a self-realizing act that "alters nothing and goes against nothing," because it works on itself, or, better yet, works on work itself, mediating between energy and actuality, energy and itself.

The dialectical alternation of currents in the energy circuit is actually a switch between two different circuits, the switch in the course of which the circuit as circuit first emerges: the enworkment of energy-actuality exchanges a straight line (whether serving as a border between subjectivity and external actuality, or denoting the subject's open-ended approach—a vector of "bad" infinity—to the outside world) for a circle, which is the same line bent and closed unto itself. (The comparison of a straight line with a circle helps us to imagine the relation between *actuality* and *actuality'* in geometrical terms.) Seen under the lens of the absolute, self-realizing activity displays a shape of energy and "has the appearance of movement [*hat . . . das Ansehen der Bewegung*]," which is perfectly circular; it "freely sets itself in motion all by itself in the void [*frei im Leeren sich in sich selbst bewegt*] and, unhindered, now enlarges and now contracts and is completely satisfied in playing only in and with itself [*in und mit sich selbst spielt]" (PhG* §396). The activation of energy-actuality spinning in a circle is its putting-into-play, full of itself, fulfilled all by itself, and free in this self-sufficiency, spinning in the void.

At the source of energy's work, then, is play, which is the hallmark of force, now bearing upon itself. This is what sets the work of energy to work, what energizes energy as it gets rerouted from the first to the second power supply no longer procured from the world outside and, therefore, making no difference whatsoever (neither altering nor opposing anything) as far as that world is concerned. In a replay of Aristotle's *energeia*, it announces the actuality of accomplishment—the plenitude of its self-satisfaction and freedom not only in the sense of autonomy, but also in the sense of leaving behind the contingency of the yet unfulfilled potentialities. To work on work is to play, freely.

Still, for this development to come to pass, for the backflow of energy that moves the entire dialectical process forward to be initiated, a new beginning is in order, one by means of which consciousness "springs afresh *from itself* and aims not at *an other* but *at itself* [*geht frisch* von sich aus, *und nicht auf* ein Anderes, *sondern* auf sich selbst]" (*PhG* §396). Just as play is necessary for the effectuation of work, so a rupture with the first beginning (the energy supply in mere being) is needed to produce the uninterrupted continuity of the circle in the second, fresh beginning (the energy provided by the concept or by self-conscious individuality). The circle both interrupts the heedless flight of a straight line and elaborates what it interrupts, bending it in such a way that its two ends meet. An open closure of this kind is the closest approximation to the figure of energy-actuality we might get.

i. The Spiritual Realm of Animals and Deception: Energy's Double Enframing

We are, at this point, well acquainted with the dialectical problem of beginnings: virtual and abstract, they have a tenuous hold on energy, even though they abound in power and/as potentiality. The fresh beginning Hegel has envisioned follows the same dynamic. The "absolute reality," *die absolute Realität,* of individuality real in and for itself remains an "*abstract universal*," *die* abstrakte allgemeine (*PhG* §397), empty of content in its formal self-fulfillment. It is an energy supply not yet tapped and deficient, because it has not been mediated, negated, and actualized. At the same time, the term "absolute reality" is notable for how it conveys the tensions and ambiguities of a beginning that is, in fact, a re-beginning, conscious of its noncoincidence with the origin, and so with its originality *as* beginning. Whereas "reality" names an actuality not yet interrelated with itself, "the absolute" signifies the relationality of relation, the rebinding of actuality's tie to actuality.

Hidden behind the oddity of "absolute reality" is the intermediary position of a fresh start situated in the no-man's-land between that which will emanate from it and the end of a preceding energy regime. This is also why the concept of individuality, into which the new circuit is plugged, is characterized in a breathtakingly self-contradictory fashion as being "initially a *result*," zunächst *Resultat* (*PhG* §398), that is, as positing the end in the beginning. Rather than a temporary hurdle on the path to clear understanding, this confusion is essential not only to the recircuiting of energy but to the very notion of energy-actuality as a mediation and the mediated, the means and the end. The overlay of the first and the last, of reality and absoluteness, goes back to the irreducible duality of *Wirklichkeit*, its double layering that may suddenly collapse into duplicity (and, hence, into deception).

My suggestion is to navigate this section in Hegel's *Phenomenology* between all those instances—doubling as the signposts for our exploration of what energy-actuality means—where *Wirklichkeit* is articulated with *Realität*, as it does indirectly in the aforementioned case of "absolute reality." The difficulty of this articulation is that it is neither entirely negative nor wholly positive. Given the tension structuring energy-actuality, the two terms are semantic friends and enemies toward one another; or, dialectically speaking, reality is and is not actuality. For instance, actuality is "reality permeated by individuality"—*der Individualität durchdrungene Realität, die Wirklichkeit*—but the evidence of this permeation is all but erased for a consciousness that commences with itself, brandishing its "determinate originary nature [*bestimmte ursprüngliche Natur*]" (*PhG* §399) and not yet recalling the *re*commencement that it is.

In its duplicity, energy-actuality spawns the myth of origins, according to which being (reality, substance, and even the subject) precedes action, with the individual "posited initially *as existing* but not yet acting [*zunächst als seiend, noch nicht als tuend gesetzt ist*]" (*PhG* §399). The circle of individuality real in and for itself remains imperceptible for the one caught up in it; the beginner unbends it into a straight line and, introducing a logico-temporal lag into energy-actuality (or overwriting its semantic lag with the logico-temporal one), assumes that actuality comes before energy. A fresh start obscures the circle as much as the discernment, which Hegel's philosophy shares with quantum physics, that at subatomic levels existence itself acts and action exists. Finally, via this detour, we pivot back to the thickness of the dialectical frame—mediation as the interrelation of the inner of the outer and the outer of the inner—slotted between the double edges of action and existence.

The framing of energy-actuality as an acting existence and an existing action temporalizes what it frames over and above a simple opposition between reality in the present and a future purpose to be achieved. (The time lag of the unbent circle is derivative with respect to this temporalization.) Taken singly, existence denotes "a present actuality," *einer vorhandenen Wirklichkeit* (*PhG* §400), a portal for nothing more than future-oriented action. Similarly isolated, action aiming at a particular end is "a completely formal actuality," *die ganz formelle Wirklichkeit* (*PhG* §400), to be concretized at a future moment once it has become present. Existence and action, "objective" actuality and energy, the present and the future are all contrasts that set reality in opposition to actuality, their terms estranged from one another and each from itself. Their dissociation is so exaggerated that it renders the pull of the extremes negligible. A virtualizing dissociation is, in turn, the breeding ground for dissimulation, surreptitiously returning to the double frame of energy-actuality.

Without naming it for what it is, Hegel has the real in mind when he cites "the semblance of present actuality [*Schein der vorhandenen Wirklichkeit*]," which becomes actually actual when one works through it, that is, in its individual repetition through action and through self-knowledge reflected in that action and its outcomes: "For what appears to be a previously found actuality [*eine vorgefundene Wirklichkeit*] is in itself the individual's originary nature, which merely has a semblance of a *being*—the semblance wherein lies the concept of a self-sundering activity [*Begriffe des sich entzweienden Tuns*]" (*PhG* §401). As the substantive aspect of energy-actuality, existence is the semblance of stationary being, an objectified splinter of activity that has torn itself into an act and actuality, the process and the product. A presumably secure origin is, therefore, the side effect (however inevitable) of an act, which has given itself time—has temporalized itself—by partitioning itself into the initial intention and the end it aims to realize.

Appearance (*Schein*) is as much a deceptive "semblance" as it is a coming-to-visibility: this insight is the genius of the *Phenomenology* (and, indeed, of any phenomenology) where the appearing truth and dissimulation are of a piece. Whereas the concept of activity is "self-sundering," its enactment, the setting-to-work of energy-actuality from the standpoint of the acting agent, is "beginning, middle, and end all in one [*ist alles in einem, Anfang, Mittel und Ende*]" (*PhG* §401). In the perspectival divergence between a self-actualizing concept and a phenomenological subject, time continues in a line connecting intentions to ends *and* disappears in a circle, which has absorbed the first and the last, converting them into the middle. Both events happen at the same time, which exceeds time. Their co-occurrence is the quasi-transcendental precondition for the double bind of dissimulation and truth.

The dialectic of energy-actuality operates within the difference between difference and indifference/non-differentiation, which, viewed strictly objectively in comparison to reality (*Realität*), amounts to nothing: "If one posits consciousness as going beyond all this [beyond reality] and as wanting to bring another content to actuality [*und einen andern Inhalt zur Wirklichkeit bringen wollend*], one then posits it as *a nothing* working toward *nothing* [*als* ein Nichts *in* das Nichts *hinarbeitend*]" (*PhG* §401). A nothing working toward nothing is an outline of time. Consciousness might still be working, setting itself to work, energizing itself, but the work of a consciousness dreaming of a content (rather than a form) distinct from that of the real, evoking or convoking an alien energy-actuality, boils down to nothing in the present. Or, more accurately stated, it boils down to the difference within nothing that is not at peace with itself, failing to coincide with itself: *a nothing*, ein Nichts, of the primary intention backed by talent, and *the nothing*, das Nichts, of its non-real goal. The movement of time is the unrest of nothing, the noncoincidence of these two nothings.

In the cycle of acting and the acted-upon, consciousness transforms reality, instead of evading it. Actualization is a *self*-realization, with an emphasis on the "self" that both rips reality up and conducts it to itself. Energy-actuality is this conduction and the destination it points to; there, "the *actual* means [*das* wirkliche Mitte] and a real transition [*der reale Übergang*] is the unity of talent and of the nature of the thing present in interest" (*PhG* §401). It is the unity of the potential (i.e., talent) and a modified actuality (i.e., our *interest* in the merely given that wrests a given actuality from its ostensibly indifferent and external givenness).

What becomes plain in the existence of the act is that the actual has always been inlayed in the real, if only by virtue of claiming our attention, which is synonymous with non-indifference. Nothing changes, nothing works, except the ostensibly trivial, belated giving-credit to what "has always been" the case. This is the difference that makes all the difference as it temporarily melts the ice of indifference. Even as nothing substantively changes, the nothing of the acknowledgment changes everything and locates energy-actuality in the real, which was previously considered purely external. "The *unity* of the outer and inner," Einheit des Äußern und Innern (*PhG* §401), which Hegel subsequently marvels at, portends not a resolved contradiction but the thickness of the dialectical frame regarded from two perspectives (energy and actuality, intention and purpose, existing action and acting existence, the actual means and the real transition) and from within the tenuous difference between the two, ready at any moment to lapse back into indifference.

The subject's energy of nothing (let's call it the "nothing-energy") resurfaces on the side of the object, of the work (*das Werk*) that determinately expresses the acting consciousness, such that "negativity, as an *existing actuality* set free from activity, is a quality in it [in that work] [*als seiende Wirklichkeit, ist die Negativität als Qualität an ihm*]" (*PhG* §402). Substantivized, energy-actuality does not backslide to positivity; it imbibes, carries on, and, of course, perverts, the disquietude, the potentialities, the talents and capacities, the nothings of the subject, and gives them existence palpable to others and to the working consciousness itself. It betrays the subject, revealing and breaking faith with the subject. Betrayal is the nexus of dissimulation and truth. In the work, an existing actuality is an objectification of the nothing-energy, but it expresses also by repressing (another double—and duplicitous—enframing): the nothing *is* something, and, moreover, something determinate and existent. The degree to which negativity is repressed in the actuality of a work then furnishes a criterion for judgment, extrapolating from what has come into being "the energy of the will," *Energie des Willens*, with its more or less "limited originary determinateness" (*PhG* §402).

Pertaining to the subject, the energy named without reference to actuality is a purely virtual and abstract moment. It belongs to the will—the bare beginning of the *Philosophy of Right*—if still without involving the efficacy of its appropriative function guaranteed by the legal institution of property. A judgment on the quality of the work marks a passage from actuality to energy, from existing *Wirklichkeit* back to *Energie* that willed it into existence, based on the limits (the scope and ambition) of a potentiality to act. It judges one aspect of energy-actuality on the basis of the other aspect, failing to register the axiological and ontological entanglement of the two, "the unity of the outer and the inner." For this reason, Hegel rejects verdicts on the goodness or badness of works that depend on the quantitative determination of "the energy of the will" they express: a work is "the self-presentation and expression of individuality and, therefore, it is all good [*sich Darstellen und Aussprechen einer Individualität, und darum alles gut*]" (*PhG* §402).

(Readers will detect in this idea a modification of the classical theological argument about the value of existence, which, as a trace of divine creation, cannot contain anything that is not good; evil is, here, the privation of being. Where Hegel departs from this explanation is in the implied meta-functionality of a work. Over and above the particular purposes it may serve, the work's meta-function is to express energy in the substantive, as actuality. And even if portions of that energy are repressed and perverted, as they invariably are, the provisional accomplishment of its self-expression, the conversion of energy into actuality is, as such, a sign of determinate being and of something good, a developed mediation and an energetic intensification.)

It is to the energy of the will—*Energie* full of empty intentions and virtual desires—that Hegel affixes the poetic description "the night of possibility," *Nacht der Möglichkeit*. An individual "can only have the consciousness of a pure translation *of itself* from the night of possibility to the daylight of the present, from the *abstract in-itself* to the meaning of *actual being* [*die Bedeutung des* wirklichen *Seins*]" (*PhG* §403). Individuality real in and for itself is the self-consciousness of a movement from energy to actuality, but it does not yet comprehend the mechanics of this working work (i.e., that it does not begin with nothing but moves within and against the actuality it tears and sews up again). Meaning, like energy-actuality itself, cracks and parts into two; "the meaning of *actual* being" is a redoubled redoubling, a necessary dissimulation and a contingent truth gradually working their way through to the necessity of contingency and a contingency of necessity.

In this sense, also, translation is genetically, from the outset, a mistranslation: for it to commence, the individual at work and individuality in the work must appear to be opposites and give "a *semblance* of opposition [*Schein* des Gegensatzes]," inviting comparisons between the intended and the realized (*PhG* §403). The appearance of opposition drives the two halves of energy-actuality apart *and* draws them together, facilitating comparisons between the non-apparent and what appears, the working and the work, the virtual and the actual, desire and the thoroughness of its fulfillment. It is a semblance both in the sense of the appearance of what is the case and in the sense of a dissimulation of reality, an actuality and a virtuality. In the end, we are nonetheless left with actuality on both sides of the divide: the shaping must be treated as an abstract and hollow shape (that is to say, a formal form; potentiality as a schema of actuality) for comparison to succeed. In lieu of acting existence and the existent act, we have an imagined potential actuality, on the one hand, and an accomplished actual actuality, on the other.

An enigmatic triumph of *Wirklichkeit* in the substantive in the midst of the individual's realization in and for itself has to do with the emphasis on realization and, more generally, the reality that tips the scales toward the actual. The implacable deception at stake is the idea that a work expresses the working transparently and exhaustively, as though there were no glitches, digressions, omissions of which dialectical energy-actuality is made: "The work is the reality, which consciousness gives to itself [*Das Werk ist die Realität, welche das Bewußtsein sich gibt*]" (*PhG* §404). Since the work is a token in the transactions that consciousness conducts with itself, its reality is closer to actuality, neither scattered nor arrow-like but self-bound, rehearsed or reiterated. Nonetheless, the self-givenness of the work oversteps the limits of consciousness by becoming phenomenal, universally accessible, exposed, available to others. Real in and for itself, individuality presents itself as an objective cipher to others, the bond of actuality unraveled: "From this perspective, actuality shows itself as having quit its concept, as a mere *previously found, alien* actuality [*nur* vorgefundene fremde *Wirklichkeit*]. The work *is*, i.e., it is for other individualities, and it is for them an alien actuality [*eine fremde Wirklichkeit*], in the place of which *they* must posit their own" (*PhG* §404).

In the sway between the real and the actual, what is one's own becomes the most alien, and oppositional energy is reawakened in the need to substitute my actuality for that of others to achieve the same effect they have—to be an individual real in and for myself. While the concept of self-making in and as a work works for an individual, it sets that individual on a collision course with all the others (more charitably, in the same paragraph Hegel terms this a "contrast," or, literally, "counterplay," *Widerspiel*, descending to the virtuality of "other powers and interests" and returning to the night of possibility from peak glow of public presence). The site of this unavoidable collision is also a place where Hegel veers off from the ideologues of bourgeois individualism. He shows, in particular, how the contradiction of one's own and an alien energy-actuality does not arise due to differences among singular individuals but, on the contrary, due to the phenomenal universality of self-expression, which is at once self-given and given to others. Concrete universality has little to do with gathering, pacification, and reconciliation; it subverts and perverts, reigniting the dialectical process.

The ontological alienation of the proper, which we have just observed, prompts us to put energy's double enframing in *its* proper place as a form of Hegel's theory of truth. A kernel of this notion of truth is hidden in the semantic contradictions of betrayal, taken as an expressive perversion and a perverted expression, without the opposite pole of a straightforward and faithful translation, which is the same perversion simply unaware of itself. Beyond the instability of the dialectical process and procedure, saying and unsaying, contradicting its previous conclusions, the concept of betrayal—for instance, the realization of individuality in a universally available work that *betrays* the individual—endows dialectics with a positive, or, at least, a fecund non-correspondence theory of truth, or in modified Scholastic terms, *inadaequatio rei et intellectus*. The double frame of energy-actuality is that of truth *and* untruth, as well as of truth *as* untruth: the work unworks itself in the workings and the workings dissolve in the work, but not without material resistance to that formal subsumption. To acknowledge the duplicity of truth as the very truth of truth is to occupy, if transiently, the place of the absolute.

It is on the basis of the absolute that one can distinguish a *tran-*

scendental deception, according to which truth is univocal and wholly opposed to untruth, from an *operative deception,* factored into the double enframing of energy-actuality. Much of Nietzsche's philosophy is geared toward exposing these two types of deception, without, at the same time, discriminating between them. Consciousness, for its part, arrives at this insight phenomenologically, by schizophrenically living through the disjunction of self-realization: it "experiences this *inadequateness* of concept and reality [Unangemessenheit *des Begriffs und der Realität*], which lies in its essence" (*PhG* §405), which is to say that it viscerally experiences a lack of fit between what is at work in it and what is substantivized in its work. Essentially disjunctive, such an experience breaks through the quasi-tautology of an actuality not yet realized and the already realized one, reestablishing the minimal difference between energy and actuality in *Wirklichkeit*. What it apprehends is that, aside from the material contingencies that make it impossible to implement a project exactly as it has been drawn up in imagination, there is a necessary self-subversion of energetic expression: faithfully realized, the concept betrays itself in a work open to others. In the experience of this "fundamental contradiction," *Grundwiderspruch* (*PhG* §406), individuality real in and for itself "becomes as it is in truth [*wird es sich also, wie es in Wahrheit ist*]" (*PhG* §405).

The double frame of energy-actuality is shaken up, betrayed as it is by a work's appearance and the self-subverting universality of givenness. But it is not entirely undone. In fact, like dialectical truth itself, this frame can only persist in a state of shakenness, neither purely static nor completely dynamic, neither fully in the work nor entirely at work. Energy-actuality shatters into "the *opposition* of willing and achievement [Gegensatz *des Wollens und Vollbringens*]," the energy yet to be expended and that objectivated in the world, a virtual actuality and an actual actuality (*PhG* §407). The twist in all this is that the scatter of energy-actuality *is* the movement-rest of (a) work. The "*vanishing work*," *das* verschwindende Werk, is a two-way street of an actuality on the path of virtualization in the act and of an act on the road to substantivation in the world. The work vanishes in the workings, even as the workings are absorbed into the work, which is why "the vanishing is itself actual and the work is tied to and itself vanishes with it [*das Verschwinden ist selbst wirklich und an das Werk geknüpft und verschwindet selbst mit diesem*]" (*PhG* §407). The individuality real in and for itself relies as much on the moment of virtualization ("the vanishing") as on the actuality of the virtual ("the vanishing is itself actual"). That is how it manages the transition from *actuality* to *actuality'*, attending to its own vanishing in the work and the work's vanishing as "*objective actuality*," gegenständliche Wirklichkeit (*PhG* §408).

The vanishing is the only thing that remains and that releases speculative energy, the atom of meaning splitting into itself and not-itself. Taken in this sense, in its non-adequation to itself, a double frame is the most adequate to a concept that does not coincide with itself. Moreover, the hermeneutical possibilities it contains are numerous, including a disarticulation of the absolute and phenomenological perspectives, of *actuality* and *actuality'*, of being-at-work and being-in-the-work, of truth and untruth, unity and contradiction. But, whatever the component parts of the double frame, its "form" no longer entails the positing of "*being-in-itself* against *actuality*." "The opposition and the negativity, which come to appearance in the work, are attached neither merely to the content of the work nor to that of consciousness, but to actuality as such [*die Wirklichkeit als solche*]" (*PhG* §408). With opposition and negativity dwelling in it, actuality *becomes* speculative energy, parting into energy and actuality. It does so at the level of its essence—the "as such," *als solche*—meaning that actuality is *essentially* a self-negation, a concept opposed to itself: actuality and non-actuality.

The fission of actuality's essence, which is also a contradiction in terms, is profoundly affected by what has transpired in existence—the coming-to-appearance of opposition and negativity in the work. In dialectics, the essential layer is not the unchangeable bedrock of epiphenomenal events, but, quite the reverse, a reverberation of these events after their passage through actuality. Add to this the insufficiency of essence as an empty and virtual category, and the "as such" of energy is altered into an intermediate link, an effect of prior existent acts, and a prelude to a further actualization-objectivation-substantivation of *Wirklichkeit*.

We ought to keep these disclaimers in mind when faced with Hegel's definition of "the thing itself," *die Sache selbst*, as being "essentially a permeation of actuality and individuality [*wesentlich als Durchdringung der Wirklichkeit und der Individualität*]" (*PhG* §409). In the thing itself, energy-actuality is substantivated differently than in the work, for, in the thing, "self-consciousness has arrived at the consciousness of its substance [*seiner Substanz*]" (*PhG* §410). Its universality hints at something other than the phenomenal shape of the work, or of energy objectivated in the work, which has scandalously given rise to a recognition of actuality as one's own *and* to the need to reject it as alien, as handed over to me from others and on to other others. The thing itself, wherein the work is sublated, flashes an image of self-consciousness before that very self-consciousness; in it, the dream of phenomenalization without exteriorization for others, an exteriority accessible to the acting interiority alone, the outer exclusively of the inner, comes true. It teaches self-consciousness that self-consciousness, too, is a thing.

Of course, the dream participates in a general deception, not only by concentrating on one aspect of the frame's thickness (the outer of the inner) at the expense of the other (the inner of the outer), but also by maintaining the illusion that self-consciousness can fully claim what is its own. The "essential permeation" of actuality and individuality, of actuality and energy flowing toward an impending substantivation, is a makeshift unity; after all, this "essence" remains an intermediate, vanishing moment both in its content (the specificity of the two terms it interrelates) and in its form (their permeation, awaiting another rift and drifting apart). Consequently, the one-sidedness of the frame, its heavy preference for the outer of the inner, catapults it into the arena of "spiritual essence," *das geistige Wesen*, which "has not yet progressed to a true real substance [*noch nicht zur wahrhaft realen Substanz gediehen ist*]" (*PhG* §410).

So, what would a "true real substance" be? As we can surmise, despite the emphasis on the "real," it is not a substance rid of all subjective overtones. The reality in question is dialectical, not ontico-empirical; it is imbued with spirit, not opposed to "spiritual essence." Positively stated, the true real substance still unactualized in real individuality is the pairing (while minding the gaps between them) of the outer of the inner and the inner of the outer, in keeping with the Hegelian double frame. It combines on an equal footing substance and non-substance, actuality and energy, energy-actuality in the substantive and verbal keys of "work." Given this combination, "a consciousness called *honest*," *das Bewußtsein heißt* ehrlich (*PhG* §411)—a consciousness that believes itself exempt from the dynamics of betrayal—will not be capable of practically interpreting the meaning of *Wirklichkeit*. Between duplicity and redoubling, honesty will be hopelessly lost. In its stead, the dialectical capacity of twisting, inverting, and perverting will do the trick much more effectively.

Lest we be too naive, an honest consciousness is far from honest: Hegel lifts the curtain on the cunning it unwittingly engages in, replaying the machinations of virtue at another level. Even if no accomplished work might come out of the purpose posited by this honest consciousness, even if its subjective energy may not attain actuality, such a consciousness "makes the *purpose* as purpose, as the *pure activity* that does nothing, into the *thing itself* [*es macht den* Zweck *als Zweck, das* reine Tun, *welches nichts tut, zur* Sache selbst]" (*PhG* §412). This is how nothing becomes something and, indeed, some thing. The primacy of nothing for the honest consciousness means that it assigns initial value to activity, to the energy of the purpose, which is actual precisely insofar as it does not act, harkening back to the nothing-energy we've invoked earlier. From this perspective, actuality is a variation on the theme of energy, regardless of whether it is objectivated in a determinate work or, conforming to its minimal substantivation, in nothing. Actuality vanishes in the purpose, which may remain forever unrealized, but whose very enunciation is already an actuality (*actuality′*) in and of itself.

Hegel openly imputes a perverse desire to the workings of the honest consciousness, which "finds satisfaction in the *vanishing* of its actuality [*findet in dem* Verschwinden *seiner Wirklichkeit noch die Befriedigung*] like bad youths who, *themselves*, take a certain pleasure in being spanked" (*PhG* §412). The affective perversion is an aftereffect of the ontologico-dialectical perversion, which obliterates actuality by setting it in motion in activity, guided by the purpose, actuality's pure form as nothing. We might say, then, that the real is to the actual as honest consciousness is to its dialectical counterpart: the first participant in each conceptual couple lacks self-relatedness, let alone the awareness of its own perversity, defining the second participant.

When we pour scorn on all ends and purposes, which we take for the anachronistic relics of old teleologies, we are no different from those bad youths who take pleasure in being spanked. We disavow the nothing which may become a self-conscious thing (the purpose) and the thing that is nothing within the purview of absolute mediation (the end). Mutatis mutandis, we find satisfaction in the vanishing of our actuality. In fact, we cannot experience actuality as anything but vanishing, having lost the sense of a project or a completed work and having begun celebrating non-realization as the highest achievement of our finitude. Our attitude, however, is symptomatic only of our not coming to terms with the end, not knowing what it signifies besides a termination of something. The non-realization of human existence in a final "product" does not mean that every single moment of a life ought to be incomplete, unrealized, and in some respect unreal. While we reveal the truth of the thing itself (of the purpose as purpose, a pure activity that does nothing), we remain in the dark when it comes to the experience of a fulfilled, energetically vibrant finitude, in which existence is set to work.

For a dialectician, an honest consciousness is in fact more perverted (and, hence, more deceptive) than cunning reason, to the extent that this consciousness implicitly trusts the double frame of energy-actuality all the while erasing one of the frame's edges. Its truth is that "it is not as honest as it seems" (*PhG* §414). In light of the odd self-satisfaction it draws from its self-abnegation, the honest consciousness foregoes substance; the thing itself is, for it, "*no work* at all [*gar* kein Werk]" (*PhG* §413)—energy without *ergon*, an act without actuality. Nor is the verbal dimension of energy important in its eyes: it elevates "*pure act*," reine Tun, into an "*empty purpose*," leere Zweck, producing "an *actless actuality*," *eine* tatlose Wirklichkeit (*PhG* §413). To obliterate one part of energy's double frame, therefore, is to interfere with the part that presumably stays intact and to disrupt the overall economy of energy-actuality. With work in the substantive thrown out the window, the verb "to work" or "to act" is deprived of its sense. A pure activity that does nothing finds its objective fulfillment in nothing, that is, both in nothing determinate and in the nothing that energy-actuality has become at the hands of the honest consciousness.

The dishonesty of honest consciousness is revealed the instant we appreciate that the nothing it has spun out of itself—its nothing-energy—is actually, in actuality, *something*. It proves, here and elsewhere, impossible to bring energy-actuality to naught, as it inevitably re-bounces, restores itself and its imperfectly overlapping frames, interspersed with the memory and the scars of the void. A vacuous "abstract actuality," *abstrakte Wirklichkeit* (*PhG* §414), which has returned to the virtual world of purposes indifferent to their fulfillment or unfulfillment, still matters only inasmuch as it depends on the individuality that has posited it. Through the individual act (be it an act of desistance), it is recovered for activity in general and for actuality determined universally, for everyone: "*actuality* is essentially *his act* as well as *activity in general*, and *his* act is equally only activity in general, hence, also actuality [ist die *Wirklichkeit* wesentlich nur als *sein* Tun sowie als *Tun überhaupt*; und *sein* Tun ist zugleich nur wie Tun überhaupt, so auch Wirklichkeit]" (*PhG* §414).

The nothing-energy is abstract activity and abstract actuality, the abstraction referring to the mutual disconnect of each term from the other and of individual energy-actuality from the universal. But the disconnect, too, is part and parcel of relation, which is how nothing becomes something, simultaneously active and actual. A conduit for this becoming is the work (without work) of individuation: when an individual decides on a purpose, if only by refraining from pursuing it, the purpose's pure activity that does nothing is appropriated into the decision ("is essentially *his*") and, thanks to this privatizing but also determining gesture, is rendered concretely universal, available to others. The opposite also holds: the individual as individual is decided into being by the purpose that, as nothing actual, works to bring individuality to actuality.

The Trojan horse of deception hides in the conduction of energy-actuality through the individual. On the one hand, in deciding on a purpose, the individual decides itself into being (or, as I've just put it) is decided into being by the purpose itself. The workings and the work of this self-realization amount to an actuality in the clasp of the potential, of potency, of a "game [the individual] plays with *his own powers* [*das Spiel seiner Kräfte*]" (*PhG* §416). On the other hand, in acting, the individual "presents and brings himself to the light of day [*sich darstellen und dem Tage zeigen*]" (*PhG* §416), substantivating the work of self-making and giving the phenomenological evidence of it to others. Even refraining from acting is an observable act that turns subjective powers inside out, betraying them. So long as one is forced to choose energy *or* actuality, a non-actual play of inner powers *or* an actual slice of *what is* processed in the meat-grinder of individual unrest, deception will be inevitable.

But this is not to say that the instant energy-actuality is integrated into a unity—assuming such integration at all possible—a non-duplicitous truth will prevail. Just as the absolute announces itself through repeated mediations within finite actuality, so dialectical truth issues from an inner elaboration of deception, its inversions and perversions pointing the way from deception's unconscious (honest) modality to one that is self-conscious. Notwithstanding an avalanche of negations and determinations that impart more and more energy-actuality to the initially abstract beginning, a double configuration, the enframing of *energeia-Wirklichkeit*, keeps a modicum of indeterminacy. Seemingly pinned down, it is already elsewhere, on the other side of the frame. A self-realizing consciousness personifies the flight of energy-actuality, whose shape it is, being "already away from here, where the others thought it was [*es ist schon da heraus, wo sie es zu sein meinten*]" (*PhG* §416).

Actualization, the becoming-actual of actuality, is putting what is one's own on display in the universal element. Putting-on-display is an appearance in the overdetermined sense of the word: a "mere" appearance that does not correspond to the essence *and* the appearing of the essence itself. Voilà the duality and the duplicity of energy-actuality. Perhaps, self-conscious reason still does not give itself the account of what is going on in *its* display, observable strictly at or after its end, from the vantage of the absolute. But it does learn something about "the *nature of the thing itself* [*die* Natur der Sache selbst]" that allows it to overcome the apparent mismatch of the two frames in question. More precisely, it learns that "neither is the thing itself a mere thing, opposed to activity in general and to individual activity, nor is activity opposed to existence [*weder nur Sache, welche dem Tun überhaupt und dem einzelnen Tun, noch Tun, welches dem Bestehen entgegengesetzt*]" (*PhG* §417). Or, to communicate this Hegelian insight with the Heidegger of "The Origin of the Work of Art," it learns that the thing has a work aspect, while the work has a thing aspect to it, and that their uneasy articulation is what makes art.

The thing itself, created almost ex nihilo, with the help of the nothing-energy invested in individual self-realization, is both more and less than the present actuality, its energy flowing to the past and the future of virtualization, subjectivation, and de-substantivation. In turn, the non-opposition of energy and actuality in the thing itself does not obviate their differences but facilitates their sharing. The conduction of energy through individual actuality similarly troubles not only the opposition of the singular and the universal, but also the immediate contrast between the *is* and the *ought*. It lets us imagine law in the form of actuality, that is, on the hither side of potency, power, play, and force—a law both at work and in the work.

ii. Law-Giving Reason: Beyond the Virtual "Ought"—Concerns with Actuality

In one way or another, contemporary theories of normativity presuppose the distinction between "facts" and "norms," between how things are (plus, how they were and will be) and how they should be. As normative assumptions, such theories freeze, stabilize, justify, and normalize the isolation of one modality of energy-actuality from the other; they keep what is in the work in the world at arm's length from what is at work in the law. As ontological postulates, they detain law in the milieu of virtuality, of a powerful but energy-less ideal possibility never to be actualized.

The normative perspective is informed by the framework of legality, if not by crass legalism, while in Hegelian dialectics the law not only *prescribes* but also *is*, its work substantivized in social, economic, and political institutions: "its existence is the *actuality* and the activity of self-consciousness [*deren Dasein die* Wirklichkeit *und das Tun des Selbstbewußtseins ist*]" (*PhG* §419). An existing act and an active (enacted/enacting) existence, the law is a thing of self-consciousness, the thing as self-consciousness, both thing and work, in the work and at work. Its display—not in the form of written statute, but in everything that in the *Phenomenology* and in the *Philosophy of Right* goes under the heading of "the ethical realm," *Sittlichkeit*—is energy in the substantive, the law actuated and phenomenally actualized. At the same time, it expresses the de-substantivation of the work in the subject who accompanies it and lends it legitimacy (*Berechtigung*) from within (*PhG* §420). Akin to energy-actuality (*Wirklichkeit*), "ethical substance" (*sittliche Substanz*) is fueled by a contradiction: the ethical moment de-substantivizes the very substance it belongs to. The limitation of the self-given and self-giving law of reason, however, is that it does not yet seize upon this contradiction, immediately accepting the law that it itself gives. It is this non-hesitancy between the workings and the work of self-legislation that launches another spiral of virtualization.

So, the law of reason is "immediately *valid*," *unmittelbar* gilt (*PhG* §421), in force and in effect without the need for external justification, let alone enforcement—that is, without the very mediations that produce the shapes of legal institutions. This sort of immediacy indicates the precariousness of law's *energy*, its mediations still only emergent. In other words, law-giving reason remains virtual, not as a mere potentiality, but as a chunk of reality that has not negated itself and has not attained actuality. The equivalent of sense-certainty with its severe energy deficit, this law immediately "*is* right and good [ist *recht und gut*]," and, shifting the emphasis as Hegel does, "indeed, it is a '*this*' [*und zwar,* dies]" (*PhG* §421). The immediate validity of self-legislation is—contra Kant—a sign of its immaturity. Its reconciliation of the *is* and the *ought* does not go beyond an empty shape of *legal* consciousness.

Despite reverting to the energy deficit of sense-certainty, of a "this" not even integrated into a thing, *this* law is a work-thing of self-conscious reason and, therefore, more than a simple "this." (In *this* law, the "this" is no longer this or that, but an excess over "thisness" that is the law itself.) In short, it is the energy deficit *of* surplus energy, the non-integration of what is at home in itself due to its failure to spot the inner contradictions that make it simultaneously possible and impossible. A recovery of the *not-yet* in the midst of the *already*, the virtual within the self-actualizing and self-actualized, the unworking within the work, negatively completes the thing itself, which is law-giving reason, its content filled out and brought to fruition (*erfüllte inhatsvolle*) (*PhG* §421). The implications of this movement for our theme are enormous: energy comes to actuality (and so, to itself) not when its two aspects are flawlessly integrated but, on the contrary, when the cracks running across and through them come to visibility, the virtual, negative element tucked into the self-relating supplement of reality, which, thanks to it, becomes actual.

If the immediate validity of law-giving reason accounts for and expresses the strange being (*als seiend ausspricht*) that is the "this," dragging behind itself the modified virtuality of sense-certainty, then it is incumbent on us to explain this being in terms of its being (*von dem Sein*) (*PhG* §422). Heidegger would have been pleased to see Hegel's articulation of ontological difference here, which, within the limits of the present study, illuminates energy deficit and excess energy in this shape of *Wirklichkeit*.

The being of this piece of law-giving reason is not unconditional: one must speak the truth *if* one knows it (*PhG* §423); one must love one's neighbor as one loves oneself, *provided that* one has enough understanding to surmise what is for that neighbor's own good (*PhG* §424). Conditional and determined, the being in question is also contingent: "Chance [*Zufall*] not only determines its occasion, but also in general whether it is a *work* [*ob es überhaupt ein* Werk *ist*] or whether it has not again dissolved and has become perverted into evil [*in Übel verkehrt wird*]" (*PhG* §424). The ontological uncertainty that shakes up law-giving reason strikes at the substantive façade of its energy, the work. At the level of its being, law-giving reason might not be *a* being at all. Specifically, it rests neither on pure potentiality and the external contingency of virtual reality, nor on the internal necessity of actuality. Perverted and pervertible by the "this" of sense-certainty, the being of law-giving reason is contingent on its necessity as a conditional command—a self-contradiction that displaces and perversely expresses the contradiction built into ethical substance.

The fact that reason immediately receives whatever it gives itself means that it takes no time to let its precepts undergo externalization, to be clothed with substance and grow in the world (it is in this sense that I have earlier invoked an inner contradiction in "ethical substance"). Easily twisted around into evil, it demonstrates that its being still borders on nothing. Hegel's coding of this perversion in his text is the reiterated word "perhaps," *veilleicht*, which upsets the work and the security of its achievement: an active response to a conditional command "is perhaps a work, perhaps it is good, but then perhaps not [*es vielleicht ein Werk, veilleicht gut ist, vielleicht auch nicht*]" (*PhG* §424). With this, Hegel subscribes to the idea that to be a work, to be in being, is good, but, at the same time, he does not, at least not for now, use the virtualization of a work as evidence for its dissipation in evil and nothing. The "perhaps" gives a dialectical half-twist, following the perverting vector a part of the way. Both worked and unworked, a work of rational self-legislation in all its indeterminacy dovetails (again, for a brief instant) with energy-actuality, the verbality and substantiality of *ergon* or of *Werk-Wirk*. It is sufficient for making the actuality of an act tremble, vibrate, quiver in its possible non-identity. But the suspension of the "perhaps" is not long-lasting: finishing the twist of perversion, Hegel translates what may or may not be a work into the absence of being-at-work and of being-in-the-work, or, in a word, into non-actuality: "such laws that remain stopped merely at the *ought* have no *actuality*, however [*solche Gesetze bleiben nur beim* Sollen stehen, haben aber keine Wirklichkeit]" (*PhG* §424). Scarcely do they have the energy to be and, therefore, to be actual or good.

Like a caterpillar in the process of metamorphosis, law-giving reason must shed the form of legality to be actualized, becoming more (and less) than law. It must leave the virtual enclosure of the *ought*, of prescription, to de-inscribe itself from the history of legal *thought*, in order to give itself actual being. Various leftist critiques of Hegel as an ideologue who raises the *ought* into the *is*, or who, conversely, treats historical reality as what ought to be, miss the mark. All Hegel is suggesting (again, contra Kant) is that on the pain of falling into irrelevance and disrepute—on the pain of lapsing into a "perhaps," which is exactly not-law—the law cannot stop at a regulative idea, an unattainable ideal without a body in the world. Its energy is nothing without actuality; its effectiveness, being-at-work, remains without effect unless it is also a *something*, being-in-the-work.

Dialectical concern with legal actuality is a concern with the middle, that is, with mediation that, above and beyond the hermeneutics of the universal law and the singular case, dismantles the illusion of immediacy as immediate applicability, the negative form of such applicability (the negation of mediacy) imperceptibly divesting the immediate of any energy it may have retained. As Hegel construes it, the law does not refer to a set of principles that are indifferent to the singularity of existence. In the work, in actuality, the law is committed to the singular and the determinate, and more than that, its commitment is as such the determining factor. As a result, the indifferent beginning of law, as well as of thinking and existence, that is consistent with energy-actuality is ever so partial and *eo ipso* not absolute.

Fast forward to today. We are politically and existentially afraid of commitment, from which we flee toward the infinity of unrealizable possibilities, eviscerating our energy (and, in fact, all energy) along the way. "What must be renounced," Hegel advises the reader, "is the appeal to a universal absolute *content*" (*PhG* §425). True: commitment is ineluctably limiting, fractional, perhaps biased, but it is an incomparably better route to the absolute than an immediate absolutization of legal (or any other) foundations. We must work at absoluteness, put plenty of energy into building it up or letting it grow by repeating the partial and the finite, connecting it to itself, plugging it into itself as other to itself in the speculative split of its identity. This work and these workings pervert the logic of expenditure, according to which the energy resources that were abundant at the outset are depleted at the end. Following the twist of perversion, the highest intensity of energy-actuality is experienced at the end, when singularity and finitude appear, without an excessively jarring contradiction, in and as the absolute.

Where does this leave law-giving reason? At an impasse, to the extent that the immediately absolute beginning, sheltered from any possible continuation, is always an impasse. Nonetheless, the first stage of negating immediate absoluteness is complete, having culminated in the renunciation of appeals to universal absolute content. What survives this renunciation is "the *pure form of universality*," *die* reine Form der Allgemeinheit (*PhG* §426), which, in the wake of absolute content and despite being caught in the virtual domain of pure form, unblocks energy-actuality by lending itself to the hermeneutic middle, where the congruence of singular laws with the universal is tested (*PhG* §427). The renaissance of *Wirklichkeit* will have taken place between the form of law (here: the principle of noncontradiction) and particular laws, on the basis of a standard (*Maßstab*), which reason finds in itself but cannot contain, bringing it to bear on things (the laws) outside it. Could it be that the act of testing, of shuttling between the formal law of law and the contents of laws, elaborates on the middle of the middle—the hyphen—in energy-actuality?

iii. Reason as Testing Laws: From De-Substantivation to Ethical Substance

Strictly speaking, for a dialectician, the principle of noncontradiction is—or should be—highly suspect, above all as a criterion for *Wirklichkeit*. Impeding the flows of energy, it does not authorize the very speculative fission of a thing against itself that is at the core of the dialectical non-principle of contradiction. Casting the iron-clad necessity of tautological identity over existence, it is ultimately contrary to everything that is in time and in actuality, everything finite that, insofar as it is, does not coincide with itself.

If so, then how can this formal and abstract, empty and virtual law of laws reinvigorate energy-actuality? By relating each law to itself and, thereby, guiding *its* virtual reality toward a self-related actuality: the "*formal* universality" of the principle of noncontradiction is compatible with each law's determinate content, "since within this universality, it [i.e., the content] is observed merely in relation to itself [*nur in Beziehung auf sich selbst betrachtet*]" (*PhG* §428). The form of law works as a channel, through which laws are conducted each to itself, attaining the self-relation of actuality in the energetic medium of the otherwise formally universal principle. Curiously, then, the principle does not precede that which is tested against it; instead of an immediate, sovereign, autonomous beginning, the law of law is a by-product, the determinate law's own self-relation mindful of its finitude yet rid of the "singularity and contingency that has stuck to its actuality [*seiner Wirklichkeit anklebenden Einzelheit und Zufälligkeit*]" (*PhG* §428).

Lest one be tempted to embrace this form of *Wirklichkeit*, Hegel points out that the self-related actuality of the law is weighed down by a tautology (*PhG* §429), which we may express in the following way: energy = energy, or actuality = actuality. A tautological criterion is not only devoid of substance, but also fails to espy the other *in the midst of a relation formally establishing exact sameness*. Insofar as energy = energy, it is precisely not equivalent to itself: at work, it is ineluctably in the work, and so entails actuality. This is also the case, mutatis mutandis, when it comes to actuality. The law that is tested, passing through the crucible of the law of laws, is not only law but also a piece of social, political, civil, or economic reality; in short, a component of ethical substance. The transition from de-substantivation to ethical substance is not a linear negation of the negation, changing around plus and minus signs in the battery of dialectical energy-actuality, but a belated realization on the part of ethical substance that, as ethical, it is inherently de-substantivized, its being-in-the-work disturbed and made possible by its own being-at-work, attended everywhere as it is by the activity of a self-conscious subject. All of a sudden, the sense of de-substantivation goes through an about-face: from the repose of an essential tautology in itself to the incessant movement of ethical life, that is, from the static to the dynamic modality of energy-actuality.

As a determining fulfillment of "empty spiritual essence [*des vorher leeren geistigen Wesens*]," ethical substance is "the *consciousness* of itself as an absolute *essentiality* [*das* Bewußtsein *von sich als der absoluten* Wesenheit]" (*PhG* §431). The fulfillment at stake here is the energetic fullness of substance, its becoming-subject or becoming aware that it has always already been subject—that its substantive work (the law) is internally de-substantivized by the workings it consists of and that, without law-giving and law-testing, laws are inert, indeterminate, inapplicable, and useless. A substance conscious of itself is "absolute *essentiality*" because it is interrelated with itself, its energy boosted. Compared to law as a spiritual thing, as energy at rest buried in the actuality of ethical substance, law-testing is an act of consciousness, energy as movement (*Bewegung*) unsettling legal determinations and making them determinate in the first place: making them determinate by unsettling them. In law considered in terms of a synecdoche for *Sittlichkeit*, the energy regime of ethical substance becomes conspicuous: "ethical substance presents itself . . . as consciousness [*sittliche Substanz sich . . . als Bewußtsein darstellt*]" (*PhG* §431), giving itself actuality in a shape of energy that is itself in movement and making itself phenomenal (exhibiting itself, even) in a non-phenomenal medium (phenomenalized solely from the standpoint of the absolute). The de-substantivation of ethical substance is, by the same token, the non-alienated substantivation of consciousness, the being-at-work of the one passing over into and mingling with the being-in-the-work of the other.

Yet, this non-alienation, this persistence of the subject in a substance that presents itself as consciousness, this ideally non-vanishing being-at-work in the work, or, succinctly put, the still rather immediate fusion of the two halves of energy-actuality, scraps the idyllic image of a singular universality which law-testing reason paints. A working and speaking *who* personally attached to its work and word is what Hegel names *honesty*, Ehrlichkeit (*PhG* §432). In light of a patently dialectical inversion, or an energetic perversion that wakes up whatever it perverts from its dogmatic slumber, honesty turns out, once more, to be thoroughly dishonest, in that it mistakes the "mingling" of different elements for their sameness, obfuscates the irreducible difference between being-at-work and being-in-the-work, and assumes that the former never evanesces from the latter. Honesty is particularly dishonest about the necessity of de-substantivation, which no actuality can simply shrug off. It takes the formula energy = energy naively, in terms of energy's equivalence to itself and the extinguishing of its constitutive difference. As a consequence, the truth of the subject is detained in the object and nothing is tested but "such fixed truth," *solcher festen Wahrheit* (*PhG* §432), which is single-heartedly committed to the substantive dimension of energy-actuality.

The immediate coincidence, to the point of non-differentiation, between the being-at-work and the being-in-the-work of reason honestly giving and testing laws produces a similarly immediate actuality of ethical substance. "Each [of the two moments] for itself *immediately* comes on the scene as *actuality* [*jedes für sich* unmittelbar *als eine* Wirklichkeit *auftreten*]," irreparably affecting "the being of actual laws," *Sein wirklicher Gesetze* (*PhG* §433). Shorn of mediations, the energy-actuality of law shatters into a myriad of shards of legal reality, which can only be experienced as an arbitrary and external imposition on the subjects of law. Completing claims to actuality de-actualize it, and "legal reality" is the outcome of that de-actualization.

Immediacy further demands that the verbal and substantive parts of *Wirklichkeit* be reversible and interchangeable among themselves: the personal element of being-at-work attached, as a presence that simply would not pass away, to the work of ethical substance creates the conditions for being-in-the-work inseparable from personal attendance. The aftermath of the reversal is "tyrannical inequity [*die tyrannische Frevel*]" (*PhG* §433), which has to do with the ontological confusion and miscommunication between the two poles of energy-actuality that end up collapsing into one another. And if one comprehends all law on the basis of "honest" law-giving, then resistance to law means a challenge thrown to tyranny, to "an alien arbitrary will [*eine fremde Willkür*]" (*PhG* §433), as a remnant of the personal being-at-work stalking, in a non-substantive form, the being-in-the-work of *Sittlichkeit*.

So, the account of how ethical substance appears in the world is a story of botched substantivations. (Of course, dialectical substance can *only* be botched by dint of being shot through with subjectivity in those spots where it is thinning and on retreat.) Complicating this already tangled narrative is the fact that such failures are signs of success in the eyes of those who value honesty, the presence or, to say it in a double negative, the non-evasion of the *who* standing by and at what has come out of his being-at-work. For Hegel, this shadowing of the substance by the subject is an obstacle to the substantivation of ethical life: "the real spiritual essence," *reale geistige Wesen* (*PhG* §434), the essence that is outwardly realized and therefore brimming with energy-actuality, is yet to announce itself where the two aspects of *Wirklichkeit* are thrown together, indeterminately, without undergoing self-negation and differentiation. My honest attachment to my legal work makes of this work a "non-actual command," *eines unwirklichen Gebots* (*PhG* §434)—full of power and force, but drained of energy, tyrannical and capricious no matter how universal I demonstrate it to be. From this dearth, spiritual energy is, nevertheless, quickly replenished, since the commanding consciousness "is not valid individually [*nicht einzeln gelten*]" (*PhG* §434), but presupposes the universality of political and legal institutions, law enforcement structures, and, in a word, the speculative doubling of force into law. Having been drained, energy-actuality rushes back and congeals into an "actual, fulfilled, self-conscious" spiritual essence (*PhG* §434).

As a nascent form of ethical substance, which in the ensemble of energy-actuality is also an act, the law that is in and for itself is still only "immediately an actuality [*das unmittelbar die Wirklichkeit ist*]" (*PhG* §435). It thus harbors a self-contradiction that may be resolved in no other manner than through its further dialectical becoming and growth, substantivation and de-substantivation. The contradiction I am referring to now—and have been for quite some time in these pages—is that *the law is immediately a self-mediation*, reality's self-relation that does not yet know itself as such. We are yet to feel the brunt of this contradiction, but, for now, "the world is merely this actuality [*die Welt ist nur diese Wirklichkeit*]" (*PhG* §435) in a non-differentiated identification with the law-giving and law-testing self-consciousness.

The utopia of self-given law as an immediate actuality, which is also its energy, is the utopia of reaching back to the state of humanity before the Fall, as though the human existed as human in that *before*. Redemption through law—through the law given by and received from oneself, bundled together with absolute honesty, innocence (*Unschuld*), and non-separation between actuality and its virtual supplement—posits a spiritualized world, which also exists. Here, the *is* is reconciled with the *ought*, and law is eternalized, frozen in a divine shape of actuality. This is the abstract, formal, and static beginning of ethical life, of crystal-clear ethical substance that corresponds to the energetic forms of understanding and the mineral world. A beginning that, like all others, awaits being unsettled, reenergized, mediated.

The immediate blending together of being-at-work and being-in-the-work is, as it turns out, not of this world, even if this world seems to be swathed in its immediacy thanks to self-legislating reason. Rather, the non-alienation of ethical substance is only possible in the sphere of "non-sundered spirits clear to themselves [*sich selbst klare unentzweite Geister*]" (*PhG* §436), where energy-actuality is gathered into itself without really having access to the "self," an identity that, splitting from and negating itself (for instance, in a clash between "energy" and "actuality"), comes back to itself across the gulf of a difference it is unable to erase.

On another occasion, it might be advisable to study the thread of divine law woven into the first fabric of ethical substance in all its fine-grained details. Though divine, it does not require faith, to the extent that faith entails the very separation that non-sundered spirits do not tolerate—an unbridgeable gap between the believing consciousness and that in which it believes. Betrayal inheres in that gap. Faith, *Glaube*, is for Hegel "the movement [*Bewegung*] of this consciousness as forever approaching that unity without ever arriving at the presence of its essence" (*PhG* §435). A movement of consciousness, faith unsettles the static order of the first beginning that aims to recapture paradise lost, where identity is immediate. It moderates the eternal actuality of its object with the ephemeral energy of the believer. Not only divine law but also the ethical mindset (*die sittliche Gesinnung*) (*PhG* §436) preclude faith, because they do not yet have an inkling of turbulent movement and its withdrawing destination, restless energy and energy at rest. Faith, in its turn, energizes religion, if not divinity itself, and is a more mature, more developed expression of *Wirklichkeit*, so long as its constitutive gap neither paralyzes action nor indefinitely defers the advent of actuality.

The unconditional positivity through which self-consciousness is related to ethical substance (it is actually doubtful that, absent the negative drive, it is, indeed, a relation) culminates in a situation of *mutual inclusion* in lieu of synergy that gathers energies from their initial dispersion. "Since right is for me *in* and *for itself*," writes Hegel, "I am in ethical substance" (*PhG* §436): my recognition of substantive right as the being-in-the-work of reason independent of my agreement or disapproval parachutes me, the one who recognizes its independence, into the thick of *Sittlichkeit*. My being-at-work diminishes to the bare minimum of what right is *for me*, namely, that it is nothing dependent *on me* but valid in and for itself. Yet, the moment of recognition that instantaneously abdicates any essential function for the one who does the recognizing is sufficient to introduce the other dimension of energy-actuality into the mix without dissolving the "I am" in the ethical substance whence it jumps. Mutual inclusion spells out mutual exclusion: I am a hole in ethical substance which is, consequently, "the *essence* of self-consciousness [*das* Wesen *des Selbstbewußtseins*], while self-consciousness is *its actuality* and *existence*, its *self* and *will* [*ist* ihre Wirklichkeit *und* Dasein, *ihr* Selbst *und* Willen]" (*PhG* §436).

Immediate mutual inclusion, which is immediately the mutual exclusion of self-consciousness and ethical substance, is none other than a hasty assemblage of energy and actuality, each accommodating the other as though it were itself, its own essence and self. A shift of perspective toward the absolute will direct attention to the *as though* of their identity and interrogate the essential and actual "ownness" of ethical substance and self-consciousness. It will thus urge an *ethical separation* instead of an immediate recognition of the one in the other as a path toward the self-actualization of energy.

Notes

Part I

1. Besides so-called traditional Marxism, I have in mind Latin American "liberation theology" and the protagonists of the decolonial struggle in Africa, such as Franz Fanon and Amilcar Cabral.
2. See Francis Fukuyama, *The End of History and the Last Man* (New York: Avon Books, 1992).
3. Michel Foucault, "Discourse on Language," in *The Archaeology of Knowledge*, translated by A. M. Sheridan Smith (New York: Pantheon Books, 1992), 235.
4. On this, see Michael Marder, *Energy Dreams: Of Actuality* (New York: Columbia University Press, 2017), esp. chap. 1.
5. Throughout, I am using this term in the sense in which Slavoj Žižek deploys it in his work. Exceptionally attentive to the inner twists and torsions of dialectics, Žižek is right to point out, with admirable consistency, how perversion is not a deviation from the non-perverse norm, but the core of dialectical "normalcy" itself.
6. Let it be noted that I am not writing these words with an intention to pass a negative moral judgment on *our* actuality; after all, perversion, *Umkehrung* or *Verkehrung*, is a better indicator of dialectical energy than negativity and sublation combined!
7. Louis Althusser and Étienne Balibar, *Reading Capital*, translated by Ben Brewster (New York: New Left Books [Verso], 1970), 15.
8. Althusser and Balibar, *Reading Capital*, 8.
9. All citations from Hegel's *Phenomenology*, abbreviated as *PhG*, are my translations of G. W. F. Hegel, *Phänomenologie des Geistes*, vol. 3 of *Werke* (Frankfurt am Main: Suhrkamp, 1970). In parentheses (or brackets), I indicate the abbreviated book title followed by the paragraph number. I have also consulted A. V. Miller's English rendition of *Hegel's Phenomenology of Spirit* (Oxford: Oxford University Press, 1977) and Terry Pinkard's excellent translation (Cambridge: Cambridge University Press, 2018).
10. Terry Pinkard, *Hegel's Naturalism: Mind, Nature, and the Final Ends of Life* (Oxford: Oxford University Press, 2012), 43 n.67.
11. Alfredo Ferrarin, *Hegel and Aristotle* (Cambridge: Cambridge University Press, 2001), 7ff.
12. Andreas Gelhard, "Abstraktion, Attraktion—Maurice Blanchot liest

Hegel," in *Der französische Hegel*, edited by Ulrich Johannes Schneider (Berlin: Akademie Verlag, 2007), 66.

13. Ricardo Pozzo, "On the History of the Concept of Effectiveness," in *On Effectiveness*, edited by Giorgio Ausenda (Woodbridge, Eng.: Boydell, 2003), 21.

14. Vladimir Bibikhin, *Energiya* (Moscow: St. Thomas Institute of Philosophy, Theology and History, 2010), 75–76.

15. Andrés Quero-Sánchez, "Sein als Absolutheit (*esse* als *abegescheidenheit*)," in *Meister Eckharts Straßburger Jahrzehnt*, edited by Andrés Quero-Sánchez and Georg Steer (Stuttgart: W. Kohlhammer, 2008), 189.

16. Meister Eckhart, *Complete Mystical Works*, translated and edited by Maurice O'C. Walshe (New York: Herder and Herder, 2009), 338.

17. Martin Heidegger, *An Introduction to Metaphysics*, translated by Ralph Manheim (New Haven, CT: Yale University Press, 1959), 69.

18. G. W. F. Hegel, *Lectures on the Philosophy of World History, Volume I: Manuscripts of the Introduction and the Lectures of 1822–23*, edited and translated by Robert F. Browne and Peter C. Hodgson (Oxford: Oxford University Press, 2011), 154.

19. See Marder, *Energy Dreams*, chap. 3.

20. This is Heidegger's central point in his book on Hegel's *Phenomenology* (Martin Heidegger, *Hegel's Phenomenology of Spirit*, translated by Parvis Emad and Kenneth Maly [Bloomington: Indiana University Press, 1988]).

21. I use the word "science" to refer to the scientific (empirical, experimental, or mathematically determined) enterprise in the usual sense of the word, not in the sense of the Hegelian *Wissenschaft*.

22. G. W. F. Hegel, *Philosophy of Nature: Encyclopedia of the Philosophical Sciences, Part II*, translated by A. V. Miller (Oxford: Oxford University Press, 2004), 67.

23. G. W. F. Hegel, *Encyclopedia of the Philosophical Sciences in Basic Outline, Part I: Science of Logic*, translated and edited by Klaus Brinkmann and Daniel O. Dahlstrom (Cambridge: Cambridge University Press, 2010), 33. (Cited hereafter as *Encyclopedia Logic*.)

24. G. W. F. Hegel, *The Science of Logic*, translated by George Di Giovanni (Cambridge: Cambridge University Press, 2010), 487.

25. Hegel, *Science of Logic*, 482.

26. Marder, *Energy Dreams*, 37.

27. Hegel, *Science of Logic*, 477.

28. See, for instance, *PhG* §770.

29. Hegel, *Science of Logic*, 482.

30. Hegel, *Science of Logic*, 465.

31. Hence, Michael Hardimon (*Hegel's Social Philosophy: The Project of Reconciliation* [Cambridge: Cambridge University Press, 1994]) is only partially correct to say that "Hegel thinks of his philosophical conception of *Wirklichkeit* as providing a philosophical account of the ordinary notion of reality" (55). Indeed, *Wirklichkeit* is not separate from the world of everyday life, but "reality" is only its truncated, substantive aspect.

NOTES TO PAGES 22–54

32. Friedrich Nietzsche, *On the Genealogy of Morality*, translated by Maudemarie Clark and Alan Swensen (Indianapolis, IN: Hackett, 1998), 25.

33. Martin Heidegger, *Being and Time*, translated by John Macquarrie and Edward Robinson (San Francisco: Harper and Row, 1962), 63.

34. Hegel, *Science of Logic*, 479.

35. Jacques Derrida, *Specters of Marx: The State of the Debt, the Work of Mourning, and the New International*, translated by Peggy Kamuf (New York: Routledge, 1994), 107.

36. In Aristotelian terms, *energeia* will be, in this way, conjugated with *theoria*: thought thinking itself will dissolve itself into and resolve the actuality of existence.

37. Hegel, *Encyclopedia Logic*, 34.

38. I warmly thank Marcia Sá Cavalcante Schuback for this wonderful etymological insight.

39. Mediated unity will permit the concept to rejoin itself after being divided in a complex synergy.

40. Hegel, *Philosophy of Nature*, 31.

41. Hegel seems to forget that the Aristotelian virtues are honed, adjusted, and steered toward "the golden mean" through repeated practice.

42. Hegel, *Encyclopedia Logic*, 50.

43. Resorting to traditional Aristotelian terms, we could say that powerlessness is a deficient—non-actualizable—potentiality; power is potentiality awaiting its actualization; and actuality is powerless otherwise, free of the need and the power to actualize itself.

44. Hegel, *Science of Logic*, 479.

45. Hegel, *Science of Logic*, 479.

46. It is not by chance that in *Being and Time* Heidegger speaks of the "existential analytic of Dasein."

47. At least formally, this idea echoes Jean-Luc Nancy's *Being Singular Plural*, translated by Robert Richardson and Anne O'Byrne (Stanford, CA: Stanford University Press, 2000).

48. Hegel, *Philosophy of Nature*, 28.

49. Hegel, *Philosophy of Nature*, 34.

50. Hegel, *Science of Logic*, 478.

51. Hegel, *Science of Logic*, 478.

52. Hegel, *Science of Logic*, 482.

53. Hegel, *Science of Logic*, 487.

54. Contemplating actual action, we come across the Aristotelian heritage that Hegelian dialectics shares with Husserl's phenomenology, where the finite intending and the intended belong together in the fullness of intuition, or, even prior to their fulfillment, in noetic-noematic correlations.

55. Marder, *Energy Dreams*, 19.

56. Naomi Klein, *This Changes Everything: Capitalism vs. the Climate* (New York: Simon and Schuster, 2014), 169ff.

Part II

1. "According [to] the quantum postulate," Bohr writes, "every observation of atomic phenomena will just involve an individual process, resulting in an essential interaction. We cannot therefore speak of independent tools of measurements." Niels Bohr, *Collected Works*, vol. 6: *Foundations of Quantum Physics I (1926–1932)*, edited by Jorgen Kalckar (Amsterdam: North-Holland, 1985), 75. See also Niels Bohr, *Collected Works*, vol. 10: *Complementarity beyond Physics*, edited by David Favrholdt (Amsterdam: Elsevier, 1999), 41.

2. If the speculative energy of the "this" propels this thing and this I out of virtual reality, today we witness the opposite tendency toward virtualization, or de-actualization. I do not mean the virtual reality spawned by computer games or the mass media, for example, even though they do contribute a fair share to the trend. What is at stake is the prevalent disconnect of "this I," of each "I," from itself as other to itself, and therefore from every other. And no extension of the communication grid will remedy a detachment that saps the speculative energy of subject-formation.

3. Refer to Patrick L. Bourgeois, *Philosophy at the Boundary of Reason: Ethics and Postmodernity* (Albany, NY: SUNY Press, 2000), 17.

Index

absolute, xiv, 8–9, 40–41, 46, 48–49, 57–62, 67, 75–76, 82–83, 87, 97, 105–6, 115, 125–26, 129, 131, 133, 143–44, 199–200, 203–4; actuality, 16, 19, 24, 45, 51, 135, 153, 212–13; art, 47–48; beginning, 6; concept, 32, 100, 102; contingency, 130; experience, 64–66, 77; finitude, 9, 153; freedom, 31, 50; knowing, 50; necessity, 15, 45, 206; reality, 228–29; reflux, 148; relation, xii–xiii, 21, 23, 51, 108, 205, 238; self-consciousness, 24; as threshold, 44; truth, 23, 39, 60, 77
action, 16–17, 35, 49–50, 77–78, 122–23, 164, 195, 198, 218–19, 229–31, 249, 253n54
actualitas, 6–8, 11, 35, 117, 213
actus, 7–8, 224. See also *purus*
Adorno, Theodor, 5, 27, 202
affect, 203, 209, 238
algorithm, 115, 170
Althusser, Louis, 5–6
ambiguity, 4, 65, 92, 166, 182–83, 195, 209, 228
anamnesis, 147
animal, animality, 9, 53, 69, 77–78, 114, 139, 160, 164–65, 228
appropriation, 62, 73–74, 135, 145–46, 149–51, 155–56, 158, 179, 202, 232, 239; energy of, 73, 149; formal, 150; self-, 80, 82–83, 150
Arendt, Hannah, 77
Aristotle, xii, xiv, 7–9, 14–15, 17, 24, 30–31, 44, 49–50, 52, 61, 65, 68, 70, 76, 102, 106, 127, 136, 145–46, 153, 155, 160, 164, 166, 173, 179, 184, 187–88, 195, 204, 208, 213–14, 223, 225, 228, 253n36, 253n41, 253n43, 253n54
Augustine, Saint, 18, 188
autotelic, 117, 160–61

beginning, 6, 12, 15, 25, 27, 37, 42, 48–50, 55, 67, 72, 77, 121, 142, 147, 226, 228–30, 240, 244–45, 248–49
Benjamin, Walter, 27
Bergson, Henri, 10, 106
betrayal, xiii, 19, 31, 42, 83, 166, 187, 218, 221, 226, 232, 234–35, 237, 240, 249
Bibikhin, Vladimir, 7
Big Bang, 19, 49, 142
biopolitics, 169
Böhme, Jakob, 18
bone, 190–95
brain, 188–91, 195

calculation, 170–72
categories 8, 15, 21, 45–46, 48, 70, 84, 127, 131, 149–50, 161, 169, 203, 236; manifold, 143, 171; pure, 195, 226; table of, 46, 171
cathexis, 81
Christianity, 4, 52, 186, 188, 190
cognition, 27–28, 58–64, 81, 95, 111, 115, 133, 150; actual, 57–60; reality of, 23, 62–63
community, 81, 196
concept, 57, 87–93, 98–100, 107–9, 121–24, 158–60, 164–66, 170–74, 196–98, 229–30, 234–36, 253n39; actual, 44, 93; becoming of, 99, 127; of concept, 162, 189, 221, 226–28; of difference, 32; energy of, 45–47, 99, 157, 167, 169; of energy, xi–xiii, 4, 7–9, 14, 26, 61, 127–28, 143, 152–54, 252n31
consciousness, 16–17, 87–89, 95–96, 99, 102, 107, 112–16, 120–21, 124–26, 133, 141–42, 145, 148–49, 155, 172–76, 215–16, 218, 221, 228–29, 235, 246, 248–49; actual, 64, 66, 75, 114, 135, 138, 193–94; honest, 237–40; idealism of, 6; legal, 242,

255

INDEX

consciousness (*continued*)
  246; mere, xiv, 63, 66–71, 78, 83, 86–87, 104–6, 136, 148, 180, 183, 197; naive, 63; natural, 118; of the object, 103; ordinary, 24; real, 61, 64–67, 71, 73, 75, 78, 84, 86, 88, 103, 114, 136, 144, 151; of self-sacrifice, 54; transcendental, 129–31; unhappy, 119, 126–29, 131–40, 142, 145–46, 204–5; work of, 159, 175, 231–33
conservation, 160–61, 167
contamination, 62, 68, 76, 102, 203
correctness, 62–65, 75

deception, 229–30, 233, 235–36, 238–40
deconstruction, 93, 170, 185, 190
de-inscription, 153, 156, 160, 163, 243
delaboration, 210–12, 214
Deleuze, Gilles, 106, 192
Derrida, Jacques, 6, 26, 133, 193
Descartes, René, 31, 120
desire, 25, 78, 106–9, 124–25, 128, 132, 134–35, 137, 140, 207, 220, 226, 233, 238; immediate, 106; object of, 110, 134, 149, 170–71, 217; for the other, 106–8; quiescence of, 108, 110, 143
difference, 60, 66, 74–76, 90–91, 94, 96–106, 108–9, 116–17, 121, 125–26, 129–30, 231, 247, 249; absolute, 11, 32, 51, 100–103, 213; actual, 84–85, 93, 166; metaphysical, 12; ontico-ontological, 68–69, 121, 242; sexual, 72; substantive, 17, 20, 42
digestion, 77, 135, 150, 164, 167, 203
digitality, 170
diversity, 25, 84, 90, 166, 169
DNA, 84, 169
double, 25, 27, 33, 38, 75, 93, 109, 118, 126–27, 174, 176, 178, 182, 196, 229–30, 232–38, 240; essence, 156; movement, xii; spectral, xiv, 32; speculative, 34–36, 66, 70, 108, 248
dunamis, xii, 35, 54, 154

Eckhart, Meister, 8–9, 49
ecology, xiii, 25, 75
economy, xi–xii, 9–10, 19, 24–25, 54, 72, 94, 199, 239, 245; political, 5–6, 10
effectiveness, 7, 10, 89–91, 101, 119, 122–24, 134, 138, 142–43, 158, 162, 188, 197, 211, 213, 218–20, 244, 252n13

eidetic, 48, 101, 171
embodiment, 42, 57, 113, 138, 145, 163, 168, 173, 188–89, 196
energeia, xii, 6–8, 10–12, 15, 17, 23–24, 27, 34–35, 44, 47–50, 52, 58, 61, 65, 99, 102, 106, 153–54, 179, 187, 188, 204, 208, 213, 228, 240, 253n36
energy: after-, 19, 76, 83, 123; amphibology of, 4, 13, 116, 195; anti-, 21, 25, 32, 37–38, 78, 89, 110, 112–13, 122, 133, 135, 216, 219, 221; atomic, xiii, 34; becoming of, 42, 54, 73; circle, 12, 14, 16, 26–27, 51, 112, 117, 152, 160, 179, 228–29; of cognition, 57–66; conception of, xi–xiv, 14, 34, 92, 127, 143, 154; deficit, 15, 65–66, 81, 84, 88, 103–5, 115, 164, 168, 174–75, 186, 224, 242; destructive, 24; duality of, 21, 65, 109, 116, 126, 134, 137, 143, 148, 150, 153–54, 170, 172, 195, 205, 234, 238, 240; finite, 9, 25, 96, 133, 147; history of, 122, 126, 154, 174; independence, 201; instinctual, 49; living, 105–8, 111, 113–14, 161, 164, 171, 173, 188; mutilated, 22, 94, 97, 211; negative, 39, 96, 135, 139, 145, 200; nothing-, 231–32, 237, 239–40; of a novice, 43, 67, 155; ontology of, 83, 158; plenitude of, 15, 64, 77, 132, 137, 145–46, 154, 246; production, xii, 52–54, 141; shapes of, 40–44, 66, 79, 95, 110, 113, 120, 147, 154, 158–59, 161–62, 169–70, 191, 201, 227, 246; solar, xiii; speculative, 32–35, 62–64, 84–85, 90, 92, 100, 103, 107–8, 127, 134, 196, 198, 207, 235–36, 254n2; supply, xii, 9, 26, 44–48, 83, 93, 121, 130, 171, 225, 228; surplus, 104–5, 107–8, 172, 242; of thought, 4, 27–32, 59, 69, 92, 118–19, 124–25, 130, 170
enjoyment, 102, 137, 139–41, 143, 201, 203–4, 218
Enlightenment, 46, 100
entelecheia, 8, 179
entropy, 4, 15, 19, 36, 49–50, 61, 73, 79, 105, 122, 125, 137, 195
environment, environmental, xi, xiii, 14, 24, 84, 115, 138, 160
enworkment, 9, 31, 59, 70, 89, 112, 116, 158, 160–61, 164–65, 170, 205, 210, 214, 217, 220, 227

INDEX

epistemology, 10, 51, 57–60, 62, 146
equality, equalization, 32, 62, 74–75, 78–79, 129
ergon, 7–8, 11–12, 21, 24, 34, 41, 45, 47, 65, 135, 178–79, 182, 184–85, 187, 198–99, 223–24, 238, 243
ergonics, 163, 165, 173, 179, 181, 188, 191
essence, 40–44, 68–73, 89–94, 121–24, 127–29, 132–35, 151–53, 160–61, 176–78, 211–13, 235–37, 246–50; abstract, 31, 85, 101, 106, 149, 164, 190; alien, 109, 118, 133, 206; categories of, 8; exposed, 53, 82, 85, 113, 142, 209, 221, 224, 248; hidden, xii, 8, 42, 53–54, 71, 75, 96–97, 115, 123–24, 141–42, 186, 224; human, 54, 116, 139; pure, 69, 73, 87, 94, 102–3, 133, 135, 141; of reason, 148, 152, 162
essencing, 42
ethical, 47, 197–201, 221, 223; life, 197, 200–201, 246–48; separation, 250; substance, 200, 241, 243, 245–50
event, 10, 19, 129–31, 230, 236
ex-ergy, 13, 109
existentialism, 24–25, 28, 38, 140, 152, 253n46
experience, 14–15, 64–65, 77–78, 123–26, 134–35, 151–52, 204–5; absolute, 64–66, 77, 151, 244; phenomenological, 58, 68–69, 75, 87, 105, 153, 159
expression, 31, 54, 80, 91–93, 133, 164, 167, 173, 182–86, 190–91, 219, 221, 226–27, 249; energy of, 29, 71, 182, 191, 235; self-, 75, 91, 98, 113, 141, 145, 180, 202, 232, 234
expropriation, 150, 179
extractivism, 51–55

facticity, 18, 60, 83–84, 209
facts, 18–19, 22, 117, 180, 192, 241
failure, 58, 64, 82, 175, 183, 206, 211, 213, 247
faith, 152, 218–20, 232, 249
fear, 110, 115–18
Ferrarin, Alfredo, 7
Feuerbach, Ludwig, 95
finitude, 8–9, 13–14, 16, 19, 58–59, 64, 93, 96, 133, 136, 141, 145, 153, 168, 209, 225, 238, 240, 244–45, 253n54
fission, 34, 64, 90, 101, 178, 193, 196, 198, 236, 245

force, 3–4, 33–36, 47, 54, 60, 73, 78, 90–97, 115–18, 126, 129, 136, 140, 143, 157–58, 161, 178, 228, 241, 248
form, xi–xiii, 11–15, 77–78, 110–12, 117–22, 125–26, 136, 146, 154, 156, 181, 195–96, 209–11, 213–14, 236–38, 243–45; dynamic, xii, 162; energetic, 11–12, 17, 28, 50, 158, 171, 204, 248; material, xi, 14–15, 25, 34, 41, 142, 173; of truth, 53, 234
Foucault, Michel, 3, 5, 7
foundation, foundationalism, 8, 11, 62, 68, 100, 144–45, 167, 182, 212, 244
freedom, 40, 48–50, 61, 63, 66, 76, 119–25, 127, 144–45, 169, 171, 209, 214, 219, 228; abstract, 30, 53, 161, 192; of accomplishment, 53; of the concept, 90; of speech, 199; of thought, 119–20, 123–24
Freud, Sigmund, 9, 25, 116
fuel, xi, 12, 46, 53–54, 110, 141, 205

Gelhard, Andreas, 7
genus, 107–8, 171–73
geometry, 12, 33, 43, 131, 227
ghost, 26–27, 108, 150, 190
givenness, 47, 67, 84, 87, 130, 175, 180, 231, 235; modes, 10; pre-, 17; self-, 22, 41, 67, 87, 175, 177, 180, 201–2, 205, 233
God, 8, 10, 14, 18, 49–50
Goethe, Johann Wolfgang, 53, 165

Heidegger, Martin, 6–7, 9–10, 23–24, 45, 68, 112, 137, 152–53, 179, 240, 242, 252n20, 253n46
Hegelianism, 3, 6
Husserl, Edmund, 61, 101, 143, 155, 161, 184, 253n54
hylomorphism, 173
hyphen, 12–14, 222, 245

ideal, ideality, xii, 4, 11, 17, 20, 30, 49, 59–60, 84–85, 88–89, 92, 95, 98, 101–2, 122, 128, 140, 150–51, 156, 162, 173, 201, 208, 241, 243
idealism, 6, 18, 28, 122, 125, 144, 147, 149–50, 201–2, 204–5, 221
identity, 31–36, 149–50, 202–3, 209–10, 217, 221, 249–50; logical, 21, 245; non-, 11, 34, 62–63, 92, 158, 167, 193, 213, 243; speculative, 27, 35, 80, 106, 135, 244

immanent, immanence, 35, 45, 75–76, 95, 106, 125, 196, 198
immediate, immediacy, 58–59, 67–69, 71–76, 78, 83–84, 97–98, 101–2, 118–21, 128–30, 152, 179, 196–97, 241–50; actuality, 28, 36, 38, 43–44, 68, 179–80, 189, 191–92, 195, 201–3, 210, 247–48; being, 47, 203, 226; fetish of, 67, 144; knowledge, 67, 147, 206; life, 106–7, 110, 118, 189, 198
indifference, 70–75, 79–82, 84–85, 99–101, 106, 120, 122, 149–50, 157, 160–61, 168–69, 171–72, 185–86, 191–92, 204, 209, 219–20; mutual, 90, 126, 160, 167, 172, 179, 193
infinity, infinite, 11, 25, 33–34, 36–38, 43, 65, 80, 99, 102, 105, 108–9, 129, 131, 148, 150, 244; "bad," 16, 52, 88, 127–28, 217, 227; of the finite, 9, 16, 41–42, 93, 153, 212; movement, 11, 106
interface, 177, 184, 186, 188

justice, 140, 145

Kafka, Franz, 140
Kant, Immanuel, 15, 21, 27, 36, 45–46, 50, 59, 117, 119, 125–26, 131, 140, 145–46, 148, 150–51, 160, 195, 207–9, 214, 224, 242–43

labor, 7, 9, 11, 112, 114, 116–17, 120, 124, 132, 134–35, 140, 146, 181, 189, 191, 199, 210, 218; division of, 94, 119; of the negative, 11, 21, 173
language, 71, 78, 213
law, 97–100, 157–59, 167–71, 174–78, 196–97, 200–201, 216–18, 241–49; and contradiction, 100; and stability, 168; discovery of, 97; of nature, 157, 159, 176; of reason, 241–44; of the heart, 205–14, 225; of thermodynamics, xiii, 14, 174
law-giving, 175, 241–44, 246–48
Lenin, Vladimir, 6, 215
Levinas, Emmanuel, 74–75, 129
liberal, liberalism, 84, 90, 199, 214
life, 53–54, 105–8, 110–15, 122–24, 160–78, 181–82, 203–5; as energy, 105–6, 108, 111, 113, 115, 167, 182, 205; biological, 74, 133, 169; ethical, 197, 200–201, 246–48; vegetal, xiii, 160, 164–65, 227

life-process, 105–6, 167
limit, limitation 36–37, 85–86, 135–36, 190–91, 196, 202, 219, 232–33, 241, 244; of energy, xiv, 26, 47, 144; of representation, 29, 157, 162; of understanding, 100, 151, 233; unsurpassable, 64
logic, 17, 19, 27, 34, 39, 45–46, 70, 125, 153–54, 221, 229, 244; formal, 21, 52, 84, 127, 175, 189; of relationality, xiii, 90

madness, 212–14, 217
Marx, Karl, 3, 5–6, 19, 50, 95, 112–13, 116–17, 140
materialism, 6, 20, 28, 147, 202, 221
mathematics, 14, 170, 252n21
matter, 9, 41, 83, 114, 128, 146, 159, 162; energy-less, 221–22; formed, 14–15, 25, 34, 41, 112, 142, 173; quantum, 34
mediation, 27–28, 30–31, 98–99, 146–49, 152, 155–56, 164, 168–69, 172, 180, 183–84, 194–96, 201–2, 207–8, 214–15; absolute, 49, 229, 238, 240; negative, 37, 41, 71, 152, 198; poverty of, 42, 46, 67, 129–30, 138, 144, 160, 192, 202, 215, 247; self-, 27, 36, 80, 248
metaphysics, 3, 5–6, 10–12, 14, 19, 32, 48, 66, 75, 132, 138, 140, 152, 170, 181, 186, 188, 224; completion of, 152; of energy, xiii–xiv, 10, 133
morality, 25, 28–29, 35, 200–201, 207–10, 216, 219, 251n6
multiculturalism, 84

negation, 19–21, 34–36, 52–53, 69–70, 84–87, 123–27, 178–79, 193–94, 205–6, 244–46; of the actual, 12, 17, 32, 108, 142, 185, 222; determinate, 19, 30, 43, 62, 80–81, 85, 87, 129–30, 141, 214, 225; indeterminate, 24–25, 125–26; self-, 17, 20, 34–35, 43–45, 52, 72, 84–85, 105, 107, 160–61, 165, 171, 236, 248; of space, 33, 43; speculative, 38
Nietzsche, Friedrich, 22, 106, 152, 178, 216, 235
nihilism, 5, 24–25, 30, 89, 114, 126, 138–39, 152
nothing, nothingness, 64–65, 76–78, 93, 95–96, 111–15, 138–40, 226–27, 231–33, 237–40; actual, 30, 52, 113, 115, 138,

INDEX

238–39; pure, 62, 71, 111, 139; subject as, 22, 231–32
nudity, 196

observation, 151–63, 173–77, 185–86, 195–96, 202, 240, 245, 254n1; of nature, 154–55, 161; of reason, 147, 151, 153, 155–59, 161–63, 167, 196; of self-consciousness, 174–77, 185, 195
organic realm, xiii, 160–74, 181, 184, 189, 191
organism, organismic, 12, 14, 54, 160–61, 163–71, 173, 184, 188–89, 192
organs, 163–65, 167–68, 179, 181–82, 184, 188–89, 191–92, 220
ousia, 68, 70

perception, 8, 23, 79–82, 85–88, 93, 95, 106, 108, 110–11, 151, 169
personality, 177, 181, 188, 195, 201, 220, 247
perversion, 5, 16, 35, 37, 92–93, 97, 101–2, 115, 119–21, 133, 135–36, 138, 142–43, 152, 158, 162, 174–79, 186–87, 190, 212–14, 216–19, 222–23, 226, 234, 237–38, 240, 242–44, 246, 251n5, 251n6
photosynthesis, xiii
phrenology, 183, 189–90, 192–94
physics, xiii, 4, 14–15, 19, 41, 49, 58, 75, 142, 153, 215, 229
Pinkard, Terry, 7, 251n9
plants, xiii–xiv, 9, 53, 114, 160, 164–65, 185, 187
Plato, 19, 48–49, 101, 140, 152, 164, 169, 171
Platonism, 60, 152
pleasure, 37, 116, 201–9, 216–18, 238; rational, 201–7
possibility, 24–26, 35–38, 42–43, 53–55, 59–60, 66, 95–96, 125–26, 152, 165, 170–72, 191–94; limitless, 36, 38, 53, 55, 74, 141, 154; meta-, 72, 130, 208; night of, 42, 233–34; of possibility, 72, 103; primacy of, 4, 122; real, 21
potentiality, xi–xiv, 24–25, 33–36, 52–55, 73–75, 83–84, 136, 154–55, 219–22, 225–28; of energy, 17, 41, 75, 128, 221, 226; individual, 16, 193–94, 231–33; pure, xi, xiii–xiv, 25, 52, 97, 219–21, 241, 243

power, 3–4, 6–7, 34–38, 85–88, 113–15, 135–39, 198–200, 203–6, 214–26, 239–41; absolute, 136–38; of abstraction, 60, 96, 163; of the negative, 6, 30, 36, 38, 114, 126, 225; play of, 88; universal, 37, 86, 100, 119, 205, 209, 217, 219
powerlessness, 34, 36–37, 113, 116, 135–37, 143, 167, 199, 215–24, 253n43
Pozzo, Ricardo, 7
pragmatism, 6, 132
principio individuationis, 48
principle(s), 8–9, 34–36, 80–82, 163–64, 215–16, 244–45; first, 8, 38, 43, 52, 185, 205; of noncontradiction, 36, 84, 149, 207–10, 212, 215, 245; pleasure, 116; rational, 52, 166
Procrustean bed, 84
psychoanalysis, 162, 214
psychology, 44, 174–75, 177, 187–88, 195
purus, 8, 204

reading, xiv, 5–7, 9–10, 65; symptomatic, 6, 9
realism, 78–79, 147
reality, 4–5, 20–24, 143–44, 146–51, 154–55, 169–70, 174–75, 196, 198–200, 209–11, 247–48; absolute, 228–29; vs. actuality, 26, 51, 63, 68, 74, 77–79, 124, 135, 144, 151, 165, 174, 199, 228–31, 233, 242; of cognition, 62–63; despair of, 77; external, 20, 66–67, 77–78, 123, 131, 226; of perception, 23, 74; virtual, 4, 22, 28, 30, 32, 36–37, 43, 69, 71, 73, 80, 83, 96, 103, 123, 148, 174, 191–93, 202, 209, 211, 243, 245, 254n2
reason, xiv, 16–17, 39, 60–61, 143–59, 161–63, 196–201, 240–49; concept of, 162; instinct of, 157; self-sufficiency of, 145–46; speculative, 60, 213
recognition, 50–51, 57, 87–89, 98, 100, 107, 109–11, 114–15, 117–18, 120, 130–31, 147, 149–50, 181, 193, 200, 211, 220, 236, 249–50
recollection, 13, 16, 40, 48–49, 194–95, 224
reconciliation, 28, 45, 87, 132, 153, 168, 172, 179, 200, 234, 242, 248
reification, 21, 50, 88, 90, 107, 123, 158, 195
relation, relationality, xii–xiii, 26–29, 37–38, 45–49, 74–81, 85–86, 112–13,

INDEX

relation, relationality (*continued*) 125–38, 143–46, 159–62, 184–86, 228–29; absolute, xii–xiii, 21, 23; meta-, 29; oppositional, 81, 106, 157, 166; self-, 21–23, 26, 28–29, 74–80, 93–94, 96, 102–3, 105–6, 112–15, 143–44; without relation, 74–75, 77–78, 82, 90, 101, 114–15, 125–27, 129–31, 195

representation, 28–31, 44, 47, 59, 61, 121, 144–45, 162, 167, 182, 226–27

reproduction, xiii, 164, 166–67, 169, 189

rest, 30, 34, 38, 44, 48–49, 97, 100–102, 104, 106, 127, 132, 145, 148–49, 154, 163, 167–72, 176–77, 183, 187, 189–92; energetic, 13, 40–41, 100, 112, 143, 152, 161, 176, 180, 246, 249

resurrection, 52, 159

revolution, revolutionary, xi, 25, 112, 167, 191

rigidity, 43, 63, 84, 87–88, 94, 131, 191

sacrifice, 34, 36, 53–54, 106, 132–33, 140–43, 188, 196, 218, 221–23

Saussure, Ferdinand de, 78, 99, 183

Scholasticism, 14, 131, 234

semblance, 130, 208, 230, 233

sense-certainty, 20, 67–79, 81, 110, 137, 146–47, 149, 182, 242–43

sensuous, sensuousness, 23, 71, 77–78, 85–86, 95–97, 101–2, 130, 153, 155–57, 159–60, 181

sexuality, 72, 164, 166, 188–89

Shakespeare, William, 191

signification, 34, 43, 99, 183–86, 191–92

simplicity, 70–71, 80, 98–99, 127, 159–60, 163–65, 172

skepticism, 66, 119, 123–27

Smith, Adam, 198–99, 223–24

soul, 8, 50, 102, 134, 160, 163–64, 180, 184–86, 188, 190

sovereign, sovereignty, 35, 245

specter, spectrality, xiv, 27, 32, 108, 158

Spinoza, Baruch, 22, 106, 120, 136, 220, 223

spirit, 9–15, 19–20, 26–27, 39–40, 43–44, 65–66, 176–77, 190–95, 201–2, 213–14, 237, 246–49; absolute, 13, 50, 154, 213; abstract, 55; actual, 11–12, 15, 20, 23, 39, 195, 213; substantive, 12, 201, 214

stoicism, 119, 121–23, 125–26

sublation, 4, 12, 31, 33–34, 43–45, 49, 52, 60, 79, 84–85, 87–88, 104, 135–36, 144, 157, 161, 168, 176, 185, 196, 201, 204, 225, 236, 251n6

substance, 14–15, 17–22, 24–26, 28, 34–35, 37–38, 47–48, 50–51, 93–95, 143, 168, 176, 181, 192–97, 200–201, 219–20, 236–38; ethical, 200, 241, 243, 245–50; evacuation of, 17, 34, 94–95, 160, 201, 245; pure, 14, 193

survival, 26, 45, 117, 121, 133, 143, 204, 244

syllogism, 24, 142

synergy, 15, 22, 26, 28, 30, 38–40, 42, 49, 52–55, 58–59, 61–62, 64–65, 71, 73, 76, 78, 86, 103, 108–10, 113, 118–19, 127, 133–34, 140–41, 155, 165, 176, 178, 189, 192, 197, 199–201, 206, 208, 226, 249, 253n39

synthesis, 30, 37–39, 49, 65, 91, 108–9, 138, 197, 203

system, 94, 215; Hegelian, 9, 12, 15, 22, 39–40, 65, 219; muscular-skeletal, 189; nervous, 164–65, 189; organic, 164–67, 192; of thought, 20, 30, 65

talent, 16, 177, 231–32

tautology, 9, 100, 104–5, 109, 186, 235, 245–46

theology, xii, 4, 9–10, 14, 18, 140, 163, 186, 232, 251n1

thermodynamics, xiii, 14, 174

thinghood, 30–31, 80–82, 85–88, 93, 106–7, 111–15, 118–21, 158, 162, 195, 197

thought, 3–7, 27–32, 37–38, 61–62, 89, 91–94, 113, 118–26, 133, 136–38, 174–76, 195; dialectical, xiii–xiv, 3–5, 9, 11, 14, 34, 181; essence of, 31, 49, 121–23, 200; freedom of, 120, 123–24; movement of, xiv, 28, 84, 120, 176, 216; representational, 30, 44, 162; thinking itself, 10, 30–31, 58, 102, 105–6, 125, 161, 253n36

thought-thing, 25, 86–87, 89, 175

transgression, 210

translation, xii, 8, 34, 99, 144, 178, 204, 213, 226–27, 233–34, 251n9; conceptual, xiv, 6; pure, 42, 227, 233

truth, 23–25, 57–58, 60–68, 70–73, 79–83, 110–11, 114–15, 125–26, 144–45,

INDEX

153, 177–78, 193–94, 218–20, 226–27, 230–36; absolute, 23, 60, 64, 66, 77; correspondence theory of, 62, 234; of knowledge, 63–64, 95, 242; non-, 62, 64, 68, 81–82, 95, 97, 194, 218, 234–36

unconditionality, 12, 25, 86, 89–90, 93, 222, 242, 249
unconscious (the), 8–9, 37, 67, 78, 99, 102, 119, 132, 157, 178, 183, 194, 197, 199, 205–6, 240
understanding, 4–5, 85–86, 88–89, 91–103, 106–11, 131–32, 168–69, 229, 242, 248; mere, 89, 98, 102, 131; self-, 5, 92, 99, 103; universality of, 85
unmoved mover, xiv, 102, 223, 225
utopia, 49, 248

vanishing, 22, 92, 94–96, 99, 112, 124, 163–64, 235, 237–38

vegetal, vegetality, xiii, 53, 139, 160, 164–66, 190, 203, 227
virtue, 35, 215–25, 237, 253n41
vision, 74, 76, 87
void, xi, 27, 74, 96–97, 99, 115–16, 118, 125–26, 128, 145, 178, 182, 201, 213, 227–28, 239

Whitehead, Alfred North, 10, 106
wisdom, 77–78
world(s), 3–5, 8–11, 18–32, 44–45, 52–53, 82–83, 94–96, 100–102, 123–24, 134–38, 140–43, 145–51, 158–61, 173–74, 201–2, 225–28, 235, 243–44; creation, 11, 18, 50; energy of, 5, 28, 89, 96, 102, 161, 181, 212, 241; possible, 19; spirit, 3, 20, 44, 66, 201, 248; virtualization, 25, 55, 170, 239; way of the, 215–23

Žižek, Slavoj, 5, 251n5